# Évangéline
## THE MANY IDENTITIES *of a* LITERARY ICON

JOSEPH YVON THÉRIAULT

*Translated from the French by*

**Aycha Fleury**

NIMBUS
PUBLISHING LTD.
— NIMBUS.CA —

Nimbus Publishing Limited
3660 Strawberry Hill Street, Halifax, NS, B3K 5A9
(902) 455-4286 nimbus.ca

Printed and bound in Canada

NB1449

Editor: Emily MacKinnon
Interior design: Rudi Tusek
Cover design: Heather Bryan

Library and Archives Canada Cataloguing in Publication

Title: Évangéline : the many identities of a literary icon / Joseph Yvon Thériault ;
    translation from the French by Aycha Fleury.
Other titles: Évangéline. English
Names: Thériault, J. Yvon (Joseph Yvon), 1949- author. | Fleury, Aycha, translator.
Description: Translation of: Évangéline, contes d'Amérique.
Identifiers: Canadiana 20200387650 | ISBN 9781771089258 (softcover)
Subjects: LCSH: Longfellow, Henry Wadsworth, 1807-1882. Evangeline. | LCSH: Acadians in literature. | LCSH: Cajuns in literature. | CSH: Acadians—Expulsion, 1755.
Classification: LCC PS2263 .T4413 2022 | DDC 811/.3—dc23

Nimbus Publishing acknowledges the financial support for its publishing activities from the Government of Canada, the Canada Council for the Arts, particularly the Arts Across Canada Translation Grant Program, and from the Province of Nova Scotia. We are pleased to work in partnership with the Province of Nova Scotia to develop and promote our creative industries for the benefit of all Nova Scotians.

*For Clara, who loves fairy tales.*

# TABLE OF CONTENTS

# INTRODUCTION

**NB:** For the sake of clarity, the publisher has employed the following styles for the spelling and treatment of "Evangeline"/"Évangéline":

- When referring to the original English-language poem written by Longfellow: *Evangeline*.
- When referring to the character herself: Évangéline.
- When referring to the French translation of the English poem: *Évangéline*.

## BETWEEN POETRY AND HISTORY

"Évangéline, here is above all the work with which I present myself to the literary world."[1] This is how Pamphile Lemay proposed to his Canadian public, in 1864, a small book entitled *Essais poétiques*. The main part of the book contains a long poem, *Évangéline*, followed by a collection of shorter poems, some of which are translations of the American poet Henry Wadsworth Longfellow. *Évangéline* is also a translation of the great American poet. Although Lemay does not hide it, he did not think it necessary to write Longfellow's name on the cover of the book, and it is only in the preface that we learn that it is a "free translation" of Longfellow's "charming poem," *Evangeline: A Tale of Acadie* (1847).

I have the feeling, in presenting my book to you, that I am following in Lemay's footsteps. I'm introducing myself as the author of the story of Évangéline, when in fact the poem was written by one of the most illustrious American poets of the nineteenth century. But is Longfellow really the author of the story of Évangéline? Pamphile Lemay believed he was, but it was also the nature of national literature to adapt foreign works to the ingenuity of each people. One could, in some way, pursue,

---

1.   "Évangéline, voilà surtout l'ouvrage avec lequel je me présente devant le monde littéraire."

enrich, or embellish the story of another author and even, as we will see, end it.

Later, French Catholics living in the old French Acadia territory, where the poem begins, would say that Longfellow, this foreigner, had only romanticized a tale rooted in the popular memory of the neutral French descendants expelled from their land of Nova Scotia and dispersed to New England in the mid-1800s. The Cajuns—the French, Catholic, white inhabitants of Lower Louisiana—would go even further, claiming that the true story of the couple Évangéline and Gabriel is that of their settlement in what has become American Louisiana.

Longfellow's work will not only have a literary continuity independent of the original literary narrative produced by its author. *Evangeline* the poem comes to be at the centre of the forging and deployment of these groups' identities: the Acadians of the Maritimes in Canada, and the Cajuns of Louisiana in the United States. Évangéline the character will become an object of identification and controversy. This was utterly foreign to the original intent of Longfellow's writing project. The latter never visited Nova Scotia and showed no particular interest in the Acadians who might continue to live there. In this story, the heroine never returns to her native Acadia, nor is she encouraged by her family to do so. She will stay only two nights in the bayous of Louisiana and will die in Philadelphia, where the American Declaration of Independence has just been signed.

Longfellow was a poet of the young American republic. The story Longfellow wanted to write was not Canadian, Acadian, or Cajun; it was American. An idyll for the "celestial mechanics" that were, for him, the United States of America in the making. The poem will be received as such. It goes on to be a huge success. Both the poem and its author will sit in the classrooms of America for the next half-century, as they are seen to describe the beginnings of the republic, the majesty of its frontier landscapes, and love in the age of democratic sentimentality.

*Evangeline* is not the only literary work to have escaped from its author and been incorporated into foundation stories. We all have in mind *William Tell* (1804), a central work in the construction of Swiss identity. Like Longfellow for Acadia, *William Tell*'s author, the German Friedrich von Schiller, is an empathetic outsider to the cause of the vanquished who has never visited the places of the story being told. Longfellow, in the case of *Evangeline*, was largely inspired by the *Saga of Frithiof*, an epic tale by the Swedish author Esaias Tegnér, which was also crucial in the construction of Swedish identity. One might also think of the *Chanson de Roland* ("Song of Roland") an epic poem whose author is unknown and which has often been referenced as an account of France's beginnings.

Therefore what appeared original to me was not the appropriation of a work of fiction for political-identitarian purposes, a common phenomenon in the construction of human societies that I will discuss again. No, it is rather the fact that the same poem has participated in the foundation and elaboration of three different narratives: the American narrative, the Acadian narrative, and the Cajun narrative. I was aware that I had before me materials of a rare singularity, a "goodie" for the sociologist that I am. Nothing is indeed more gratifying in sociological work than to be able to tell the story of the beginning of societies. There is a kind of ecstasy in seeing these moments when society takes on meaning and form. Usually, these beginnings are lost in the mists of time, difficult to decipher.

*Evangeline* is a foundational poem dating from the mid-nineteenth century, a period both close and easily accessible to us. It is also the founding story of white American groups, new societies born with modernity.

But *Evangeline* in not only a story of founding; it is a work that remains enlightening to this day. I felt I could tell the story of the beginning and development of three different social groupings through the voice and eyes of Évangéline. Although all three were communities of history and memory, they were very different from each other. Their difference spanned the entire spectrum on which sociologists distribute ethnocultural identities in modern societies: the ethnic, the national minority (nationalitarian), and the nation. The Cajuns are the prototype of an "ethnicity," a grouping based on the memory of immigration and which constructs a symbolic boundary with other groups in its environment. The Acadians are grouped as a "national minority," a grouping that draws from its own history the narrative of its foundation (self-referentiality) and aims at a high level of historicity, i.e. to equip itself with the tools to make its own history. The

Americans form a "nation," the place par excellence of society in modernity, the only grouping endowed with high historicity (capacity to orient its history) and whose memory is nourished by history.

Following the path of these three societal groupings, from the voice and the gaze of Évangéline, the history of America's identity was taking shape. Évangéline's tale sent me back to the American story of its founding, the story of Acadia, and the story of the Cajun country. It introduced me to the construction of their national narratives in the nineteenth century. That led me to the transformations of these narratives through Canadian and Quebec history—the Canadian confrontation of French- and English-Canadian nationalism (and American history), the frontier experience, the Civil War, the postbellum South—to the building of nation states, of ethnicity, to the deployment of multiculturalism and the "roots" phenomenon, to the advent of what some today call "postmodernity." In short, *Evangeline: A Tale of Acadie* became *Évangéline: contes d'Amérique* ("Tales of America"), which was translated into *Évangéline: the Many Identities of a Literary Icon*. The story of America's identity told from its centre, American America, and from two of its margins, Maritime Acadia on its northeastern border and Cajun country in the Deep South of the United States.

The book is built around these three stories: Évangéline the American, Évangéline the Acadian, and Évangéline the Cajun, followed by an afterword: Postmodern Évangéline. These stories can be read separately, but they are complementary. My method was limited to letting myself be guided by Évangéline's voice and gaze. The "voice" is that of the poem and its interpreter through time. It indicated to me the "creation's work," (that is to say, how, from the poem itself and its interpretations and reinterpretations, from its translations and reworkings, from its use and its forgetting, *Evangeline* was an evolving work that participated in defining the meaning and shaping of the social groups studied). All these voices are the narrative authors.

The "gaze" is the referral by the performers of the tale that had to be observed in order to grasp the narrative entirely. As you may have guessed, my project was not mainly to understand the work's influence but, above all, to grasp the type of society that the "creation's work" helped build. It is a historical sociology work rather than a historical work. Each time I left Évangéline's narrative to enter into history, into the sociological description of the communities targeted by the narrative, it was Évangéline's gaze that led me there. Évangéline's viewpoint is the story's explanatory tracks.

One could call this method "cultural history of societies," "history of ideas," or even "intellectual history." I prefer to call it, borrowing the expression from the French historian Pierre Rosanvallon, "conceptual history of politics" (from "histoire conceptuelle du politique"). The point is to see that ideas, in this case a work of fiction—a poem—do not sit above societies as ideologies, myths or inconsequential rantings. Ideas serve to shape societies and participate in society's work on itself; if they are social objects, it is in this sense that they are political. They contribute to shaping and making sense for the social. They are not only abstract things; they are part of historical reality. I do not wish to substitute an ideological interpretation with a materialist interpretation of societies. I am well aware societies are also born of economic and social history, interactions, and relations of domination. Nevertheless, ideas are part of history and are a privileged entry point to its understanding.

This is especially true when we are interested in communities of history and memory, which are the ethnocultural groupings that concern us here. "A people is a population, plus contours and storytellers," said the essayist Régis Debray.[2] Human groupings can sometimes be formed mechanically by belonging, by simple interaction, as with crowds, workers of a company, customers of a shopping mall, inhabitants of a neighbourhood, and even citizens of a state. But it takes more for them to form a community. So, as Fernand Dumont said, "belonging" must become a "reference." A community is created and perpetuated because someone has given meaning to our multiple belongings, to the plurality of our lives. Meaning is not automatically born of existence. Even historical events only appear when an enunciator gives them significant meaning to a certain public. Memory is forgetful; it needs a narrative to last. We will see it in the "expulsion" of the French Catholics of Nova Scotia in the middle of the eighteenth century from their lands in the former French Acadia. For

---

2.   "Un peuple, c'est une population, plus des contours et des conteurs"

this event to be meaningful, the advent of the poem and the production of narratives were necessary.

The narratives of modern societies are particular. They must be confronted with history. Already, in Greek antiquity, Aristotle distinguished poetry and history in *Poetics*. He thought poetry manufactures the new and says what should be according to necessity; its affirmations are more general, of the verisimilitude order. On the contrary, history is interested in what is made; it says what is regardless of the necessity, and its assertions are more precise. History seeks the truth.

Aristotle preferred poetry to history; he preferred the storyteller to the scholar. For a long time, these two orders of fact were opposed. As modernity has seen the imposition of the historical narrative, the storyteller must now rely on history. Today, many would like history to be completely detached from the storyteller, abolishing the narrative, so to speak. But this is impossible in itself, as made-up things have no meaning without a storyteller, without being inscribed in a narrative. This does not mean that historical truth disappears from the narrative. What distinguishes the modern narrative from the ancient one is that it is now measured by the yardstick of history—poetry and history intermingle, while opposing each other at the same time. Longfellow conducted historical research to write Évangéline's idyll, and from the moment it was published, the work was at the heart of a polemic between poetry and history.

I wanted to fully assume this difficult tension between poetry and history, which is characteristic of modern narrative. I wanted to write a story, or even three. I tried to keep the tone of the original. After these few clarifications, this book does not include long theoretical passages, as a scholarly work would have. I have not included footnotes that constantly refer the reader to the possibility of verifying the truth of the facts. The ambivalence between poetry and history must be maintained. The conceptualization and veracity of the facts must flow from the enunciators of meaning that are the authors of this triple story of *Evangeline*. That said, I have great respect for my sources. They are usually obvious because the narrative continually forces one to recall *who* is speaking and *why* (the voice and the eyes). I have indicated after each chapter the main references that allowed me to reconstruct the story. In the end, everything in this book is true, except for its beginning, which is a work of poetry.

As for the narrator of this book, he has kept a low profile. This is not a book with a thesis, other than the one I have just stated, according to which ideas participate in the making of societies, and narratives are necessary for their understanding. Through the voice and the eyes, I wanted to follow the trail of the stories of the men and women who made up *Evangeline* and, thanks to this trail, understand the worlds they were helping to build. I have a particular affection for Acadia, and through the work of this book, I have acquired a great empathy for the Cajun country. I do not think, however, that I have been complacent about either of these realities. I am aware, in writing *Évangéline: The Many Identities of a Literary Icon*, that I am adding another layer to the poem's sedimentation. In short, I am aware, as we shall see, that I am doing "evangelism." I could not write the story of Évangéline without paying this price.

In writing this book, I wanted, above all, to avoid pitfalls that I believe are recurrent in contemporary social sciences. Today, we all know that societies are constructed things and that traditions are invented. Many, because of this, conclude that society is a "pious lie," a "fakelore," as the Cajun historians would say—that it only remains for the social sciences to unmask the impostor, to deconstruct the narrative. My approach does not aim at deconstructing the narrative but at seeing how the narrative is constructed and how it participates in creating a world of meaning, shaping, and making society from the infinite human plurality. There are no societies without storytellers and no humanity without societies.

I have not sought the truth about the poem *Evangeline*; what I want is its social effectiveness. That is why this book is not the result of archival work, or a small lost-and-found book that challenges the historical interpretation. Rather, I am interested in the public statements to which the story's authors refer. Meaning is not constructed without the knowledge of the actors; it needs a word that states it. I did not want to rewrite the poem, but rather the narratives emanating from it throughout history.

I also avoided, as much as possible, the association of the poem with myth. A myth has something structuring, static, as if the world it built was forever forced to turn on itself. For me, *Evangeline* was a political text, evolving according to the context of those who took its voice and its gaze. Of course, one cannot make *Evangeline* say anything—the work informs the narrative—and it is a mark left on reality rather than a structural effect.

I also did not want to make an aesthetic analysis of the original work; I would have been unable to do so. Évangéline had a literary career of her own, which was also immense. There are several other stories of Évangéline; different from the ones I am about to tell you. I was only interested in the poem's influence on social imaginaries, and in *Evangeline* as a builder of history and memory communities. That's already a lot.

And now, let's hear the story: "Once upon a time, the Americas...."

# PART I

## ÉVANGÉLINE THE AMERICAN

# ÉVANGÉLINE THE AMERICAN

♦ indicates a publication.

## XV CENTURY

### 1492
Europeans discover America through Christopher Columbus.

### 1497
John Cabot lands in Newfoundland and establishes a British presence in North America.

## XVI CENTURY

### 1524
Giovanni da Verrazzano explores the West Coast of the Atlantic in the name of the king of France. He names the present Virginia and Maryland coasts "Arcadia."

## XVII CENTURY

### 1607
John Smith becomes the founder of the Jamestown Settlement (Virginia).

### 1614
The Dutch become the founders of the New Netherlands.

### 1454
Gutenberg introduces printing to Europe with the printing press and typography.

### 1517
♦ Ninety-five Theses, Martin Luther.
Birth of Protestantism.

### 1530
♦ On the Revolutions of the Heavenly Spheres, Copernicus.

### 1619
First Black slaves arrive to the Jamestown plantations.

### 1620
The Mayflower lands in Cape Cod with 100 Pilgrims (the Pilgrim Fathers) who established the Plymouth Colony.

### 1624
The Dutch settle New Amsterdam (future New York).

### 1640
The Beaver Wars.

### 1682
William Penn founds Pennsylvania.

### 1682
René-Robert Cavelier de La Salle sails to the Mississippi River Delta.

### 1621
First Thanksgiving is celebrated in Plymouth.

### 1633
The Church condemns Galileo Galilei for "vehement suspicion of heresy" regarding his position that the earth rotates around the sun.

### 1636
Harvard College (later Harvard University) is founded.

### 1662
♦ The Day of Doom, Michael Wigglesworth.

### 1692
The Salem witch trials (Massachusetts).

## XVIII CENTURY

**1738–50**
First Great Awakening.

**1754–63**
Seven Years War.

**1763**
Treaty of Paris (end of the Seven Years War). France gives Canada to England and Louisiana (Mississippi) to Spain.

**1775**
Beginning of the American Revolutionary War.

**1776**
United States Declaration of Independence.

**1783**
Treaty of Paris (end of the American Revolutionary War).

**1789**
The first president of the United States, George Washington, is elected.

**1793**
Yellow fever pandemic in Philadelphia.

**1758**
◊ *The Way to Wealth*, Benjamin Franklin.

**1766–67**
Daniel Boon makes his way to Kentucky.

**1776**
◊ *Common Sense*, Thomas Paine.

**1782**
◊ *Letters from an American Farmer*, J. Hector St. John de Crevecoeur.

**1783**
◊ *Remarks Concerning the Savages of North America*, Benjamin Franklin.

**1787–88**
◊ *The Federalist Papers*.

## XIX CENTURY

**1800–40**
Second Great Awakening.

**1801**
Thomas Jefferson is elected president of the United States.

**1803**
The United States buys Louisiana from France.

**1812–14**
The War of 1812 between the United States and Great Britain.

**1819**
Spain gives Florida to the United States.

**1820–60**
Two hundred thousand Irish immigrate to the United States.

**1828**
Andrew Jackson is elected president of the United States (Jacksonian democracy).

**1807**
Henry Wadsworth Longfellow is born in Portland, Maine (known as Massachusetts at the time).

**1814**
◊ *The Star-Spangled Banner*, Francis Scott Key.

**1819**
◊ *Rip Van Winkle*, Washington Irving.

**1828**
◊ *American Dictionary of the English Language*, Noah Webster.

**1834**
Anti-Catholic protest, Ursuline Convent riots in Somerville, Massachusetts.

**1845**
Annexation of Texas.

**1846–48**
Mexican-American War.

**1860**
Abraham Lincoln is elected president of the United States.

**1861**
Beginning of the American Civil War.

**1865**
Abraham Lincoln abolishes slavery.

Assassination of Lincoln.

End of the Civil War.

**1866.**
The Ku Klux Klan is created.

**1870**
Fifteenth amendment passes "The right of citizens of the United States to vote shall not be denied or abridged by the United States or by any State on account of race, color, or previous condition of servitude."

**1834**
♦ *History of the United States of America*, George Bancroft.

**1835**
♦ *Outre-Mer: A Pilgrimage Beyond the Sea*, Henry Wadsworth Longfellow.

♦ *La démocratie en Amérique* (1st American edition: 1841), Alexis de Tocqueville.

**1836**
♦ *Nature*, Ralph Waldo Emerson.

**1842**
♦ *Poems on Slavery*, Henry Wadsworth Longfellow.

**1845**
♦ *Manifest Destiny*, John L. O'Sullivan.

**1846**
♦ *The Philosophy of Composition*, Edgar Allan Poe.

**1847**
♦ *Evangeline: A Tale of Acadie*, Henry Wadsworth Longfellow.

**1850**
♦ *The Scarlet Letter*, Nathaniel Hawthorne.

**1851**
♦ *Moby-Dick*, Herman Melville.

**1852**
♦ *Uncle Tom's Cabin*, Harriet Beecher Stowe.

**1855**
♦ *Hiawatha*, Henry Wadsworth Longfellow.

**1858**
♦ *The Courtship of Miles Standish and Other Poems*, Henry Wadsworth Longfellow.

**1863**
♦ *Tales of a Wayside Inn*, Henry Wadsworth Longfellow.

**1876**
♦ *Adventures of Tom Sawyer*, Mark Twain.

**1882**
Death of Henry Wadsworth Longfellow.

**1893**
♦ *The Frontier in American History*, Frederick Jackson Turner.

## XX CENTURY

### 1904

The Jim Crow Laws are created to marginalize African Americans by denying them the right to vote, hold jobs, get an education, and other opportunities.

### 1909

W. E. B. Du Bois founds the National Association for the Advancement of Colored People (NAACP).

### 1917

The United States declares war against Germany (First World War).

### 1929

Wall Street crash (beginning of the Great Depression).

### 1941

The Japanese attack Pearl Harbour. The United States enters the Second World War.

### 1945

The US drops atomic bombs on Hiroshima and Nagasaki, Japan.

### 1955-56

Rosa Parks and the Montgomery bus boycott.

### 1960

John F. Kennedy, the first Catholic president of the United States, is elected.

### 1960

Kennedy is assassinated.

### 1964

The Civil Rights Act is published. Martin Luther King Jr. is assassinated.

### 1973

End of the Vietnam War.

---

### 1903

♦ *The Call of the Wild*, Jack London.

### 1908

♦ *The Melting Pot* [play], Israel Zangwill.

### 1911

First Hollywood film studio.

♦ *The Genteel Tradition in American Philosophy*, George Santaya.

### 1915

♦ *Democracy Versus the Melting-Pot*, Horace Kallen.

### 1919

*Évangéline* (movie) is produced by the Fox Film Corporation, directed by Raoul Walsh, starring Miriam Cooper.

### 1929

*Évangéline* (movie), is directed by Edwin Carewe, starring Dolores del Río.

### 1960

Andy Warhol launches the pop art movement.

### 1969

Woodstock Music and Art Fair.

### ♦ 1976

*Roots: The Saga of an American Family*, Alex Haley.

### ♦ 1979

*La condition postmoderne*, Jean-François Lyotard.

---

NB: These historical and cultural landmarks are meant to help the reader situate *Évangéline* and its legacy within the landscape of the American cultural imaginary. They are not meant to be exhaustive nor holistically representative of American or Canadian history. This logic applies to the timelines in sections two and three as well.

# LONGFELLOW AND THE AMERICAN TALE

*The author has done himself justice, and has regard to his well-earned fame; and, by this work of his maturity—a poem founded on American history, and embodying itself in American life and manners—he has placed himself on an eminence higher than he had yet attained, and beyond the reach of envy. Let him stand, then, at the head of our list of native poets, until someone else shall break up the rude soil of our American life, as he has done, and produce from it a lovelier and nobler flower than this poem of Evangeline!*

—Nathaniel Hawthorne
"Review of Evangeline," *Salem Advertiser*, November 13, 1847

## The Enlightenment in America

With this profoundly American poem, Henry Wadsworth Longfellow raises himself to the first place of our national poets. Thus spoke Nathaniel Hawthorne—one of the greatest novelists of the first part of the nineteenth century, who would go on to write *The Scarlet Letter* (1850), a masterpiece of American fiction—in the *Salem Advertiser* a few months after the 1847 publication of the poem *Evangeline: A Tale of Acadie*. More than an Acadian odyssey, writes Hawthorne, Longfellow's work is a great American tale, for, despite what its title suggests, the story depicts the United States of America while simultaneously contributing to its identity. It is a tale that establishes Longfellow as the first great national lyricist.

7

Hawthorne was a long-time friend of Longfellow's. More than twenty years prior, they had both attended Bowdoin College, located in northern Massachusetts, which was renamed the state of Maine in 1820, where Longfellow was from, and from which you could almost see the old French Acadie. Hawthorne even acted as a go-between in the genesis of the poem. Initially, it was he who had been asked to write a novel about a couple separated in Acadie during the Seven Years War. Not feeling inspired by the eternal quest of a lover lost in the midst of human tragedy, Hawthorne passed the baton to Longfellow. This is why Hawthorne stressed in his review how difficult it was to elevate the topic to the level of national literature, as it could easily fall into a sorrowful pathos, which was "not to be trusted in the hands of a ordinary writer." In transforming the couple's romantic idyll into an epic narrative of America, Longfellow became one of the top national poets.

In 1847, Hawthorne and Longfellow were mature authors, renowned in the American cultural milieu even though their great works had yet to be published. Their works were integral parts of the literary effervescence that overcame the young republic in the first part of the nineteenth century, including New England with Boston as its epicentre. They fought for the creation of a national literature…a uniquely American literature. This fight was initially rooted in nationalist inspiration, though it cannot be reduced to it, as we will see.

This project began in the wake of the American War of Independence. In 1783, the year the Treaty of Paris ended the war, Noah Webster, a lexicographer whose name has become synonymous with the dictionary, affirmed that, "America must be as independent in literature as she is in politics." The War of 1812–1814 against Great Britain kindled the desire for nationalist literature. Such affirmations marked the period, which is known as *antebellum*, that is, the period between the last war against the ex-homeland (1812–14) and the Civil War (1861–65). In 1847, at the heart of the Young American Movement, Cornelius Mathews published—the same year *Évangéline* was published—*Nationality in Literature*, a work in which he pleads for a radical separation from British-inspired literature. In his words, America needed "home writers…home themes, affording opportunity for descriptions of our scenery...events... [and] the manners of the people all 'penetrated and vivified by an intense and enlightened patriotism.'"

This literary effervescence wanted the young republic to have a literature that was distinct from—yet worthy of—European literary trends. It aimed to give Americans an image of themselves. The period indeed provided a legacy of portraits, which, more than two centuries later, still leaves a mark on the American imagination. Consider "the grotto" in *Rip Van Winkle* by Washington Irving (1819), the "last of the Mohicans" in the eponymous book by James Fenimore Cooper (1826), the "white whale" in *Moby-Dick* by Herman Melville (1850), the "austerity of the small Puritan towns of New England" in *The Scarlet Letter* by Nathaniel Hawthorne (1850), or "the case of Uncle Tom" in the famous novel by Harriet Beecher Stowe (1852). Each of these tales describes the setting, natural environment, and anguish of a young nation in development. *Évangéline* would become a part of this pantheon of founding images of America.

Poetry also had its place in this budding national literature. It was a prized genre, attuned to the temperament of the period, where a romantic fog that had drifted from Europe had established itself on the young continent. Poets and essayists like Edgar Allan Poe, Ralph Waldo Emerson, Henry David Thoreau, and Henry Wadsworth Longfellow were often more popular than authors of literature proper. In a narrative style—such is the case with Longfellow and his epic poems, like *Évangéline*—they strived to reveal the impressions and sentiments of the natural surroundings and inhabitants of this new continent. Hawthorne, who, as we saw earlier, was well established in this literary movement, did not hesitate in 1847 to include the long narrative poem *Évangéline* at the forefront of this new national imagery.

More than a prosaic description of American life and nature, these authors shaped a romantic narrative of the foundation of a nation. And they were not the only ones; the period also saw the first truly national historiography, also born out of New England, at the college of Harvard. Both political and religious discourses contributed to the elaboration of the narrative, which evolved closely with the great socio-political transformations that followed the independence of the thirteen North American British colonies: a wind of change for religion, enthusiasm for popular democracy, the opening of the Western frontier, and the forthcoming confrontations between the South and the North. The foundational narrative grew from each of these sources of which *Évangéline* was a part.

To understand the scope of the growing foundational narrative of the time, we must look to the societal discourse that preceded it. Until the beginning of the nineteenth century, the United States of America did not possess a historical consciousness. It did not have its own story. Indeed, there was no pressing need for one during the colonial period, for several reasons. For one, there was no existing United States—or American societal reality—in the colonial period. The thirteen colonies were largely disparate administrative units with little commerce between them. When trade opportunities transcended the colonies, they were directed to the homeland. Certain colonies were created out of mercantile interests (the Southern colonies), some out of religious dissidence (those of New England), and others, like Maryland and Pennsylvania, were established as quasi-colonial kingdoms. Though British settlers were predominant, other groups also colonized America. New York was a Dutch colony at first, and there were many German settlements throughout the territory. There was a strong diversity of religions—not only Protestant, as Maryland was initially a Catholic colony—and languages within most colonies.

When this diversity first gained meaning during the colonial period, the distinct groups did not rally around a collective cultural imaginary nor continental geography, but rather around a shared contribution to the British Commonwealth. The filiation was thus eminently political at this point. The English colonies were seen as settlement colonies and therefore a sort of transatlantic extension of Great Britain. In this context, American settlers assumed they held the same rights and privileges as British citizens. They had inherited the English freedom as conceived of in the *Magna Carta* of the Glorious Revolution. No need, then, for an autonomous political conscience. Future Americans were transatlantic Britons. As the future leader of the fight for independence, Benjamin Franklin stated at the time of the conquest of Canada by the British in 1760, and less than twenty years prior to the Declaration of Independence: "No one can more sincerely rejoice than I do, on the reduction of Canada; and this is not merely as I am a colonist, but as I am a Briton."

The political debates that led to the War of Independence were never in the name of what would later be called the "national sentiment." The British Enlightenment would come to name the motifs of the rebellion as the corruption of republican virtues, the failure to respect the freedom of the English—no taxation without representation—and the advent of a democratic people who opposed the patriarchal legitimacy of the British monarchy. Political essays such as John Locke's "Two Treatises of Government" (1684) or Thomas Paine's "Common Sense" (1776) paved the first affirmations of the American people; these essays were usually written by political philosophers of English origin who attempted to frame, in an essentially contractual or political manner, the nature of the political regime that arose out of opposition to the faltering forces of the monarchy. These were thinkers of the new political liberty, not of the burgeoning American nation. The idea of an American nation with its own history, its own narrative, has yet to be designed.

The first few years following the American Revolution were similar this way. The new independent states largely remained separate units. "America" was not yet a nation. The Founding Fathers undertook the task, a radically new one in history, of inventing a political regime whose legitimacy rested exclusively on the contractual willingness of its adherents. Facing the divided nature of the participating societies—the pro-slavery south and the commercial universe of the peasants in the north, among other issues—the growing strength of the people frightened the new leaders, and the Founding Fathers hesitated. Was the desire to be free from England sufficient to ensure the stability of the new country? They initially turned to the laws of the ancient republics to alleviate the anxieties that arose from the revolutionary rupture, and they believed they had found a tradition they did not have. This tradition was liberal and republican; it was not rooted in a specific national history. The new regime would be the result of delicate political gymnastics combining the guarantees for freedoms within a procedural republic with divided powers such as had designed Montesquieu, which would consequently limit social power, including that of the lower classes.

The *Federalist Papers* written in 1787–88 by eminent members of the new political elite—James Madison, Alexander Hamilton, John Jay—are exercises in classical political science. Using laws inherent to politics, they attempted to define the best government and not deprive the regime of the qualities and history specific to the "American" people, as the next generation would come to do. Jefferson, who consolidated the institutions of the new republic through his presidency (1801–09), remained a fervent partisan of the Enlightenment into the beginning of the nineteenth century. He believed, above all, that a democracy is better protected by a constitution and proper laws than by the attribution of direct power to the people. The years of his presidency, both in history and literature, are still marked by neoclassicism where the search for pure forms, such as the imitation of the ancient republics, surpassed a truth which would emanate from the people. At the time, there was neither historical nor cultural definition of the American people, who were known only as a disparate group of men and women brought together by laws. There was no romance in the narrative of America.

Everything changed at the beginning of the 1800s. This formal manner of conceiving politics, and the society that proceeded from it, changed drastically. From this point on, the laws governing the states and the reasoning behind them would be drawn from within society's history, culture, and soul. Montesquieu had written about how one could best understand law by studying a people's customs. Philosophers of the Enlightenment searched for truth in the ability to remove oneself from the world, in theoretical universalism—the concept of human rights, and the idea that human nature was universal throughout history—is one such example. In contrast, the historical period that followed rooted its quest for truth—as applied in both laws and institutions—in the history of those people it served.

## The Romantic Era in America

This change in thinking can be considered Romantic, though it must not be reduced to the sole opposition between sentimentality and reason. Romanticism was society's revenge for the Enlightenment's abstraction.

As such, it was a phenomenon in all registers of human experience: in religion, art, politics, and the law. More than just an opposition to the rationalism of the Enlightenment, it was a shift through whereby what used to be *cause* became *effect*. In the rationale of the Enlightenment, reason, form, and pure thought derived from history, humanity, and progress (the cause), whereas the Romantics considered these artifices of human thought as consequences of history (the effect). History, society, culture, the enhanced feeling created by the experience a place or a moment, then became a bridge to the shared living experience of a society. Romanticism was not opposed to reason or progress; it did, however, refuse to see these two elements as autonomous principles, conceiving of them instead as deriving from the spirit of a people.

Romanticism took form at the same time as the Enlightenment reached its peak, at the moment where it seemed to materialize into the politics of the American and French Revolutions. It was no coincidence, for the tension between the concept of a humanity built on universal reason and one drawing its origins upon a culture that existed throughout the modern history was exacerbated when democratic revolutions attempted to institutionalize modern reason. Romanticism was a response to the failure of modern, enlightened reason. Its abstract and artificial nature provoked an empty dissatisfaction, or "malaise," as philosopher Charles Taylor called it. Rationalized modernity did not fill individual and collective needs for expressiveness, hence Romanticism.

Romanticism thus appeared as a quest for settled conscience and authenticity that would fill the void left by the modern condition. In art, it asserted itself through the artistic singularity of expression, the birth of artistic genius, and artists able to instill feelings, as opposed to artists capable of reproducing a trend or form—classicism—that defined beauty. In religion, it contributed to a movement that rejected institutional forms of belief and the authorities that defined it, supporting instead faith as mediated by individuals. Such were the religious movements of early nineteenth century America. In politics, it sounded the awakening of cultural nationalities and the understanding that the state does not create the nation; rather, the nation equips itself with a state. History as a discipline would be made responsible for the arduous task of making known the people's spirit—the genuine substance that fuelled progress. History derived from Romanticism, even though, as with all modern disciplines, it also emanated from a movement of rational thought preferring to claim it as its own progeny. But at the beginning of the nineteenth century, modern history embraced its double origins drawing from both science and Romanticism, and sought to demonstrate how modern progress needed the vehicle of a national, Romantic narrative.

This Romantic shift did not only occur in America. Indeed, its epicentre was in Germany. One of the main paradoxes of Romanticism was to appeal to individual or collective distinctive characteristics, as opposed to the universal abstraction of the Enlightenment, all the while remaining a universally applicable movement. All modern societies were swept away by Romanticism, though each one experienced it differently.

## When the *Mayflower* Meant Everything

American Romanticism had the difficult task of creating a national narrative consistent with the spirit of the people in a society that had, through the revolution, abandoned its homeland and thus rejected all filiation with its past. For this new society, Independence Day would be considered the "Day of Deliverance," in the words of John Adams. The bearers of Romanticism also needed to provide cultural coherence to a very fragmented people where modern individualism was especially exacerbated…to ascribe meaning to a heterogeneity that was largely sanctified by a constitution that had, in a way, made its foundation by way of federalism, division of powers, and protection of individuals. Romanticism would thus need to negotiate the presence of religious pluralism where dominant Protestants were resistant to symbolism and ritual, which happened to be central to the Romantic rhetoric.

Why then attempt to create a national narrative in a place that seemed reticent to such a project? There was, at the time, a generalized malaise deriving from modern politics that was not strictly American: all modern societies had to deal with the disquiet caused by the fragility of modern social ties. But America had, by establishing its independence and democratic constitution, emphasized this requirement, and thus needed to establish a "people" out of what was still then a heterogeneous population. America was, indeed, a *land* in the imaginary of immigrants who settled there, not a *society*. Choosing the way of democracy, the new republic had made its people a mandatory reference for each political process. It quickly became apparent that the people lacked consistency and had no reason to act cohesively. If the people needed to rally together to defend the nation from its enemies, external and internal, or to support its leaders' Western expansion project, then the people needed to share something more than submission to the same legal system. The national narrative would give America the cultural and motivational substance that the newly formed rule of law could not.

In its first few years of existence, young America was thusly haunted by the fear that the Union might dissolve. The stark opposition between the southern colonial economy, which relied considerably on large operations and slavery, and the smaller-scale productions of the northern economy that would prove a fertile ground for the development of a modern capitalist economy, rapidly became apparent. The continual displacement of the western border, a reality enhanced after the American government purchased Louisiana in 1803—that is, the entire basin west of the Mississippi, from Lower Louisiana to Illinois Country, which nearly doubled the nominal size of the young republic—intensified the malaise of the shared living experience.

Western migration disrupted the communities of New England, which had been founded on a Protestant ideal of order. What status should be given to the new states that joined the Union following the purchase of pro-slavery Louisiana? The politically and economically dominant south's hegemony was slowly erased at the expense of the westward expansion and the flourishing industrial society of the north. From New England came the idea that America was born from the *Mayflower*, a ship that brought Puritan Pilgrims to Plymouth, south of the Boston Bay, in 1620. Choosing this location was detrimental to Jamestown, Virginia, a somewhat shady merchant colony founded in 1607, and to New Amsterdam (today's New

York), established in 1614—and even, as the Cajuns of Louisiana might timidly claim, to their own settlement on American soil which can be traced back to the *Jonas*, a ship steered by Poutrincourt that brought the first Acadian settlers in 1607.

The birth of America on the *Mayflower* gave a religious and even messianic character to the foundation of the United States. Plymouth would not be the only American settlement established for religious reasons. The South Carolina Huguenots, the Pennsylvania Quakers, the Maryland Catholics also sought refuge in the New World for religious reasons. Considering the *Mayflower* Pilgrims as the founders of the United States had the advantage of a more secular historical basis: the group had left Europe for America not mainly because of religious prosecution, but rather in the hopes of finding a promised land, a new Jerusalem likely to welcome a new chosen people. The Pilgrims became the first actors in the American narrative.

And what is more, before landing on American soil, the small group of settlers had decided to sign an agreement among them—the *Mayflower* Compact—in which they willingly "combine[d them]selves together into a civil body politic" to manage the colony. This was a bold choice for such pious people, as it disassociated them from the religious community responsible for their salvation, the same salvation that had led them to settle in America. They were also distancing themselves from the religious community that was designated as a political entity meant to ensure order. Though this covenant was largely attributable to the necessity for the Pilgrims to get along with the foreign merchants who accompanied them aboard the *Mayflower*—thus making it more utilitarian than properly democratic—this document was considered a founding act of democratic America. It foreshadowed the Constitution by combining, in an original manner, the providential mission of creating a new heavenly city, and the advent of a new civilian power known as democracy.

The story of the *Mayflower* closely associated religion with democracy in a way that still marks the American narrative to this day. Democracy and religion were bound on the *Mayflower*. American democracy was the embodiment of the city of God on Earth, and the American people were chosen to build the democratic society requested by God in the New World. This association was a creative solution to the rupture at the heart of revolutionary America's discourse. The challenge then became to reconcile to the fact that the revolution had been an act of rupture from old Europe and from monarchy; that the "Day of Deliverance" was synonymous with the creation of a new American society. How could a history of division align with the cherished Romantic idea of the continuity of the world, of a humanity that transcended the immediacy of our lives, of the need to be part of a tradition? The Revolution re-established a continuity much older than that of the ties to England. Indeed, the democratic rupture was in line with an earlier rupture, that of the Protestant Reformation. Continuity and rupture were thus in paradoxical harmony.

In the American narrative, the rupture would no longer be tied to the Revolution, which would become the confirmation, or consecration, of a rupture already present in the founding act of America by the *Mayflower* Pilgrims whose covenant merged the religious and democratic goals for the new land. The Pilgrims left a corrupt Europe to establish a new society. The source of this rupture was found in the Calvinist tradition of the Protestant Reformation, which was itself tied to the Anglo-Saxon culture that drew from Germanic and Teutonic populations of Northern Europe. There, in ancient societies that preceded the corruption of papist or Anglican churches and European monarchies, there, they found an authentic culture where communal egalitarianism heralded the ideal of American democracy. The Protestant Reform thus reiterated an even older quarrel between the artificialism originating from Roman civilization—the Latin people—and the authenticity of the people from Northern Europe—the Germanic tribes.

America could thus divorce from its British past without losing its European filiation. The origins of America could be found in the Teutonic forests, a place synonymous of religious and democratic authenticity. The *Mayflower* Pilgrims, though of English origin, had lived a few years in Leyde, Holland, on the Continent, where they believed they had found a place more open to their separatist goals of creating an authentic Christian community in a corrupt world. In the end, America had been the land of refuge for these Pilgrims, and by extension, for the Protestant Reformation. As such, the American rupture was not a true rupture, but rather a reconciliation with the true nature of humanity whose religious and democratic truth could be found in the Nordic forests cherished by the Romantics. The genesis of the American narrative was set in these forests, and its tale would echo throughout the vast wilderness of the new continent in a way that is reminiscent of the famous first lines of *Evangeline*:

> *This is the forest primeval. The murmuring pines and the hemlocks,*
> *Bearded with moss, and in garments green, indistinct in the twilight,*
> *Stand like Druids of eld, with voices sad and prophetic,*
> *Stand like harpers hoar, with beards that rest on their bosoms.*
> *Loud from its rocky caverns, the deep-voiced neighboring ocean,*
> *Speaks, and in accents disconsolate answers the wail of the forest.*

## Populist Democracy and Religious Renewal

The goal of this narrative was not exclusively to provide an explanation for the origins of the American people and thus bring coherence to the post-revolution American identity. The Romantic quest to find human roots was not only an intellectual trend, but also a popular, societal pursuit as seen in the transformations of democracy and the religious sentiment of the antebellum period.

The first phases of American democracy were republican in their attempt to define institutions (the constitution, the law) and procedures (indirect election), which would allow for the expression of a political power legitimized by the very people it kept a certain distance from. The following period, after the turn of the nineteenth century, saw the birth of the idea of the "real" people at the heart of the democratic imaginary. America got wrapped up in democracy, and made it one of the key elements of its identity. It was no longer the republic that was virtuous, but rather the individual citizen. The ordinary man, proud and independent, became the true hero of democracy. This corresponded with the extension of voting rights to all white men. The period also championed the idea of the "small town" where ordinary citizens with ties to their family and their church participated in their community.

The first phase of American constitutionalism had been defined by the elite's fear of the people; the second phase would be characterized by the critique of institutions and a corrupt elite that was not representative of the people—a change that led to the election of judges. This "Jacksonian" democracy—so named after Andrew Jackson, Democrat president-elect of 1828 with a populist agenda—would impress Frenchman Alexis de Tocqueville, the author of *De la démocratie en Amérique* (later translated as *Democracy in America*), during his travels in America at the beginning of the 1830s. In the introduction to his work, Tocqueville made connections between the enthusiasm for popular democracy he saw in America and those gatherings of believers that had been at the heart of community living for the first Pilgrims. Tocqueville thus borrowed from the burgeoning American narrative the idea of the religious and democratic dual origin of the nation. Religion had its place in the democracy that criticized institutions to valorize the common man.

As discussed earlier, Protestantism, through its rejection of corrupt religious institutions and its individualization of faith, could be interpreted as a source of modern democracy. Furthermore, with its anti-institutional beginnings and the free will it advocated, Protestantism was in a way destined to a perpetual self-questioning that would result in the multiplication of factions and sects, as every attempt to institutionalize a Church or sect was immediately criticized. From the beginning of the eighteenth century, American Protestantism was therefore periodically confronted to evangelical awakenings whereby established religions were criticized in the name of the conversion to a more personal faith. In both religious and political fields, a shift from institutions in favour of the genuine man meant that truth would henceforth emanate from the common man.

At the beginning of the nineteenth century in New England, evangelical awakenings moved in two main directions. A "Unitarian" version of the Church, more liberal and with universal aspirations, emphasized the Christian nature of faith. The second, "Orthodox," was congregationalist, more conservative, and with sectarian aspirations, insisted rather on distinguishing between the converted and those who weren't. The Orthodox vision, though conservative, was closer to a church of the people, like a religious adaptation of the Jacksonian democracy, while the Unitarian design was carried forth by the Boston elite, which was mostly formed of educated Whigs who were dosing the evangelical awakening with the perspective of the Enlightenment. There we find Longfellow.

Members of the Unitarian Church were indeed the ones who championed the Protestant birth of America. In the Pilgrims' borderline sectarian and fanatic Protestantism, they saw a progressive egalitarianism that had led to the democratization of America and the development of a sort of civic religion. Their Romanticism served to halt the popular and populist impulses of the Orthodox followers, for such waves were often affirmed with virulent attacks on the old religions, including Catholicism. Their vision also allowed them to fulfill the need for tradition while giving enlightened reason a platform. Longfellow would succeed in this vein by daring to make the protagonist of his American narrative, Évangéline, a Catholic. And many others would do so, such as his transcendentalist friends, led by poet Ralph Waldo Emerson who conceived of a sort of religion of humanity that extended beyond Protestantism.

This is a central debate in the American narrative: at its core, the nature of American democracy was perceived as a fulfilled promise by Unitarians and a broken promise by Orthodoxes. For the latter, the need for reconversion always reminded them of the corrupt nature of the current regime. The reminder of their Puritan ancestors felt, in a conservative sense, like a return to their roots. For the Unitarians, the Protestant past heralded above all the genesis of a democratic America and by extension, an American civil religion.

## The Providential Mission of America

The American narrative did not assert itself without first sparking debates and controversies. It created oppositions between Orthodox and Liberal Puritans, conservatives and progressives, nationalists and cosmopolitans, partisans of an open America and those desiring a radical rupture from

Europe: the then-president of Harvard University apparently stated that he hoped to never receive a letter from Europe. Despite the contention, the progressive and Romantic vision of an America seeking to achieve universality and become the only society in the world with a history full of nothing but progress would prevail.

The progressive and Romantic vision had its own talented historian, the first great narrator of the new republic, George Bancroft, whose first volume was titled *History of the United States of America. From the Discovery of the American Continent*, was published in 1834, with the last of the seven volumes published in 1874. Bancroft studied in Germany, where he trained in the Romantic school. The genius of America was liberty, he claimed. He confirmed the Germanic roots of American democracy through erudite scholarship, asserting that the idea of liberty was brought to America by Puritans of the Nordic forests. The geography and nature of America, themes dear to Romantics, had set the stage for this blooming liberty. At the same time New England was being established, Bancroft introduced the notion of America as an open frontier where unbounded borders did not, like those of Europe, hinder the liberal implementation of progress. The continual displacement of the Western border sealed the alliance between American nature and democracy, an alliance introduced by those Puritans who crossed the waters.

In a canonical text titled *The Significance of the Frontier in the American History*, historian Frederick Jackson Turner summarized in 1893 the impact of the Western frontier on American history. The border did not enclose as it did in old Europe, he claimed, it instead represented movement, a window to the vastness of the continent. The point of contact between untamed nature and civilization was not a site of confrontation, but a place of regeneration where the culturally restricted men of old Europe could transform into a new open-minded mixed race. The frontier, where civilization was restored to the conditions of primitive existence, revealed the democratic individual. Thusly defined, the frontier was but the pursuit of a mission that had begun aboard the *Mayflower*.

A new formula, known as *The Manifest Destiny*, summarized the American narrative and struck the collective imagination in this first part of the nineteenth century. The formula was very successful and is still applied to this day. The idea came from Jacksonian democrat journalist John L. O'Sullivan in 1845 in the context of a fervent plea published in the *Democratic Review* where he lobbied for the annexation of Texas to the United States through an act of war. The formula aimed to justify American expansionism—the annexation of Texas, and the southwestern Mexican territories which would indeed become American in 1848—as a providential mission which destined the States to continental expansion. The formula encompassed even further notions. The perpetually extended border meant America was not like other societies, these closed societies with a defined national history. O'Sullivan legitimized "America's exceptionality," for as he wrote in 1839, the high destiny of America was to be "the great nation of futurity." A nation unlike any other…a hybrid of all races and cultures…a nation of nations…without an aristocratic past. O'Sullivan argued that America had "been chosen" to abolish the monarchies and oligarchies of this world, for it was "the nation of progress, of individual freedom, of universal enfranchisement."

America thus came to be known for its exceptional destiny whose peculiarity was to achieve universality. With this vision, it foreshadowed the cosmopolitan humanity of the future.

## Longfellow and the "Celestial Mechanics" of America

We are now better positioned to understand what Hawthorne meant when he said that the American tale *Évangéline* had hoisted Longfellow among the great writers of national literature. He is considered the first author to write a major work about the American narrative, but is he really? Where does Longfellow fall within the construction of the American narrative? For such a task, we should not put undue reliance on the word of his schoolmate, Hawthorne, who is also a contender for the position of author of the great American novel.

Though Longfellow was not the most gifted poet and novelist of the budding American literature, he was certainly the most popular. It is difficult to imagine the level of fame he enjoyed at the time, for poetry as a literary genre is marginalized nowadays, and his life's work paled almost into oblivion in the wake of the pantheon of American inventors that followed him in history. We will learn why later on, but for now, let us explore his rather surprising notability.

Longfellow, as his most recent biographer Christopher Irmscher reminds us, can be considered the first American "pop star." He was adored during his lifetime. In 1881, the year preceding his death, his birthday was celebrated nationwide with performances and recitals in every school. It is estimated that he received over 20,000 letters from his admirers throughout his life. His home, Craigie House, which Washington had incidentally used as general headquarters during the War of Independence, was a national icon…almost a place of pilgrimage where one would go see the house of the poet. The house was depicted on a variety of commercial products, from children's candy to cigar boxes. Construction plans to build replicas were available for purchase through the catalogue of the large retail chain then known as Sears, Roebuck and Company. Imitations, theatrical and cinematographic adaptations, musical renderings, and images of his works number in the thousands.

Throughout the course of a century, he was the most famous American author—all genres included—in America, the Anglo-Saxon world, and beyond. His popularity transcended classes and artistic milieus. French poet Charles Baudelaire adapted Longfellow's *Song of Hiawatha* into *Le Calumet de paix*. Hungarian composer Franz Liszt set the prologue of Longfellow's *The Golden Legend* into music. The Brazilian emperor Dom Pedro II requested to dine with the poet during a visit to the United States, and to thank Longfellow, he translated *King Roberto of Sicily* into Portuguese. Queen Victoria, who hosted Longfellow for dinner during his travels to England in 1868, and Charles Dickens were both impressed by his enormous popularity among the "servants and workers." He was a poet for all classes, as attested by the candid remarks of an Irish worker who happened upon him in Cambridge, Massachusetts: "I am proud to meet a poet. My own brother, who works at the docks, is a drunk and a poet."

Longfellow created the status of professional writer, managing his royalties and the rights to his works like an entrepreneur more than a

Romantic. The first American author to make a living from his writing, he quit his post as professor of modern languages at Harvard in 1854 to focus on his family and his writing. His characters (Paul Revere, Hiawatha, Évangéline) and descriptions of the lifestyle and villages of New England (*The Courtship of Miles Standish, The Village Blacksmith*), Mississippi (*Évangéline*), and the Atlantic coast (*The Tide Rises, The Tide Falls*) inspired the imagination of Americans.

Though it is an exaggeration to say he was "*The Man Who Invented America*," as the title of a recent exhibition on his work suggested, Longfellow was nevertheless the first to put a human face on the devoted Pilgrims of the *Mayflower*. He did so in his poem entitled *The Courtship of Miles Standish*. Even though Longfellow has since been forgotten and rejected by literary critics, the modern poet Dana Gioia reminds us that without us always knowing the author, people aged over sixty can still recite from memory the first lines of his most famous poems, including those of *Évangéline*—"*This is the forest primeval. The murmuring pines and the hemlocks. / Bearded with moss, and in garments green, indistinct in the twilight*"—and that some of his verses have come into everyday use in the English language: ships that pass in the night; footprints on the sands of time; when she was good, she was very good; the patter of little feet.

But Longfellow was not a man of the people. In his second marriage, he wed Fanny Appleton, the daughter of a rich industrialist from Boston. His own middle-class family had settled in New England at the beginning of colonialism. He lived lavishly at Craigie House in a manner that impressed his less-fortunate friends. In the summer of 1853, Emerson wrote with irony: "If Socrates were here, we could go & talk with him; but Longfellow, we cannot go & talk with; there is a palace, & servants, & a row of bottles of different colored wines, & wine glasses, & fine coats." He was a part of a caste known as Brahmin, made up of those old families from the first Puritan settlements that still dominated New England financially, intellectually, and politically. Others from this group included William Hickling Prescott, George Bancroft, John Lothrop Motley, and Francis Parkman. The four great historians were essential to the development of the historical foundation of the American narrative that would transpire in the peregrinations of Évangéline. Later, as Longfellow's fame subsided, he was lumped in with his poet friends who were also Harvard professors—notably Oliver Wendell Holmes and James Russell. He was further associated with the genteel tradition of this generation of poets who were too rich to be truly talented, sentenced to write insignificant short tales, and destined to be remembered as "the fireside poets."

Nor was Longfellow a populist. He did not take the floor in public and avoided gatherings. He did not preside over organizations other than the "Dante Circle" that, near the end of his life, rallied some of his friends to join his project of translating *The Divine Comedy*. (Of note, contemporary author Matthew Pearl wrote a fascinating and fictional murder mystery titled *The Dante Club*, which places a serial killer in the setting of Longfellow's Boston.) Back to Longfellow: he quit his teaching post at Harvard as soon as he could, complaining of the distractions it provided and expressing relief for no longer having to speak in public. "I like intimate footings; I do not care for general society," thus he was reputed to have spoken while he was a young professor at Bowdoin. He projected the image of a bard inhabited by a muse. The loss of two wives had conferred upon him a tragic personality. His face was scarred from the fire that killed his second wife—he had attempted to save her from the flames sparked by the curling iron used on their daughter's hair. After this fateful event, he kept a long beard that seemed to confer upon him a certain inwardness. Widowed, he lived as a recluse in his home, praising the merits of a Victorian democracy that was both imbued with egalitarianism and principles of honour (*The Children's Hour*, 1863).

## A Cosmopolitan Nation

Longfellow rarely commented on his own artistic or political trajectories. Only a select few essays, such as "Defense of Poetry" (1832) which we will address later, provided his opinions on the ties between poetry and the development of the national narrative. His written outlooks on politics proper are rarer still. He claimed he was not interested in politics. However, very early on, he positioned himself as an abolitionist, as attested by his

*Poems on Slavery* (1842) and his longstanding friendship with Senator Charles Sumner, one of the first anti-slavery politicians. It is not known if he had any other political interests. His journal is filled with reflections on everyday life, but does not provide biographers with indications regarding his intellectual process, nor any means of considering him a political poet. Using these arguments, some 1920s and 1930s critics successfully dislodged him from his status as a national poet by claiming that such innocent goodness had no ties to the real world. It was, as they argued, difficult to find someone as detached from politics, indifferent to social issues, and isolated from the influences of his time.

Today, these judgments seem unfair; Longfellow's works contain political notions that explain why readers of his time admired his writings. The poet's apparent silence on worldly issues is typical of Romantic attitudes whereby one rejects the artificial and frivolous aspects of the modern world preferring instead to focus on inwardness, which is representative of a more tangible dimension of the human condition. This Romantic attitude draws us to a community based on a literal "communion," as opposed to the public arena that focuses on "communication." According to Longfellow, the role of an artist was not to be an avant-garde who enlightened the people with reasoning, but rather to distance himself from the public so as to better express through sentiment an inner and profound universal truth. Such practices do not make the Romantic attitude undemocratic, as they contribute to strengthening the otherwise frail social ties within a society of individuals.

Such were Longfellow's Romantic ways. As he wrote his review titled "Defense of Poetry" (1832), artists must relinquish being useful, and instead trust in their own expression, for this leads to the expression of something along the lines of a national authenticity. We mustn't therefore look for an explicit national narrative in the works of Longfellow, but rather for the intuition of one, something that appears naturally or unwittingly, as the poet would have us believe. By removing himself from the public and insisting on inward sentiments, Longfellow manages to communicate to a public of individuals who do not know each other, the expression of a shared experience. Scholar Mary Louise Kete calls such work on society as was practised in Longfellow's poetry "sentimental collaboration." It was the fabrication of a sentiment whereby all worked toward a common goal in an America that invented its national reality at the same time as it underwent, through its experience of the frontier, a new interior dislocation.

Was it truly, then, a "national" sentiment? Longfellow's readers at the time—like his literary colleagues, as we saw in Hawthorne's statement—believed so, and considered him the first great American poet. Modernist literary critics at the beginning of the twentieth century later rejected him as a minor poet, not American in inspiration, and thus removed his works from the nation's literary canon. Recent biographies (Irmscher, Calhoun), published after over forty years of near silence on Longfellow's contributions, portray the poet as a precursor of multiculturalism and cosmopolitanism. Gioia, who presided over the National Endowment for the Arts, wrote "Longfellow in the Aftermath of Modernism" in *The Columbia History of American Poetry* (1993), in which she made a virulent and convincing plea for the reintegration of Longfellow among the great poets who contributed to the development of the national American imaginary.

The strictly aesthetic value of Longfellow's oeuvre is not debated here. What is more relevant in this case is whether his works derived from outdated Europeanism, fostered American nationalism, and eventually brought about forms of multiculturalism or cosmopolitanism. The seemingly contradictory opinions regarding his career are mainly attributable to the fact that Longfellow was indubitably the most Europeanist poet who participated in the development of a national literature. Longfellow's singular rapport to Europe made him stand out from the New England writers, including the Brahmin poets, who were passionate about European culture and worked tirelessly to create a non-British, though European, past for America (and who must be differentiated from those more nationalist movements that desired an authentically American national culture).

This seems unsurprising for a modern languages professor who was fluent in European languages other than English (French, Spanish, Italian, German), and who was knowledgeable in Danish, Finnish, etc. Through his translations of these languages, he was in constant dialogue with their cultures. His rapport to Europe could therefore not be one of pure rejection. The type of Romanticism he practised incited him to maintain this openness. His Romanticism would not lead him to adopt the posture of singular individuality, a pure subjectivity that, in the name of artistic inspiration, allows for the rejection of all forms and all artistic traditions. His Romanticism was tinted with Classicism, as we can see in his incessant play with different poetic forms (from the sonnet to the hexameter), and his constant borrowing of classical poetry themes—these practices even led Edgar Allan Poe to view Longfellow as a plagiarist. Though the contents of his narrations became American, their form remained European.

The same was true for politics. Longfellow's perception of democracy was always marked by conservatism, as his nationalism was with prenationalism, which is what allows us today to paradoxically view him as a precursor of postmodernism. In time, he nuanced his initial plea for a New World national literature, proposing instead a sort of great novel of humanity, a Goethe-style "Weltliteratur" where humanity replaced the nation as the foundation and horizon of literature. New World literature nonetheless remained the inspirational genius of a new universal dialectic. In 1847, the year *Évangéline* was published, he insisted "We have or shall have, a composite one [literature]; embracing French, Spanish, Irish, English, Scotch, and German peculiarities. Whoever has within him most of these is the truly national writer—in other words whoever is most universal, is almost the most national."

In his novel *Kavanagh* (1849), Longfellow had his alter ego say, "Simply, that a national literature is not the growth of a day. Centuries must contribute their dew and sunshine to it [...] As the blood of all nations is mingling with our own, so will their thoughts and feelings finally mingle in our literature. We shall draw from the Germans, tenderness; from the Spanish, passion; from the French, vivacity—to mingle more and more with our English solid sense. And this will give us universality, so much to be desired."

Must we then see a project for a cosmopolitan literature that rejected nationalism? Not if we follow the trail of the American narrative. America, in the national narrative, was the first society in the world whose tradition was to integrate all traditions, the first society where the claims to nationalism drew on cosmopolitanism. Indeed, it was the first society to, somehow, not really "be" a society, for it rather constituted the prefiguration of human emancipation. Thus, as a cosmopolitan nationalist, Longfellow could not be any closer to the heart of the American tale of the early nineteenth century. What was peculiar about America was its ability to be universal, to embody the first humanity, to use the language of the Romantics. "Be patient with America. The idea, the meaning of America is very grand. She is working out one of the highest problems in the 'celestial mechanics' of man," replied Longfellow to an English colleague who had complained of America's lack of maturity.

# References

ARVIN, N. *Longfellow, His Life and Work.* Boston, MA: Little, Brown & Co., 1962.

BUELL, L. *New England Literary Culture: From Revolution Through Renaissance.* Cambridge, UK: Cambridge University Press, 1986.

CALHOUN, Charles C. *Longfellow: A Rediscovered Life.* Boston, MA: Beacon Press, 2004.

FRANCHOT, J. *Roads to Rome: The Antebellum Protestant Encounter with Catholicism.* Berkeley, CA: University of California Press, 1994. ark.cdlib.org/ark:/13030/ft1xonb0f3/

GIOIA, D. "Longfellow in the Aftermath of Modernism." *The Columbia History of American Poetry.* Jay Parini (Ed.), New York, NY: Columbia Press, 1993. pp. 64-96.

HOWARD, D. *Aux Origines de la pensée américaine.* Paris, France: Buchet-Chastel, 2004.

IRMSCHER, C. *Longfellow Redux.* Chicago, IL: University of Illinois Press, 2006.

KETE, M. *Mourning and Middle-Class Identity in Nineteenth-Century America.* Durham, NC: Duke University Press, 2000.

LACORNE, D. *De la religion en Amérique. Essais d'histoire politique.* Paris, France: Gallimard, 2007.

LEGROS, R. *L'idée d'humanité: Introduction à la phénoménologie,* Paris, France: Grasset, 1993.

LIND, M. *The Next American Nation.* New York, NY: Free Press, 1995.

LIPSET, S. *American Exceptionalism: A Double-Edged Sword.* New York, NY: W.W. Norton and Company, 1996.

MARIENTRAS, É. *Nous le peuple: Les origines du nationalisme américain.* Paris, France: Gallimard, 1998.

MORENCY, J. *Le mythe américain dans les fictions d'Amérique: de Washington Irving à Jacques Poulin.* Montréal, QC: Nuit blanche éditeur, 1994.

PHILBRICK, N. *Le Mayflower: L'odyssée des Pères pèlerins et la naissance de l'Amérique.* Paris, France: JC Lattès, 2009.

TAYLOR, C. *Le malaise de la modernité.* Paris, France: Éditions du Cerf, 1992.

TOCQUEVILLE, A. *La démocratie en Amérique.* Paris, France: Flammarion, 1981.

WAGEKNECHT, E. *Henry Wadsworth Longfellow: Portrait of an American Humanist,* New York, NY: Oxford University Press, 1966.

WILLIS, L. *Looking Away: The Evasive Environmental Politics of American Literature.* Ph.D. Dissertation, University of Florida, 2006.

# ÉVANGÉLINE,
# THE FIRST WOMAN

*There from the troubled sea had Evangeline landed, an exile,*
*Finding among the children of Penn a home and a country.*
*There old René Leblanc had died; and when he departed,*
*Saw at his side only one of all his hundred descendants.*
*Something at least there was in the friendly streets of the city,*
*Something that spake to her heart, and made her no longer a stranger;*
*And her ear was pleased with the Thee and Thou of the Quakers,*
*For it recalled the past, the old Acadian country,*
*Where all men were equal, and all were brothers and sisters.*

—Henry Wadsworth Longfellow, *Evangeline: A Tale of Acadie*

On February 27, 1847, Longfellow wrote in his journal partly in French, partly in English: "Aujourd'hui j'ai quarante ans, une femme et deux enfants. Evangeline is ended. I wrote the last lines this morning."[1] At the time, he was a mature man living a happy period of his life. For almost ten years, he had been a professor of modern languages at Harvard University. In 1844, he had married Fanny Appleton after having maintained a long and platonic relationship with her since their first meeting in Switzerland shortly after the death of his first wife. Their marriage brought him joy, for when he had alluded to this love, not yet requited, for Ms. Appleton in one of his writings (*Hyperion*, 1839), he had described it as nearly impossible. The fact that such a pretension had been shared with the high society of Boston had shocked the beautiful heiress. Some saw in *Évangéline*—a hymn in praise of feminine virtue and fidelity—signs of Longfellow's love for Fanny, at long last mutual.

---

1. "Today I am forty years old. I have a wife and two children."

He was already a known author, though his first prose essays—
*Outre-mer* (1834) and *Hyperion* (1839), which recount his first stays in
Europe—did not get much traction, much like his very first works on
French and Italian grammar meant for his students at Bowdoin College.
His collections of poetry, on the other hand, were received with more enthusiasm. These were short poems largely inspired by European themes,
such as *Voices of the Night* (1839). *Poems on Slavery* (1842), on the other
hand, was a small work of thirty-six pages with a more political than
aesthetic contribution, that brought together eight short poems on the
situation of enslaved Black Americans. To make his mark on the literary
movement of burgeoning America, he still needed to write a major, and
inspired, American work. *Évangéline* would be this work, and the first
of a series of long poems—*The Song of Hiawatha* (1855), *The Courtship
of Miles Standish* (1858), and *Tales of Wayside Inn* (1863)—that would
ultimately make Longfellow a great American poet.

*Évangéline* became the first American bestseller in verse since Michael
Wigglesworth's *The Day of Doom,* which was printed in 1662. Published in
1847, *Évangéline* was a long poem of 1,399 verses, spanning 160 pages in its
original version, and written in English hexameters without rhymes. Less
than a year later, the book was already in its sixth printing. Throughout the
following century, there came to be more than 270 editions in the United
States alone, and at least 130 translations published in other countries. In the
one hundred years following its original publication, there were countless
theatrical adaptations, musicals, nineteenth-century–style French operettas
(opéra-bouffe), films—among the first in the Hollywood industry—and a
wide usage by the tourism industry that highlighted the poem's significance
for the American collective imaginary. The poem's fame is consecrated by
its long and overarching presence as mandatory reading in schools. At the
beginning of the twentieth century, it was the most commonly assigned
reading in Anglo-American schools throughout the world. The level of fame
achieved by *Évangéline* propelled Longfellow's career, making him a star of
the burgeoning American literary industry and a world-renowned poet.

But beyond its popularity, what of the poem's contribution to the great
American narrative? To understand how *Évangéline* participated in this

tale, we need to distance ourselves from Longfellow's own oft-repeated affirmations, which were repeated by critics: that he had little interest in politics. We also need to distance ourselves from the intentions that the author wanted to inscribe into the poem. Longfellow allegedly said, "It is the best illustration of faithfulness and the constancy of woman that I ever heard of or read," in 1840 during a dinner at Craigie House with Nathaniel Hawthorne when Pastor Connolly recounted the story of this legend of supposed Acadian origin. In the story, in the hasty expulsion of Nova Scotian French Catholics during the Seven Years War, a young woman was said to have searched her whole life throughout New England for her long-lost lover, only to find him at long last on his deathbed in old age. Longfellow made a claim to this intention—writing a poem that exuded the Romantic sentiment of fidelity and love between a man and a woman—and he instills this intention into his poem, attempting to convince readers in the final couplet of the introduction: "Ye who believe in affection that hopes, and endures, and is patient, / Ye who believe in the beauty and strength of woman's devotion, / List to the mournful tradition still sung by the pines of the forest; / List to a Tale of Love in Acadie, home of the happy."

Did Longfellow want to write a poem on the principles of fidelity and love between a woman and a man? Certainly, but readers need not venture far into the work to understand that *Évangéline* was not meant only for such limited interpretations. The great American narrative is everywhere, sometimes unwittingly, sometimes explicitly. In this way, the work conforms to its Romantic roots by absorbing the spirit of its times.

Exploring the poem further, we shall thus discover the presence of the American narrative by analyzing the following themes: 1) the foundation of America; 2) the epic tale: the odyssey of a chosen people; 3) democracy in America; 4) the frontier; and 5) the Catholic ballad of American Protestantism.

## Évangéline, the Founder

Consider the heroine's first name: Évangéline. One might think Longfellow created it. If similar forms existed in New England before the poem was published, it was not part of the French tradition prior to 1847, notably in Acadie. Longfellow hesitated to choose it, having first titled his work *Gabrielle*, then thinking of *Celestine* before finally settling on *Évangéline* and relegating masculine form "Gabriel" to the heroine's absent lover. All three names are biblical: Gabriel(le) is the angel who proclaimed the good news, Celestine is reminiscent of the divine nature of the character, Évangéline (from the Greek *evangelion*) is, herself, "the good news." In French, it is patronization and feminization of the word "*Évangile*" (meaning Gospel). In English, it is a contraction of *Eve*, the first woman and founder of humanity, and *Angel* (an Eve who, like an angel, did not succumb to temptation or, in all likelihood, an Eve who suffered through the ordeal of damnation to enter into the age of redemption). The final words of Évangéline were indeed Christ-like. Pressing the lifeless Gabriel to her bosom, she said, like Jesus on the cross: "Father, I thank Thee!" thus announcing the end of an old world and the foundation of a new Jerusalem.

Évangéline is thus the good news, the promise fulfilled, the one who, as the *Mayflower* Pilgrims did, contributes to the foundation of the promised land. To ensure the metaphor is not hidden, Longfellow saddled the lovers with surnames that were not used in Acadie and that echo the source of life: Évangéline "Bellefontaine" (lovely fountain), Gabriel "Lajeunesse" (youth). And much like the *Mayflower* Pilgrims, this female founder was banned, exiled, and cast onto the American coast because of the corruption of the Old World: "But in the course of time the laws of the land were corrupted; / Might took the place of right, and the weak were oppressed, and the mighty / Ruled with an iron rod."

Though the setting of the story Connolly had told Longfellow was limited to New England, Évangéline's odyssey embraced the entire United States. The goal here, in the same manner as those historians of the American narrative, was to reproduce the essence of the *Mayflower* Pilgrim experience of America. Évangéline landed in Philadelphia and crossed the Appalachian Mountains to reach Ohio. She then followed the river down to Mississippi and continued the path it set all the way to southern Louisiana. She did not settle in Louisiana, staying only two nights. She went back up the great river, the central artery of the new America, then changed course toward the Ozark Mountains, the last mountainous area before the western plains, considered the final frontier at the time, which she trampled. She went again farther north, to Michigan, near the Great Lakes and the Canadian border, which did not seem to instill in her a desire to return home. She long erred in cities and the country of an America where the War of Independence was in full swing. She finally returned to the place where, like a wreck, the maleficent powers of monarchical Europe had first abandoned her: Philadelphia, "Penn's city," wrote Longfellow, in honour of another founding Pilgrim of America. Most importantly, Philadelphia was the city where, below the bell tower, the independence of America had been affirmed in writing.

This journey, this topography of the United States of America, particularly that of the new border, this vast territory of the old French empire that the young republic is preparing to colonize, takes place during the War of Independence. Évangéline's quest begins in 1755 with the episode of the Grand-Pré peasants being evicted from their ancestral land by the British, and culminates with the death of Gabriel, in 1793, the year of the yellow fever in Philadelphia. The revolution is not directly integrated into the setting with the exception of this single line where we see Évangéline "Now in the noisy camps and the battle-fields of the army."

And yet, the odyssey that is *Évangéline* is indeed one of taking possession. Her arrival in Louisiana, in the middle of the poem, has the allure of a military parade associated with a religious procession. The Acadian group travelled like Americans would, down the Mississippi, through the heart of the United States. To welcome them, nature suddenly transformed herself into a cathedral or a triumphal arch. At the very place where the majestic river, which originates at the northernmost border of the United States, swallows numerous waterways from the east and the west, and transforms into bayous upon reaching the Atchafalaya Basin before leisurely completing its long voyage in the Gulf of Mexico. There, at the southern border of the United States, the rowboat transporting the poor Acadian pilgrims is welcomed as one welcomes conquerors seeking divine blessings for their new possession.

*Soon were lost in a maze of sluggish and devious waters,*
*Which, like a network of steel, extended in every direction.*
*Over their heads the towering and tenebrous boughs of the cypress*
*Met in a dusky arch, and trailing mosses in mid-air*
*Waved like banners that hang on the walls of ancient cathedrals.*

*[...] Then in his place, at the prow of the boat, rose one of the oarsmen,*

*And, [...] blew a blast on his bugle.*

## The Odyssey of a Chosen People

The name "Évangéline" is reminiscent of the foundation of a new world, and so is the literary form of the poem. Longfellow chose to write a poem in English dactylic hexameter without rhymes. The hexameter was the metre valued by the Ancients, both Greeks and Romans, in their epic poems; Homer and Virgil wrote in hexameters, for example. The Romantic period, believing in the authenticity of first experiences, which contrast with the artificiality of the modern world, resuscitated this form of writing, in particular in the Nordic and Germanic world where Romanticism was strong and where the young American democracy was trying to find its roots.

Longfellow had, a few years prior and before entering Harvard, travelled Europe as part of the "Grand Tour" (1835–36). These journeys wealthy youth would undertake at the beginning of the nineteenth century were intended to complete their education. Where his first trip (1826–29) had taken him mostly throughout Latin Europe—France, Spain, and Italy—this second one would introduce him to Nordic languages, and was thus mainly focused on northern Europe and Germany. This was where Longfellow lost his first wife and where, a few months later, he met Fanny, the woman he would yearn for from that moment on. He also borrowed the form and a little of the substance of *Évangéline* from these northern parts of Europe. Similarities were sought, found—and used to criticize him—with *Hermann and Dorothea* by Goethe, and *Frithiof's Saga* by Swedish author Esaias Tegnér, two epics from the Nordic Romanticism written in hexameters.

Also, by looking deeper into the past of the German forest, critics found similarities with the medieval tale *Der arme Heinrich*, which was recorded by Hartmann von Aue around 1200. The Germanic influences are so strong that in Germany, *Evangeline* was almost considered a German poem, part of the national repertoire, and that, for a long time, the visual representations of Évangéline and her native Acadie—in the United States, abroad, and even in Acadie—put the tale and character in a Germanic setting.

This should not be interpreted as a lack of imagination on Longfellow's part. Borrowing from the German tradition the hexameter, the pastoral scenery of the Nordic forest, the theme of the young woman separated from her lover, was not fortuitous. After all, the idea of a couple separated by destiny, so universal, could easily have been concealed. Longfellow borrows abundantly, but his plagiarism is never camouflaged. In a thesis of over 700 pages published in the early 1900s, Paul Morin documented thousands of these imitations. Like Hansel and Gretel, the author left markers indicating how to trace the sources. In *Évangéline*, the borrowings lead back to the Teutonic Forest, the birthplace, as we have described, of the (Protestant) Revolution that put an end to the Old World.

Nor was it fortuitous that Longfellow's work recalled the great epic poems of the antiquity. The destruction of Grand-Pré had all the bearings of Troy. Évangéline, whose name originates from Greek, was an American Penelope, and her country, the bucolic A(r)cadia. But she was not as passive as her Greek alter ego who incessantly repeated her work on the loom as she awaited Ulysses's return. The American Penelope travelled far and wide across horizons to the new frontier, actively searching for her lover. Évangéline was thus a strong female figure typical of the democratic Romanticism that would paradoxically be interpreted in the Acadian tale as a symbol of resignation and even obstinacy.

More fundamentally, for Longfellow, the hexameter was a foundational form of writing suitable for narratives about origins. The hexameter "is the only way to translate Homer," said Longfellow once. In response to the insistent advice of his friends—notably Charles Sumner, the Boston anti-slavery politician—who all pleaded for him not to use this form of writing, Longfellow affirmed that it seemed the only appropriate form for such a poem. The issue was that the hexameter was frowned upon in the English tradition. In England, at a time when English was being consolidated as the national language (sixteenth and seventeenth centuries), some attempts were made to incorporate it in the new poetic writing; but the hexameter was quickly rejected as it was deemed improper for the genius of the English language. A few English Romantics endeavoured to use it at the beginning of the nineteenth century, but the verdict remained unchanged, as stated in the *Edinburgh Review* in 1821: "The hexameter line can never be made a legitimate English measure." All the more reason for Longfellow, who wished to write a great American epic poem, to employ the hexameter; he could thus show how the genius of new countries eclipsed that of the old monarchical societies.

The opinions of critics were varied when it came to Longfellow's success at integrating the verses of Homer and Virgil into American poetry. But the popular success of *Évangéline* was undeniable. The American version of the English hexameter, with its long lines and absence of rhymes, is a cross between prose and poetry. The poem is a quasi-novel with exacerbated musicality. It is reminiscent of the oral tradition of fairy tales and popular romances, all of which, as we will later see, is absent from the French-Canadian translation of the poem. It seems a sort of democratic form of writing that is specific to the Romantic era. Readers raved and cried. However, these features also conferred a serious, sorrowful, and occasionally flat tone, which, as interest in Romanticism faded, indisputably became irritating to the hedonistic ears of our contemporaries.

Even so, the Acadian odyssey is neither a German, nor a Greek story. As we will see later on, Longfellow deliberately blurs the lines leading back to the origins of Acadians. More than anything, the odyssey that is told in *Évangéline* is that of the chosen people. The tale is constructed like a biblical triad: a first part, "Heaven on Earth," the land of Cocagne, the bucolic life of Acadian peasants; a second part, the "fall," the corruption of the Old World, the expulsion of Acadians; then a third part—the longest of the narrative—"redemption," the long crossing of the desert to arrive at the promised land, America, the new Jerusalem. Longfellow used the image of Agar and his son Ishmael, chased away by Abraham, to foreshadow the terrible fate that awaited Évangéline, on the eve of her engagement, the eve of the fateful day when the men would be locked into the Grand-Pré church, the eve of the day she would be chased from her home and separated from her lover: "As out of Abraham's tent young Ishmael wandered with Hagar!" Longfellow did not expressly name Israel when he described the ships laden with poor Acadian peasants disappearing behind Cape Blomidon and officially leaving the Minas Basin, but he did write: "Bearing a nation, with all its household gods, into exile. / Exile without an end, and without an example in story."

In this passage, Acadia represented something more than just Acadia. The odyssey was "without an example," for it was that of humanity sailing toward the celestial city. Longfellow repeated the exodus metaphor at the end of the poem, when Gabriel died, writing, "Hot and red on his lips still burned the flush of the fever, / As if life, like the Hebrew, with blood had besprinkled its portals."

## Democratic America

The promised land was obviously America. Throughout the poem, Longfellow maintained the confusion between the Acadians expelled from their land and welcomed in America, and the idea of a people working toward realizing the promise given at the origins of humankind. The poet struggled with bouts of fiction to set the historic Expulsion of Acadians at the northeastern border of New England and present it as a confrontation between the British Old World and the idyllic society at the border. The event had actually taken place during the French and Indian War, an expression designating, in the new early nineteenth century American historiography, the tumultuous period that had occurred shortly before the Revolution and had worn out the French empire in America and the alliance between French Catholics and Indigenous populations at the American border.

The French and Indian War (1756–63) opposed France and England, and resulted in the Paris Treaty in 1763, which officiated the transfer of vast Northern territories like the American West to England and surrendered the French-occupied territory of the Mississippi basin to Spain. By focusing on the French and Indian War the burgeoning American historiography wanted to show that these conflicts were not just colonial wars, but also had an eminently American dimension. These were the wars of the frontier that had instilled national sentiment in the new Republic. Hadn't George Washington himself played an important role in these battles?

On this matter, the episode of the displacement—the removal—of French neutrals, a term used in eighteenth-century New England to designate the Nova Scotian French Catholics, posed a problem for the young historiography. The Expulsion had taken place on the territory of Nova Scotia, once known as Acadie, which had been under British rule since 1713 and was governed from Boston as an extension of the colony of Massachusetts. It concerned British subjects who believed they had been authorized to stay on these lands all the while practising their Catholic religion without having to bear arms against their old masters, the French—hence the expression "French neutral." The event had taken place before the outbreak of the Seven Years War and was mainly due to the New England settlers' desire, against the mild English response, to deal once and for all with the threat of the French and Indigenous presence at the border.

In 1755, Massachusetts militia formed by Governor William Shirley travelled to Nova Scotia to assist the colony's administration in destroying Fort Beauséjour, which the French Canadians had erected in the Chignecto Isthmus, and which they considered the border between the French and English territories. The French had planned to build a new Acadie just north of this line. While the Massachusetts militia was in place, it was decided that some eight thousand French neutrals remaining on British land, accused of collaborating with the French and refusing to take an oath of allegiance to the Protestant king, would be displaced throughout other New England colonies. The other Acadians, approximately equal in numbers, then lived on the French side of the border.

With all the excitement of the young national historiography for the French and Indian War, the events came to be known and discussed in New England. Thomas Hutchinson, who at the time of these events was a member of the colonial council and who would later become governor of Massachusetts (1771–74) had, in his history of the colony titled *The History of the Colony of Massachuset's* [sic] *Bay*—written in the 1760s though the third volume describing these events would only be published in 1828, justified the act of expulsion by arguing that the French inhabitants of Acadia were objective allies of the French and a danger to the peace of the New England colonies. Their displacement and integration into the American colonies, he continued, would be done as humanely as possible.

It was only when George Richards Minot, in his *History of the Insurrection in Massachusetts* (1788), sourced information from the journal of Lieutenant-Colonel John Winslow, commander of the Expeditionary Force of American Militia in Nova Scotia, that the true events were unveiled, as the journal described the events of 1755 more explicitly. Thomas Chandler Haliburton, in *An Historical and Statistical Account of Nova Scotia* (1829)—a book that Longfellow claims to have used as inspiration to describe the episode of the Expulsion from Grand-Pré—also draws on Minot's book and Winslow's journal to recount with much empathy the injustice suffered by these poor peasants. In early nineteenth century America, this event was already considered cruel and unnecessary, intolerable by the standards of justice of the times. The judgment by American Robert Walsh, US Consul General in Paris, was more severe. In 1820, he compared the treatment of Acadians to the slave trade, calling it a "sin of inhumanity," a "crime."

In 1841, prior to the publication of *Évangéline* but at a moment when Longfellow was already preparing to write the poem, George Bancroft, the first of the great national historians, wrote in *The Token*—a collection which also had Longfellow as a contributor—an article titled "The Exiles of Acadia" that would later be published again in his general history of the United States. In this article, Bancroft wondered if there had been, elsewhere in history, a similar example of such abominable and intentionally inflicted punishment. Friend and writer Hawthorne, who had declined to write a novel recounting the story of a couple separated during these events, a story supposedly told by Reverend Connolly, wrote instead the same year a work titled *Famous Old People*. This collection included a short story titled *The Removal of the Inhabitants of Acadia* about the distress of those Acadians exiled in Boston. The same year, Catherine Arnold Williams published a novel which was not very successful, *The Neutral French, or the Exiles of Nova Scotia*, but that faithfully represented the Acadian exodus from the perspective of the American narrative: deported by the English, the story's heroine was welcomed and harmoniously integrated into the high society of Boston. We can thus see how this small community of New England writers, though not at the heart of the events of the Great Upheaval (*Grand Dérangement*) of 1755, had created a compounded effect of publications that publicized the crisis and the implications of Bostonians in the disastrous adventure.

How could this tragedy be integrated into the American narrative? Historians would first need to lay the blame on the British, converting the events into a prominent example of the treachery of English colonialism. To do so, Americans could base themselves on a few anticolonial European works such as Guillaume-Thomas Raynal's (abbé de Raynal) work entitled *Histoire philosophique et politique des établissements et du commerce des Européens dans les deux Indes* (1770). This work presented the expulsion of Acadians as proof of the absurd colonial logic of both English and French monarchies. Politician and philosopher Edmund Burke intervened twice on this issue, in 1757 and 1780, insisting each time on England's inability to ensure an organizational order instilling loyalty, and that these shortcomings had provoked the colony's "inhumane" actions toward Acadians. Though historian Bancroft recognized that Winslow was an American commander, he limited to this very fact the role New England settlers in the expulsion and concluded that the crime was on the hands of the English officers who led the expulsion.

The second step was to suggest that Acadians had been welcomed in democratic America, land of asylum for all the refugees of the world. Then again, the historical documents available at the time, such as a letter from exiled Acadians to the governors of Philadelphia, which served as a basis of Longfellow's character notary Leblanc—the only historical character of the poem, along with Lieutenant-Colonel Winslow, whose name was, however, not stated—showed that Acadians had, as Catholics and Frenchmen, been an embarrassment and victims of hostility. They eventually left, in large groups, the English colonies where the Deportation had abandoned them. By 1793, when Évangéline found Gabriel, there had not been any Acadians in Philadelphia for quite some time already. After years of trauma, between 1766 and 1770, where their children were taken from them by the authorities under the pretext of incapacity, "they all went off in body to the bank of the Mississippi," affirmed John Watson in the *Annals of Philadelphia and Pennsylvania, in the Olden time*, a work Longfellow had read. They also fled Massachusetts, an area where life was more promising than others, returning to Canada as soon as the English governor of Quebec, James Murray, gave them permission to, immediately following the Paris Treaty of 1763. Hawthorne's short story, which was set in Boston, was nevertheless presented as a form of living memory; that of his Bostonian grandfather who remembered the sympathy he felt for these exiled strangers and the hostility he carried through life toward the Englishmen responsible for the drama, especially Governor Shirley. This memory was specific to the American narrative.

*Évangéline* became a part of this movement: it amplified and ultimately incorporated the Great Upheaval into the American narrative. The poem had no traces of American responsibility, no mentions of the recurring confrontations between New England and what used to be known as French Acadie, no indication of rejection or negative feelings toward the exiled Acadians. The domination was British, and so were the persecutors of the Acadians: "Down with the tyrants of England! we never have sworn them allegiance! / Death to these foreign soldiers, who seize on our homes and our harvests!" It was Basil the blacksmith, Gabriel's father, who thus spoke to the "English" officer who had come to proclaim the seizure of property and deportation of the inhabitants—in reality, the Lieutenant-Colonel Winslow from Massachusetts, whose words Longfellow borrows almost verbatim then strengthens so as to highlight the cruelty of the old regime. The same Basil, who later in the poem had become the owner of a herd in the "Eden of Louisiana," sang the praises of his new homeland, America: "Welcome once more to a home, that is better perchance than the old one!—[...] No King George of England shall drive you away from your homesteads, / Burning your dwellings and barns, and stealing your farms and your cattle."

This was the same warm welcome that would incite Évangéline to return to live and die in Philadelphia, in that place where the equality of the primeval forest and the equality of democracy converge. Her travels in America culminate in the discovery of a democratic attitude, a democracy of sentiments, a sort of return to her origins, to the equality of the old forest that had been transported into the New World: "Something that spake to her heart, and made her no longer a stranger; / And her ear was pleased with the Thee and Thou of the Quakers, / For it recalled the past, the old Acadian country, / Where all men were equal, and all were brothers and sisters."

## The Frontier

It was through the experience of the frontier, the border, that the young American democracy defined, in the first part of the nineteenth century, the struggle that transformed the old European tradition into a new democratic one. Bancroft had already designated the experience of the *Mayflower* Pilgrims as a cathartic experience, an experience of the frontier. But it was in the shift that opened up the vast western and northwestern territories through the purchase of Louisiana from France (1803) which the French had only just recovered from Spain; the shift that opened all the territory of the central Mississippi Basin to colonization, and the annexation and conquest (1848) of the southwestern territories—Texas, New Mexico, California—that the experience of the frontier in constant westward movement, found its true meaning. Longfellow was writing *Évangéline* while these events were unfolding.

*Évangéline* was undoubtedly a tale of the frontier. It began, as previously stated, in the historical times when America was still a British colony, and, through the Seven Years War, proceeded to mark the sites for its future expansion. But in Longfellow's work, the frontier did not bear the same cathartic strength as it did in the works of the main glorifying American writers. In *Évangéline*, the border's liberating dynamic was seemingly toned down by the Romantic nostalgia of the poem, the one that Europe had possessed before the age of progress, in the old days. This was why there are at least three settings (the different experiences of the frontier): the Acadian border, the European border of the primeval forest, and the American border. Three distinct sites that would become interlaced, recalling the curious rapport that Longfellow maintained, in the young American literature, with regard to the European continuity within the American experience.

Acadia was the first site of the border in the poem. Évangéline was born there and lived a happy youth until the eve of her wedding. The episode of the deportation of the inhabitants and the destruction of Grand-Pré took place there. But in 1755, the year of the Great Upheaval, Acadie no longer existed as a political and administrative entity. Acadie was the old name that the French used for this Canadian territory, an extension to the northeast of the New England coast, though separated by the Appalachians from the St. Lawrence River basin as well as that of the Great Lakes and the Mississippi. For, since 1713, due to the English occupation of 1710—long before the birth of Évangéline—the Acadian peninsula had been passed on to England, and the territory had been renamed Nova Scotia. From that moment on, it was mainly managed as a province of the colony of Massachusetts, from Boston. Évangéline was thus truly a frontier girl.

In the tumult that followed the publication of the poem (see chapter three—"A Memory from Beyond the Grave"), the American historian Phillip H. Smith said about Acadie, in 1884, that it was "a lost chapter of American history." He was referring to the episode of the Expulsion, but the same can be said about Acadia as a frontier. The western and northern borders were those that, for the most part, attracted the attention of the authors of the American narrative in its political, literary, and historical dimensions. In 1755, the surprising defeat of Braddock, who lost Ohio to the Indigenous and the French armies, was the event that fascinated American historians, not the Battle of Fort Beauséjour and the expulsion of the inhabitants of Nova Scotia, even though this defeat contributed to accelerating the events at the northeastern border (Acadie).

Longfellow was not the first to instill the conscience of a northeastern, Acadian, border, even though his poem was its epicentre. We saw how these events had been discussed in Boston intellectual communities, notably after the publication of Haliburton's history of Nova Scotia (1829). Furthermore, Acadia had long shared kinship with the collective imaginary of New England. Its name had been assigned by the Italian explorer who worked for France, Giovanni da Verrazzano, who named "Arcadie," during an expedition in 1524, a large portion of the northeastern coast of America that touches on New England—from Virginia in the south, to the new lands. "Arcadie," for the beauty of its trees and the luxuriousness of the setting, which reminded him of the descriptions of the mythic Greek *Arcadia*. It was, in a way, the first name attributed to the United States. Samuel de Champlain, a French cartographer who established the first European colony north of this territory in 1604, kept this name, minus the "r." Some say the name used by Champlain was instead borrowed from the Indigenous language of the Mi'kmaq, for whom "Acadie" means a place, as demonstrated by numerous toponymies still existing in the region: Tracadie, Shubenacadie. One explanation does not invalidate the other, and Champlain may have decided to keep Verrazzano's borrowed Greek word because the name sounded like the Indigenous word. We can nevertheless be certain that the dual nature of the border as both a frontier of wilderness and a metaphysical frontier with antiquity fascinated Longfellow.

In 1620, when the *Mayflower* Pilgrims established themselves nearly a thousand kilometres south of Acadie in Plymouth, they did not consider the name. The boundary between the English colony and the French settlements remained ambiguous at the time. The small Acadian colony changed hands at least six times between 1604 and 1701. The two histories were intermingled: "our friends the enemies" (*nos amis les ennemis*), as people would say in Acadie to define the relations with the New England Protestants. When William White wrote, in 1827, one of the first local histories of Maine titled *A History of Belfast*, he introduced the history of Maine through the history of Acadie without explaining how Acadians had disappeared.

Lieutenant-Colonel Winslow, who had presided over the displacement of the Grand-Pré Acadians, was from the family of Governor Winslow of the Plymouth colony at the time of the *Mayflower*. His ancestors and those of notary Leblanc, the only historical characters of the poem, thus lived, in 1755, on adjacent territories for over 150 years. The story of Longfellow's family, whose origins also go back to the beginnings of the American colony, is also intertwined with the French Catholics from the North. His great-grandfather drowned in the St. Lawrence River in Quebec City in 1690, during the William Phips expedition, when the French governor named Frontenac uttered his famous reply: "Je vous répondrai par la bouche de mes canons"—"The only response I have for your general is through the muzzles of my cannons."

The French settled into the centre of what is now Maine. They claimed the Kennebec River, built a fort on the Bagaduce River, a tributary of the Pentagouet (Penobscot) River, where the baron of Saint-Castin, a French nobleman who became a sachem through his marriage to the daughter of a Pentagouet chief, and who, with the help of his Indigenous allies, terrorized the Protestant populations of New England during the second half of the seventeenth century.

Longfellow had spent his youth in Portland, a few hundred kilometres from this region. He would later recount the story of the Baron of Saint-Castin in a tale from the collection *Tales of Wayside Inn* (1863): "The Baron of St. Castine." It was a region he knew well. During the War of Independence, at the time of the disastrous expedition of Bagaduce—known as Castin today—his maternal grandfather, Peleg Wadsworth, had been taken prisoner by the English army. In 1830, before having been told the legend of *Évangéline*, he had considered writing a poem about Acadie called *Down East: The Missionary of Acadie*. In 1843, in speaking of a friend who lived in this region, Longfellow said she enjoyed living in the "solitudes of Acadia."

It comes to no surprise, then, that the story of Évangéline was framed into the poem—through couplets in the introduction and conclusion— with a description of the settings of New England rather than historic Acadie. For even if Acadie and New England straddle the border, their geographical landscapes are distinct. The Acadian settlements were found well into the French bay—known today as the Bay of Fundy—where Acadians had found lowlands that were protected from the wrath of the ocean and where they could cultivate on dried marshlands. But in the opening line of the poem that would become one of the most famous English lines in the world, Longfellow wrote: "This is the forest primeval. The murmuring pines and the hemlocks," and for the closing lines that seem to echo the opening ones, he chose: "While from its rocky caverns the deep-voiced, neighboring ocean / Speaks, and in accents disconsolate answers the wail of the forest." As such, the tale of Évangéline was enclosed in a natural setting that was reminiscent of the forests of Maine and its rocky coasts.

Yet there were no tall pines, no deep-voiced ocean sounds, nor rocky caverns in the Acadian ecological niche. And Longfellow knew this, as he immediately continued his tale with a rather exact description of the village of Grand-Pré that sat on the border of the Minas Basin where vast prairies extended out to the dykes built by its inhabitants to intercept turbulent tides and where villagers planted wheat and orchards. In Longfellow's version of these Acadian prairies, turkeys strutted and the peasants, descendants of the French region of Normandy, drank beer—nay, ale—rather than cider from their orchards, as though they were common Saxons.

But the parallel between Acadians and New England settlers remained incomplete. Acadie is a mythical place situated in the "primeval forest" where trees "Stand like Druids of eld, with voices sad and prophetic." In the original title *Evangeline: A Tale of Acadie*, the word "Acadie" was chosen over "Acadia," as if to signal to Anglo-American ears a foreignness, pointing to an "other" place, the place of "another race, with other customs and language." The place of the primeval forest was the Europe of before the age of progress, before the age of corruption, and was also the luxuriant forest of ancient Arcadia. There was a border here that was not the same as that of the French and Indian War. In this primeval forest where druids, as in the Teutonic Forest, swung from tree branches, life was bucolic, peaceful, and happy. There, people lived in neat houses and sang songs from Normandy and Burgundy, women and girls wore bright skirts in all colours, there were no locks on the doors, the harvest was bountiful. "There the richest was poor, and the poorest lived in abundance [...] Every house was an inn, where all were welcomed and feasted."

The border was not, however, the American frontier—the West—the place where society started from year zero. In Acadia, life was organized, rhythmically structured around, "the bell from its tower," around the villagers' celebrations, and religious events, "thronged were the streets with people"; priests, blacksmiths, notaries officiated village life. Even Évangéline's heifer seemed to be a part of a human chain in harmony with nature. "Foremost, bearing the bell, Évangéline's beautiful heifer, / Proud of her snow-white hide, and the ribbon that waved from her collar, / Quietly paced and slow, as if conscious of human affection. / Then came the shepherd back with his bleating flocks from the seaside." Even so, the American border was not far away. The evening of the Deportation, when the inhabitants of Grand-Pré were assembled on the shore waiting to board the ships, the militia set fire to the village. The humanized nature of the primeval forest was transformed into the wilderness of the American frontier. Longfellow described what the Acadians heard that night as they waited on the bank of the Minas Basin:

*Then rose a sound of dread, such as startles the sleeping encampments*
*Far in the western prairies or forests that skirt the Nebraska,*
*When the wild horses affrighted sweep by with the speed of the whirlwind,*
*Or the loud bellowing herds of buffaloes rush to the river.*
*Such was the sound that arose on the night, as the herds and the horses*
*Broke through their folds and fences, and madly rushed o'er the meadows.*

The trial of the American frontier awaited them.

Longfellow, like his fellow countrymen, was besotted with the adventure of the Western frontier. His journal is scattered with notes from adventurers and conquistadors who recount the story of its occupation. From Grand-Pré, he had Évangéline transition directly to the West, on the Ohio River, where she would have taken the same path as General Braddock had during his infamously failed battle against the French army in the summer of 1755, though omitting to describe the exiled Acadians' forced travels by sea and their unfortunate stay in Philadelphia. If the border was a required passage, it was also an evanescent place, inhabited by the shadows of the peoples it had wounded. "As the emigrant's way o'er the Western desert is marked by / Camp-fires long consumed, and bones that bleach in the sunshine." Those were the wounded shadows of those immigrants who had been swallowed by the frontier, and the shadows of the "Canadiens," those coureurs des bois (unlicensed fur traders) who failed to give the country a soul. They were like the untraceable Gabriel who had himself become a coureur des bois, and who, "weary with waiting, unhappy and restless, / Sought in the Western wilds oblivion of self and of sorrow." The surname Lajeunesse, which the author attributed to Gabriel, was not meaningless, but also not of Acadian origin. Longfellow borrowed it from the description of a coureur des bois—Basil Lajeunesse—in the narrative of Captain John Charles Frémont, commander in chief for the American government, who, in 1845, published *Report of the Exploring Expedition to the Rocky Mountains in the Year 1842, and to Oregon and North California in the years 1843–44*. Longfellow used Basil Lajeunesse as the name for Gabriel's father.

The American frontier is also, and above all, the burial ground of Indigenous peoples. "Over them [the prairies] wander the scattered tribes of Ishmael's children." The deadly destiny of the Acadian people and the Indigenous peoples is fused together through the meeting between Évangéline and an Indigenous woman: "She was a Shawnee woman returning home to her people, / From the far-off hunting grounds of the cruel Camanches, / Where her Canadian husband, a Coureur-des-Bois, had been murdered." They shared stories of their suffering through the night. The Indigenous woman told Évangéline the legend of Mowis and that of Lilinau. Évangéline wondered whether, "like the [Indigenous] maid, she, too, was pursuing a phantom." For the frontier could be a mirage for those who thought they had found the primeval forest, one would often be guided there by "the magic Fata Morgana."

The frontier was a return to raw nature. And in the tale of *Évangéline*, nature did not have its own dynamic, nor did it have the transcendence in the works of Longfellow as it did in those of his friend Emerson. It appeared as a décor, a majestic setting, like Bonvard's moving diorama (a three-mile-long canvas) of the Mississippi that Longfellow saw in 1846 to describe the long river. Évangéline explores nature "alone," without a family, without a homeland. She does not find what she is looking for. As Longfellow had said about the glory of a nation and its literature, nature is not sufficient; it has to be given a "soul," assigned a "moral nature." This can be done, as the stay in Louisiana demonstrated. It was indeed a frontier, as Basil Lajeunesse stated: "Here, too, numberless herds run wild and unclaimed in the prairies; / Here, too, lands may be had for the asking, and forests of timber / With a few blows of the axe are hewn and framed into houses." But it was an inhabited frontier. The druids of the ancient forest had accompanied the Acadians to their new home, the Eden of Louisiana: "Garlands of Spanish moss and of mystic mistletoe flaunted, / Such as the Druids cut down with golden hatchets at Yule-tide."

Basil Lajeunesse welcomed Évangéline with a patriarchal demeanour, mounted on a horse and bearing a Spanish sombrero. The experience of the frontier had transformed him from a blacksmith to a rich livestock owner in the plains of the Opelousas, west of the Atchafalaya—the patriarch of the first American cowboys. For the descriptions of Évangéline's stay in Louisiana, Longfellow took much of his inspiration from a work he acclaimed, which was entitled *Life in the New World* (1844), written by Charles Sealsfield, the pseudonym of a refugee Austrian monk who wrote novels and travel accounts praising the democratic virtues of the New World and the regenerative virtues of the frontier. Sealsfield had visited the southwest of Louisiana and the Texas border in the 1820s. It was one of the rare texts at the time that described the setting and everyday life of Acadians who had settled in Louisiana after 1755.

Though Longfellow accurately reproduced Sealsfield's descriptions of nature as the "paradise of Louisiana," and the "Creole ball," the poet completely transformed the descriptions of frontier Acadians. Sealsfield described Acadians as poor little peasants who faced the hostility of rich Creoles—the great landowners of French descent—who treated them like "negroes."[2] They had a reputation for being wild fighters, drunks,

---

2.   Translator's note: Sealsfield weaved into his fiction numerous representations of enslaved Black people, which he described as "negroes." He marked a clear distinction between Black and white inhabitants, describing Black people in a variety of offensive and deprecating ways, which makes the unfortunate novel particularly challenging to read.

and barbarians. The American settlers who squatted the lands near the Texas border apparently feared Acadians more than the "ferocious" and "unpredictable" Mexicans.

Longfellow could not reuse this description of the experience of the frontier. In his work, the frontier needed to lead to a sort of recovered harmony, after the age of corruption, with the primeval forest. Hence the idyllic portrayal of Acadians in Louisiana. They were the projection of the American narrative, transformed by the frontier, though representing modern democratic equality and liberty. As in the land of Penn, where Évangéline chose to settle in the end, nature had reconciled with society: "There all the air is balm, and the peach is the emblem of beauty, / And the streets still re-echo the names of the trees of the forest, / As if they fain would appease the Dryads whose haunts they molested."

## The Protestant Romance of American Catholicism

A final element, and perhaps the most original, which marks the inscription of *Evangeline* into the American narrative, is its eponymous Catholic character. *Evangeline* was the first widely read American work with a Catholic main character. Such a peculiarity deserves a few explanations, for, as we have seen, the American narrative aimed mainly at establishing a link between the exceptionality of the American democratic adventure and the Protestant origins of its colonizers. The hatred for Catholics and the association between papists and the corruption of the Old World were considered in part the most important motivations that had led the *Mayflower* Pilgrims to the coast of Arcadia.

Yet the Pilgrims had encountered these Catholics in the New World, notably in the French American empire that surrounded their settlements on the Atlantic coasts, thus limiting their opportunities for continental expansion. The zeal and success of those Frenchmen in converting the "savages"[3] and rekindling political and economic alliances with them was

3.   Translator's note: The terminology employed throughout the text is representative of the phrases and expressions that were frequent in early nineteenth-century North America. The goal is not to validate a Eurocentric vision of the crimes committed against Indigenous peoples in America, but rather to translate the European depiction of such historical events.

a prime example of the idolatrous nature of Roman Catholicism. At least, such were the premises of American historians—we will see this further on, in Part II, in the writings of Parkman, for instance—who strived to integrate the French and Indian War into the national narrative. The wars for the ownership of America had been, for the inhabitants of New England, a sort of holy war against the corruption of the Old World, against Catholicism.

Anti-Catholicism persisted throughout the colonial period and during the American Revolution. It was even exacerbated at the beginning of the nineteenth century by the Second Great Awakening, which, by accentu-ating the anti-institutional nature of Protestantism, also associated the progressive routinization of Protestantism with a papist downward spiral. In 1834, less than ten years before Longfellow began to write *Évangéline*, a popular revolt in the Boston region had resulted in the arson of an Ursuline convent. The furious crown, mainly made up of a Scottish Presbyterian brigade, wanted to liberate the girls of good-standing New England fam-ilies from the claws of the nuns, who were themselves prisoners forced to serve priests—even, allegedly, in a sexual way. By imprisoning women and girls outside their family environments, this foreign religion—foreign to the national narrative, but also submitted to a foreign power, the pap-acy—was said to be incompatible with the values of liberty and respect for family and paternal authority which were specific to Protestant and democratic America.

Such ideas were features in a popular "anti-convent" literature, which often used the tone of a personal story. These romanticized, anti-Catholic lampoons were spectacularly popular in the Boston area. In 1834, *Convent's Doom: A Tale of Charlestown* sold more than 40,000 copies. Despite hav-ing been published shortly after the fire of the convent (1835), Rebecca Reed's *Six Months in a Convent*—more than 10,000 copies sold in the first week following its publication—had been circulating prior to the tragic event and would come to be exposed as the source of the popular upris-ing. Rebecca Reed told of how she had been abused during her stay at the Ursuline convent. The most successful book, however, was attributed to Maria Monk, *Awful Disclosures of the Hotel Dieu Nunnery of Montreal*

(1836), which sold 300,000 copies in the twenty years following its initial publication. Its popularity was only surpassed at the time by *Uncle Tom's Cabin* (1852) by Harriet Beecher Stowe. Maria Monk, a Canadian of Irish origin, recounted the story of her life as a nun with the Sisters of Charity at the Hôtel-Dieu in Montreal—the Charlestown Ursulines had fled to Canada in 1838 following the fire that destroyed their convent. By the author's account, the environment was vicious, a map of the subterranean tunnels was provided, Sisters of Charity and Sulpicians fornicated, the children born from these unions were baptized and slaughtered, a non-consenting sister was assassinated under orders from the Mother Superior, others disappeared. The quasi-pornographic book circulated and fuelled the convictions of working-class Protestants regarding the decadence of Roman Catholicism despite its implausibility. These rumours went around Boston at a time when waves of poor Irish immigrants—Catholics, as it happens—were landing, carriers of a resolutely un-American religion.

By making Évangéline a Catholic heroine, Longfellow clearly placed himself in a difficult position amid these events. What is more, Évangéline finished her life as a nun with the Sisters of Mercy in Philadelphia, within a religious order created specifically to take in women of ill repute—prostitutes—who, in Maria Monk's story, were affiliated with the sisters themselves. The reference was not gratuitous, for in 1793, the year of the plague in Philadelphia when Évangéline takes care of the sick with Quakers, there were no female Catholic religious orders in Philadelphia. The situation was pure fiction from Longfellow. The "convent," a foreign hotspot for Catholic corruption in the popular imagination, was thus magically transformed by the author into an institution of divine mercy, into a hot spot of American egalitarianism.

This was how Longfellow integrated Catholicism into the American narrative. He would be the first to do it, the Catholic effusions of Hawthorne in *The Scarlet Letter* (1850) and Stowe in *Agnes of Sorrento* (1862) came along after, as did the historical works of Parkman and Prescott on the "Catholic" past of America. Longfellow inaugurated a process that would last almost 150 years, and that could only be completed in 1960, with the election of the first Catholic president, John F. Kennedy, an event that consecrated Catholicism's place in the American collective imaginary.

Longfellow's empathy for Catholicism predates *Evangeline*. At the age of twenty-two, landing in France and entering the cathedral of Rouen, then a young ascetic Protestant taught to distrust ostentatious Catholic rituals, was dumbfounded: "There was an air of antiquity about the whole city that breathed of the Middle Ages; and so strong and delightful was the impression that it made upon my youthful imagination, that nothing which I afterward saw could either equal or efface it."[4] During the same stay in Europe, he reacted similarly while attending midnight mass in Genoa. He was dazzled by the solemnness of the light that shone from the altar and reverberated unto the kneeling worshippers. Throughout his travel narrative (*Outre-mer*), he was filled with wonder when discovering Catholic rituals, funerals, processions, Extreme Unction, all things foreign and new for this grandson of New English Puritans. "There is much in the Catholic worship which I like," he said during his second stay in Europe, when referencing a mass that he had attended following the death of his first wife.

It was his Romantic nature that made Longfellow this sensitive to the expressiveness of Catholicism. He would never join the Church, but he liked the idea, the communion, the push toward achieving a certain transcendence. The de-ritualization of Protestantism brought the individual down to the lowly world, but the Romantic individual wished to be in communion with that which is universal, to connect the individual to a notion of the universe as a whole. Incidentally, that was how, in the middle of the nineteenth century, certain progressive intellectual circles of New England came to flirt with a form of pantheism (the group of transcendentalists around Emerson, for instance), a natural religion, which promoted immediate communion between the individual and nature. Others, more Europeanist and closer to the Unitarian Church, including Longfellow, reconciled with the expressiveness of traditional Catholicism, in particular that of the Middle Ages. This "abstract" Catholicism became

---

4.  This passage appears in Longfellow's (1835) *Outre-mer: A Pilgrimage Beyond the Sea*, volume I, p. 25.

a sort of universal receptacle for the forsaken souls of lonely Protestants—and lonely cowboys; we must not forget the thriving imaginary of the frontier at the time. This foreign Church referred to the memory of a universal community that the American narrative wanted to recreate. Constructed in this way, Catholicism could enter into the blended religion—largely Judeo-Christian—that America was getting ready to adopt as a quasi-civilian religion. It was, to borrow from Jenny Franchot, the "Protestant romance" of American Catholicism.

*Evangeline* was the first of such Protestant romances of American Catholicism. We have already highlighted the fact that the poem, through its structure and narrative, echoes Christlike redemption and the exodus. Paul Morin identified nearly twenty lines deriving directly from the Bible. Yet the poem is not only Judeo-Christian in a general sense, it is Catholic, and ultimately, Protestant. Longfellow did not hide the Catholic origins of the inhabitants of Grand-Pré, though he took care to situate the village at the boundary of the early days, the border with Europe, with the primeval forest. "Under the Sycamore-tree were hives overhung by a penthouse, / Such as the traveller sees in regions remote by the roadside, / Built o'er a box for the poor, or the blessed image of Mary." This Catholicism still had the power to structure, rhythmically, community living, a world reminiscent of the Middle Ages, of the world that preceded the individualism of Jacksonian democracy.

> *As in a church, when the chant of the choir at intervals ceases,*
> *Footfalls are heard in the aisles, or words of the priest at the altar,*
> *So, in each pause of the song, with measured motion the clock clicked.*
>
> *[…]*
>
> *Softly the Angelus sounded, and over the roofs of the village*
> *Columns of pale blue smoke, like clouds of incense ascending,*
> *Rose from a hundred hearths, the homes of peace and contentment.*

Longfellow's description of the role of Catholic clergy in Acadie was also imbued with empathy. One of the reasons to evict Acadians from the territory had been, according to the leaders of the colony, the disruptive role of the French Catholic clergy, inciting the Indigenous populations to resist the English and the Acadians to cross over into Catholic territory. Besides, by September 1755, there were no priests left in Grand-Pré, as they had all been chased out of Nova Scotia a few months prior by colonial authorities. Longfellow might not have known this, for his only historical documents were lieutenant-colonel Winslow's recollections of the events—the "real" history was only found later, after the poem had been written—but he knew of the religious rivalries that were at the heart of the French and Indian War. Winslow, who at the time of the events lived in the presbytery and occupied the church, made no mention in his memoirs of the presence of the clergy. Longfellow created the character of Father Felician, "Priest and pedagogue both in the village, had taught them their letters." Rather than intervening to incite anti-British rage, Father Felician tended to appease the Acadians, preaching Christian resignation. Addressing the Acadians who were imprisoned in the church and applauded Basil the blacksmith's call to arms, the priest said, with grave and solemn emphasis: "'what madness has seized you? [...] Have you so soon forgotten all lessons of love and forgiveness? / Let us repeat that prayer in the hour when the wicked assail us, / Let us repeat it now, and say, 'O Father, forgive them!'" [...] But on the shores [...] Wandered the faithful priest, consoling and blessing and cheering."

In this description of Catholicism prior to the age of corruption, Longfellow did not hide the artifices of Catholicism associated with Catholic idolatry by Protestants. The clouds of incense exit the chimneys. "Solemnly down the street came the parish priest, and the children / Paused in their play to kiss the hand he extended to bless them." Or in the Grand-Pré church, on the night of September 5 when the men were held prisoners: "Then came the evening service. The tapers gleamed from the altar. / Fervent and deep was the voice of the priest and the people responded, / Not with their lips alone, but their hearts; and the *Ave Maria* / Sang they, and fell on their knees, and their souls, with devotion translated, / Rose on the ardour of prayer, like Elijah ascending to heaven." This religiousness did not carry the sadness associated with Protestant communities. "Many a youth, as he knelt in the church and opened his missal, / Fixed his eyes upon her [Évangéline], as the saint of his deepest devotion."

However, the American Évangéline did not carry with her religious artifacts: neither altar candle, rosary, scapular, nor images. She was a Catholic "saint" whose Catholicism had transformed into a sort of humanitarianism. Quite a difference from the image of her native land, Acadie, where: "Fairer was she when, on Sunday morn, while the bell from its turret / Sprinkled with holy sounds the air, as the priest with his hyssop / Sprinkles the congregation, and scatters blessings upon them, / Down the long street she passed, with her chaplet of beads and her missal." Even Father Felician, whose hand was kissed by parishioners in the streets of Grand-Pré became, in America, a sort of Protestant pastor: "…the priest, her friend and father-confessor." He accompanied the heroine, did not sprinkle anyone with holy water, did not officiate mass, participated in the Creole ball, watched over her, asked her to be patient, all this without the pomp of the Old World Church.

There are two mentions of processions in the poem. The first described the departure of the prisoners from the church to the banks where the ships were waiting for them. This was Grand-Pré on September 10, 1755. The atmosphere was all-Catholic—so much so that it was reminiscent of the Christ King who saw the community in hierarchical ranks call for its saviour:

*[…] On a sudden the church-doors*
*Opened, and forth came the guard, and marching in gloomy procession*
*Followed the long-imprisoned, but patient, Acadian farmers.*
*Even as Pilgrims, who journey afar from their homes and their country,*
*Sing as they go, and in singing forget they are weary and wayworn,*
*So with songs on their lips the Acadian peasants descended*
*Down from the church to the shore, amid their wives and their daughters.*
*Foremost the young men came; and, raising together their voices,*
*Sang with tremulous lips a chant of the Catholic Missions:*
*"Sacred heart of the Saviour! O inexhaustible fountain!*
*Fill our hearts this day with strength and submission and patience!"*

*Then the old men, as they marched, and the women that stood by the*
*wayside*
*Joined in the sacred psalm, and the birds in the sunshine above them*
*Mingled their notes therewith, like voices of spirits departed.*

And then...there is the procession we mentioned above: the arrival of the cortège of Acadians in the *Eden of Louisiana* where the cypress "Waved like banners that hang on the walls of ancient cathedrals," and where one could hear the blast of the horn "that resounded / Wildly and sweet and far." This second procession was more civil than religious, the entrance into the new Jerusalem. In the American part of the tale, the old religion was rarely mentioned. It appeared like an evanescent shadow on the western frontier "Hearing the homelike sounds of his mother tongue in the forest," when Évangéline, for instance, met with the Jesuit missionary, a meeting that is reminiscent of the Franco-Catholic dream and the world of the Indigenous Shawnee that were both crushed by the experience of the frontier.

There are no more living memories of the Church from the old Acadie in the American idyll, only those unnamed graves—"Under the humble walls of the little Catholic churchyard"—in Philadelphia.

# References

ARVIN, N. "Acadian Idyll," *Longfellow: His Life and Work*. Boston, MA: Little Brown and Company, 1962, pp. 101–115.

FRANCHOT, J. *Roads to Rome: The Antebellum Protestant Encounter with Catholicism*. Berkeley, CA: University of California Press, 1994. ark.cdlib.org/ark:/13030/ft1x0nb0f3/

GRIFFITH, N. "Longfellow's Évangéline: The Birth and acceptance of a Legend." *Acadiensis*, Vol. 11, No 2, pp. 28–41. Fredericton, NB: University of New Brunswick Press, 1982.

HAWTHORNE, M. and Dana Henry Wadsworth Longfellow. "The Origin of Longfellow's Évangéline." *The Bibliographical Society of America*, 41, 1947.

HERBERT LUSSIER, M. *From Acadian to American: The Literary Americanization of Cajuns*. Ph.D. dissertation, Chapel Hill: University of North Carolina, 2005.

MARTIN, E. *L'Évangéline de Longfellow et la suite merveilleuse d'un poème*. Paris, France: Librairie Hachette, 1936.

MORIN, P. *Les sources de l'œuvre de Henry Wadsworth Longfellow*. Paris, France : Librairie Éditions, 1913.

SEELYE, J. "Attic Shape: Dusting Off Évangéline." *Virginia Quaterly Review*, Vol. 60, 1984, pp. 21–44.

VIAU, R. *Les visages d'Évangéline. Du poème au mythe*. Montreal, QC: MNH, 1998.

WILLIS, L. E. "Henry Wadsworth Longfellow, United States National Literature, and the American Canon's erasure of material nature." *Looking Away: The Evasive Environmental Politics of American Literature, 1823–1966*. Ph.D. dissertation, Gainesville, FL: University of Florida, 2006.

# A MEMORY FROM
# BEYOND THE GRAVE

*Side by side, in their nameless graves, the lovers are sleeping.*
*Under the humble walls of the little Catholic churchyard,*
*In the heart of the city, they lie, unknown and unnoticed.*
*Daily the tides of life go ebbing and flowing beside them,*
*Thousands of throbbing hearts, where theirs are at rest and forever,*

—Henry Wadsworth Longfellow, *Evangeline: A Tale of Acadie*

## Longfellow at the Mercy of Modernist Critics

As meteoric as Longfellow's rise to popularity had been, his eviction from the pantheon of great national writers was equally rapid. The advent of modernism in arts and culture at the beginning of the twentieth century brought on the fall. Modernism, in poetry and other art forms, was characterized by a cult of the *new*, and the praising of creative, avant-garde artists. This artistic sensitivity was particularly critical of the narrative dimension associated with the poetic universe, for poetry needed to be a more complex form of expression, more unique, more creative, more focused on the future. The Romantic Period could not be considered modern because of its attachment to the past. Though a few nineteenth-century poets were safe from this ravenous criticism and maintained their status as great national poets (Emerson, Whitman, Dickinson), this was not the case for Longfellow. Our poet even served as the main scapegoat, for he represented the aesthetic form that modernist critics particularly liked to condemn.

Everything that had made Longfellow a great poet was suddenly being used against him to marginalize his place in American poetry. His works were now described as simple little stories lacking depth, leaving little space for imagination, filled with dated Victorian morals, and largely modelled after European works. As the novelist and literary critic Ludwig Lewisohn stated in 1932: "Who, except wretched schoolchildren, now reads Longfellow?" Longfellow was thus pejoratively categorized among his friends the Brahmin poets of New England, alongside the fireside poets, or as George Santayana would say, alongside those poets of the genteel tradition, too rich to grasp the tragic sense of the modern world, too aristocratic to relay the democratic nature of America. In Santayana's words, "To minds concerned with the imaginative interpretation of man, for nature and of human life, Longfellow has nothing left to say."

At first, strong criticism had been taken from the eminently hostile Longfellow biography by Herbert Gorman, published in 1926. From then on, biographical works on the poet became increasingly rare. The important 1963 biography by Newton Arvin, eminent biographer of nineteenth-century American authors, has been deemed an oddity. It nevertheless helped give a lasting lustre to the works of the old Romantic poet even though Arvin took care not to praise Longfellow, and even hesitated to reintegrate him among the pantheon of great national poets. Readers would have to wait more than forty years for a renewed interest in the biographical history of *Evangeline*'s author, but we will address this later, in the final section.

Similarly, after the 1920s, Longfellow's poems began to disappear from the great anthologies of American poetry and critical works. Longfellow had become a minor poet. Dana Gioia has claimed that this treatment was unfair and that his works should be rehabilitated. Gioia stressed the fact that this banishment was largely decided on by professional critics and literature professors—and yet, Longfellow was the first great American poet who was both professor and professional poet. His works would have survived in popular memory, Gioia argued, because Longfellow remains one of the few nineteenth-century poets that a majority of Americans can still quote—notably the opening lines of *Evangeline*—without ever having read.

And what about *Evangeline*? The poem certainly had another fate. We could even say that it had two fabulous destinies: one in northern Acadie—in Canada—and the other in southern Acadie—in Louisiana. The following sections of this book will address each of these destinies. But the American fate of *Evangeline* was largely sealed in the end of the 1920s; the zeal for the poem had faded at the same time as the appreciation for Longfellow. Schools and operas would no longer be named after the American heroine, nor would there be any new theatrical adaptations or paintings. Slowly, the mandatory reading of *Evangeline* was phased out of Anglo-American schools.

Even those foreigners who were interested in the marvellous continuance of a poem—that is, the work's reception and continued use outside of the United States—were conscious that the American story of *Evangeline* and its author were a thing of the past. Such was the case for Paul Morin, this literary man from Montreal who produced, in 1913, a monumental doctoral dissertation in Paris on the sources of Longfellow's works. Morin also published, in 1924, a literal translation of *Evangeline* into French. In the introduction to this translation, Morin wrote: "Our century no longer praises the moral elevation that is characteristic of his [Longfellow's] works. Furthermore, the repeated discoveries by modern philologists of Longfellow's extraordinarily unconscious borrowing of texts, figures, ideals, and sentences, have had a somewhat chilling effect, even among his fellow countrymen, on the enthusiastic admiration that he once inspired."[5] This judgment properly summarizes the largely shared sentiment of twentieth-century critics regarding the author of *Evangeline*.

The same was said by Ernest Martin, a Frenchman of Acadian descent and professor of English literature in France, who published in 1926, *L'Évangéline de Longfellow et la suite merveilleuse d'un poème*. Recalling how Longfellow had been "the most popular" American poet, he quickly added: "Nowadays, his glory has much faded. America and the world in general have moved on from the times when Voices of the Night and The

---

5. "Notre siècle n'a plus de lauriers pour l'élévation morale qui caractérise son oeuvre. D'autre part, les découvertes répétées des philologues modernes, relativement à son extraordinaire inconscience comme emprunteur de textes, de figures, d'idées, de phrases, ont quelque peu refroidi, même chez ses compatriotes, l'enthousiaste admiration qui lui fut jadis prodiguée."

Golden Legend were published."[6] But one poem, he insisted, had outlived him: *Evangeline*. The poem's survival, as we will see, would no longer be dependent on its ties to the American narrative.

## From the *Mayflower* to Ellis Island

To grasp how the perception of *Evangeline* came to change, we will explore, within the context of the American narrative, the disappearance of Longfellow—and *Evangeline*—from the national consciousness. It was not only the dated aesthetics, as literary critics claimed at the time, that led to the rejection of Longfellow, but rather a specific conception of the American identity. Early twentieth-century America had been profoundly transformed since the antebellum period when the poem was written. *Evangeline*, as we have previously stated, was a combined representation of the American identity, a democratic Anglo-Protestant character. By the early 1920s, the United States entered into a pluralist phase. The fading interest for *Evangeline* was closely tied to the transformation of the great American narrative.

National narratives, from the United States and other modern democracies alike, tend to attribute a depth of identity and history to democratic societies where spontaneity usually leads to individualism and presentism, and as such, amount to an existential emptiness that is detrimental to communal solidarity. Without narrators of history, it is challenging to transform a multitude of presumably autonomous individuals into a group that is sufficiently solitary to act collectively. Without meaning makers, it is difficult to compensate the deficits of a society of individuals. National narratives tend to make connections between two relatively contradictory yet essential characteristics of modern democracies: the self-constructed nature of the democratic people—the people being nothing more than an immediate willingness—and the cultural nature of the people, which is also constructed, but which gives a depth to the vacuity of the immediate willingness.

These two trends in constructing the identity of democratic societies

---

6.   "Aujourd'hui cette gloire a bien pâli. L'Amérique et le monde en général ont marché depuis le temps où parurent *Les Voix de la Nuit* et *La Légende dorée*."

lead to antithetical conceptions of the community we live in, two forms of modern national identity. Since the publication of Werner Sollors's *Consent and Descent in American Culture* in 1986, it has become habitual to question whether the United States form a community of descent or a community of consent, with a net presumption that they are essentially a community of consent. What this means is that, in a purely constructed or democratic sense, the community is constantly building itself, becoming, and "consenting" to the characteristics of the new world. The opposing view is that the community is evolving with its memory of the past, establishing ties of filiation, continuity—"descent" by inheritance of the characteristics of its ancestors. This old, yet still relevant, distinction was a reiteration of what Frenchman Ernest Renan had called in 1882, the "civic nation" and the "ethnic nation." According to Renan, the civic nation was an everyday referendum, whereas the ethnic nation was rooted in "ethno-cultural" descent. Scholars have long opposed these two elements, but I believe that since the advent of modernity, every community is constituted of a mix between consent and descent, evolving amid a tension between an outlook on the future and a narrative of its past.

In a society like the United States of America, borne from a rupture of the homeland and a democratic revolution, continually swept by influxes of new immigrants, a society with fluid borders in continuous expansion, the memorial definition of a "descent" was particularly problematic. What did a common history look like for a society that defined itself as a new world? This concordance was at last found, as we have previously stated, in a particular strategy at the heart of the American narrative, in the exceptionality of the first Americans, the *Mayflower* Pilgrims, whereby their "descent," the Protestant revolution, was nothing but a beginning, the future of humanity, of democracy. The American descent was actually ascendant. The modern principles of universalism were thus incarnated into a specific people. This was how "nativism"—a movement aiming to make the United States unique, often at the expense of newcomers—was combined with a perception of the community as one of "consent."

But the American narrative is ever changing, and the ties between the community that is becoming—the "consenting community"—and the original community—the "descending community"—fluctuated over time. As with all contradictory associations, these ties oscillated between more "nativist" (descent) periods such as the generalized fear of Black people and "inassimilable" immigrants—which initially included Catholics—that swept large parts of the United States following the American Civil War, and that continued into the first part of the twentieth century; and, enthusiastic "universalist" (ascendant) periods, such as Longfellow's Romantic era or contemporary multiculturalism. Such oscillations are just that—oscillations: they in no way contradict the representation of the identity of an America whose distinctive characteristic is that of being universal.

Regardless of oscillations, consenting America would always be dressed in descent. From the first formulations of the national narrative in the first half of the nineteenth century, the exact period when Longfellow wrote *Evangeline*, when the Anglo-Teutonic origins of the American people were celebrated through the celebrations of multiculturalism in the 1960s, the descending community was nevertheless transformed. At the beginning of the nineteenth century, the aim was to tie the descent to the Pilgrim refugees who disembarked from the *Mayflower* in Plymouth— and we argue, in light of our reading, that Évangéline was a poetic and Catholic version of these refugees. In 1960, the pluralist descent of America became the norm, and it was therefore open to an ethno-racial pantheon that aspired to be universal. The image of Ellis Island—the island in the port of New York where one can see the Statue of Liberty, and which was the entry point to America for more than a century for millions of mainly European immigrants—came to replace that of the *Mayflower*. From the *Mayflower* to Ellis Island, the same idea remained: that of an America born from successive waves of immigrants chased out of the old world and looking to create a new society.

What changed between the *Mayflower* and Ellis Island was the pluralist conception of the American identity. The *Mayflower* was an avant-garde Anglo-Protestant melting pot. The Pilgrims inaugurated a nation into which other immigrants would have to insert themselves while adding their collective memory. There was no doubt that, until the beginning of the twentieth century, the nation being built, the consenting nation, despite a de facto pluralism, was an Anglo-Protestant one. All immigrants were "invited" to assimilate the English language, and religions coalesced around a sort of civic religion with a definitively Protestant matrix.

This was the reason the image of the melting pot—which gained a foothold thanks to the 1908 eponymous play by Jewish-American playwright Israel Zangwill—harkened to an already-outdated reality when it was first formulated. America no longer assimilated was the claim at the time; it produced difference. At the time, this new representation of the national identity could be seen in the birth of American sociology. This field, following the publication of the foundational work *Folkways* (1907) by William Graham Sumner, was particularly interested in the formation of identity in modern societies. As early as the 1920s, Chicago sociologists showed how the American culture defined itself by maintaining differentiated cultures within populations of immigrant origin. Such readings inaugurated a tradition whereby the American society would be seen as a society where there were a variety of persistent ethnic groups. At the beginning of the twentieth century, this statement of diversity and its problematization prevailed over the idea of a fusion, or a melting pot, which was already considered outdated at the time.

Some people were against this change and were nostalgic of an America descending from those populations of the Teutonic forest. This was the case with the nativists who successfully imposed the Johnson-Reed Act in 1924, which restricted the entrance to new immigrants in the name of Anglo-Protestant values. But the consensus was no more: the cohesive, unified vision of an Anglo-Protestant America was called into question. Though some, such as Israel Zangwill, author of the melting pot formula, would propose to maintain the old dream of a unified people, the goal was to expand the idea to include all Judeo-Christian peoples, including Catholics, Caucasian populations, and southern Europeans. Zangwill challenged Anglo-Protestant America, preferring instead a Euro-America: a white America of Judeo-Christian ascent and descent.

A third trend, which can be traced back to the works of essayist Horace Kallen (*Culture and Democracy in the United States*, 1924), further strengthened the pluralist descent and attempted to make it the formula of the future. According to Horace Kallen, America was, from a cultural standpoint, not a true nation, but a "nation of nations," a pluralism that needed to be maintained and preserved. In this new formula, descent changed from Anglo-America to a pluralist America, but the idea that the United States was a consenting society rooted in democracy persisted. This final trend was confirmed in the passion for multicultural pluralism in the 1960s. Rather than rooting the original American diversity in Anglo-Protestant culture (White Anglo-Saxon Protestants, or WASPs), or in the Euro-American melting pot, America's ascendant community must blossom in a societal pluralism.

The erasure of Longfellow and *Evangeline* from American consciousness corresponded to this process: from the *Mayflower* to Ellis Island. At its peak in 1880, when Longfellow died, the poem's popularity faded around the 1920s, when the idea of an ethnic America began to predominate. Ron McFarland's recent study of representations of Évangéline in print and popular culture of the Anglo-American culture—*The Long Life of Evangeline* (2010)—presented an interesting portrait of this evolution. The first figurative representations appeared as soon as 1850 in England. Évangéline was presented as a Romantic virgin. This was the case for the first illustrated edition of *Evangeline* with forty-five wood engravings by Jane E. Benham, Birket Foster, and John Gilbert (1850). Longfellow is said to have found this representation a little gloomy. The one he particularly liked, and which is to this day the great Romantic representation of Évangéline, was the portrait by Thomas Faed (1855), which was engraved by his brother James Faed.

The American representations that came later inserted *Evangeline* into America's landscape and history. In 1866, Felix Octavius Carr Darley was the first American to represent the figure of Évangéline—his was livelier, less iconic than the English Romantic representations. Évangéline was inducted into a society that was sometimes depicted as the "primeval forest," and at other times as New England. The Englishman John Gilbert, who in 1853 represented Évangéline as a saint living in the primeval forest, and portrayed Évangéline's father, Benedict Bellefontaine, the rich farmer of Grand-Pré, as a bourgeois of New England, was already introducing the confusion between the primeval forest and the place where the first American Pilgrims had settled.

This integration of Évangéline into America and the narrative of its Anglo-Protestant fusion was felt with more panache near the end of the nineteenth century. The history of Acadians became less visible in the representations, and "Évangéline, the American" appeared in all its splendour. She was more spirited, more joyful, sometimes even drinking beer, or even seen happily serving the divine liquid to English soldiers in a tavern (Hines, 1895). The more she became a popular icon—think of the French operetta *Évangéline* (1874) by Edward Everett and John Cheever Goodwin—the more she was portrayed as having a given sensuality, even some sort of modern sexuality. The American landscape, the Mississippi, the West, and Louisiana, overpowered the image of the "primeval Acadian" forest. The superb 1905 illustrated edition of *Evangeline* by Howard Chandler Christy was the best example of this American Évangéline, remaining faithful to the religiousness of the primeval forest all the while integrating feminine sensuality and the *joie de vivre* of the American dream. It seemed that Christy's Évangéline, a blended figure representing the Romantic Teutonic forest—and proudly wearing a Norman cap—and modern America, even served as the image of Évangéline that the Louisiana Cajuns chose around 1920 for their portrayal of the heroine.

Thus, as they took on a more American style, the figures of Évangéline became more ethnic, detached themselves from a cohesive, fusional image of America, and portrayed an image of a multicultural America. The cinematic evolution of *Evangeline* attested to this. The illustration of Évangéline by Faed portrayed the heroine without any specific ethnic features, aside from some generic European origins: "Fair was she to behold, that maiden of seventeen summers. / Black were her eyes as the berry that grows on the thorn by the wayside, / [...] Wearing her Norman cap and her kirtle of blue, and the ear-rings, / Brought in the olden time from France...." In the first Hollywood movie, produced in 1919, actress Miriam Cooper often appeared as a rather modern American, even somewhat emancipated. But in 1929, Mexican star Dolores del Río portrayed Évangéline. The film was shot in the heart of Cajun country, in Louisiana. In this production, the tale was clearly no longer set in Longfellow's cohesive white America, but in the ethnic narrative of a new America.

In 1947, for the hundred-year celebration of the poem's publication in Cambridge, Acadians, Quebecers, and Louisianians flocked to the ceremony. At the time, the American public seemed to have forgotten that Évangéline was one of their founders. She had become an ethnic figure. Furthermore, in 1963, when John F. Kennedy travelled to Ireland for one of the first official visits of an American president to Ireland, Kennedy recalled his double allegiance to Ireland and to the United States, in what was considered by some as the first political gestures of contemporary multiculturalism. Évangéline was, for all intents and purposes, forgotten. Yet it was she who, more than a century prior, had secured a place for those Catholics from Ireland and abroad within the American national narrative.

However, in 1962, Howard Mumford Jones, professor of literature at Harvard and specialist of narratives of the American origins, wrote in an introduction to a revised edition of the poem *Evangeline: An American Idyll* designed for American students: "This poem, if it is to be understood and valued, must be read from a certain point of view and in a certain way. *Evangeline* is not a story by Hemingway. It is a legend, poignant and beautiful, out of American history."

## "Written their history stands on tablets of stone in the churchyards"

The American Évangéline was a daughter of the *Mayflower*, not of Ellis Island. She was a character of pre-ethnic America. Her destiny was to blend into Anglo-Protestant America, not to carry on into a diverse America. Though pluralism was foundational in Longfellow's works, it was not the way of the future. Indeed, *Evangeline* was the first significant American work centred on a Catholic main character. As a founding narrative for America, it expanded the descent identity beyond that of Anglo-Protestants. However, as we saw in the previous chapter, Évangéline's Catholicism was inserted into the America setting without the superstitions—images, rituals, devotions—which are usually associated with this religion. The divinity that Longfellow attributed to his heroine did not derive from some mystical activity, but rather from faithfulness to ordinary human relations—and an entirely ascetic resignation to the earthly destiny.

In the course of her tribulations, Évangéline met numerous immigrants, each representing different degrees of religious faithfulness. On the one hand, there were the Pennsylvania Quakers, direct descendants of Penn the Apostle, and who echoed the democratic equality of the new America—these immigrants would have descendants, for they were the future of democratic America. On the other hand, the Shawnee Indigenous woman whose memory, like that of Évangéline, was drawn from the grave, painful, even phantasmagorical, and did not serve to build a society—the descent of these women was a thing of the past. "A breath from the region of spirits / Seemed to float in the air of night; and she felt for a moment / That, like the [Indigenous] maid, she, too, was pursuing a phantom." The other immigrants (of European origins) appear only as an elusive décor within the setting of America's nature.

An unlikely transformation allowed Basil the blacksmith, father of Gabriel, to retain visibility as an immigrant in the tale. He became, in the Eden of Louisiana, a rich livestock owner with a Spanish flair: "Mounted upon his horse, with Spanish saddle and stirrups, / Sat a herdsman, arrayed in gaiters and doublet of deerskin. / Broad and brown was the face that from under the Spanish sombrero / Gazed on the peaceful scene, with the lordly look of its master. / Round about him were numberless herds of kine, that were grazing." But the metamorphosis of the Grand-Pré blacksmith into a grand livestock owner was more representative of his successful integration into the American culture than proof of a lived ethnicity—he was already constructing the identity of his descent, much like the contemporary cosmopolitans. With this example, Longfellow was referencing the Mexican-American War (1846–48), which began after the annexation of Texas (1835), and which was ongoing when he wrote *Evangeline*. Here, too, at the southern border, Mexican Catholics were called, without a living memory of their descent, to become full-fledged Americans.

In the tale of *Evangeline*, the destiny of Acadians was not to bear children and establish their culture in America. Their reality was essentially a recollection of the past, with no predispositions allowing them to become a community of consent. This fate was affirmed in the opening verses of the introduction to the poem: "Naught but tradition remains of the beautiful village of Grand-Pré." Further in the text, Longfellow wrote: "Fair was she and young; but, alas! before her extended, / Dreary and vast and silent, the desert of life." And, concluding the poem, Longfellow reminded readers that America, without consideration for the memory of Acadians, trampled on the unmarked graves of the lovers, at long last reunited, and resting unnoticed in the small Catholic cemetery, while:

*Daily the tides of life go ebbing and flowing beside them,*
*Thousands of throbbing hearts, where theirs are at rest and forever,*
*Thousands of aching brains, where theirs no longer are busy,*
*Thousands of toiling hands, where theirs have ceased from their labors,*
*Thousands of weary feet, where theirs have completed their journey!*

The idea of those founding groups who shared the fate of melting into Anglo-Protestant America was strange to Longfellow. Theirs was a story without filiation—a memory from beyond the grave. It was not a story of absence, but one of death. Évangéline expressed it so, while thinking of the way she herself conceived of her quest to find Gabriel: "He had become to her heart as one who is dead, and not absent." This was why the story of these groups needed to be told even though they had no proper descendance. Therein lies the Romantic ambiguity of the past: it is neither our master as it would be from a wholly conservative perspective, nor is it to be rejected as it would be from a purely modern perspective. The past was dead, yet still present. Only the "celestial mechanics" of America could simultaneously articulate both memory and future in a delicate operation, which left no room for any other than Protestants.

A telling feature of this rapport to a memory that promised no future is the omnipresence of cemeteries throughout the poem. In the cemetery near the church of Grand-Pré, Évangéline and the other women realized that the men were being held prisoner. It was also there that Évangéline understood the inescapable fate of her people, for, with her cries unanswered, "Came from the graves of the dead, nor the gloomier grave of the living." Later on, during her exile in America, her lack of future was again mapped out through the image of the cemetery. "Fair was she and young; but, alas! before her extended, / Dreary and vast and silent, the desert of life, with its pathway / Marked by the graves of those who had sorrowed and suffered before her." And when, by chance, she met other Acadians during her travels, because she was in exile, it was to remind us that those pilgrims would only become a part of America if they repressed their experiences into a memory from beyond the grave. "Friends they sought and homes; and many, despairing, heart-broken, / Asked of the earth but a grave, and no longer a friend nor a fireside. / Written their history stands on tablets of stone in the churchyards."

The portrait by Scottish brothers Thomas and James Faed (1855) illustrated this well. Évangéline is depicted in front of a tombstone. At the time, it was one of the most well-known images of Évangéline, and so it remains today. We can associate it with the description by Longfellow of the long wanderings of the Acadian exiled in America: "Sometimes in churchyards strayed, and gazed on the crosses and tombstones, / Sat by some nameless grave, and thought that perhaps in its bosom / He was already at rest, and she longed to slumber beside him."

In the illustration by the Faed brothers, as in the cited verses, tombs are "nameless," clearly recalling the memory without filiation. This had already been announced, from the early scene of the banned Acadians standing on the banks of the Minas Basin in Grand-Pré. Évangéline's father, Benedict Bellefontaine, died and was buried there without a grave to commemorate his passing. "But without bell or book, they buried the farmer of Grand-Pré." The future of Évangéline would not hinge on any kinship. This was not the only place in the works of Longfellow where the image of the cemetery was tied to the absence of a future. It was a recurring theme, inherent to the fusional conception of America to which the author adhered. We will recall two other such examples.

In a short poem written in 1858 and entitled *The Jewish Cemetery at Newport*, Longfellow recalled with empathy the tragedies of the history of the people of the Exodus. However, the journey to America seemed to be their last. America would assimilate them: "Closed are the portals of their

Synagogue." The Jewish cemetery and its dusty tombstones attest to the disappearance of the group, to its fusion with the new chosen people. For Longfellow, the Jews were no longer a nation, their past being evanescent and their future, cosmo-politically American.

> *But ah! What once has been shall be no more!*
> *The groaning earth in travail and in pain*
> *Brings fort hits races, but does not restore,*
> *And the dead nation never rise again*
> *(The Jewish Cemetery of Newport)*

But it was in *Hiawatha* (1855), an epic poem recounting the tragic odyssey of the Indigenous peoples of America, that the idea of a descendance with no future is most clearly presented. For Longfellow, the memory of Indigenous peoples was but the long complaint of a lost land. This was partly the reason why *Hiawatha* was never reclaimed as a great narrative by Indigenous peoples—in the poem their destiny was but to carry the burden of their painful history. With the encounter between the exiled Acadian and the Shawnee woman in *Evangeline*, Longfellow had already explicitly associated the history of Indigenous peoples with that of the Acadians. He had drawn a parallel between what he saw as two histories where filiation upheld no future, and two people with nameless graves.

> *On the grave-posts of our fathers*
> *Are no sign, no figures painted;*
> *Who are in those graves we know not*
> *Only know they are our fathers*
> *(Hiawatha)*

There is the destiny of *Evangeline* in America: the heroine was among those anonymous founders of America, an America whose future reconnected with the democratic reality of the forest primeval. In Longfellow's America, descendance disappeared, leaving in its place a nameless future.

*Still stands the forest primeval; but far away from its shadow,*
*Side by side, in their nameless graves, the lovers are sleeping.*
*Under the humble walls of the little Catholic churchyard,*
*In the heart of the city, they lie, unknown and unnoticed.*
*Daily the tides of life go ebbing and flowing beside them,*
*Thousands of throbbing hearts, where theirs are at rest and forever,*

In contrast to Longfellow's works about the children of Israel and the Indigenous peoples of America, *Evangeline* had a bright future of literary fame. Indeed, the work was re-appropriated as a narrative of the future.

# References

GIOIA, D. "Longfellow in the Aftermath of Modernism." *The Columbia History of American Poetry.* New York, NY: Columbia University Press, 1993, pp. 46–96.

HOLLINGER, D. A. *Post-ethnic America: Beyond Multiculturalism.* New York, NY: Basic Books, 1995.

JACOBSON, M. F. *Roots Too: White Ethnic Revival in Post-civil rights America.* Cambridge, MA: Harvard University Press, 2006.

KALLEN, H. M. *Culture and Democracy in the United States.* New York, NY: Boni and Liveright, 1924.

KAUFMANN, E. "Nativist cosmopolitans: Institutional Reflexivity and the Decline of 'Double-consciousness.'" *American Nationalist Thought, Journal of Historical Sociology,* Vol. 14, No. 1, March 2001, pp. 47–78.

LACORNE, D. *La crise de l'identité américaine: Du melting-pot au multiculturalisme.* Paris, France: Fayard, 1997.

LIND, M. *The Next American Nation.* New York, NY: Free Press, 1995.

MCFARLAND, R. *The Long Life of Évangéline.* Jefferson, NC: Jefferson, McFarland & Company, 2010.

MARTIN, E. *L'Évangéline de Longfellow et la suite merveilleuse d'un poème.* Paris, France: Librairie Hachette, 1936.

MORIN, P. *Les sources de l'oeuvre de Henry Wadsworth Longfellow.* Paris, France: Librairie Éditions, 1913.

SEELYE, J. "Attic Shape: Dusting Off Évangéline." *Virginia Quarterly Review.* pp. 21–44, 1984.

SOLLORS, W. *Beyond Ethnicity: Consent and Descent in American Culture.* Oxford, UK: Oxford University Press, 2006.

THÉRIAULT, J. Y. "Au-delà du multiculturalisme: le cosmopolitisme." *Sociologie et Société,* Vol. 44, No. 1. pp. 17–33, 2012.

# PART II

## ÉVANGÉLINE THE ACADIAN

♦ *indicates a publication.*

## XV CENTURY

**1492**
Europeans discover America through Christopher Columbus.

**1497**
John Cabot lands in Newfoundland and establishes a British presence in North America.

## XVI CENTURY

**1524**
Giovanni da Verrazzano explores the east coast of the Atlantic in the name of the king of France. He names the present Virginia and Maryland coasts "Arcadia."

**1534-38**
Jacques Cartier explores the coasts of what will become Acadia and Canada.

## XVII CENTURY

**1603-13**
Samuel de Champlain names Maine and Nova Scotia "Arcadia" then "Acadia."

**1604**
Acadia is founded with the installation of a first settlement on Sainte Croix Island.

**1605**
Port-Royal (capital of Acadia) is founded.

**1606**
Samuel de Champlain establishes the Order of Good Cheer.

♦ *Le Théâtre de Neptune en Nouvelle-France* [first play in Classical French], Marc Lescarbot.

**1608**
Quebec is founded.

**1613**
Port-Royal is destroyed and the British take control of Acadia.

**1621**
The king of England claims Acadia and names it Nova Scotia.

**1628**
Sir William Alexander Jr. establishes a settlement of seventy men in Port-Royal, renamed Fort Charles.

**1629**
Treaty of Suza: Nova Scotia is given back to France. Acadia and Port-Royal keep their names.

**1632**
Isaac de Razilly arrives with three hundred French settlers.

**1654**
England declares that Acadia is "illegally taken by the French." Major Sedgwick attacks and conquers Acadia.

**1667**
Treaty of Breda: England gives Acadia (Nova Scotia) back to France.

**1680**
Pierre Thérriot and a couple of other Acadians leave Port-Royal for Grand-Pré.

**1690**
Admiral Phips takes control of Port-Royal.

**1697**
Treaty of Ryswick between France and England: Acadia becomes French once again.

## XVIII CENTURY

**1710**
Port-Royal surrenders.

**1713**
Treaty of Utrecht: Acadia is definitively surrendered to England, and is renamed Nova Scotia.

**1719**
French settlers start building Louisbourg on Cape Breton Island.

**1720**
Settlers colonize Île Saint-Jean (Prince Edward Island) and a New Acadia emerges in French territory.

**1745**
English settlers attack and conquer Louisbourg.

**1748**
Treaty of Aix-la-Chapelle: Louisbourg is given back to France.

**1749**
Foundation of Halifax: Nova Scotia is under a new colonization plan.

**1751**
Construction of Fort Beauséjour.

**1755**
The English seize Fort Beauséjour and force Acadians to swear fealty to the English crown.

Deportation of Nova Scotian Acadians.

**1756-63**
Seven Years War. English settlers seize Louisbourg, Île Royal, and Île Saint-Jean. New Acadian deportations.

**1763**
Treaty of Paris (end of the Seven Years War). France gives Canada to England and Louisiana (Mississippi) to Spain.

American settlers (Planters) establish settlements in Grand-Pré. Beausoleil-Broussard leaves Halifax for Louisiana with six hundred Acadians; three hundred of them will get there.

**1763-85**
Acadians come back to the old Acadian territories.

**1769**
Prince Edward Island separates from Nova Scotia.

**1783-85**
Thirty thousand American Loyalists make their way to the Maritimes.

**1784**
New Brunswick and Cape Breton separate from Nova Scotia.

**1789**
Nova Scotian Catholics are granted the right to vote.

**1763**
Acadians from Philadelphia sign a petition presented to the King of England.

**1794**
◊ *Histoire philosophique et politique des découvertes et établissements des Européens aux deux Indes,* l'abbé Raynal.

## XIX CENTURY

**1827-32**
Abolishment of the laws preventing Catholics to occupy electoral ranks.

**1836**
Election of the first Acadian deputies in Nova Scotia: Simon d'Entremont and Frédéric Robichaud.

**1838**
Rebellions in Upper and Lower Canada.

**1840**
Union of the Canadas.

**1846**
Election of the first New Brunswick Acadian: Amand Landry.

**1851**
Creation of the Nova Scotia Archives.

**1854**
Election of the first PEI Acadian: Stanislas-François Poirier (Perry).

**1829**
◊ *An Historical and Statistical Account of Nova Scotia,* Thomas Chandler Haliburton.

**1847**
◊ *Evangeline: A Tale of Acadie,* Henry Wadsworth Longfellow.

**1848**
◊ *Histoire du Canada,* vol. 3, François Xavier Garneau.

**1859**
◊ *La France aux colonies. Études sur le développement de la race française hors de l'Europe. Les Français en Amérique, Acadiens et Canadiens.* François-Edme Rameau de Saint-Père.

**1864**
Foundation of the University of St. Joseph's College (Memramcook, New Brunswick).

**1867**
Canadian Confederation (New Brunswick and Nova Scotia sign).

**1874**
Foundation of Saint-Louis de Kent College by Marcel-François Richard (closed in 1882).

**1875**
Riot in Caraquet to oppose the Common School Act.

**1885**
Nomination of the first Acadian senator: Pascal Poirier

**1890**
Foundation of Collège Sainte-Anne (Sainte-Anne University) in Church Point, Nova Scotia.

The first Acadian judge is nominated: Pierre-Amand Landry.

**1899**
Foundation of the Collège de Caraquet (College of Bathurst).

**1865**
♦ *Évangéline*, transl. Pamphile Lemay.

**1866**
♦ *Jacques et Marie*, Napoléon Bourassa.

**1867**
Foundation of the first French-language Acadian newspaper by Israël Landry, *Le Moniteur Acadien*.

**1874**
♦ *Origines des Acadiens*, Pascal Poirier.

**1875**
♦ *Les Acadiens à Philadelphie*, Pascal Poirier.

**1877**
♦ *Une colonie féodale en Amérique: l'Acadie*, François-Edme Rameau de Saint-Père.

**1881**
First national Acadian convention in Memramcook. Establishment of a national celebration (l'Assomption, August 15) and of a Patron Saint (Notre-Dame de l'Assomption).

**1884**
National anthem of the Acadians becomes *Ave Maris Stella* and the Acadian flag is raised (tricolour flag) during the second national Acadian convention in Miscouche, PEI.

♦ *Montcalm and Wolfe*, Francis Parkman.

**1885**
Foundation of the newspaper *Le Courrier des Provinces Maritimes* by J. Théophile Allard, A. A. Boucher, and Valentin Landry.

**1887**
Foundation of the newspaper *L'Évangéline* by Valentin Landry.

**1888**
♦ *Un pèlerinage au pays d'Évangéline*, Henri-Raymond Casgrain.

# XX CENTURY

**1903**
Foundation of the Société Mutuelle de l'Assomption in Waltham, New England.

**1912**
Nomination of the first Acadian Bishop, Edward Alfred Le Blanc, at the Roman Catholic Diocese of Saint John, NB.

**1920**
Nomination of a second Acadian Bishop, Patrice-Alexandre Chiasson, at the Bathurst Diocese, NB.

**1920**
Unveiling of the statue of Évangéline and creation of the Grand-Pré Heritage Site.

**1922**
Benediction of the Grand-Pré chapel.

**1924**
Foundation of two religious Acadian congregations: Filles de Marie-de-l'Assomption and the Sisters of Notre-Dame-du-Sacré-Coeur.

**1936**
Foundation of the first Acadian credit union. Creation of the Archdiocese of Moncton.

**1946**
Foundation of Collège Saint-Louis, Edmundston, New Brunswick.

Federation of the Acadian credit union.

**1905**
Fifth National Acadian Convention, Caraquet, New Brunswick.

**1907**
♦ *Henry Wadsworth Longfellow: sa vie, ses oeuvres littéraires, son poème Evangeline*, Philéas Bourgeois.

**1922**
♦ *Le Grand dérangement. Sur qui retombe la responsabilité de l'expulsion des Acadiens*, Placide Gaudet.

**1937**
Tenth National Acadian Convention, Memramcook, New Brunswick.

**1954**
The French division of the CBC/Radio-Canada is permanently established in Moncton.

**1955**
Bicentennial of the Acadian Deportation.

**1960**
Election of Louis J. Robichaud, first Acadian elected as prime minister of New Brunswick.

**1963**
University of Moncton is founded.

**1968-1969**
Student strikes at the University of Moncton.

**1972**
Creation of the Acadian party.

**1973**
Founding of the Société des Acadiens du Nouveau-Brunswick (SANB).

**1977**
Official opening of the historical Acadian village in Caraquet, New Brunswick.

**1971**
♦ *La Sagouine*, Antonine Maillet.

**1972**
The opening of the first Acadian publishing house, Les Éditions d'Acadie.

**1974**
The National Film Board of Canada establishes a film studio in Moncton.

♦ *Mourir à Scoudouc*, Herménégilde Chiasson.

**1975**
♦ *L'Acadie du discours*, Jean-Paul Hautecoeur.

**1981**
Ruling of Bill 88, recognizing the equality of two language communities in New Brunswick.

**1982**
The Canadian constitutional law recognizes the right to be taught in French.

**1992**
Inclusion of the principle of the equality of French and English in New Brunswick within the Canadian Constitution.

**2003**
Nomination of Herménégilde Chiasson, artist, to the role of lieutenant-governor of New Brunswick. Royal proclamation of July 28 as a commemorative day of the Grand Dérangement of the Acadian people.

**1978**
♦ *L'Acadie perdue*, Michel Roy.

**1979**
♦ *Pélagie-la-Charrette* [recipient of the Goncourt Prize], Antonine Maillet.

National Acadian Convention, Edmundston, NB.

**1982**
Closure of daily newspaper, *L'Évangéline*.

**1994**
First International Acadian Congress (southeast of New Brunswick).

**1997**
First edition of *À l'ombre d'Évangéline*, project of the art gallery of the University of Moncton. The objective is to invite artists to create, each year over thirty years, three art pieces following on the theme of Évangéline. The first three were produced by Francis Couturier, Herménégilde Chiasson, and Roméo Savoie.

**1999**
Second International Acadian Congress (Louisiana).

**2004**
Third International Acadian Congress (Nova Scotia).

**2009**
Fourth International Acadian Congress (Acadian Peninsula).

**2012**
Grand-Pré is granted the status of UNESCO World Heritage Site.

**2014**
Fifth International Acadian Congress (Quebec, Maine, and New Brunswick).

# THE BATTLE OVER LOST SOULS

*And forth came the guard, and marching in gloomy procession*
*Followed the long-imprisoned, but patient, Acadian farmers.*
*Even as pilgrims, who journey afar from their homes and their country,*
*Sing as they go, and in singing forget they are weary and wayworn,*
*So with songs on their lips the Acadian peasants descended*
*Down from the church to the shore*

—Henry Wadsworth Longfellow, *Evangeline*

## The Facts

On September 5, 1755, Lieutenant-Colonel John Winslow, who was born in Marshfield, Massachusetts, into one of the most prominent families of New England—his grandfather and great-grandfather had been governors of the Plymouth Bay colony—wrote in his journal: "Thus ends my Memorable fifth of September, a Day of great Fatigue for me and Trouble."

Lieutenant-Colonel Winslow was the leader of the American militia charged by Governor William Shirley of Massachusetts with recruiting two thousand men in support of the lieutenant governor of Nova Scotia's efforts to solve, once and for all, the problem of the French neutrals, the French-speaking inhabitants at the northern border and those living on English lands. This militia, in the spring of 1755, captured Fort Beauséjour, the fortification that had recently been built by the French to limit English invasion into Acadian territories of the Nova Scotian peninsula. Afterwards, Winslow moved into the Minas Basin to oversee, with Colonel Murray, the deportation of its inhabitants into New England.

Concerned with his legacy to future generations, Lieutenant-Colonel Winslow kept a detailed diary with the orders he received, the documents justifying these decisions, and specifying his actions and intentions. He described the order he received to evict the inhabitants of the Grand-Pré region and the ruse—the convocation of the men and children in the church under a false pretext—that he used to lock all men aged over ten years in the church to inform them that they had been stripped of their lands and made prisoners. He took care to write down the words he used to announce the terrible news. He described the cries of women and children while the captured men walked down the rough, mile and a half-long road separating the church and the banks: "The Which they then did, though Slowly, and they went singing and crying and praying, being met by the Women and Children all the way (the road is rough and a mile and a half long) with great lamentations and upon their knees" (Journal of John Winslow, September 10, 1755). Winslow kept a detailed register of the livestock found, the number of burned buildings, and lastly, the number of inhabitants made prisoners as well as their projected destination.

Winslow expressed some compassion for the situation of these poor peasants. As he told them, he was but a messenger carrying out the decisions of Governor Lawrence in the king's command, who, in the last fifty years, had given them opportunities to prove their loyalty. The "duty" assigned to him was "very disagreeable to [his] natural make and temper." He told them he understood their pain, they who were of the same "specia" (species).

The day of September 5, which for Winslow ended with "great Fatigue... and Trouble," was meant for more than the evacuation of the inhabitants of the territory. It was the "great and noble scheme" announced by the authorities of Nova Scotia in the *Pennsylvania Gazette* the day before, informing the citizens of Philadelphia of the imminent arrival of the exiled neutral French.[1] The "noble scheme" would eliminate the threat

---

1.  "We are now upon a great and noble Scheme of sending the neutral French out of this Province, who have always been secret Enemies, and have encouraged our Savages to cut our Throats. If we effect their Expulsion, it will be one of the greatest Things that ever the English did in America; for by all Accounts, that Part of the Country they possess, is as good Land as any in the World: In case therefore we could get some good English Farmers in their Room, this Province would abound with all kinds of Provisions."

of these domestic enemies and provide the opportunity to expand the Anglo-Protestant colony. Their lands were confiscated, their buildings burned to the ground, they were deported and dispersed in such a manner to prevent them from rebuilding communities, and ultimately, to ensure they would assimilate. What is more, the authorities took care to redesign the territory, retracing villages and renaming places in English fashion to erase from the old French Acadie not only its inhabitants, but also the memory of their presence. In this "noble scheme," not only were Acadians made to disappear, but also the mere memory of Acadie.

\* \* \*

In the year 1770, the first edition of an anonymous book entitled *Histoire philosophique et politique des établissements & du commerce des Européens dans les deux Indes* was printed in Amsterdam. Subsequent editions confirmed the author to be Guillaume Thomas Raynal, more commonly known as Abbé Raynal (Father Raynal), a French priest who was strongly influenced by the philosophical ideals of the Enlightenment. His very successful book was a "postcolonial" critique before its time. Raynal vilified European nations and monarchies for the devastations they caused in their colonies. His printed words ultimately led to his expulsion from pre-revolutionary France.

Raynal writes a few pages on Acadie in his *Histoire philosophique et politique*. Unlike the few, mainly English, existing references at the time— notably the writings of philosopher Edmund Burke—which described the Deportation within the context of British military history, Raynal ventured a socio-historical explanation. France had quickly abandoned its settlement at Port Royal. As it was distant from Quebec, this allowed the few thousand French inhabitants—there were at least four thousand when Acadie was surrendered in 1713—to spread out liberally over the land. Their dispersion even accelerated after 1713. The English then only saw in Port Royal a small garrison, with most Acadians living farther and farther away from any colonial administration.

The relative abandonment of Acadie by colonial authorities had the effect of creating a society without hierarchies, a sort of "state of nature" as Jean-Jacques Rousseau would describe. This society without political structure or nobility was egalitarian and had peaceful customs. There was no crime, no illicit trade between sexes, noted Raynal. As for commercial trade, it was reduced to its simplest form—a few exchanges of rare goods with the English in Annapolis Royal (Port-Royal) or with the French at Louisbourg. The Acadians did not use money; they lived self-sufficiently in a regime of community partnership. The greed of colonial authorities, their religious and national fanaticism, would put an end to this idyllic state. England tried in vain to populate this country with Protestants though Acadians were peaceful subjects. Raynal wrote: "French priests who were overcome with their own enthusiasm or by the incentives of the administrators of Canada, persuaded them of everything they wanted against the English they called heretics."[2] They attempted to convince the Acadians to come join them in their Canadian territories. Ultimately, England preferred an empty land to one inhabited by French Catholics. Thus ended the quiet pastoral society with peaceful customs.

\* \* \*

In 1829, *An Historical and Statistical Account of Nova Scotia* was published in Halifax, Nova Scotia. The author, Thomas Chandler Haliburton, was the grandson of New England Loyalists, who, in 1760, settled on the lands made available through the expulsion of Acadians. He wrote about his country, as he noted in the epigraph, "This is my own, my native Land." He was born in Windsor, Nova Scotia, located deep in the Minas Basin—a place that used to be named Pesaquid in French Acadie—and where the English established Fort Edwards after 1713. He practised law in the small town of Annapolis Royal (Port-Royal), which had been the capital of Acadie until 1713, and of Nova Scotia until 1749 when Halifax was established. Haliburton was a member of parliament for the region, and went on to

---

2.   "Des pasteurs échauffés par leur propre enthousiasme, ou par les insinuations des administrateurs du Canada, leur persuaderent tout ce qu'ils voulurent contre les Anglois qu'ils appelloient hérétiques." (Raynal 1770, *Histoire des deux Indes*, volume 6, p. 6.)

become a judge and immigrate to Great Britain where he was also elected MP. Mainly, though, he became famous throughout the British Empire for his series of popular novels featuring the character Sam Slick.

Thomas Chandler Haliburton wrote that when he had decided to draft an account of the events that led to the expulsion of the French inhabitants of the province in the mid-eighteenth century, he realized there were no traces of such events in the colonial archives of Nova Scotia that could help him reconstruct the events and understand the decisions that were made at the time. All the correspondence between the London Board of Trade and Governor Lawrence from December 1754 to August 1756 was unavailable. Was this deliberate? Were the authors of these actions "ashamed of the transaction"? Haliburton reconstructed the events with great difficulty.

He found a marginal reference in *History of the Insurrection in Massachusetts* (1788) by Richard Minot, which mentioned the journal of Lieutenant-Colonel Winslow, leader of the militia, that showed an account of the expedition to Nova Scotia in 1755. Haliburton obtained a portion of this manuscript and a copy of the petition that a group of Acadians exiled in Philadelphia had submitted to the authorities of the colony in 1756. To this day, the 1756 petition remains the principal historical document by Acadians recounting their experience, their point of view on their historic rights and the injustice that was imposed on them when they were evicted from their lands. It is also in this document that we find the first reference to the notary named Leblanc who, having been imprisoned by the French for collaborating with the English, was transported with the others to New York, then to Philadelphia, without his whole family—it is specified that he had twenty children and more than one hundred and fifty grandchildren.

Haliburton was a reformist spirit. He gave an eloquent speech at the provincial legislative assembly in favour of the political emancipation of Catholics in the wake of London Parliament's 1829 Catholic Relief Act, which lifted the last restrictions preventing the election of Catholic members of parliament. Such changes led to the abolition of the Test Act in Nova Scotia in 1830, and later in the rest of the Maritime provinces, which would allow Catholics—including Acadians—to be elected. The new legislation eliminated the problematic clauses of the oath of allegiance forcing Catholics to renounce their faith, an oath that had been at the heart of the conflict leading to the banishment of Acadians from the region. This was the last in a long list of measures that were in place since the middle of the eighteenth century and that had progressively prevented Catholics from living in the colony, owning land, voting, and finally, electing representatives.

Haliburton's plea was not purely theoretical. He knew that some Acadians had survived the Deportation of 1755. In the southwest of his county of Annapolis, in the parish of Clare, there was a community of nearly three thousand descendants of the old inhabitants of Nova Scotia. For the most part, their ancestors returned in 1766 from their involuntary exile in Boston, having received the permission from colonial authorities to settle on this long sandbank, as their previously owned lands were occupied. The historian maintained a good relationship with the priest of Clare, Father Sigogne, who officiated in this region since he had left post-revolutionary France. This population massively supported Haliburton in the elections of 1826. These Catholics, he said, did not have specific demands, had peaceful mores, and requested only to live according to their traditions. In his opinion, they were quite like the depiction that Abbé Raynal had made of their mores and customs before 1755. For this reason, he concluded, even though Acadians had their faults in complying with their Canadian compatriots, the way the issue had been resolved was quite "embarrassing."

\* \* \*

In the spring of 1840, during a dinner at Craigie House—the Longfellow residence in Cambridge, Massachusetts, where sat Nathaniel Hawthorne—Reverend Horace Lorenzo Connolly, then pastor of St. Matthew's Episcopal Church in Boston, told Longfellow the following story. During the Seven Years War in Nova Scotia, all the men of the village, French neutrals, were assembled in a church and were then transported to New England to be dispersed. Among them, on separate ships, a couple was to marry that same day. The fiancée spent her entire life until her old age travelling New England to find her lover. Pastor Connolly recounted that this story came to him from one of his parishioners, the wife of George Mordaunt Haliburton (nephew of Thomas Chandler Haliburton), a French Canadian, according to whom this story was truthful—it seems, however, that the wife of G. M. Haliburton was not indeed a French Canadian.

We know what happened next, Longfellow covered the story. According to his own affirmations and the books he borrowed at the Harvard library, he used two sources for inspiration: Raynal's work for the simple and pastoral life of Acadians, and that of Haliburton for their eviction, their banishment.

## *Evangeline* and the French Canadian Narrative

With this part of the story in mind, we can investigate how the tale of Évangéline arrived in Acadie. But before landing in Acadie, the tale transited through French Canadian territory, a process that considerably modified the American reception of the work.

*Evangeline: A Tale of Acadie* was first published in 1847. This was the time of the unification of Lower and Upper Canada. It was a pivotal period for the establishment of the French Canadian nationhood. The "Canadiens" as the francophones of Lower Canada liked to call themselves, had just suffered a bitter defeat. Their parliament was suspended, they were forcefully united with Upper Canada, the French language had lost its official status, and their political elite was either discredited by the English authorities or exiled. Antoine Gérin-Lajoie wrote in 1842 the words to the song "Un Canadien errant" lamenting the misfortune of the exiled Canadians who had participated in the Lower Canada Rebellion (known as the *Rébellion des Patriotes*, 1837–38).

During the years preceding the rebellions of 1837–38, a specific idea of nationhood had taken form. For the most part, it hinged on the existence in Lower Canada of a people with a distinct nature who collectively had the same rights as those of the English. The brutal response of the English colonial government to these aspirations of independence blocked the political track to the affirmation of the "Canadienne" nation. From then on, after 1840, the idea of nationhood became more impressed in cultural endeavours. The intellectuals of French Canada insisted on their French and Catholic origins. When they were offered to assimilate to the Anglo-British civilization, they promptly refused. They also declined when some of their leaders, who were disappointed with the British response, proposed an association with the great American democracy. Étienne Parent, one of the first French Canadian intellectuals, impressed on them to be wary of the rapid Anglicization of the French in Louisiana under the reign of the great Republic. They affirmed that they were a civilization, like the Anglo-American civilization, but whose providential destiny—or manifest destiny—was not to achieve democracy, nor to become subjected to the love of material goods, but rather to spread across the territory of America the spiritual values of the French and Catholic civilization.

Many saw this discourse as a retreat into old-fashioned values, with French Canadiens retreating into "a long winter of survival"[3] in the words of Fernand Dumont, one of the most supportive of this tradition among contemporary readers. Some of this may have been true, yet the tale of the humble folk descending from French settlers who were called to impart the greatness of French Catholicism across America could not merely be reduced to backward tradition. Such a transition from a political nation to a cultural nation was not unique to Quebec, nor to small societies. This process was part of the great Romantic shift at the beginning of the nineteenth century, which, as we have seen, also produced the American national narrative. "Canadiens" looked to the United States of America not only to construct their democracy, but also to elaborate their national narrative.

This French Canadian narrative, which reached its full maturity at the beginning of the twentieth century was in the heart of its construction phase by the middle of the 1840s. All the core elements were already there, they just needed to be aligned. Such was the narrative that would embrace and "translate" *Evangeline*, contributing to define the new Acadie of the north in the process.

---

3. "un long hiver de la survivance."

Acadie used to be part of Nouvelle-France, the French colony in America, though it was separated by the practically insurmountable Appalachian Mountains. The geographical border gave this region of Canada much autonomy, and its proximity to New England was deemed dangerous. The defeat of France in Acadie and the setbacks of the Acadian people were critical events that led to the fall of Quebec in 1759 and the handing over of Canada to the British in 1763. Indeed, between 1750 and 1763 when the population of Canada (Quebec) was of approximately seventy thousand, the conflicts in Acadie led some three thousand Acadians to seek refuge to the west of the Appalachians. A group of Acadian refugees arriving from the east even fought in the Battle of Quebec under the leadership of Boishébert. Some memos reiterate the destitute nature of these people who managed to cross the Appalachians or follow the banks of the St. Lawrence River to rejoin their Canadien brothers. The expression "Cadie" or "Petite-Cadie" (petite meaning little) was long used throughout the nineteenth century to describe the localities where these Acadians mainly settled—near Trois-Rivières in Nicolet, or along the Richelieu River, near Saint-Jean.

These Acadians, despite having gathered in Petite-Cadie, rapidly blended into the Canadien population with whom they shared their French origins, language, and religion. This was not the case for Quebecois Acadians who settled at the border with the Acadie of old—the Acadians of Chaleur Bay and those of the Magdalen Islands who, for the most part until the middle of the twentieth century, shared a way of living and collective imaginary with the Acadians of the Maritimes. In either group, the notion of the Expulsion as the central phenomenon that put an end to Acadie, was not part of the collective imaginary before the romance of *Evangeline* came along. Indeed, the poem and its translation introduced Acadie as a theme of French Canadian nationalism…and later on, of Acadian nationalism.

In 1843, four years before *Evangeline* was released, Michel Bibaud published *Histoire du Canada sous la domination française*. He insisted heavily on French attempts after 1748 to create a new French Acadie, to the north, along the coast of the Gulf, at Île Saint-Jean (today's Prince Edward Island) and at Île-Royale (today's Cape Breton). Bibaud recounted the zeal, which he considered exaggerated, of Abbot Le Loutre, who tried to convince the Acadian populations of Nova Scotia to migrate to these new settlements. He described how Le Loutre had the village of Beaubassin burned to the ground after having displaced the Acadian people to the French side. Bibaud read Raynal and Haliburton. He wrote on how the British chased the Acadians from the territory, but offered few details. The Expulsion was not yet part of the narrative. Bibaud did not describe the scene in Grand-Pré, nor the expulsion of Acadians toward the United States. He rather insinuated that Acadians had either returned to France or reached Canada where they "found the much needed assistance for their misfortunes" (*les secours dus à leurs infortunes*).

Bibaud had also published in 1830 a short poem titled "Les moeurs acadiennes," in what should be considered the first book of poetry published in French Canada, under the title *Épîtres, satires, chansons, épigrammes et autres pièces de vers*. The poem played on the analogy between "l'Acadie perdue" (the lost Acadie) and "l'heureuse Arcadie" (the merry Arcadia). The pastoral description of the Acadian customs was that of Raynal. The old man recounted his lost paradise and his youthful love, and though he spoke of wars, there was no mention of an exile caused by a deportation.

Though we cannot consider Bibaud a proper poet, historian, nor great intellectual of the French Canadian narrative, it can be said of François-Xavier Garneau, who first published his *Histoire du Canada* in 1845. This work was the first true national history of French Canada. Garneau wanted to restore the confidence of his compatriots, who were going through a great period of uncertainty. Unlike "the Germans, Dutch, Swedish [who] settled in groups in the United States, and who indifferently melted into the masses without resistance, without a single word revealing their existence to the world," the descendants of the French settlers established a nation.[4] As the great historian Jules Michelet did for France, and as the historians were doing in the United States, Garneau wanted to present the history

---

4. In Garneau's words: "des Allemands, des Hollandais, des Suédois [qui] se sont établis par groupes dans les États-Unis, et se sont insensiblement fondus dans la masse sans résistance, sans qu'une parole même révélât leur existence au monde."

of his people according to "the principle of the modern school of history, which takes the nation as a source and aim of all power."[5] Though he saw a great destiny for the French Canadian people, he did conclude with a word of caution. The population of this small nation did benefit from the same cheerful presumptions as big democracies; its "preservation" would always remain its main priority.

Insofar as the history of Acadie was a part of that of Nouvelle-France, Garneau wrote of it in his history of French Canada. The third volume of his work was published in 1846 and covered the period ending in 1755. Like Bibaud, he insisted on French efforts to align the Acadian "neutrals" with the French, to bring to the new Acadie, farther north—a project Garneau felt was hardly justifiable. The establishment of Halifax in 1749 increased the pressure on Acadians, who migrated closer and closer to the French side, with some reaching Quebec. All these events hinted at the upcoming war between both groups, but nothing announced the fatal blow the Acadians would suffer.

Volume IV of his *Histoire du Canada* came out in 1848—a year after the publication of *Evangeline*. The tone had changed. After describing how, following the defeat at Fort Beauséjour, the French had to evacuate the French part of the Acadian territory and leave "the inhabitants of this province to the mercy of the English," Garneau wrote: "What we have yet to tell of this interesting people, calls to memory a painful tragedy the likes of which are rare even in the barbaric periods of history, at a time when the laws of justice and humanity were yet to be birthed with the enlightenment of civilization."[6] He borrowed entire pages from Raynal to reaffirm the gentle nature of the Acadians. Garneau wrote again on the events leading up to 1755 using Haliburton's writings as a foundation, and on the Grand-Pré episode with Winslow's diary as a source document, adding pathos that was more characteristic of the poem than of Winslow's

---

5. Garneau wrote: "le principe de l'école historique moderne qui prend la nation pour source et pour but de tout pouvoir."

6. "Ce qui nous reste à conter de ce peuple intéressant, rappelle un de ces drames douloureux dont les exemples sont rares même aux époques barbares de l'histoire, alors que les lois de la justice et de l'humanité sont encore à naître avec les lumières de la civilisation." (Garneau, *Histoire du Canada*)

restraint. He related the scene where prisoners were displaced toward the beach, a "sorrowful procession" with the cries of women and children in lieu of a hymn. "The men were brought aboard ships, the women and children were placed on others, indiscriminately, without the least regard for their comfort."[7] He reused the misfortunes of notary LeBlanc, who "died of sorrow" in Philadelphia even though he was a friend of the English.

Garneau did not research his own facts about Acadie, even making the same factual errors as Haliburton had. Having only had access to some passages from Winslow's diary, he assumed September 10 was the day of the expulsion. Rather, this was the day Winslow described having sent the men, with the youngest in the lead, aboard the ships, to avoid trouble inside the church. But the departure of the vessels came later...in October and even in December. It was this description of the procession that led to the strong conviction that the Acadian prisoners had been separated into age groups before boarding the ships. Longfellow needed this hypothesis to explain the separation of the Évangéline and Gabriel: "Wives were torn from their husbands, and mothers, too late, saw their children / Left on the land, extending their arms, with wildest entreaties." And Garneau amplified the pathos by adding: "In an act of unprecedented barbarism, families were separated and dispersed onto different vessels."[8] Much like in the poem, he turned the tragedy of Grand-Pré into a condensed version of the process of expulsion: "On that very day, at that very time, the same desolate spectacle took place in all Acadian settlements."[9]

In his works, Garneau specified that exiled Acadians were welcomed to the United States with humanity, though some went on to settle in Louisiana, France, Guyana, and so on. He did not write of Acadians who returned to Acadie, for he was of the opinion that Acadie was a dead society with the majority of descendants having chosen the "Canadien" side prior to 1755. Garneau did, however, innovate by introducing two elements

---

7.  "Les hommes furent mis sur des vaisseaux, les femmes et les enfants sur d'autres, pêle-mêle, sans qu'on prît le moindre soin pour leur commodité." (Garneau, *Histoire du Canada*)

8.  In Garneau's words: "par un raffinement de barbarie sans exemple, les mêmes familles furent séparées et dispersées sur différents vaisseaux."

9.  "Tous les autres établissements des Acadiens présentèrent le même jour et à la même heure le même spectacle de désolation." (Garneau, *Histoire du Canada*)

of the Expulsion that were not included in the narrative constructed by Raynal, reworked by Haliburton, and finally integrated into Longfellow's *Evangeline*. The first element was the covetousness of the American colonies for the fertile lands of the old Acadie. "Many schemers and adventurers eyed these beautiful Acadian farms with envy."[10] Therein lay, or so it seemed, the fundamental reason for this odious act. The second element was the widespread dispersion of the nation. "When came the time board the vessels, leaving the homeland forever, distancing themselves from their kin and friends without hope of seeing them again, to go live dispersed within a population that was a stranger to their language, customs, mores, and religion, their courage forsook them, and they fell victim to unbearable pain."[11] Actually, for Garneau, the Expulsion was an "expatriation," such was the term he used to designate it, as it was the "complete destruction of a people" (*la ruine totale d'un peuple*). The Acadian nation no longer existed, but it gave a "new motive to Canadiens, if they needed one, to defend their country with all the energy they could muster."[12]

## Évangéline Misses Her Homeland

What truly marked the consecration of *Evangeline* into the "Canadien" collective imaginary, however, was the translation of the poem by Léon-Pamphile Lemay and the publication of a novel titled *Jacques et Marie* by Napoléon Bourassa—two works that came to market within a few months of each other in 1864.

Pamphile Lemay was part of the Quebec Literary School (École littéraire de Québec), which was also known as the Quebec Patriotic School

---

10. Garneau wrote: "Beaucoup d'intrigants et d'aventuriers voyaient ces belles fermes acadiennes avec un oeil de convoitise."
11. "Lorsqu'il fallut s'embarquer, quitter pour jamais le sol natal, s'éloigner de ses parents et de ses amis sans espérance de ne jamais se revoir, pour aller vivre dispersés au milieu d'une population étrangère de langue, de coutumes, de moeurs et de religion, le courage abandonna ces malheureux, qui se livrèrent à la plus profonde douleur." (Garneau, *Histoire du Canada*)
12. In Garneau's words: "un nouveau motif aux Canadiens, s'ils en avaient besoin, de défendre leur pays avec toute l'énergie dont ils étaient capables".

(École patriotique de Québec). In the wake of the socio-historical works by François-Xavier Garneau and Étienne Parent, this group of literati headed by Father Antoine Henri-Raymond Casgrain (1831–1904) met regularly in the back room of a bookstore owned by Octave Crémazie. The group notably brought together talented authors like Pierre-Joseph-Olivier Chauveau, Joseph-Charles Taché, Antoine Gérin-Lajoie, Louis-Honoré Fréchette, and Léon-Pamphile Lemay, all of which were important figures of the burgeoning "patriotic" literature. They wanted to infuse a national dimension into the emerging French Canadian literature. In contrast to the Liberals united around the Institut Canadien—also a patriotic cultural and political organization—their inspiration is more Romantic, Catholic, and conservative.

Literature, as Casgrain noted, "is the reflection of the customs, character, abilities, genius of a nation."[13] Octave Crémazie complained in 1867 that there was yet to be, among the French Canadians, the likes of Fenimore Cooper (*The Last of the Mohicans*, 1826), capable of describing the "grandiose nature of our forests," the "legendary feats of our trappers." They were fascinated by the birth of an American national literature, though noting that the United States was a land of greed, eroded by the egoism of merchants, the antipode of the spiritual values of French Canada. They developed a literature, which, despite referring to French Canadian themes, remained largely defined by the literary code of France. It was, in reality, a reversed copy, but a copy nonetheless, of the project put forth by the Brahmins, the literary group from New England that Longfellow defended and whose vision of nationalism similarly maintained a filiation to a certain idea of Europe.

In 1864, Pamphile Lemay was a young poet making his first foray in literature. He would go on to become an important writer of French Canadian literature (known then as "Canadian" literature) and serve for twenty-five years as the first librarian of the new legislature of Quebec. His translation of *Evangeline* was the central part of his work titled *Essais poétiques*, which included a few original poems and a few other translations

---

13.  In Casgrain's words: "la littérature est le reflet des moeurs, du caractère, des aptitudes, du génie d'une nation" (*Le mouvement littéraire en Canada*, 1866).

of Longfellow's works. He presented himself before the literary world with his translation of *Evangeline*. For him, in a country indifferent to poetry, writing was a national imperative. "I hope to have served my country by doing this work! May my book shine a reflection of glory on my dear Canada."[14]

The cover page announces only Lemay as the author of *Essais poétiques*. It is only in the preface to the reader that we learn that *Évangéline* is a translation of the "charming poem" by Longfellow. Lemay's translation is largely an appropriation of the poem or rather, a "(re)Canadianization" of *Evangeline*. Lemay did not shy from this, reminding Longfellow in a letter he sent him in 1865 alongside a copy of his *Essais poétiques* and "his" *Évangéline*. He reaffirmed in the presentation of the subsequent editions of the poem (1870 and 1912) that his work was a liberal translation ("traduction libre"). Literature being, for him, a representation of national realities, it was evident that a work of translation was a sort of rewriting. "English poetry is more sober and less lively than ours," he pointed out. In 1878, he wrote Longfellow again, this time sending copies of his two novels, *Le Pèlerin de Saint-Anne* (1877) and *Picounoc le maudit* (1878), and asking whether he could intercede with an American author on his behalf so his works might be translated. Lemay added that these were "faithful portraits of the [French] Canadian habits and customs" which would need to be Americanized in the same way he had "Canadianized" *Evangeline* ten years prior. It seems as though Longfellow never responded to his request.

Longfellow, himself a great borrower who had been deemed the "king of plagiarists" by Edgar Allan Poe, had, however, responded with restraint to Lemay's first letter. His "only reservation," he wrote, was that "you had Évangéline die." Evidently, having Évangéline die of sorrow in the arms of Gabriel—"Her painful life had ended" ("*Elle avait terminé sa douloureuse vie*")—meant Lemay was breaking with the American narrative. Évangéline needed to die quietly in the welcoming democratic society of the Quakers. Lemay rapidly corrected this issue in subsequent editions, which were more directly marketed as translations of Longfellow's work.

14.   In Lemay's words: "Puissé-je avoir servi mon pays en faisant ce travail! Puisse mon livre faire rejaillir un reflet de gloire sur mon cher Canada" (*Essais poétiques*, 1865).

Yet, the fact that the poor exiled Acadian woman died of sorrow was most definitely not the only infringement on the American narrative within Lemay's version of *Evangeline*. His strategic adaptation was even analyzed by scholars of translation studies.

And yet, Lemay did not betray Longfellow's narrative. The story remained the same, and most of the verses, with the exception of a few notable oversights, were faithfully reproduced. Lemay even said he respected the sentiments of the American poet throughout the work, and the facts appear to prove him right. Lemay's version of the poem remains a great Romantic poem, an ode to love and fidelity, and his translation, which he reworked with each new edition, was quite successful.

What changed was the national narrative within which the story was inscribed. This was how Lemay initially modified the writing format. Rather than using the English dactylic hexameter without rhymes that Longfellow chose in order to echo the great foundational epic narratives, Lemay chose the French alexandrine verse, which he deemed more consistent with French prosody. The hexameter without rhymes gave the English original a rhythmic continuity with a stylistic lightness and softness similar to that of a fairy tale, but the rhythmic break caused by the alexandrine gave a more solemn character to the French translation, with irregular verses appearing more weighted, grave, and memorable. While Longfellow's version was a Romance well suited to the democratic nature of the American society, Lemay's version resembled more the biblical Sermon on the Mount, a testament to the Acadian tragedy.

Hexameters being longer than alexandrine verses, Lemay deemed it practical to translate each hexameter with two alexandrines on average. This had the effect of more than doubling the length of the poem—Longfellow's *Évangeline* had 1,399 verses; Lemay's *Évangéline* had 2,894 in the 1865 edition. The supplementary verses gave Lemay the space to enrich the poem using a "Canadianizing" lens. This practice was occasionally made explicit, as in the final verses of the prologue, where Lemay announced that the poem was "a love story *for* the Acadian land" while Longfellow had made it "a love story *set in* Acadie." In Lemay's work, the place, the scene, became the subject of the poem.

| | |
|---|---|
| *List to a tale of Love in Acadie, home of the happy* | *Écoutez une histoire aussi belle qu'ancienne,* |
| Longfellow | *Écoutez une histoire d'amour de la terre acadienne* |
| | Lemay |

Similarly, when came time to leave the banks of Grand-Pré, the women turned around to look at their homes, which Longfellow had called "dwellings," but in Lemay's vision were transformed into an Acadian village universe.

| | |
|---|---|
| *Pausing and looking back to gaze once more on their dwellings.* | *Et puis, de temps en temps, elles s'arrêtaient toutes* |
| Longfellow | *Pour regarder encore une dernière fois* |
| | *Le clocher de l'église et leurs modestes toits* |
| | *Et leurs paisibles champs et leur joli village* |
| | Lemay |

In Longfellow's poem, the procession of men leaving the church and treading toward the beach and ships was depicted as sorrowful and religious, while in Lemay's rendering, it had the allure of a military parade where the Acadians sang patriotic songs under the watchful eye of the dishonourable soldiers. These men leaving Acadie were beaten, yet they marched on as valiant soldiers with their head high and will strong. One should recall that in Longfellow's work, it was only when Évangéline arrived in Louisiana that such a procession was transformed into a military parade.

| | |
|---|---|
| *Followed the long-imprisoned, but patient Acadian farmers.* | *Mais voici qu'aussitôt, le front haut l'âme forte,* |
| *Even as pilgrims, who journey afar from their homes and their country,* | *Les pauvres Acadiens défilent deux à deux.* |
| *Sing as they go, and in singing forget they are weary and way-worn,* | *Mille ignobles soldats se tiennent auprès d'eux.* |
| Longfellow | *Comme des pèlerins, bien loin sur quelque rive* |
| | *Vont ensemble chantant une chanson naïve,* |
| | *Un air de la Patrie, un antique refrain,* |
| | *Pour calmer la fatigue et l'ennui du chemin.* |
| | Lemay |

Occasionally, Lemay's work appeared like an extended accentuation of a description already present in Longfellow's poem. Such was the case for scenes where the evicted boarded the ships and the families were separated. The four verses where Longfellow recounted this episode became a pale description of the barbarity of the events that unfolded. The "charming poem" took on an apocalyptic tone.

*There disorder prevailed, and the tumult and stir of embarking.*

*Busily plied the freighted boats; and in confusion*

*Wives were torn from their husbands, and mothers, too late, saw their children*

*Left on the land, extending their arms, with wildest entreaties.*

Longfellow

*C'est alors que l'on vit au bord des sombres flots,*

*Un spectacle navrant. Les grossiers matelots,*

*En entendant les cris des malheureuses femmes,*

*Plus gaîment replongeaient dans les ondes leurs rames :*

*Par d'horribles jurons les soldats insolents*

*Des prisonniers craintifs hâtaient les pas trop lents.*

*L'époux désespéré parcourait la pelouse,*

*Cherchant, de toutes parts, sa malheureuse épouse.*

*Les mères appelaient leurs enfants égarés,*

*Et les petits enfants allaient, tout effarés,*

*Pareils à des agneaux cherchant leurs tendres mères!*

*Femme, cesse tes pleurs et tes plaintes amères :*

*Car tes pleurs seront vains et tes cris superflus!*

*Ton enfant bien-aimé tu ne le verras plus!*

*Et toi, petit enfant, tu commences la vie*

*Et déjà pour jamais ta mère t'est ravie!*

*On sépare en effet les femmes des maris;*

*Les frères de leurs soeurs, les pères de leurs fils.*

*Sur le sein de sa mère en vain l'enfant s'attache,*

*Aux baisers maternels un matelot l'arrache*

*Et l'emporte, en riant, jusqu'au fond du vaisseau.*

Lemay

That same evening, in Longfellow's depiction, those prisoners who had remained on the beach could hear, while their village burned, sounds of wild horses and buffalos of the American west foreshadowing their crossing into the American border. Lemay translated this passage without specifying the location of the prairie and took care to invert the order of the description. Longfellow had begun with a mention of the villagers of Grand-Pré, "We shall behold no more our homes in the village of Grand-Pré!" which immediately called to mind their travels to the western frontier. Lemay transformed this reference into a vague image and made it a simple prelude to the complaint of the lost Acadian country. The final image of the Acadians in Grand-Pré was no longer the American frontier, but rather the refusal of an imposed exile.

And there is more. Lemay, by adding simple adjectives to the passage, made the English soldiers "cruel," "ferocious," "sinister," "without shame," and "joyous" in the barbarism. The English were more present; they were the true tyrants, which diminished the poem's critique of democracy. Évangéline was no longer a victim of the tyranny of the old European oligarchies; she and her people were subjected to the oppression of the English. Her exile was no longer unnamed. The figure of the west became evanescent, as Lemay did not have the same fascination as Longfellow for the American frontier. Évangéline, now the "exiled Acadian" or the "virgin of Acadie," wandered for years on end throughout America. When she reminded the Shawnee woman of the pain of the separation that appeared in the Longfellow original as the loss of her lover, in the French version, she specified it was because, "for months—Very far from her homeland was she exiled" ("depuis des mois—Bien loin de sa patrie elle était exilée").

In the Canadian narrative, Évangéline never integrated into American society. While the egalitarianism of the Quakers was "Something that spoke to her heart, and made her no longer a stranger," in Lemay's poem, this phrase disappeared leaving in its stead a reference to the memory of her homeland. "It was in this city that the virgin found / Most memories of her homeland" ("C'est dans cette cité que la vierge trouvait / Le plus de souvenirs de sa terre natale"). When Longfellow showed Évangéline and her escort in awe of the American success story that was Basil Lajeunesse, "Much they marvelled to see the wealth of the ci-devant blacksmith / All his domains and his herds, and his patriarchal demeanor," Lemay attenuated the achievement and thought it useful to remind readers that it had been achieved "abroad": "They, however, admired the tranquil existence / That lead abroad their old friend Basil," ("Ils admirent pourtant l'existence tranquille / Que passe à l'étranger leur vieil ami Basil"). The "Spanish sombrero," sign of his acculturation to America, was not mentioned in the description of the initial meeting with Basil the "herdsman." And when Basil welcomed them into this home, which might be better than their old one, Lemay omitted the last part of the sentence to recall that the old Basil had not forgotten his homeland of Acadie.

| *Welcome once more to a home, that is better perchance than the old one!*  Longfellow | *Je vous le dis encore : soyez les bienvenus! L'âme du forgeron ne s'est pas refroidie! Il se souvient toujours de sa belle Acadie Et de l'humble maison qu'il avait à Grand-Pré!*  Lemay |
|---|---|

As Lemay noted in a letter to the reader printed in the second edition of his translation: "very few of the exiled Acadians were able to praise the generous hospitality, riches, and liberty of the great English colony like Basil Lajeunesse, one of the protagonists of the poem. On the contrary, the majority were pushed away with malice, ridiculed, and mistreated. In Pennsylvania, they tried to force these poor deportees into slavery. Such is not the way the exiled are welcomed into the great republic today." It was probably for this reason that, in the subsequent edition (1912), Lemay did not revisit the death of Évangéline. He did, however, specify that it is on "foreign beaches" ("d'étrangères plages") that the betrothed sleep side by side.

The religiousness of the poem also changes tones. Évangéline the "saint," the "virgin," much like the "noble shepherd," the "saint priest" who accompanied her, maintained in their American voyages the Catholic practices that Longfellow had concealed. Évangéline the American was Catholic, but of a quasi-Protestant Catholicism, purified of its religious knick-knacks. Lemay put Évangéline's Catholicism back on track. And so, before beginning the meal which reunited the characters on the property of Basil Lajeunesse, Lemay added these lines: "The good father Felix, standing near the table / Recited aloud the Benediction / And all responded 'amen' with humility" ("Le bon père Félix, debout près de la table / Récite à haute voix le Benedicite / Et chacun dit: 'amen' avec humilité"). Similarly, when Basil left the Jesuit mission in the deep American west, Lemay took care to remind readers that these old Canadians had not lost their Catholic piety.

| | |
|---|---|
| *Mounting his Mexican steed,*<br>*with his [Indigenous] guides and*<br>*companions*<br>*Homeward Basil returned, and*<br>*Évangéline stayed at the Mission.*<br>                  Longfellow | *Le lendemain matin, revêtu de son aube,*<br>*Le prêtre dit la messe à la clarté de l'aube;*<br>*Et quand fut consommé l'holocauste*<br>*divin,*<br>*Basil fit seller son coursier mexicain*<br>                  Lemay |

Lastly, where the Deportation announced in the American narrative the passage to the Promised Land, it hearkened in the French-Canadian narrative the wrath of God. When the English commander finished reading "his Majesty's mandate," Longfellow wrote in six lines that the notice fell on the Acadians like a sudden storm. Lemay used twenty-three lines to translate the scene and the analogy with nature was made to resemble the divine response that followed the crucifixion of Christ.

| | |
|---|---|
| *As, when the air is serene in sultry solstice of summer,* | *En été quelquefois quand le soleil de juin,* |
| *Suddenly gathers a storm, and at the deadly sling of the hailstones* | *Par l'ardeur de ses feux dessèche les prairies;* |
| | *Que les fleurs des jardins, que les feuilles flétries* |
| | *Tombent, une par une, au pied de l'arbrisseau;* |
| *Beats down the farmer's corn in the field and shatters his windows,* | *Qu'on n'entend plus couler le limpide ruisseau;* |
| | *À l'horizon de flamme un point sombre, un nuage,* |
| *Hiding the sun, and strewing the ground with thatch from the house-roofs,* | *Portant dans son flanc noir le tonnerre et l'orage,* |
| | *S'élève tout à coup, grandit, grandit, toujours.* |
| | *Le soleil effrayé semble hâter son cours.* |
| *Bellowing fly the herds, and seek to break their enclosures;* | *Il règne dans les airs un lugubre silence;* |
| | *Le ciel est noir; l'oiseau vers ses petits s'élance;* |
| *So on the hearts of the people descended the words of the speaker.* | *Et la cigale chante et l'air est étouffant;* |
| | *Le tonnerre mugit, le nuage se fend;* |
| Longfellow | *Le ciel vomit la flamme; et la pluie est grêle* |
| | *Sous leurs fouets crépitants brisent l'arbuste frêle,* |
| | *Et le carreau de vitre, et les fleurs et les blés.* |
| | *Dans un coin du clos un moment rassemblés,* |
| | *Les bestiaux craintifs laissent là leur pâture.* |
| | *Puis bientôt en beuglant ils longent la clôture* |
| | *Pour trouver un passage et s'enfuir promptement.* |
| | *Des pauvres villageois tel fut l'étonnement* |
| | *À cette heure fatale où le cruel ministre* |
| | *Eut sans honte élevé sa parole sinistre.* |
| | Lemay |

## Gabriel Goes Off to War for the Homeland

The task of reinstating the romance of *Evangeline* into the French Canadian narrative was, however, taken up by Napoléon Bourassa (1827–1916) and his novel titled *Jacques et Marie: Souvenir d'un peuple dispersé*, which was printed a few months prior to the publication of Pamphile Lemay's *Évangéline*. *Jacques et Marie* appeared as a series in *Revue canadienne* in 1865, then in book format the following year. Literary critics never received it as a great novel, but it was quite popular and was likely more widely read in both Quebec and Acadie than the fancy poetry by Lemay.

Napoléon Bourassa was firstly a painter and religious architect who travelled and studied in Europe with masters of the German Nazarene movement. Profoundly religious, he was also active in the French Canadian national awakening notably by leading the *Revue canadienne* from 1860 onward. His personal journey was reminiscent of the national narrative of Quebec that had turned into a discourse on French Canada. He married Azélie Papineau, daughter of Louis-Joseph Papineau, who was the leader of the Parti canadien, known as the Patriotes, and who was behind a push for a secular republican nationalism in Lower Canada. Bourassa and his family even lived in the Papineau family manor in Montebello. One of his sons, Henri Bourassa—founder of the newspaper *Le Devoir*—would come to define the cultural (religious) and political parameters of French Canada.

*Jacques et Marie* was the only novel written by Napoléon Bourassa. It was an overtly engaged historical novel, which aimed to give French Canadians a national tradition. The work was based on historical facts that were known at the time regarding the expulsion of Acadians, notably through the writings of Haliburton and Garneau. In the prologue, Bourassa did not mention Longfellow's poem, though he owned a copy. Rather, he stated that he wanted to pay tribute to the inhabitants of Petite-Cadie, a geographical name ascribed by Acadians who, after 1760, had settled along the Montreal Petite Rivière in the Richelieu Valley (known today as the Acadie River). There, they established the parish of Sainte-Marguerite-de-Blairfindie, which became the municipality of Lacadie in 1926, and is known today as L'Acadie. This was the birthplace of Napoléon Bourassa. Drawing a parallel with the practices of exiled Acadians, Bourassa wrote in the prologue to *Jacques et Marie* that Trojans "assigned meaningful names to unidentified areas where they had come in search of a new homeland." His novel paid homage to the grandchildren of those banned Acadians who inherited the memories and virtues of their forefathers. Bourassa hoped their "faith and virtues" would set an example for readers in the "difficult circumstances" still ahead for the French Canadian nationality. The Richelieu Valley had been a place of momentous confrontations between the Patriots and the British authorities in 1837 and 1838. Bourassa compared the burning houses of the Richelieu Valley during these battles to those of Grand-Pré in 1755, and saw a correlation between the resistance of the Patriots and those of his protagonist.

Though Bourassa did not make it explicit, most critics were right in interpreting *Jacques et Marie* as the French Canadian (or Quebecois) version of *Evangeline*. The crime against humanity outlined in the American tale became a "national crime." The story is that of a pair of young lovers, Jacques Hébert and Marie Landry, inhabitants of Grand-Pré at the time of the events that led up to the Deportation of 1755. Their trajectory, however, followed that of the French Canadian narrative, not of the American idyll.

Jacques and his family left Grand-Pré for the region of Beaubassin on the Chignecto Isthmus in 1749, when tensions had begun to rise between Acadians and the British authorities. The clashes at the border of Acadie (Nova Scotia) and the new French Acadie prevented Jacques from returning to Grand-Pré. His family participated in the burning of the Beaubassin village under the leadership of Father Le Loutre in 1750. Jacques then crossed over to the French side of the border, joined the French army, and was there for the surrendering of Fort Beauséjour in the spring of 1755. The Acadian border had disappeared. He secretly returned to Grand-Pré in September 1755 to warn the villagers of an imminent threat of imprisonment and bring Marie back into French territories. He found her attracted to an English soldier, who proposed to marry her in exchange for the protection of her family and…that of notary LeBlanc, her uncle.

Taken prisoner, Jacques could no longer reach Marie. By the time he managed to free himself, he saw that the villagers had been taken aboard the ships. He fled west to the French territory, as he was now prey in a ferocious war. He joined the expeditionary force of Boishébert, which brought together the French military and exiled Acadians. They later retreated toward Canada, participated in the Battle of Quebec (1759), and those of Levy and Montreal (1760). The hostilities ended, and Jacques learned from the lips of Marie's British suitor—who asked to convert to Catholicism as he lay dying on the Plains of Abraham—that Marie had not betrayed her people and he had been unable to prevent her deportation to Boston. Jacques set out to find her in the Canadian establishments where Acadian refugees had settled. He found her in the Petite-Cadie of the Richelieu Valley, where deportees to Massachusetts had found a home while searching for friendly faces that did not bear "the mark of a national crime." They had managed to cross the Appalachians, and reaching Lake Champlain, had been welcomed into a Jesuit mission on Canadian soil, their new homeland. They got married and had many children.

The American travels in Bourassa's novel were but a digression. Marie was deported there but was just as quickly rejected into "Canadian" territory, her true homeland. Through the love triangle—Jacques, Marie, and the British soldier—the story of faithful love became a dilemma of homeland and family. Would Marie, niece of notary LeBlanc, friend to the British, succumb to the soldier's proposal to save her family, or would she remain loyal to Jacques, who represented French patriotism? In the end, the homeland came out victorious. But the Acadian homeland was not at the heart of the debate; it was the old "French" motherland. Acadians were a reminder of the love for Catholic France at the heart of the French Canadian genesis. And in any case, Acadie had disappeared. "Acadie was deserted and ready to receive another race; it had lost its name from the moment it lost its first inhabitants,"[15] wrote Bourassa to close out the episode of the French defeat in Acadie. And in the prologue, he reminded readers that he had collected "like debris from a still-life" drawn from legends of his village, the story of Acadians—that is, "the ephemeral existence of a people whom Providence had seemed to destine to a longer and happier national life."[16] "Besides, Providence let Acadians disappear, we [French Canadians] were preserved despite having lived through similar circumstances."[17]

---

15. "L'Acadie était déserte et prête à recevoir une autre race; de ce moment elle avait perdu son nom en perdant ses premiers habitants."

16. "l'existence éphémère d'un peuple que la Providence semblait destiner à une vie nationale plus longue et plus heureuse"

17. "D'ailleurs, la Providence qui a laissé les Acadiens disparaître, nous [les Canadiens français] a conservés au milieu de circonstances analogues."

## The Quarrel of the Historians

Father Henri-Raymond Casgrain (1831–1904), in *Un pèlerinage au pays d'Évangéline* (1887), brought the Canadian genesis of the *Evangeline* poem by reinstating it within a typical historiographical debate on core differences between the two Canadian nations. As previously noted, throughout the end of the nineteenth century, Casgrain was the leader of the Quebec Literary School (*École littéraire de Québec*), a movement meant to give "Canadians" a national literature and to which Pamphile Lemay participated. Father Casgrain was a historian particularly interested in putting together profiles of important French Canadian Catholic figures. His enthusiasm for *Evangeline* and Acadie came late in his career, following a disagreement with a historian of New England named Francis Parkman with whom he shared sympathy for the historical importance of Catholicism in America.

But the dispute with Parkman was preceded by another historiographical debate this time regarding the chronicles of America, and the emerging historiography of Nova Scotia. The immense popularity of the poem and its description of a historic crime, which was said to have been perpetrated by the British authorities, shook the burgeoning historiography of Nova Scotia. In 1847, the year *Evangeline* was published, Nova Scotia was preparing to celebrate the centennial of the city of Halifax, founded in 1749, and considered to be the true birthdate of the colony. However, the accusations put forth by Longfellow, Bancroft, and other zealous writers of the American national narrative, associated this act of creation with an immoral one—the deportation of its Franco-Catholic inhabitants—thus rendering the foundation illegitimate. The problem was emphasized by the fact that the accusations emanated from the most illustrious of their citizens, Thomas Chandler Haliburton, author of the first historical annals of the colony. Not only did Haliburton look down on the "crime," but he also wondered whether the perpetrators had had a guilty conscience afterwards. Had they deliberately hidden the evidence?

Accounting for the American interest in the history of Nova Scotia, Thomas B. Akins, a lawyer with a passion for history, had a law passed at the colony's legislative assembly in 1857 that allowed for the creation of a governmental section for archives. These became the first public archives in British North America, and Akins was appointed their first commissioner. By 1869, he had gathered in the Archives of Nova Scotia a voluminous compilation of 755 pages bringing together everything he had found on the relations between the old Acadians and the colonial authorities after 1713. Akins did not have a belligerent temperament and presented his work as one of pure archival research.

At the same time, in 1866–67, his cousin and mentor Beamish Murdoch, using this material, published his *History of Nova Scotia*. Murdoch, in writing the history of his province, explicitly attempted to relieve his ancestors of the responsibility of those terrible crimes, which had been attributed by Raynal, Bancroft, and Longfellow. The Acadians had never been those idyllic peasants described by those authors, and they had not respected the treatises requiring them to swear allegiance to the British Crown or leave the territory. They had remained faithful to France, notably by participating in the defence of Fort Beauséjour in the sprint of 1755, and they had remained allied with Indigenous peoples who were known enemies of the English. The permission given to Catholic priests to officiate on British territory had been co-opted by the priests to incite Acadians and Indigenous peoples to sedition or to encourage them to settle in French territories. The Expulsion, or Deportation, had been a "cruel but necessary" act.

The documents used as reference for such affirmations had never been hidden and Haliburton's allusion to their absence was more proof of his incompetence as a historian than of the shame of the authorities of those times. Even Haliburton's son gave a statement regarding the new archival proof that his father, then a well-known author in London, had changed his opinion as to the necessity of such a military operation. Finally, Murdoch reminded Bancroft and Longfellow that the operation was more "American" (New England) than British, writing "We Nova Scotians knew all these things."

The effort of elite Nova Scotians to restore their honour was well received. As soon as 1870, the president of the Literary and Historical

Society of Quebec, W. J. Anderson, in a conference titled: *Evangeline and the Archives of Nova Scotia; on the Poetry and Prose of History*, presented the research of Akins as an eloquent demonstration of the superiority of the work of historians over those of poets with regards to historical truth. In 1881, the major work of synthesis *Narrative and Critical History of America* asserted that Akins's selection of texts was the most significant contribution to historical knowledge on the expulsion of Acadians. In the field of Canadian (English) archives, Akins is still considered a pioneer. But at the time, the most important validation of his compilation no doubt came from the great American historian Francis Parkman.

Francis Parkman (1823–93) was, like Longfellow, of the New England Brahmin caste: he was a historian and briefly a professor of horticulture at Harvard University. He also adhered, like Longfellow to what Jenny Franchot has called "the great American romance of American Catholicism."[18] He was the great specialist of the Catholic past of the North American continent, having taken a keen interest in the evangelization efforts of the Jesuits and the confrontations between British and French powers that he saw as a clash between political and religious systems. In his opinion, the war between Protestantism and Catholicism was not confined to the Teutonic forest; the formation of America was also the stage on which it played out.

Parkman described the work of Jesuits with great empathy, so much so that the very Catholic Casgrain was initially astonished by his accounts. Parkman was fascinated by the success of the French in the religious conversion of Indigenous peoples and the political coalitions that ensued, which explained the strength and longevity of the French Empire. But such alliances, he concluded, were more attributable to ad-joining of the persistent idolatry of Catholicism and natural barbarism of the native populations. According to Parkman, the cruelty of the French, which so frightened New Englanders and explained their fanatic desire to finish them off, was the result of the meeting of these cultures. This alliance could not prevail upon the superior British political system and Protestant rationalism, which generated American democracy. Parkman

---

18.   "la romance américaine du catholicisme américain."

argued these flaws lead to the collapse of the French and Indigenous alliance.

Parkman was from a generation younger than that of Bancroft and Longfellow, and was not as influenced by the Romantic period as they were. He considered his American narrative more "objective," descriptive even, in the scope of work of historians. He wanted to put this perspective forward in his monograph *Montcalm and Wolfe* (1884), wishing to distance himself from overly romanticized visions of history. "The conflict in Acadia has a melancholy interest, since it ended in a catastrophe which prose and verse have joined to commemorate, but of which the causes have not been understood," he noted in the introduction to a section dedicated to Acadie. And he concluded the chapter on the Expulsion by recalling that the American tale of *Evangeline* was ultimately unfair to the British past of America: "New England humanitarianism, melting into sentimentality at a tale of woe, has been unjust to its own." Parkman, a historian of facts, was conscious that he could not scrub the implication of American settlers in the Expulsion of Acadians.

In his account of the events that led to the Expulsion, the renowned historian drew on the documentation presented by Akins and the diary of Winslow. He therefore supported the radicalized version of Nova Scotian historians. France, Quebec, and Catholic priests were, in his opinion, the main culprits in the misfortune of Acadians. They had prevented them from becoming loyal British subjects. They incited Indigenous peoples to attack those Acadians who collaborated with the British. In addition, the clergy rendered fanatical by Catholicism and the alliance with the Indigenous peoples transformed Acadians into veritable rebels of colonial power. Parkman claimed that while the colonial authorities had no choice but to approve these actions, they took care to tend to the consequences of such a decision as humanely as possible.

Henri-Raymond Casgrain was shocked to learn of the prestigious American historian's endorsement of the conclusions drawn by "local" anglophone historians, and this incited him to launch a full-fledged crusade against Parkman. Fellow historian Casgrain became a rival of Parkman, with a project that made him into a figure against the American narrative. His goal was to recall the glorious past of Catholicism in America through biographical portraits of the great Canadian Catholic figures. This past was still alive, as Casgrain was one of the instigators of the providential mission of French Canadians, a mission devoted to reproducing on American soil the great Catholic and French civilization, a sort of continuity of the Crusades. In this effort, Parkman saw a continuation of the religious wars stemming from the Protestant Reformation. The defeat of the French in America may have been providential by planting in the heart of Protestantism the seeds of Catholicism. Casgrain dreamed of the day when Spanish Catholics from the south and French Catholics from the north would meet on the banks of the Mississippi and put an end to the mercantile civilization of Anglo-American Protestantism.

Because of their mutual interest for the history of Catholicism, Parkman and Casgrain had long been correspondents. Casgrain, who taught at Université Laval in Quebec City, regularly sent the American historian documents on the history of Catholicism at the time of New France (Nouvelle-France). He thought he had found in Parkman's first writings an objective ally, a historian capable of describing the grandeur of the civilizing mission of Catholicism in America. He even published a book on Parkman (1872), and while putting it together, he and Parkman met Longfellow, whom Casgrain deemed "the American [Alphonse de] Lamartine."

Casgrain progressively became disheartened; over time, he lost faith in the Boston historian whose steely gaze prevented him from understanding the originality of this civilization. The first squabbles over Acadie began in 1877, when Parkman published in *The Nation* an unfavourable review of the book by Frenchman François-Edme Rameau de Saint-Père titled *Une colonie féodale en Amérique: l'Acadie*. Parkman contested the pro-French bias of the work and affirmed the necessity for British authorities to evict the French. He would later reuse and document these arguments in his book *Montcalm and Wolfe* (1884), as previously stated.

Alerted by Rameau himself, Father Casgrain, of poor health, nevertheless prepared a vigorous response to Parkman. He went on a "pilgrimage" in the old French Acadie and all the way into Louisiana to track down the former excluded, attempting to document testimonies more than 120 years after the events. He visited places of remembrance of the old French Acadie to collect his thoughts and appropriately measure the scope of the tragedy. He spent time in London and Paris where, with Rameau de Saint-Père, he scoured the archives to find proof that the colonial authorities had manipulated Acadians by preventing them to leave the territory after the Treaty of Utrecht (1713), then promising them the right to neutrality, and finally, when their presence was no longer useful, in an act of horrible barbarism, deporting them.

In 1887, Casgrin published his research outcomes in a book with a revealing title: *Un pèlerinage au pays d'Évangéline* ("a pilgrimage to the Land of Évangéline"), and for which he won a prize from the prestigious Académie française the following year. It was a strange book, somewhere at the crossroads of a travel log, commemoration, chronicle, and political tract. The figure of Évangéline was everywhere, sometimes appearing to confirm the memory of those lovers separated because of the tragedy, and at other times to validate the existence of a real little girl named Évangéline. He met some of "notary LeBlanc's" grandchildren; he recognized in the son of ex-Governor Mouton of Louisiana the proud blacksmith named Basil who Longfellow had transformed into a proud herdsman resembling Mexicans at the border with Texas; he vouched for the disappearance of Acadians in the old territory of Grand-Pré. Parkman had based his argument that Acadians had not been welcome in Quebec on a note from Bougainville, exclaiming: "What a country! What morals!" To this, Casgrain responded that, on the contrary, Acadians had been rejected from the United States, that not a community had survived, that in Philadelphia, the city where Évangéline supposedly lived in the equality of the Quakers, "nostalgia killed them as much as misery did; like the famous exile, they died with their eyes turned toward their homeland."[19] Borrowing the words of Parkman, this time to speak of the United States, Casgrain wrote: "*Quel pays! Quelles mœurs!*"

Though Casgrain refuted Parkman's arguments on the clergy's role

---

19. "la nostalgie les tuait autant que la misère; comme l'exilé antique, ils expiraient en tournant les yeux vers leur patrie"

in the expulsion of the Acadians, his main retort was that Parkman had relied on truncated documents. Casgrain insisted that Akins and the Nova Scotia historians had voluntarily eliminated documents that supported the incriminating claims of Acadians. He reiterated this accusation of historical falsification during a conference at The Royal Society of Canada in 1888, which promptly set off a passionate public outcry in Nova Scotian newspapers. For Casgrain, the responsibility of the expulsion fell on the local authorities, Governor Lawrence supported by the Protestant fanaticism of New England. The British authorities were barely involved, the Board of Trade had even, until the end, tried to moderate the anger of opponents of Franco-Catholics on this side of America.

By drawing such conclusions, Casgrain kept the Acadian question within the war of Canadian nationalities. The enemy that should be feared was less the British English or Anglo-American than the Canadian English. Since 1867, Nova Scotia was effectively a Canadian province. And the quarrel of the historians made waves throughout English Canada. While novelists, and female novelists in particular, embraced the bucolic romance of Evangeline—dozens of English Canadian novels on the theme of Évangéline and Grand-Pré were published at the turn of the century—political centres were wary of the deformed image the tale projected onto the history of the British Empire. At the beginning of the twentieth century, Evangeline was banned from schools in British Columbia. And in 1924 the president of the Board of Governors of the University of Toronto, H. J. Cody, launched a campaign to ban the poem from all Canadian schools.

Unlike Garneau, Bourassa, and Lemay, Casgrain was well aware of the surviving Acadian communities in the Maritimes. Acadians were not, however, the population at the core of his quest about the history of Acadie. The Deportation was a battle on the memory front that engaged the memory of New France and its rapports with the Anglo-Protestant universe, the Acadian tragedy was a weapon that could be wielded in the fight against the Anglo Canadian nationality. In his travels throughout Acadie, he became more interested in French Acadie, now sparsely populated by Acadians, than in the new Acadie, which was located just north of the old one, precisely near where the French had wanted it to develop after 1713.

His work nevertheless had an impact in Acadie. He was the first French Canadian historian to produce new knowledge on Acadie. He expanded the historical understanding of Acadie beyond the Deportation. The major conventions of the end of the nineteenth century praised the salutary nature of his work. And the Acadian senator Pascal Poirier could still say in 1907 that Akins the archivist, in trying to hide the historical truth, was crueller than Governor Lawrence who had signed the order of expulsion. Was "negationism" more cruel than the "historical fact" for those who came from this tradition?

# References

BLODGETT, Edward Dickinson. "Translated Literature and the Literary Polystem: The example of Lemay's Évangéline." *META*, vol. XXXIV, No. 2, 1989.

BOURASSA, Napoléon. *Jacques et Marie. Souvenir d'un peuple dispersé*, Montreal, QC: Fides, 1976 [original edition, Montreal: Sénécal, 1866].

CASGRAIN, Henri-Raymond. *Un pèlerinage au pays d'Évangéline*. Quebec City, QC: Imprimerie de L.-J. Demers & frère, 1888.

CUTHBERTSON, Brian C. "Thomas Beamish Akins: British North America's pioneer archivist", *Acadiensis*, Fredericton, vol. 7 (1977–1978), no 1, p. 86–102.

DUMONT, Fernand. *Genèse de la société québécoise*, Montréal, Boréal, 1993.

GARNEAU, François-Xavier. *Histoire du Canada*, 4 volumes, Québec, Imprimerie N. Aubin, 1845, 1846, 1848, 1852.

GOUPIL, Mylène. *La construction du récit du "Grand dérangement" de 1757 à 1890*, Masters thesis, Département de Lettres françaises, Université de Sherbrooke, Sherbrooke, 1999.

HALIBURTON, Thomas Chandler. *An Historical and Statistical Account of Nova Scotia*, Halifax, Nova Scotia, Published for J. Howe, 1829.

IRMSCHER, C. "Chapter 4, 'It Whirls Me Away': Longfellow and Translation." *Longfellow Redux*. University of Illinois Press, 2006, p. 218-273.

LE MOINE, R. *Napoléon Bourassa: L'homme et l'artiste*. Ottawa, ON: Éditions de l'Université d'Ottawa, 1974 [Chapter 5, "Jacques et Marie," pp. 100–135].

LEMAY, Léon-Pamphile. *Essais poétiques*, Québec, Desbarats éditeurs, 1865.

MORENCY, Jean. "Postface", *Évangéline*, translated by Pamphile Lemay, (bilingual edition), Montreal, Boréal, 2005, p. 229-247.

NOVA SCOTIA ARCHIVES. *Acadian Heartland: Records of the Deportation and Le Grand Dérangement, 1714–1768*. Nova Scotia Historical Society, 2020, online: https://archives.novascotia.ca/deportation/.

PARKMAN, Francis. *Montcalm and Wolfe*. Boston, MA: Little, Brown, 1884.

Taylor, Brook. "5, The Maritimes opt out." *Promoters, Patriots and Partisans: Historiography in Nineteenth-Century English Canada*. Toronto, ON: University of Toronto Press, 1989, pp. 181–230.

THÉRIAULT, Joseph Yvon. *Critique de l'américanité, Mémoire et démocratie au Québec*. Montreal, QC: Québec Amérique, 2002.

VIAU, Robert. *Les visages d'Évangéline: Du poème au mythe*. Montreal, QC: MNH, 1998.

# THE ACADIANS
# RECEIVE *ÉVANGÉLINE*

*And on the deserted edges of the resounding Atlantic*
*We see, from place to place, a rustic peasant.*
*It is a poor Acadian whose plaintive ancestor*
*Did not want, for sepulchre nor shroud,*
*The land of exile so heavy and so fatal,*
*And who returned to die on his native shore.*

—Henry Wadsworth Longfellow, *Evangeline*

## Rameau Sets Foot in Acadie

In September 1860, a Frenchman, François-Edme Rameau de Saint-Père (1820–89), set foot in the Public Archives of Nova Scotia. He gained access through his "friend," the historian Beamish Murdoch. The chief archivist, Thomas B. Akins, was absent that day. The clerks received Rameau coldly, setting onto a table in the middle of the room a series of documents that he would only be able to consult under the watchful eye of all present, and without the authorization to take notes. This manner of proceeding reminded him of a note by Haliburton in *An Historical and Statistical Account of Nova Scotia* (1829) describing the difficulty of obtaining information on the deportation of Acadians. Could this have been attributable to the shame of communicating certain documents? "Such were the conditions under which I was able to consult the Archives during the eight to ten days that I spent in Halifax," wrote Rameau to Father Henry-Raymond Casgrain. Casgrain added this letter to the file of accusations against Nova Scotian historians regarding their attempts at historical negationism, as put forth in *Pèlerinage au pays d'Évangéline*.

Rameau de Saint-Père did not make a case of this incident. Nearly twenty years later, while the quarrel of the historians was raging, he stated that the story of Murdoch and the publication of the *Archives* by Akins largely made accessible the documentation that was available and necessary to the understanding of the events that led to the expulsion of Acadians. For him, this quarrel was a secondary consideration, for his project was not the restitution of Acadian nationalism. In 1859, the year preceding his first travels to America, he had published a book titled *La France aux colonies, Études sur le développement de la race française hors de l'Europe. Les Français en Amérique, Acadiens et Canadiens* (which translates as "France in the colonies, Studies on the development of the French race outside Europe. Frenchmen in America, Acadians, and Canadians"). The idea behind this monograph stemmed from his interest in the French colonial ventures, which France was vested in throughout the mid-eighteenth century. Rameau believed that the nature of great nations was spread their civilizing mission throughout the globe.

Rameau even tried out the colonial experience for himself in Algeria by acquiring a few small landholdings, which he considered to be the justified foundation of all colonies. His experience was a failure, much like the Algerian colonial project had been. It was there, however, that in 1854, he met missionaries who spoke of the forgotten daughter of France, the French Canadian society that resulted from the seventeenth-century French colonial venture in America. Rameau decided to assess the overall experience of French colonial history. He started with Acadie and Canada, and in the end, his project was limited to these two cases. He mostly studied Acadie and devoted most of his time to this case, as he thought he found in Acadie a pure model of the colonial experience.

His reading of the history of Acadians and Canadians was not only informed by his interest in colonialism. Rameau's interpretations were a curious blend of intellectual traditions that were reflected in his portrayal of these societies. He was the son of a small-town aristocrat who left him a small inheritance that he used to finance his Algerian adventure and his passion for North American French descendants. He tried his hand at a variety of professions working as an amateur journalist, archivist, etc., and upon his arrival in Paris—where he studied the law without ever practising it—he spent time with Proudhonnian[20] self-governing socialists (the first anarchists). He was active in politics among revolutionary democrats, at the time of the July Monarchy, the proclamation of the Second Republic (1848), and Louis-Napoléon Bonaparte's coup d'état (1851). He was incarcerated for a few months during this last event, but afterwards maintained relations with aristocrats of the Second Empire whose influence he used to support his "Acadian work."

His Proudhonism was always strongly tainted with Catholicism, associating him with a sort of Christian democracy. He criticized the aristocratic Republic in the name of old Christian values and associationist egalitarianism. As he aged, he became more conservative, but he never recovered from his aversion for modern state structures and aristocratic materialism. He later adhered to the ideas of sociologist Frédéric Le Play (1806–82), who practised an empirical form of sociology and believed societies were born from the extension of family structures. For both Le Play and Rameau, the idea was to study different types of families so as to understand the implementation of modern societies (or nationalities).

To understand how Rameau, the first historian and sociologist of Acadie, conceptualized society, we can look to the ideologies that inspired him. He adhered to anti-statist associationism (Proudhon), saw in the evolution of model families (Le Play) the source of progress, and considered Christian egalitarianism to be the key to social revolution. These ideas, Rameau believed, were what pre-revolutionary France could have shared with the world. He eventually found a society reflective of this ideology in Acadie, and published a second monograph in two parts (1877 and 1889) titled *Une colonie féodale en Amérique: L'Acadie.*

As for his book *La France aux colonies*, published in 1859, Rameau wrote it without ever having set foot in Acadie or Canada. His journey in 1860, which included the problematic visit to the Halifax Archives, was his first encounter with the American continent. Prior to this, he had explored the colonial archives in Paris, and applying Le Play's notion of

---

20.  Translator's note: in relation to the ideology and political philosophy of the French journalist Pierre-Joseph Proudhon (1809–65).

model families, he had studied the demographic evolution of families by researching surveys and parish registers. During the period that followed the French regime, he established correspondences with whomever was literate in French Canada: Parent, Papineau, Garneau, Ferland, Chauveau, Morin, Viger, Cherrier, Casgrain. So much so that Quebec sociologist Fernand Dumont said that *La France aux colonies* remains to this day the best summary of the state of mind that governed the birth of the French-Canadian nation. Rameau's significance in the genesis of the Acadian national narrative is even more essential, for he was the first to publish the affirmation that the Acadian nation had survived the Expulsion of 1755. His works were also the first endogenous studies of Acadian culture.

Though Rameau admitted to not knowing a thing about French Canada prior to 1854, this was even truer for Acadie. He read the poem *Evangeline* from which he gathered, like everyone, that the old French colony named Acadie had faded out of existence following the expulsion of its inhabitants by the British in 1755. His knowledge of the works relating the French Canadian national narrative, such as his correspondence with its authors, taught him that the disappearance of Acadie was "dead" proof of the greed of the English.

Rameau's oeuvre was very much aligned with the *Evangeline* times and the reception of the poem in French Canada. He introduced his chapter on the deportation of the inhabitants that describe the never-ending exile of a nation: "Exiles without an end, and without an example in story." He further affirmed that this was a history that could only be written by counting those who had passed: "Written their story stands on tablets of stone in the Church yards." This last verse was featured on the title page of the second volume of *Une colonie féodale en Amérique*. Rameau stated that with the "fantasy pastoral" of Raynal, the "sparse traditions" of Haliburton, and the "touching poem by the most distinguished of American poets"—Longfellow—this was all that was left of the history of the Acadian people, at least until the publication of his own book. He did not hesitate to use the verses of *Evangeline* as historical data. In *Une colonie féodale en Amérique*, he cited Longfellow directly to attest to the pastoral nature of Acadian life. And, when relating the "procession" of deportees exiting the Grand-Pré church and treading toward the ships, he thought it necessary to relay the American poet's moving description of this "heinous tragedy" ("drame odieux"):

*Ainsi s'avança le triste cortège, et il y eut un grand désordre; dans le tumulte de l'embarquement, des femmes furent séparées de leurs maris, et des mères s'apercevaient trop tard qu'elles avaient laissé sur la grève des enfants qui, dans un amer désespoir, leur tendaient les bras.*

*Évangéline,* translated by Rameau

*Thus to the Gaspereau's mouth moved on that mournful procession.*
*There disorder prevailed, and the tumult and stir of embarking.*
*Busily plied the freighted boats; and in the confusion*
*Wives were torn from their husbands, and mothers, too late, saw their children*
*Left on the land, extending their arms, with wildest entreaties.*

*Evangeline,* original verses by Longfellow

These borrowings were misleading. By structuring his narrative around *Evangeline* and its French-Canadian translation—the Lost Acadie—Rameau significantly modified the storyline. For one thing, the Acadian people survived the Deportation. By carefully studying data from surveys and registers, he estimated that by the mid-1800s, more than eighty thousand descendants of Acadians were living in French Catholic communities on the lands of the old French Acadie. He rapidly communicated with Father Hubert Girroir, the parish priest of Arichat in Nova Scotia, one of the few priests of Acadian origin—there were four at the time. With this preliminary information, he painted a rather accurate portrait of the state of these communities in the middle of the nineteenth century. The work of 1859 largely focused on the post-deportation recovery of the Acadian people. Rameau was stupefied. By what inexplicable manner had this small French colony survived such a horrible fate?

This unexpected revelation—the survival of the Acadian people—explained his ongoing fascination with Acadie. In 1859, he only had an intuitive explanation for their survival: a fidelity to their religion, and love for the old French civilization. But at the time, he already supposed that there must have been something in the history of this old French colony that could explain its endurance. For this reason, when he arrived in Quebec during the summer of 1860, he chose to spend most of his time visiting Acadie, a nation from which he "had much to learn." His intuition took on the form of *Une colonie féodale en Amérique*, which was published at the beginning of the 1880s. For Rameau, Acadie was a pure case of the development mode of European colonies in the New World—a sort of laboratory attesting to the strength of the European style of (French) feudal family.

Though other colonies, including Canada, were established through the settlement of small estates managed by a lord, these colonies usually fell victim to corruption, as had been the case in Europe, due to the appetite of lords for royal commissions and material gains. The Acadian settlement having been so small—only forty-seven families settled for at least one generation (according to the 1671 census) made up the basis of the Acadian people, specified Rameau—and having been isolated under both French and English rule, meant that the feudal family evolved according to its natural gradient and hierarchies until it became its own form of democracy. The lord never took on a role more central than that of a purveyor of communal services as a sort of *pater familias*.

The prodigious demographic development of Acadians, claimed Rameau, would have been achieved thanks to the social power of families brought on by this type of settlement. The sixteen thousand Acadians in 1755, and the seventy-one thousand in 1850, despite the immense losses caused by the deportation, were almost all borne from the original forty-seven families, a mere four hundred inhabitants. The deployment of French Acadie beyond its initial implementation zone—from Port Royal in the Minas Basin to Beaubassin—had these founding families reproducing through a village implementation model that resembled the mild hierarchy of the French feudal commune—Village des Hébert, Village des Forest, Prée des Bourgs, Prée aux Richard.

It was the strength of familial organization that allowed Acadie, despite its small number of inhabitants, despite it being abandoned by colonial powers, to defend itself for more than a century from its neighbours, who were one hundred times as many in numbers and oh-so jealous of its riches. It was also thanks to the strength of this familial organization that a new Acadian society emerged from the debris of the Deportation, belying the verse of the poem whereby "Naught but tradition remains of the beautiful village of Grand-Pré."

To understand Rameau's interpretation of Acadian and Canadian history, it is useful to look back on his intellectual project. In a barely hidden reference to Tocqueville, who had just published *La démocratie en Amérique*, Rameau recalled that societies did not appear fully formed with philosophical speculations like those seen with the Pilgrims of New Plymouth and the democratic foundation of the United States. Following the empirical traces of populations was a means of discovering another path to social progress, a social progress more aligned with tradition and less inclined to the materialist excesses of Anglo-America. Both Acadians and French Canadians had a "providential" mission on the American continent different from the individualistic American democracy: they were carriers of a distinct civilization project.

As bearers of the same providential mission as that of French Canadians, Acadians were nevertheless a different people. This affirmation was Rameau's great intellectual innovation. He wrote that French Acadia formed a colony separate from Canada, which was largely ignored by colonial authorities in Quebec; that its people were more tied to familial land ownership; and that its isolation produced a more "homogeneous" type of French family. On one side, in Acadie, "liberty, to not speak of abandonment, and on the other, [in Canada] governmental leadership."

In 1755, Acadians already formed a society distinct from those of Canadians and the French. Their society was more wholesome than what the feudal family was thought to generate. According to Rameau, the Expulsion broke the traditions of this colonial treasure on American soil. His words could not sufficiently deplore this tragedy. As Rameau was less involved in the controversy raging among North American historians, he did not seek to find "the" culprit, instead choosing to multiply accusations of responsibility against Nova Scotian colonial authorities, Governor Lawrence and his New England accomplices, the perfidious England, and finally, the French administration, who endangered this population without providing the resources required for its protection.

Acadie was not dead. Rameau urged Acadians to rebuild what the Deportation had destroyed: to rebuild their society. Not in the old Acadie, the basin of the French Bay—known today as the Bay of Fundy—but farther north where one could find the scattered debris of the old Acadie. From his vantage point at the Paris Archives, before having even set foot in the country, he had already begun imagining on the coasts of the Gulf of St. Lawrence—from Cape Breton to Miramichi via Prince Edward Island, and from Miramichi to Chaleur Bay—a continuity of settlements that would reconnect with Acadians who had settled in Canada, those of Gaspésie, and those of Madawaska who already shared a border with the French Canadians of Témiscouata. "I will rebuild the Acadian nation or I will die trying,"[21] wrote Rameau in his travel diary from 1860 to 1861.

He thus began sketching out for Acadians a veritable social project consistent with his idea that societies were born of the organizational strength of family ties. First through the colonization of the land, which would ensure the continuity of settlements and would allow Acadians to leave the coasts where they landed after the Expulsion, and where they remained at the mercy of British and Jersey merchants. In Rameau's view, the true strength of extended family resided in land ownership and agriculture. Investing in educational institutions was also a way for a population to ensure its social and moral progress. Creating a veritable Acadian clergy that would be a vector of social progress, for the then-recent history had revealed that the only parishes that had developed were those where French Catholic priests had been involved. And finally, to tie everything into one Acadian society, there was a need to develop national institutions, notably a national newspaper, as the French Canadians had done with the *Societé Saint-Jean-Baptiste*, a national organization.

---

21.  In Rameau's words: "Je relèverai la nation acadienne ou j'y perdrai la vie."

## Before the National Reference

After the publication of Longfellow's *Evangeline* in 1847, the works of Rameau became the first interpretations that could be considered endogenous to Acadie. The previous references were based on an external point of view, exogenous: that of the colonial wars (Burke, Raynal), of the French and Indian Wars (Bancroft), of the history of Nova Scotia (Haliburton, Murdoch), and that of French Canada (Garneau, Casgrain). Rameau, as a sociologist and historian, was the first to take interest in the development of a society among Acadians. He reconstituted the history of French Acadie from within the natural deployment of families to better affirm the longevity of the society following the Deportation.

What made his work an endogenous narrative was the perspective he took of Acadie as an evolving entity and ascending society. The historical narrative he established was reused after 1860 by the first Indigenous narrators of the Acadian narrative. The story written by Rameau was the first scholarly mediation, the first description of the "charming work of art" of the American poet that was historically contextualized from the internal point of view of Acadie. For Rameau, the Acadian narrative was complete as of 1860 and ready to be appropriated by a people still in the process of becoming. The narrative changed very little over time.

Before Longfellow, before Rameau, and since the events that had led to their expulsion from Nova Scotia in the middle of the eighteenth century, Acadians did not have a collective memory of their history and particularly of the central event—the Deportation—that would then become the key to their identity reference. Acadie had literally been destroyed by the Seven Years War, and there remained instead an empty society devoid of any Acadian memory. In Rameau's words, there remained only "scattered debris" of this old French colony. The (re)settlement in the region, following the Treaty of Paris (1763), of a few thousand original Acadians, resembled in a way the "debris" of an explosion. Nothing remained of the French and Catholic core, of Port-Royal and the Minas Basin. These lands had been emptied, restructured, and recolonized as soon as 1760 by another people who spoke another language and practiced another religion.

*Still stands the forest primeval; but under the shade of its branches*
*Dwells another race, with other customs and language.*

*Evangeline,* original verses by Longfellow

Farther away from the epicentre of the tragedy, the debris was even more scattered. A few dozen families had settled in southwestern Nova Scotia on the sandy coasts of St. Marys Bay (Baie Sainte-Marie), and another dozen were established even farther in the old fiefdom of the d'Entremont family, on Pubnico Point. Fewer still could be found to the south, in Chezzetcook, near the new capital of Halifax, and a few more were hundreds of kilometres to the east on the old Île-Royale that would become Cape Breton. Other establishments were farther north, at the old French border in what is now New Brunswick, and were more spread out but more numerous. Dozens of families could be found in the old region of Fort Beauséjour and up where the Saint-Jean River flows into the small Madawaska River. More still to the north and south of Chaleur Bay, more than one thousand kilometres away from the French Bay, with others on the coasts and islands of the Gulf of St. Lawrence, the east coasts of New Brunswick, and Prince Edward Island—then known as Île Saint-Jean—and on the Magdalen Islands. In total, there remained four thousand Acadians in 1763. Three quarters of those present in 1755 had disappeared, some who had been spread out across the continent, others throughout the islands of the Gulf of St. Lawrence. This population was distended over more than 130,000 square kilometres, divided by straits, sounds, and still wild forests. This space had been "made available" by the new colonial powers for Anglo-British emigration and welcomed American Loyalists with the explicit goal of making it an Anglo-Protestant society that would assimilate what remained of French Acadie. As of 1764, the French neutrals had been authorized to resettle in this space under certain conditions—the legal restrictions included a ban on Catholicism and a variety of land ownership problems, which endured for nearly a century.

The Acadian society was no more in the old French Acadie after the definitive surrendering of territories to England in 1763. Had there been one before then? Longfellow had described the exile of "a nation, with all its household gods." Rameau had confirmed that such a society did indeed exist, and even stated that elements sufficient to its reconstruction had survived the annihilation efforts. Later on, at the end of the nineteenth century, the Acadian narrative anchored itself in this validation to affirm the renaissance of the Acadian people. Still today, historians assert that the reconstruction of Acadie is due to the development, prior to 1755, of a sentiment of collective identity.

These opinions, however, need to be emphatically nuanced. The Acadie of before 1755 was a colonial society, practically feudal in its organization. This type of society did not produce a self-reflective national sense of belonging like those of the modern and Romantic periods. The concepts of family, village, and "country," as old France used to call a geographical space with its own customs, set the foundation for an anthropological culture, an anchoring of belonging. In Acadie, the religious universe represented a second sphere that tied the initial culture of belonging to an existing civilization: the Catholicism of the kings of France.

In Europe, a national reference had been developing over a few centuries and eventually imposed itself as a vehicle of culture and civilization while remaining the ideal marker for identity. But Acadie did not have the same socio-political ideology in 1755. There existed an Acadian "land" insofar as it was understood in Old France, that is, the rural identity of those peasants from Poitou who had settled in America more than one hundred years prior and who had become inhabitants of another "land." But this country was not a "society," let alone a "nation." Its marginality, its essentially rustic nature, its demographics that would never reach twenty thousand inhabitants, would prevent it from reaching such a status. French Acadie was a human community that had not developed its own cultural, religious, or political infrastructures, and especially, that did not have a collective representation of itself. This community was, as Longfellow stated, far from having its "household gods."

The behaviour of Acadians at the time of the events they deemed the Grand Dérangement (known as the Great Upheaval, but meaning the great disruption)—we will come back to this—reveals the lack of an

Acadian society at the time of the French colony. There are no references to Acadie in the letters or documents produced by Acadians, nor any nostalgia for this Acadie as a "homeland," "land of our ancestors," or any such expression. As emphasized in the petition sent to the English authorities by a group of Acadians in Philadelphia (1756), they felt they had been treated unfairly and had been unjustly dispossessed of their property. But they did not demand the restitution of their lands, nor their return to Acadie. They requested to be considered as "French" prisoners, and to be returned to the protection of their Catholic king. More than anything, they wanted to be reunited with their families. When Acadians were given the opportunity, as in Massachusetts, to choose their new place of settlement, the majority chose Canada (Quebec) rather than Acadie. Others, like the six hundred Acadians under the leadership of Joseph and Alexandre Broussard, also known as Beausoleil, who were prisoners in Halifax in November 1764, traded Halifax for Santo Domingo, never to return. They did not, however, stay in the Caribbean, moving instead to Louisiana, a territory they still believed to be under French rule—this group was the first significant contingent of Acadians to settle in Louisiana, but theirs is another tale we will address later. Some returned to France—almost four thousand of them—but they struggled to adapt to the habits and customs of their old country. Another sixteen hundred Acadians settled in Louisiana in the middle of the 1780s. Very few returned to Acadie.

Of course, some did return—dozens of families that had been deported to Massachusetts arrived in 1767 in the old French Bay, which was now known as the Bay of Fundy. In the years that followed, a few families travelled with fish merchants, returning from their exile in France. Others still, from Canada, joined family members who had settled on the coasts of Chaleur Bay and the Gulf of St. Lawrence. For the most part, the Acadians from the Atlantic coast that Rameau documented in his history of 1859 were descendants of the thirty-five hundred Acadians who had managed to avoid the successive deportations from the years 1755–64, or who had migrated to the French part of Acadie prior to 1755. The "deported" never returned.

By 1785, the Acadian populations had re-stabilized following the disturbances of the three previous decades. Their descendants were distributed across the land, with a third of them in the old Acadie (six thousand), another third in Canada/Quebec (six thousand) and the final third was in Louisiana (thirty-five hundred), in France and the West Indies. In the turmoil, almost eight thousand Acadians had disappeared. It was the poem *Evangeline*, not history, which crystallized the idea of a return to the national territory in the collective imaginary of nineteenth-century Maritime Acadians. Longfellow had, perhaps inadvertently, instilled this idea into three short verses at the end of the poem:

*Only along the shore of the mournful and misty Atlantic*
*Linger a few Acadian peasants, whose fathers from exile*
*Wandered back to their native land to die in its bosom.*

*Evangeline*, original verses by Longfellow

The Acadians who had settled in the old French Acadie had not committed to memory this deportation that Longfellow immortalized in his poem. This was first noticed in the notes of travellers who were in contact with Acadians prior to 1847. In 1790, Reverend Andrew Brown met with some of the Acadians established near Halifax, in Chezzetcook. Brown wanted to write a history of Nova Scotia by relating the expulsion of the French. He was surprised by how few recollections Acadians had of the loss of the ancestral lands and even noted indifference toward the suffering caused by their expulsion. The documents of Reverend Brown (the Brown Papers) were part of the controversy between Father Casgrain and archivist Akins. Casgrain accused Akins of not reproducing all the documents compiled by Reverend Brown, including documents found in 1852 and preserved at the British Museum. These apparently described Acadians as not very belligerent and thus not much of a threat to the British authorities. Between 1811 and 1815, Plessis, bishop of Quebec, travelled three times to visit the Catholics of the Gulf of St. Lawrence and eastern colonies, which are today the Maritime provinces. Bishop Plessis kept a journal, which was edited and published after 1860. His writings can be considered as the first monograph describing post-Expulsion Acadians. He visited each parish, relating the way of life, marginality, and poverty of the Acadian communities. Throughout the Magdalen Islands and on Prince Edward Island, he noted persistent conflicts regarding land ownership where Acadians had settled—and this was more than fifty years after the expulsion. Plessis attributed these disputes to the short-sightedness of Acadians regarding land registration. In other cases, he recalled the proscriptions that prevented Catholics like them from holding public office. He found Acadians to be "relatively impervious to these deprivations" ("peu sensibles à ces privations"). Hardships that he saw as an opportunity better tend to the affairs of the religion.

When Plessis visited Nova Scotia, he referenced the Deportation of the old Acadians, though he quickly emphasized the challenges he faced when collecting witness statements from a few octogenarians. He even wrote in his journal that the difficulties of these poor inhabitants under British occupation were due to their lack of understanding of the religion ("une religion mal entendue"), with some Acadians believing it impossible to practise the true religion after swearing allegiance to a heretical prince. This position, conciliations of British powers, was typical of the "Canadian" clergy at the turn of the nineteenth century, who wished to preserve their alliance with the English civil authorities that had been consecrated in the Quebec Act (1774). Rameau stressed in *Une colonie féodale*, that Bishop Plessis saw the considerable advantages that the Catholic Church could gain from an English Catholic hierarchy in the Maritimes. Bishop Plessis's focus on the memorial vacuum appeared to be validated by the Acadians' lack of memory.

At long last, in 1829, Haliburton published his history of Nova Scotia, which was strongly influenced by Longfellow's narrative, and he told of the challenges he came across while trying to find sources that explained the reasons for the Deportation and the way the French neutrals had been banished. He noted that the Acadians of the municipality of Clare (St. Marys Bay) had neither specific complaints nor hostility toward the government of Nova Scotia—if anything they desired to be loyal subjects.

Haliburton knew these people well, for he had been their political representative. Using his sharp observation skills, Haliburton found that they did not retain painful memories of the expulsion.

The non-existent memory of the Expulsion prior to 1847 was again confirmed by the absence of references to it in popular culture. After the letters and petitions of the first few years where the deported complained of having been unjustly defrauded of their lands and separated from their families, the memory dissipated. Ethnologists, folklorists, and historians alike could not find accounts, laments, popular tales, or even songs associated with these events having circulated prior to the publication and circulation of *Evangeline* in Acadie—and, as we will see, the situation was similar in Louisiana. In the century of oral literary traditions that followed the destruction of the old French Acadie, the theme of love was most prevalent according to Marguerite Maillet author of *Histoire de la littérature acadienne* (1983). In his notes, Reverend Brown recalled three songs that attested to the French Catholic culture of Acadians at the end of the eighteenth century: *Faux plaisirs, vains honneurs*; *Tout passé*; and *Vive Jésus*. These are far from the patriotic songs that Lemay attributed to Acadians in their march from the church of Grand-Pré to the ships that would sail them into exile. Longfellow had also specified that their songs were hymns.

> *Even as pilgrims, who journey afar from their homes and their*
> *country,*
> *Sing as they go, and in singing forget they are weary and wayworn.*

*Evangeline*, original verses by Longfellow

## Recollections of the Wars and the Great Upheaval

There is a word that circulated prior to the poem and that harkens to a "popular" memory of the events that led to the disappearance of the old French Acadie. The expression is "dérangement," which means "disruption" or "disturbance," but is officially translated as "upheaval." The first occurrence is documented in 1773, only ten years after the definitive transfer of the territories to England. Individuals of Acadian origin who had settled on the islands of Saint-Pierre and Miquelon—the small archipelago near Newfoundland that France kept following the treaty of 1763—referenced a period of "dérangement par les guerres" (disturbance caused by the wars), a period preceding the signature of the Paris Treaty and the dispersion of some of their old acquaintances to New England, like those of Île Saint-Jean (now PEI).

In 1803, missionary Antoine Bédard, of the New Brunswick Richibucto-Village mission, asked his bishop in Quebec City if those of his parishioners who found goods in caches that dated from "after the dérangement of Acadie" could keep such items. Did they owe the poor some form of charity? At the time, the expression "dérangement" or its plural form "dérangements," referred to a period that seemed to begin around 1749–50—the founding of Halifax, the construction of Fort Beauséjour. This period continued after the end of the Seven Years War in 1763 and into 1785, the year a group of Acadians from the village of Sainte-Anne on the Saint John River was displaced northward, near the Madawaska River, under pressure from American loyalists who had settled there after the American Revolution. This was the period that came to be defined as that of the grands dérangements, and eventually as the singular "Grand Dérangement," or Great Upheaval.

Recalling a few historical facts about these disturbances might help us better understand the context. Between 1749 and 1755, Acadians began leaving English Acadie—the Nova Scotia peninsula—to settle in the new French Acadie: Île Saint-Jean (PEI), Île-Royale (Cape Breton Island), and the current territory of New Brunswick. Those who stayed in the English part of Acadie were expelled shortly after the capture of Fort Beauséjour by the British in 1755. The Franco-English war that began shortly after (1757–63) led to the fall of Louisbourg in the northeast of Acadie and the extension of the conflict to the entire French Acadian territory. Some Acadians under the direction of Boishébert participated in these wars, notably the group led by Beausoleil-Broussard. The English rapidly defeated them and set to the task of depleting the rest of the territory of its

French-speaking inhabitants. Some Acadians hid in the woods or along the coasts farther north of the old Acadie, others ran off to Canada or to the Saint-Pierre and Miquelon islands, and still others went to France with the French army. The British deported three thousand Acadians from Île Saint-Jean (PEI) to France in 1758, and more than half of these people died during the voyage from disease and shipwrecks.

After 1763, the Acadians who had been expelled from English Acadie and were still in the United States—nearly thirty-five hundred souls—travelled to Canada or back to the old Acadie. As for those who were farther south, they made their way to Louisiana, occasionally stopping on the then-French island of Saint-Domingue, which is now Haiti. As early as 1755, Virginia had sent off a group of more than one thousand Acadians to England; Massachusetts, refusing to take any more in after 1755, returned a group of fifteen hundred newly deported Acadians to the Halifax prison in 1762. This did not, however, mark the end of the migrations. The Acadians who were prisoners in England were "returned" to France, those who had sought refuge in Saint-Pierre and Miquelon were deported to France in 1778 as a form of English retaliation against France—a nation that had supported the American Revolution.

Some of the Acadians transported to France managed to settle there, though others returned to Saint-Pierre and Miquelon, Gaspésie, or the coasts of the Gulf of St. Lawrence. The French tried to dispose of other Acadians by leaving them on Saint-Domingue or elsewhere in the West Indies, all the way to the Falkland Islands, but many of them, approximately sixteen hundred, were finally transported to Spanish Louisiana in 1785. With the northward displacement to Madawaska in 1785, of Acadians who had (re)settled at the base of the Saint John River, the period known as the "dérangement par les guerres" (disturbance caused by the wars) came to an end.

The Deportation of 1755 appears in this fuzzy recollection of the "disturbance of Acadie" as one episode among other disruptions that led to the downfall of French Acadie. The expression "dérangement" remained vague, and was not indicative of the accuracy of historical recollection that people had of these events; it had not yet become a reference. We can see it in the story of the old Acadian woman who, in 1812, recounted to

Bishop Plessis her life's peregrinations since her birth in Louisbourg. She was of the same age the poem's heroine Évangéline would have been—born around 1735—and had lived her youth in Grand-Pré. Her story preceded the publication of *Evangeline*, and though it is representative of the "dérangement" or disturbance, it was not a tale of a people and their return from exile. Here was the account of their meeting by Henri Têtu, biographer of Bishop Plessis:

> *Chose remarquable, dit Monseigneur, j'ai rencontré à Chétican, isle du Cap Breton, au mois de juillet 1812, Jeanne Dugast, âgée de 80 ans, veuve de Pierre Bois, laquelle m'a dit être née à Louisbourg, avoir été de là à l'Acadie, au lieu nommé le Grand Pré (Horton), puis être revenue au Cap-Breton, puis avoir demeurée à l'Île Saint-Jean, ensuite à Remshic en Acadie, puis encore au Cap-Breton, de là encore à Remshic, puis à l'Île Saint-Jean pour la seconde fois, puis une troisième fois à Remshic, de là à Restigouche, de Restigouche à Halifax, de là à Arichat, puis aux isles de la Madeleine, puis à Cascapédia, et de Cascapédia à Chétican, et ne s'être jamais couchée sans souper.*

Original French

> *A remarkable thing, said the Bishop, I met in Cheticamp, Cape Breton Island, in July 1812, an eighty-year-old named Jeanne Dugast, widow of Pierre Bois, who told me she was born in Louisbourg. She said she was there in Acadie, at the place called Grand-Pré (Horton), that she came back to Cape Breton, lived on Île Saint-Jean, then Remshic in Acadie, then again in Cape Breton, from there back to Remshic, then Île Saint-Jean for a second time, then a third time in Remshic, and from there Restigouche, from Restigouche to Halifax, and from there to Arichat, then to the Magdalen Islands, then Cascapedia, and from Cascapedia to Cheticamp, and that she never once went to bed without dinner.*

Transl. Fleury

Some tried to explain this strange silence and claimed it was the result of a post-traumatic recollection; a repression needed in order to forget a tragedy that no one could do anything to prevent. The victims were ashamed of the degrading situation that was brought on by the oppression they suffered. Silence would have been a way of being forgotten so that such dreadful events would never again be repeated. Memory or recollection would require a period of mourning to accept such a terrible loss. Recent examples include how the first generation of Holocaust survivors in the twentieth century would not, or could not, share memories of the extermination camps. Indeed, some of these explanations are plausible, but they do not exactly apply to the case of Acadie or the memory of the Expulsion. In this case, the period of mourning lasted more than a century and surpassed the social structures of three generations, which meant that by 1850, very few people could know someone who had actually survived these events. This was more a case of forgetting than extended bereavement.

The explanation might even be simpler than that. After 1860, the Acadians of the Maritime provinces who structured their collective memory around the Expulsion could not pass on a living memory of this event because, for the most part, those who were alive at the time had not suffered through exile, but rather the experience of an upheaval (dérangement).

While there could not be a first-hand account or lived memory, there was a secondary—collective, reflexive—memory of a different nature. This type of memory needed a "society" to produce the necessary mediations and transform it into a narrative—tales, legends, myths of origin in traditional societies; history, literature, press and media coverage in modern societies. The Acadians from before 1860 did not form a society. They lived in scattered clusters on the margins of a society of "Maritimers" who simultaneously rejected and ignored them. They were tolerated mainly for their use in the colonial fishing commerce that took place on the coasts of the Gulf of St. Lawrence. As a result, that further amplified the perceived eccentricity of Acadians in relation to the society that was being built around them.

## A Society Awakens in the Light of *Evangeline*

In other words, for a century, nothing banded Acadians together. They did not occupy a specific geographical area either. They lived under the jurisdiction of five distinct colonies or provinces if we include the Acadians of the Gulf—Magdalen Islands—and of Chaleur Bay—Gaspésie—under "Canadian" jurisdiction, and those of Cape Breton, which was an independent colony from 1784 to 1820. There were also the Acadians of Newfoundland—which remained an English colony until 1949—and those of Saint-Pierre and Miquelon, which are still French territories. Despite speaking the same language, they did not share a common communicational space—there were very few ties between the different clusters, no newspapers nor commerce. Acadians had neither memory of their common origins nor institutions of any kind—political, economic, social—to tie them together.

Church was the only connection, but it was a tenuous one until the 1860s. There were passing missionaries who took interest in Acadians and Indigenous peoples until the end of the eighteenth century. A few French priests fleeing the French Revolution resided there until the turn of the nineteenth century. "Canadian" priests replaced them, but nothing resembled a common religious space before 1860. At the time, Acadian adherence to Catholicism was a result of old colonial strategies, and did not yet emanate from society itself.

A society, defined as an articulation of different social elements—a morphology, as sociologists call it—did not exist in Acadians prior to the dissemination of *Evangeline*. The attribution of meaning to the society through a narrative preceded its physical consecration in the form of Acadie. One thing must be made clear: *Evangeline* did not create Acadie. The Deportation at the heart of the tale really did happen. A few tens of thousands of descendants of the old inhabitants of French Acadie, still French-speaking Catholics, lived in the old territory of French Acadie by the middle of the nineteenth century, but they did not form a society. *Evangeline* and the narrative of the Expulsion provided the first articulated connection of a society that would go on to build itself.

The structuring capacity of the poem derived from particular circumstances that brought about change on the sidelines where the outcast of the previous century had been marginalized. At the beginning of the nineteenth century, Irish Catholic immigrants, and also Scottish, began settling in the neighbouring regions of the re(populated) Acadian clusters. Catholicism was invigorated by these influxes. Peninsular Nova Scotia was detached from the Quebec diocese in 1816 (Halifax) and the rest of the Maritimes (Charlottetown) in 1829. Around the 1830s, colonial authorities lifted the bans that prevented Catholics from holding office. From then on, Catholics could become civil servants and members of legislative assemblies. With its newly anointed legitimacy and the population growth among Catholics, the Catholic Church saw an opportunity to expand its organization. After Halifax and Charlottetown, Catholic dioceses were created in the regions of Fredericton (Saint John) and Arichat (Antigonish).

The recognitions that impacted Catholics were not made for Acadians, even though they still represented a majority among the Maritime Catholics. With the blessing of the bishop of Quebec, it was a group of bishops of Irish and Scottish origin that organized the Catholic expansion into the Acadian populations in the middle of the nineteenth century. With Acadians being mostly uneducated and disconnected from the power relationships of the "English" society that was being established near them, few of them initially took advantage of their new political rights. A few individuals of Acadian origin became representatives before the 1860s—Simon d'Entremont in Nova Scotia (1836), and Amand Landry in New Brunswick (1846).

The integration of this marginal population into the surrounding society was bound to happen at some point. What was unscripted was the way Acadians integrate. Would it be through cultural, religious, or linguistic assimilation? Or would it come about through a differentiated ethnic or nationalist integration? By opening up the region to British Catholic immigration and emancipating Catholics in general, the colonial authorities had in some way renounced the religious assimilation of these populations.

Linguistic and cultural assimilation, though, were non-negotiable. To the English colonial society in the making, the French heritage and worn-out character of their customs and traditions were foreign features. It was agreed upon that Acadians would be assimilated as they exited the side-lines of society. Everything was lining up for the "scattered debris" of French Acadie to integrate the majority by way of English-speaking Catholicism. The Irish and Scottish leaders of the Catholic Church had seen an opportunity to expand their herd by unifying these lonely souls to their cause.

With this in mind, we can understand the mandate of the arch-bishop of Halifax. In 1855, Father Walsh was marking the centennial of the Deportation, which seems to be the first commemoration of the event. This gesture was part of the reactions of the Nova Scotian elite to the American reprobation that followed the publication of the poem *Evangeline*—Akins was named the archivist in charge of shedding light on the historical documentation in 1857. The archbishop of Halifax drew on the biblical dimension of Longfellow's narrative. The Acadians were likened to the Hebrew people.

*Voici ce que dit le Seigneur Dieu: « Je vous rassemblerai du milieu des peuples, je vous réunirai des pays où vous avez été dispersés, et je vous donnerai la terre d'Israël » (Ezéchiel 16, 17). C'est à la même fin, N. T. C. F. [nos très chers frères], qu'il vous a ramenés, « pour que vous ôtiez du milieu de vous tout ce qui peut être un sujet de chute, et toutes les abominations, » pour que vous receviez de lui « un même cœur, et [que se] répande dans vos entrailles un fruit nouveau, pour qu'il ôte de votre chair le cœur de pierre, et vous donne un cœur de chair; afin que vous marchiez dans la voie de ses préceptes, que vous gardiez ce qu'il vous a ordonné et que vous le fassiez; que vous soyez son peuple; et qu'il soit votre Dieu ».*

Original French

*Thus saith the Lord God: "I will even gather you from the people and assemble you out of the countries where ye have been scattered, and I will give you the land of Israel" (Ezekiel 11:17). It is to this same end, very dear brothers, that he has brought you together, so that you might "take away all*

*the detestable things thereof and all the abominations thereof from thence,"*
*so that you may receive from him "one heart, and for Him to put a new*
*spirit within you; and take the stony heart out of your flesh, and receive a*
*heart of flesh, that you may walk in His statutes and keep His ordinances,*
*and do them. And you shall be His people, and He will be your God."*

Transl. Fleury

The people mentioned by the Scottish bishop was not yet the Acadian people, it was the people of God, a chosen people, Catholic, who would soon speak English. This was what the Comte of Gobineau noted when he met with Acadian descendants in 1859 while travelling through Cape Breton to Newfoundland (a travel narrative he published as *Voyage à Terre-Neuve* in 1861). Their story, he said, had been told by Longfellow the American. Their story had lost "all national colour" ("toute couleur nationale") amid the tales that were recited to him, and had instead become the story of Catholics of Acadian, Irish, or Scottish origins. Upon hearing the tales, he said, it was difficult to distinguish myth from historical fact.

Events did not unfold as Father Walsh and Comte Gobineau had anticipated. At the turn of the 1860s, history unfolded rapidly. The railroad and the integration of the Maritime colonies to the Canadian Confederation (1867)—which made the construction of the railway possible—created the opportunity for an initial convergence of Acadians. A new physical proximity was achievable thanks to the railway, even though the geographical marginality of the Acadian populations meant that the "tracks" were mostly laid far from the clusters of Acadians. A cultural convergence was also opportune among Acadians and with French Canadians who, since the failure of the rebellions in 1837–38, were busy building a new identity and a new project.

A few Canadians came to the old French Acadie, and were surprised, like Rameau had been, to find persisting clusters of French speakers. These newcomers joined the few members of the Canadian clergy who, despite the Irish turn in Catholicism, had persisted, mainly in New Brunswick, to offer services in French to the old Acadians. In 1864, Father Lefebvre from the province of Quebec, established the first college with bilingual instruction in Memramcook, southern New Brunswick, set in the middle of an Acadian, French, and Catholic population. In 1867, Israël Landry, another Quebecer, established a French-language newspaper named *Le Moniteur acadien* in Shediac, a town also located in southeastern New Brunswick. The first editions reproduced, with great fanfare, the new translation of *Evangeline* by Pamphile Lemay. The poem was at last delivered to the Acadians.

The French Canadians who arrived in Acadie brought parts of the French Canadian project: build a French-speaking society in North America. Father Lefebvre established his college's Saint-Jean-Baptiste Society to initiate his young pupils to the work of the French Catholic civilization. At the same time in New Brunswick in particular, the Francophone clergy who were mainly of "Canadian" origin or trained in Quebec seminaries began to complain about the habit of Irish-Scottish bishops to assign priests who did not speak French to Acadian parishes. Would the Acadians assimilate to the Irish culture, or would they participate in the French-Canadian civilization project?

This first tension between Irish and French Catholics was in part stirred by the refusal of the Anglo-Protestant majority to welcome Acadians within their institutions. Despite the abuses toward Catholics having officially ended, Acadians could not manage to occupy public positions in those communities where they were the majority. The anglophone elites maintained their control over economic power all the while eliminating or marginalizing the appointment of Acadians to elected positions. The rare few Acadians who managed to make their way into the system were ridiculed by the English press who saw them as a backwards population manipulated by a foreign clergy. The Acadian marginality was being transformed into a rejection based on ethnicity.

During the 1866 election, a few representatives from Acadian regions of New Brunswick found themselves practically alone against the Canadian confederation even though the motives of their position remain nebulous. For the anglophone majority, this was perceived as a sign that the Acadian population did not adhere to the political values of the majority.

It was a first moment of political awareness of Acadians: they came to understand that they were a distinct people. The same thing happened in 1871–75 with the Common Schools Act that aimed to establish a secular, government-run schooling system. Acadian members of parliament and a few Irish MPs were opposed to the project because it prevented religious education. The conflict led to a fight in the Acadian community of Caraquet, in northern New Brunswick. In 1875, an English militiaman and an Acadian lost their lives in what is known as the Louis Mailloux Affair. The situation ended in a compromise that satisfied Irish Catholics, but that did not resolve the issues of language, which left a bitter aftertaste among the burgeoning Acadian elite.

Acadians were once again isolated. Even within French Canada, they did not receive the support needed to convince them that their fight was the same as that of the French Canadian brothers they had only just rediscovered. Commenting the work of Rameau de Saint-Père in the newspaper *Le Pays*, journalist and essayist Arthur Buies mocked the pretension of Rameau who claimed he had found a people along the coasts of the Gulf of St. Lawrence: "No, whatever degree of sympathy we might have for this small people, swarm dispersed along the wild coasts of the Gulf, descendants of those exiled in 1755, milk kin of the [French] Canadian people, we cannot do it the honour of believing it a nationality."[22] When Louis Riel was arrested during one of the North-West insurgencies in Saskatchewan (1885–86), the Quebec press spoke of a "political servitude" to describe the laxism of Acadian representative Pierre-Amand Landry who, condemning the actions of Riel, supported the Canadian government.

The idea that the Acadians were lacking in nationalist convictions due to their proximity to the English-speaking world—their habit of integrating English words into their spoken French attested to this closeness—was widespread among French Canadian nationalists. Such was the theme of the novel by nationalist historian Lionel Groulx titled *Au Cap Blomidon* (1932), which he wrote during a pilgrimage to Grand-Pré at the

---

22. In the words of Athur Buies: "Non, quelque sympathie que nous ayons pour ce petit peuple, essaim parsemé sur les côtes sauvages du golfe, descendant des exilés de 1755, frère de lait du peuple canadien, nous ne pouvons pas cependant lui faire l'honneur de le croire une nationalité."

beginning of the twentieth century. The first Acadian leaders—Father Marcel-François Richard, Pierre-Armand Landry, Pascal Poirier—complained that they did not always receive the attentive listening of (French) Canadians in matters relating to schools of the French-speaking clergy. This latent tension between half-brothers would soon be intellectualized through the prism of distinct nationalities.

Rejected by the Anglo-Protestant majority, marginalized by Irish Catholics, viewed as nothing by the French Canadians, the few Acadian elites who surfaced in the middle of the nineteenth century were forced to develop their own national reference. *Evangeline* would provide them with the framework.

## The Delegate of the "Little Nation"

The contentions of Father Marcel-François Richard (1847–1915) with his bishop of Irish origin, Father Rogers, in the second part of the nineteenth century, were indicative of the formation of the Acadian identity. Marcel-François Richard was the first Acadian nationalist, the first who identified the cause as one of a people. He was born in 1847—the year *Evangeline* was published—in the parish of Saint-Louis-de-Kent in the eastern region of New Brunswick. Too old to attend the college of Saint-Joseph, which was established in 1864 and would become a veritable nursery for the first generation of Acadian nationalists, Father Richard began his schooling in an Irish setting at St. Danshai's College in Charlottetown in 1861. He then studied at Montreal's Grand Séminaire, where Father Ignace Bourget formed his army of French Canadian prelates entrusted with the mission of spreading the French Catholic civilization across North America.

The spirit of Catholicism had profoundly changed in the province of Quebec since the beginning of the century when Father Plessis, visiting Acadians, had extolled the virtues of submitting to English colonial powers. The Church took charge of the destiny of the French Canadian nation and resolutely connected the French nationality to the Catholic mission in America. French Canadian nationalism and ultra-montanism—that is, the adherence to the Church of Rome beyond political institutions—curiously came together in a way that would distinctly mark the French Canadian nation-Church during the following century.

Upon his return from Canada in 1870, Father Richard strived to transplant Catholic institutions of French Canada as a parish priest in his native town of Saint-Louis-de-Kent. He invited the nuns of the Notre-Dame congregation from Quebec to settle there; he founded Saint-Louis College in 1877 for the education of boys, which he modelled after French Canadian schools. Father Richard quickly learned that the Franco-Catholic Church in Acadie did not benefit from the same hegemony it had acquired in the province of Quebec.

The bishop for the region, Father Rogers, was of Irish origin, and had recently assumed his role in the new diocese of Chatham (1860), a region with a Franco-Catholic majority, and saw Father Richard's initiatives as obstacles to his own project. Rogers instead proposed to establish an ecumenical Catholic Church, that is, a Church that did not distinguish between nationalities—French, Irish, Scottish, or English. As a vehicle of communication, his Church would use English, the language of the British Empire and American continent, and the vehicular language accepted by the Irish and Scottish. Father Rogers raised barriers to the ambitions of the young priest by refusing to give him the resources he needed to build his college, and discouraging him from acquiring the resources from Quebec, supporting the grievances of Anglo-Catholics regarding the excessively French nature of the small institution.

Father Richard was walking a tight line, stuck between his placement in an Anglo-Irish Catholic Church and his conviction that the future of the French language and the Catholic religion were intimately related. He sought support in Quebec, but the modest help he got came from a clergy who did not want to exacerbate conflicts between the French Canadian Church and the hierarchy of the (Irish-Scottish) Church of the Maritimes. Richard turned to France for help, through Rameau, who had called on Acadians to imitate the [French] Canadians and to build their own institutions. He received the help of a French abbot named Biron, who would become the director of his college. Father Biron was a correspondent of Rameau who had stayed at Father Lefebvre's Saint-Joseph College in Memramcook, and who thought they spoke too much English at the school. But it was all in vain; in 1882, barely five years after the college had opened, Father Richard, under pressure from Rogers who considered the establishment "too frenchy," was forced to close the institution. Father Biron was forced to retreat to France. The event was deemed "the death of a national institution," according to local newspaper *Le Moniteur acadien*.

Soon after, in 1885, the bishop moved the rebellious priest whom he accused of "infusing national sentiment" in the back country colonial missions where Acadie was still trying to (re)take hold following the project of Rameau. Ironically, these parishes were called "Rogersville" in honour of Father Rogers—the bishop against Acadian nationalism— and "Acadieville" in honour of the new Acadie that Father Richard was fighting to create. Rogers understood the bonds that tied Father Richard to Rameau. He accused him in 1890 of having inspired the "poisoned chapter" of Rameau's last book in which the author described the "nefarious" ("infâme") role of the Irish prelate in the refusal to build Acadian institutions.

This did not, however, stop Father Richard who had taken up other battles from the list Rameau had elaborated in 1859 to promote the rebirth of Acadie. At the same time as he was fighting for the survival of educational institutions, he was the great instigator and champion of the Acadian nationality during the first national conventions organized by Acadians as of 1881. Richard pleaded strongly for a national holiday that was distinct from that of the French Canadians—the Assumption instead of the Saint-Jean-Baptiste—and he was the inspiration behind the national anthem—*Ave Maris Stella*—as well as the designer of the Acadian flag—a replica of the French Republic flag adorned with a Marian star. Here again, we can see the strange influence of Rameau, who saw in feudal Acadie the microcosm of a Catholic egalitarian republic. Richard was invested in the colonization of the inland areas especially after his forced nomination in the missions of Acadieville and Rogersville, attempting to rally the debris of French Acadie onto one territory...again, with limited success.

Father Richard was mostly, from the 1880s, the first combatant who was in the front lines of the great battle of this generation: the Acadianization of the Catholic clergy. He travelled to Rome twice to demand the nomination of an Acadian bishop, in a crossover with his own bishop and all of the Catholic hierarchy of the Maritime provinces. As Richard prepared his final trip to the Vatican in 1910, Father Casey, bishop of Saint John had advised his colleague—and Richard's immediate superior—Father Rogers to "watch out for the 'delegate of the little nation.'"

Richard would not become the first Acadian bishop. He was given the honorific title of Monseigneur in the hopes that this recognition would suffice to calm the priest's militant passions. Instead, in 1912, a more discreet Acadian was made bishop, and taking excessive precautions, he was assigned to an anglophone diocese far from the places where Acadie was developing its institutions. But the barriers were broken in 1936 when the creation of the archdiocese of Moncton confirmed the autonomy of the Acadian Church-nation. Through a few dioceses, a handful of parishes, convents, colleges, and other religious institutions, and, of course, the spiritual direction of the now-Acadian souls, the Church-nation had succeeded in transforming the "scattered debris" from Rameau's accounts into a "petite nation." Such was the only decisive victory of this generation, but what a victory it was.

## The Children of Évangéline

Though he was the first and most ardent militant, the "delegate of the little nation" was not alone in his fight. Through the years, a small Acadian elite mainly coming out of the first generation of students from Saint-Joseph College in Memramcook created in 1864, had joined forces with him. These were the first literate men of Acadie. They were few of them, barely a dozen, and they were all born in the years following the publication of *Evangeline*. Pascal Poirier (1851–1933), the leader and most intellectual of the group, who dallied with literature; Pierre-Amand Landry (1846–1916), the first true Acadian politician; Placide Gaudet (1850–1930), the great trailblazer of Acadian genealogy; Valentin Landry (1844–1919), who founded the newspaper named *L'Évangéline* (1887), a paper that would become the official body of Acadian patriotism; Philéas Bourgeois (1855–1913), priest-teacher-literary person, somewhat distanced from the Acadian movement, but among his generation, he knew the works of Longfellow best.

To these rare literate laypeople, we must add a few priests—who became more important as time went on—more builders than ideologues: Hubert Girroir (1825–84), priest of Arichat (Antigonish) in Nova Scotia—one of the first correspondents with Rameau; Father Stanislas Doucet (1847–1925), fellow in struggle with Father Richard in northern New Brunswick, and who had trained with him in Montreal at the seminary of Father Bourget; and a few politicians marginally connected to the Acadian cause, including Gilbert A. Girouard (1846–85) and Urbain Johnson (1824–1917).

French Canadians, both priests and laypeople, had preceded them and accompanied them in what this generation would come to call the "Acadian Renaissance": Father Camille Lefebvre (1831–95), founder of the first Acadian college—Saint-Joseph College; Israël Landry (1843–1910), founder of the first Acadian newspaper, *Le Moniteur acadien*; and Ferdinand J. Robidoux (1849–1921) who succeeded him at the *Moniteur* and would act as the scribe of the Acadian Renaissance for a generation.

These were the people who stood in 1881 on the podium of the first national convention of Acadians, a gathering that inaugurated these grand patriotic assemblies that would become, at regular intervals and until today—there had been ten by 1937 and a few others after 1955, following a break—key events of Acadian nationalism. There, people gathered together like at high mass, to celebrate the survival of a people and to establish projects for the future.

In 1881, the Acadian society was strong enough for the new Acadian elites to be able to mobilize nearly five thousand participants from the parishes that now structured the scattered debris of the old French Acadie. In the first instances, the goal was to confirm the very existence of the Acadian reference, and such was the objective of the first commission of the convention. "Should we share a national holiday with French Canada?"

"Are we, as Rameau described, a nation in its own right?" "Are we, like the French Canadian odyssey of the *Evangeline* poem suggests, a mere reminiscence of the French Acadie whose debris would be better served by a fusion with French Canada?

## Rameau against *Evangeline*

Was Acadie an ascending nation, able to "build a society," or a descending community, that is, a people essentially made of memories from the past and incapable of becoming a nation? "We are decidedly still too weak to ride alone,"[23] affirmed the political leader Pierre-Armand Landry—the symbolic union with French Canada would come to seal the political union with the Canadian Confederation. And Philéas Bourgeois further opined that: "We can affirm our existence in the face of other nations, but we would not yet know how to show our strength, our organizational power, and our independence."[24] He considered that this was tied to the fact that Acadians were the children of Évangéline: "in God's plans, perhaps Acadie was always meant to bear the scars of a great wound. She was destined to be the land of Évangéline."[25]

If we are all of the same nationality, responded Father Richard, where were our French Canadian brothers at the time of the Confederation, when they did not even think to extend to Acadians the education rights of known Catholics offered to both Canadas? We are, on the contrary, "convened here," he continued, to perform a task of utmost historical importance, "I would not want history, when recounting these events (…) to have to describe how a son of Acadie was denied the right to join the army and defend his nation from invasions."[26] The task was in fact "to affirm our existence as a people and apply all measures to preserve

---

23. "Nous sommes décidément encore trop faibles pour faire cavalier seul."
24. "Nous pouvons affirmer notre existence devant les autres nations, mais nous ne saurions encore témoigner de notre force, de notre pouvoir d'organisation, de notre indépendance."
25. "dans les plans de Dieu, l'Acadie devait peut-être porter pour toujours les cicatrices d'une grande plaie. Elle devait être la terre d'Évangéline."
26. "je ne voudrais pas que l'histoire qui racontera ces événements (…) ait à signaler le refus d'un enfant de l'Acadie de s'enrôler sous le drapeau national et le défendre contre toute invasion."

our nationality."[27] And nationalities, added his colleague Father Doucet, were not artificial groupings: "It is because of the circumstances tied to its [Acadie's] origin and surrounding its existence are different from those that forged the character of the other peoples"[28] that Acadie forms a distinct nationality than that of French Canadians. We cannot help it.

Rameau was the great winner even though he could not attend the convention due to illness. Pascal Poirier consecrated the great helmsman of the Acadian Renaissance by urging each delegate to make a financial contribution so that the historian could finish the book *Une colonie féodale en Amérique*—the version published in 1877 documented the history of the people until 1755. It was a national imperative, for, as Poirier argued, no one among them could continue the work Rameau had begun. Earlier, in 1874, Poirier had reminded his peers that Rameau was among those historians capable of inspiring a people: "Rome needed the words of Livy, Canada, those of Garneau, Acadie, those of Rameau."[29]

The rest of the convention, after the confirmation of the national reference, was dedicated to the reiteration of the program dictated by Rameau from 1860 on: acquiring a clergy, investing in education, agriculture, colonization, a national press. The orators, one after another, attested to the "miracle," the "Acadian Renaissance," they were dazzled, perhaps too much so, by the successes accomplished over the preceding twenty years. "A phoenix-like people born again from its ashes,"[30] proclaimed genealogist Placide Gaudet in 1907 while commenting the work of the generation to which he belonged.

---

27. "d'affirmer notre existence comme peuple et prendre tous les moyens de conserver notre nationalité"

28. "C'est parce que les circonstances qui se rattachent à son origine [l'Acadie] et qui ont entouré son existence sont différentes de celles qui ont formé le caractère des autres peuples"

29. In Poirier's words: "Il faut à Rome la plume d'un Tite-Live, au Canada celle d'un Garneau, à l'Acadie celle d'un Rameau."

30. "Un peuple phœnix qui renaît de ses cendres."

## The *Evangeline* Moment

This was the *Evangeline* generation. Even though they had ratified Rameau's audacious plan to make a nation, they would not be able to shake off the weight of the poem. These first Acadian nationalists were born around 1847, the year Longfellow's *Evangeline* was published. Their idea of nationality was structured around the tragedy of Grand-Pré which had been overlooked in Acadie prior to the translation of the poem by Pamphile Lemay. Their understanding of history followed the narrative of *Evangeline*, the trace of its French Canadian interpretation and its inflection by Rameau, according to whom Acadie was indeed a society distinct from that of French Canadians, a society that had survived the Deportation. In *Origine des Acadiens* (1874), the first work written by an Acadian about the history of Acadians, Pascal Poirier proclaimed the profoundly different nature of the Acadian people compared to French Canadians due to what he called the "racial purity" of Acadians. In Canada, colonization had provoked race-mixing (métissage), whereas in French Acadie, it had created an agricultural society in direct filiation with France. To prove his point, Poirier had to go against the words of Rameau, who considered the founding miscegenation of Acadie to be proof of the strength of the French family type capable of transcending "racial impurity."[31]

For the tragedy of Grand-Pré to become central to the identity of this resurgent people, there would need to be proof that Acadians returned from the Deportation. The first Acadian writings were fascinated by the travels of Acadians to the United States. In 1875, Pascal Poirier presented in Ottawa a theatre production he had written titled *Les Acadiens à Philadelphie* (*Acadians in Philadelphia*). The funds from this play would finance the legal defence of Acadians arrested during the recent troubles linked to Catholic schools in Caraquet, New Brunswick. Around the same time, Poirier wrote a short "rural sketch" (saynète champêtre) titled *Accordailles de Gabriel et Évangéline* (published posthumously), that described

---

31. Translator's note: The racial ideology of nineteenth-century historians and scholars has been under scrutiny for decades. Readers are encouraged to read recent publications which challenge obsolete—though unfortunately long-accepted—statements on miscegenation, that is, on procreation between people belonging to different ethnic groups.

the engagement of the couple immortalized in the bucolic land of pre-Deportation Acadie.

Like Napoléon Bourassa had done in *Jacques et Marie* (1866), Poirier built the intrigue of his play titled *Les Acadiens à Philadelphie* around a love triangle. His triangle was made up of an Acadian couple also called Jacques and Marie, separated by the Deportation, and one Englishman, governor of the colony, who was in love with Marie. Unsurprisingly, notary LeBlanc, the only "historical" character of the poem *Evangeline*, was present. To save her family, would Marie renounce her love and, above all, her nation? Jacques was an Acadian "patriot" who took up arms against the English. Unlike the novel by Bourassa, where the lovers eventually met up in Quebec—and the poem by Longfellow where the lovers died in Philadelphia—Jacques went to Philadelphia, where Marie and the Acadians were held prisoners, to bring them back to Acadie.

In 1908, Poirier presented a more scientific study at the Royal Society of Canada, *Des Acadiens déportés à Boston en 1755* (*On Acadians Deported to Boston in 1755*), in which he recounts in strong words the inhuman nature of the suffering that the inhabitants of the American colony imposed on Acadians: "A nasty wind blew over Massachusetts at that moment, impacting Puritan souls in the same way the sight and smell of blood affects wild animals."[32] He noted that the twelve hundred Acadians who had remained in the Boston area until 1766 had finally sought refuge in Lower Canada. But he ended his text by describing how two hundred of them returned to Acadie. Having little information of the subject, he inserted a long quote from Rameau which recounted, in an almost biblical manner, the return of Acadians to the old French Acadie—the procession, according to Rameau, brought together nearly eight hundred Acadians. Rameau based his narrative on the witness statements collected from the grandchildren of the deportees who had settled in the region of Clare/Baie Sainte-Marie, Nova Scotia, the same location that the historian Haliburton had described to Longfellow as a French settlement on the territory of the old Acadie.

It was, however, Placide Gaudet who inaugurated the tradition of an

---

32. In Poirier's words: "Un souffle mauvais passa sur le Massachusetts, à ce moment-là, produisant dans les âmes puritaines l'effet que la vue et l'odeur du sang produisent chez les fauves."

Acadian historiography grounded in genealogical research and a constant preoccupation of a return to the country. In the end he published few historical works, for he led a scattered life working as a teacher and journalist in different parts of Acadie. But he was a tireless genealogist interested in restoring the history of Acadian families since the seventeenth century. Subsequent historians would be inspired by his work. He notably published parts of his research in Acadian newspapers, thus contributing to the collective memory of Acadians.

We can thus understand the fascinating memory of certain Acadians who, at the end of the nineteenth century, meticulously described the Deportation of the preceding century through the lens of their family narratives—notably to Casgrain, who documented them in *Un pèlerinage au pays d'Évangéline* (1887). For instance, Euphrosine LeBlanc, a "descendant" of notary LeBlanc, recalled the discouragement of her great-grandfather on the day of the proclamation by Winslow in the Grand-Pré church, and a descendant of Michel Bastarache alias Basque related the travels of his ancestor between 1755 and 1763 from the Carolinas to Lake Ontario, then to Canada, and finally back to Acadie.

Later on, Gaudet was appointed to the National Archives of Canada and published, in 1906, a four-hundred-page document titled *Généalogie des familles acadiennes* (*Genealogy of Acadian families*) which represented a sort of travel narrative of the deportees. In 1921, he also published a small book, *Le Grand Dérangement*, which was ordered by the project promoter of the Grand-Pré church reconstruction. Gaudet was also the one who merged, in the popular memory, the idea of the "dérangement des guerres" (disturbances of the wars) and the more literary *Evangeline*, daughter of the "Deportation," into the formula of the "Grand Dérangement" (the Great Upheaval).

This generation would participate further in the *Evangeline* moment by interfering in the battle of historians that followed the 1857 creation of the Nova Scotia Archives. The role of the Archives, as was stated in the previous chapter, was to shed light on the events of 1755 following the publication of the poem and the response by French Canadian historians like Henri-Raymond Casgrain's *Un Pèlerinage au pays d'Évangéline*. In this fight, the *Evangeline* generation generally chose to follow the interpretation initiated by Rameau and Casgrain. These two historians were considered the heralds of the Acadian people. On many occasions, Poirier emphasized how the Deportation was principally caused by the greed of the English who desired above all the prosperous agricultural lands occupied by the French in the old Acadie. Again in 1907, he insisted that Akins, the Nova Scotian archivist, was more cruel than Governor Lawrence for trying to hide these facts. In his history of the Deportation—Le Grand Dérangement—Gaudet, like Casgrain, drew attention to the responsibility of the clique of colonial administrators and particularly that of Lawrence, who was lieutenant-governor of Nova Scotia between 1753 and 1760.

None of the artisans of the Renaissance would, however, come to produce a great original work on Acadie. The response to the works of Nova Scotians Murdoch and Akins and to the American Parkman would come in the lengthy work by Édouard Richard (1844–1904): *Acadia, Missing Links of a Lost Chapter in American History* (1895). The work was published in English in New York, and was addressed to the American public as an explicit reply to the thesis of the great historian of religion in America, Francis Parkman, according to whom the Acadians were themselves responsible for their expulsion because they had broken their neutrality under the direction of French priests. The subtitle "A Lost Chapter in American History," was borrowed from American historian Philip H. Smith (1884) who, beyond the sentimentalism of the verses of *Evangeline*, but also in its wake, had wanted to offer—as the first generation of American Romantic historians had done—a reading that supported the Acadian cause.

The book by Édouard Richard had some impact in American and Anglo-Canadian historiography, which was seen as the national response to the quarrel of historians. But Richard was an Acadian of Quebec origin (born in Plessisville) who lived in western Canada for a long time, very close to the federal political milieus. He was careful to rehabilitate historical Acadie, of which he said he had memories through his family stories, all the while defending the reputation of the British Crown which was then associated with Canadian nationalism.

Though Richard borrowed the "discoveries" and arguments of Casgrain regarding the good faith that Acadians had in the English regime, as well as the responsibility of the local elites in the Deportation, he did considerably soften the implication of English colonial authorities. His cousin, a French Canadian nationalist named Henri d'Arles who lived many years in the United States, in his introduction to the French version destined to a French Canadian public (*Acadie. Reconstitution d'un chapitre perdu de l'histoire d'Amérique*, 1917), thought it useful to modify this interpretation slightly under the pretext that he was correcting the imperfections of the author's written French. The publication revived the debate on the responsibility of the Deportation (British, American, Nova Scotian), and also brought forth the notion that French Canadian nationalists considered Acadians to be a little sentimental in their historical interpretations.

## *Evangeline*: Calling Card or National Heroine?

It should nevertheless be noted that the Acadian nationalist elite showed restraint in their reception and use of *Evangeline* at the time. Only one text of importance from the children of *Evangeline* was directly related to the poem. Written by Philéas Bourgeois for the centennial of the birth of the poet (1907), it was a conference paper of a few pages titled *Henry Wadsworth Longfellow: sa vie, ses œuvres littéraires, son poème Évangéline* (*Longfellow: his life, his literary works and his poem Evangeline*). The text was symptomatic of the ambivalence with which Acadian nationalists of the times received the poem. *Evangeline* was clearly presented by Bourgeois as a foreign work with the great merit of having introduced Acadie to Americans, and by extension, the English-speaking world. Pascal Poirier had said the same thing in his introduction to the book *Origine des Acadiens* (1874): we need to thank *Evangeline* for "having made us known to the world." While the fathers of the Renaissance considered the American tale as a means of recognition, a sort of calling card to be proudly displayed, "I am a child of *Evangeline*," they still recognized the foreign nature of the gaze that fell upon them.

Bourgeois specifically insisted on the Romantic and Christian nature of the work, and in this regard partially distanced himself from the overly activist translation by Pamphile Lemay; he preferred the one published by Henri Gautier in Paris, for "it better grasped the beauty of the original text." Similarly, in his preface to the French translation of *Evangeline* by A. Bollaert, Poirier wrote that Lemay had created "an elegant paraphrase," but that Bollaert was more successful in bringing out the beauty of the poem. Édouard Richard, in his preface to the 1912 edition of Lemay's translation, highlighted that one of the great merits of Longfellow's text was that unlike Harriet Beecher Stowe, author of *Uncle Tom's Cabin*, the poet had managed to avoid "political convulsions." In Richard's words, we can see a criticism of the first versions of Lemay's translation which were deemed overly activist and a call to see value in an interpretation of the work as one that promoted victim and memorial acceptance, far from the "political convulsions." The accusation that *Evangeline* instilled an outright Christian resignation in Acadian nationalism would, as we will see, be frequently borrowed later on.

The children of *Evangeline*, explicitly, speak very little of the poem, except to occasionally recall the short passages of the "delightful" poem by the "great" poet that raised awareness on their cause in the world. During national conventions, it was more common for foreigners (Canadians) to draw attention to the great emotion they felt being in the land of Évangéline. Newspapers, *Le Moniteur acadien* then *L'Évangéline*, published the first editions of the poem—in 1867, *Le Moniteur acadien* published the translation by Pamphile Lemay; in 1887, *L'Évangéline* published the translation by Frenchman A. Bollaert. After this, during almost a century, it sufficed them to periodically reproduce a few short pastiches or parodies of the national heroine often written by foreigners to Acadie. They related the far-reaching echoes of the poem, be it on the occasion of celebrations organized in the United States to commemorate the great poet—and the poem, notably at the centennial of its publication—or to relay the identity development or awakening of Louisiana Acadians, where *Evangeline* also played a central role.

Despite the restraint of the children of *Evangeline*, the poem became an essential element of Acadien culture. Pascal Poirier recounted how, as a young student at St. Joseph's College in the middle of the 1860s, he carried in his jacket, on his heart like an icon, the translation of *Evangeline*. The poem was introduced in the French reader—*French Reading*—distributed in the schools of New Brunswick and Nova Scotia, where a certain level of French teaching had managed to be introduced. The poem was thus known to all Acadian men and women. Acadian girls proudly bore the name of the Grand-Pré virgin. The song "Évangéline" written in 1917 by Father Thaddée Bourque (see lyrics on the following page), which lamented the loss of pastoral Acadie all the while assimilating the pain of Évangéline's lost love to the quest of the country, practically became a national anthem. It was sung in all the Acadian gatherings.

All of these uses, until the first decades of the twentieth century, remained largely patriotic. The neighbouring anglophone communities, as we will see, would be the first to draw on *Evangeline* for promotional, popular, touristic, and folkloric means. *Evangeline* arrived in Acadie like a secondary—perhaps even intellectual—culture, more than popular culture. The poem had a structuring, foundational effect in Acadie before—as most previous analysts have suggested—a sort of popular and quasi-religious devotion. The heroine did not arrive in Acadie as would a pop star; rather, the narrative initially worked to transmit information, and its character would have to wait before becoming a living legend.

The foreign gaze on Acadie, as previously mentioned, strengthened the popular buzz of the poem's arrival. For instance, Ernest Martin, a French professor of English literature, published in 1936 a book titled *L'Évangéline de Longfellow et la suite merveilleuse d'un poème* (*Longfellow's Evangeline and the wonderful afterlife of a poem*). In his opinion, all Acadians worshipped Évangéline, and even wanted her to be canonized a saint. Martin's informer on the canonization project appears to have been an English-speaking teacher from Halifax; we have not found any historical trace of Acadians expressing such a desire. On the whole, the work by Martin sought to demonstrate that the Longfellow's poem was of a great historical truth and that it was received as such by Acadians.

In his *Histoire des Acadiens* (1955), the Quebecker Robert Rumilly reused this same analysis: "[For Acadians,] Évangéline is not a legend, and it is something other than a symbol. It is a historical character who truly existed, that truly suffered and personifies Acadie."[33] Others would go on to say that for Acadians, Évangéline was the equivalent of what the *Song of Roland* or *Joan of Arc* had been for the French: the great narrative of their national epic.

| | |
|---|---|
| **Évangéline** <br> Lyrics: André-Thaddée Bourque | **Evangeline** |
| **Couplet 1** <br> *Je l'avais cru ce rêve du jeune âge* <br> *Qui souriant m'annonçait le bonheur,* <br> *Et confiante en cet heureux présage* <br> *Mes jeunes ans s'écoulaient sans douleur.* <br> *Il est si doux au printemps de la vie* <br> *D'aimer d'amour les amis de son cœur,* <br> *De vivre heureux au sein de la patrie* <br> *Loin du danger à l'abri du malheur. (bis)* | **Verse 1** <br> *I believed in this dream of youth* <br> *It had smiled at me, calling for happiness,* <br> *And, as I trusted it would unfold* <br> *My youth passed by without pain.* <br> *It is so sweet, what life's spring brings,* <br> *To love dearly thy closest friends.* <br> *To live happily in the heart of our nation* <br> *Far from danger and misfortune. (repeat)* |
| **Chœur** <br> *Évangéline, Évangéline!* <br> *Tout chante ici ton noble nom,* <br> *Dans le vallon, sur la colline,* <br> *L'écho répète et nous répond:* <br> *Évangéline, Évangéline!* | **Chorus** <br> *Évangéline, Évangéline!* <br> *Everything here sings your noble name,* <br> *In the valley, on the hill,* <br> *Echoes repeat, answering our cries:* <br> *Évangéline, Évangéline!* |
| **Couplet 2** <br> *Qu'ils étaient beaux ces jours de notre enfance,* <br> *Cher Gabriel, au pays de Grand-Pré,* <br> *Car là régnaient la paix et l'innocence,* <br> *Le noble amour et la franche gaîté!* <br> *Qu'ils étaient doux le soir sous la charmille* <br> *Les entretiens du village assemblé!* <br> *On n'y formait qu'une aimable famille* <br> *Sous ce beau ciel, sous ce ciel adoré! (bis)* | **Verse 2** <br> *How wonderful were the days of our youth,* <br> *Dear Gabriel, in the land of Grand-Pré* <br> *For there ruled peace and innocence,* <br> *Noble love and true happiness!* <br> *How pleasant were the nightly conversations* <br> *Of our people beneath the tree tunnel!* <br> *United we were in one loving family* <br> *Beneath the beautiful blue skies we adored! (repeat)* |

---

33.  In Rumilly's words: "Évangéline [pour les Acadiens] n'est pas une légende, et c'est autre chose qu'un symbole. C'est un personnage historique qui a vraiment vécu, qui a vraiment souffert et incarne l'Acadie."

**Couplet 3**

Là les anciens devisant du ménage,
Avec amour contemplaient leurs enfants,
Qui réveillaient les échos du village
Par leurs refrains et leurs amusements.
La vie alors coulait douce et paisible
Au vieux Grand-Pré, dans notre cher pays,
Lorsque soudain, notre ennemi terrible
Nous abreuva de malheurs inouïs! (bis)

**Couplet 4**

Hélas! depuis sur la terre étrangère
J'erre toujours en proie à la douleur,
Car le destin dans sa sombre colère
M'a tout ravi, mes amis, mon bonheur.
Je ne vois plus l'ami de mon enfance
À qui j'avais juré mon tendre amour,
Mais dans mon cœur je garde l'espérance
De le revoir dans un meilleur séjour. (bis)

**Chœur**

Évangéline, Évangéline!
Tout chante ici ton noble nom,
Dans le vallon, sur la colline,
L'écho répète et nous répond:
Évangéline, Évangéline!

**Verse 3**

There, the old folks chatting with family
Lovingly contemplated their children
And brought life to the echoes of the village
With their choruses and laughter.
Life then was easy and calm
In old Grand-Pré, our beloved country
When suddenly, our terrible enemy
Brought upon us terrible woes and misfortunes! (repeat)

**Verse 4**

Alas! Now from estranged lands
Forever I err, a prey to pain
For destiny, in its dark anger
Stole from me my friends, my happiness.
I no longer see that friend of my childhood
To whom I had sworn my tender love,
But in my heart I keep hoping, that
I will see him again in happier times. (repeat)

**Chorus**

Évangéline, Évangéline!
Everything here sings your noble name,
In the valley, on the hill,
Echoes repeat, answering our cries:
Évangéline, Évangéline!

Excerpt from: André-Thaddée Bourque, *Chez les anciens Acadiens: Causeries du grand-père Antoine*. Moncton, Presses de l'Évangéline, 1911, pp.147–48.

The intellectuals of the Acadian Renaissance were more modest regarding the role of *Evangeline*. The poem drew the eyes of "foreigners," the "others," to the Acadian reality at the risk, as is often the case with recognition by others, of producing a stereotype, a caricature of the people. The men and women of the end of the nineteenth century knew, as we do, how to distinguish between fiction and reality.

The foreigner's gaze was discussed at length in light of the American provenance of the poem, and the agents of the Acadian Renaissance, as previously stated, were well aware of this. It might be useful to recall that it was Father Walsh, the bishop of Halifax of Scottish origin, at the beginning of the Nova Scotian archive crisis, who first called upon Acadians to commemorate the Deportation. In 1881, Father Rogers—who was in a dispute with his subordinate, the "delegate of the little nation" named Father Marcel-François Richard—gave him permission to preach in Saulnierville and urged him to speak of the poem in his address to the inhabitants, for in so doing, he would "honour the nationality that the famous poet Longfellow immortalized in his *Evangeline*."

It was through an interest in the American poet Edgar Allan Poe that the French specialist of American literature, Émile Lauvrière, discovered Longfellow—the literary enemy of Poe—and, consequently, the poem *Evangeline* and the existence of Acadie. In the end, he devoted the better part of his career to producing in the first part of the twentieth century, a monumental work on the "Acadian tragedy." *Evangeline* was therefore much more than the words of foreigners whether American, French Canadian, English from the Maritimes—which was often Scottish or Irish—or French from France…words received in Acadie.

The foreigner's gaze also carried a fatalist image that the character of Évangéline imposed on Acadians. For Longfellow, Acadie was a community of memory, living only through its memory, dead but not forgotten.

*Still stands the forest primeval; but far away from its shadow,*
*Side by side, in their nameless graves, the lovers are sleeping.*
*Under the humble walls of the little Catholic churchyard,*
*In the heart of the city, they lie, unknown and unnoticed.*

*Evangeline*, original verses by Longfellow

Acadie was a dead society, or at the very least, it was too broken to claim to be a nation, according to French Canadian nationalists (some of whom still believe this to this day). The fatalistic image project by foreigners did however echo a partial truth that was considered as such in the Acadian collective imaginary: fragility. Let us recall the words of Philéas Bourgeois at the 1881 Convention: Acadie "forever bears the scars of a great wound. She was destined to be the land of Évangéline."[34] Despite the

---

34. "dans les plans de Dieu, l'Acadie devait peut-être porter pour toujours les cicatrices d'une grande plaie. Elle devait être la terre d'Évangéline."

triumphant word, the children of *Evangeline* noticed that the program outlined by Rameau had its failures. Acadie was not, and would never be, the province of Quebec. Acadians were destined to be a minority and the dream of a nation would forever remain a dream. Assimilation was eroding its borders. In Nova Scotia and Prince Edward Island, the numbers were decreasing. The colonization strategies implemented in New Brunswick managed to consolidate the space of a nation, but the populations remained largely poor, uneducated, and at the mercy of an English-speaking capitalism. The fight for French Catholic schools was a failure.

Some persons of note managed to hold public office, though it was often acquired in exchange for a co-optation that weakened Acadian activism. When Poirier was twenty-one years old, he was appointed to a position at the Canadian Parliament, and in 1885 when he was only thirty-four, he became a senator in Ottawa—to represent Acadie, by all accounts. His involvement in federal politics meant that he was distanced from the cultural battleground. At one point he was even forced to give up the presidency of the National Society (1904–13), giving into the pressures of the Irish clergy who considered him too involved.

Pierre-Amand Landry was an important provincial minister, but the position of prime minister was unattainable because of his identity, despite the compromises that he accepted to make, notably concerning matters of education. Father Richard complained in 1879 of the lowliness of the gains in the "French department" of the "Acadian" minister. "They are getting us to swallow the pill with jam,"[35] he said begrudgingly. Still young, Pierre-Amand Landry traded politics for a position as a judge, thus distancing himself from turbulence. The battle raged on in the Church, and it was only there that Acadie acquired its true autonomy. But in the north, far from Grand-Pré, the poem always drew Acadie back to the memory of its past…"dead, but not forgotten."

*Evangeline* was, then, always in a relational position. It was the gaze of the other—of the foreigner—on the Acadians, and at the same time it was an integral part of their identity. There was a rift between the

---

35.    In Father Richard's words: "On s'efforce de faire avaler la pilule au moyen de confitures."

antiquarian work on memory of the first Acadian intellectuals—the intellectual contribution of Poirier was his *Glossaire du parler acadien* (*Glossary of Spoken Acadian*), and that of Gaudet was his *Généalogie des familles acadiennes* (*Genealogy of Acadian Families*)—and the conviction with which they spoke at the national conventions, proclaiming the strong future of the nation. There was a tension, an abysmal distance perhaps, between the projected image of Acadie and the image interiorized by Acadians, the pathos of a society that would never be—the land of *Evangeline* forever bore "the scars of a great wound," as emphasized by Bourgeois—and the project of a society established by Rameau—the Acadie nation—incarnated in the figure of Father Richard to create a new Acadie, farther north.

The first affirmation referred to Acadie as a victim, that of the memory, unable to immerse itself into the world; the second referred to an ascending Acadie, which had the pretension of every great nation of the world to become a society. *Évangéline* provided them with the reason for the incapacity, Rameau the reason for hope. And yet they were inseparable, the project of building a society in Acadie had no other roots than that of creating what Longfellow claimed to have been lost: Acadie.

## *Evangeline* settles once again in Grand-Pré

This tension, between "Évangéline" as seen by the other and "Évangéline" as appropriation, or Acadianization, can still be retraced in the events of the beginning of the twentieth century that led to the development of a memorial park in Grand-Pré.

After the period of turmoil and denial that had accompanied the publication of the poem in Nova Scotia and the disclosure by Akins of the archives of Nova Scotia, the anglophone elites reconciled with the narrative of the American poet. The thing was that Nova Scotia had rapidly become a place of Romantic tourism, particularly for Americans, but also English Canadians. *Evangeline* was the first film produced in Canada, in 1912, by The Canadian Bioscope Company established in Halifax (there are no remaining copies of the film). "Acadia," "Nova

Scotia," "Longfellow," and the country of *Evangeline* blended together to produce the image of pastoral country of Arcadie.

As soon as 1859, at the same time Acadians were learning through the work of Rameau that they had survived a deportation, the American naturalist Frederick S. Cozzens published in New York a travel narrative on Nova Scotia titled *Acadia or a Month With the Blue Noses*. Travel narratives recalling the bucolic *Arcadia* as well as novels set in "The Land of Évangéline" began to multiply. Still in 1859, when the train arrived in the old region of Grand-Pré (Horton), a long banner awaited visitors with the following inscription: "Welcome to the Land of Gabriel and Évangéline." The company had chosen, as an image for its business, the already famed painting by the English painter Thomas Faed, representing the Romantic image of the heroine in a cemetery. "Written their story stands on tablets of stone in the church yards." And, in 1869, when the company extended its service to the old capital of French Acadie, Port-Royal now named Annapolis, the new locomotives were named in honour of Longfellow: "Évangéline," "Gabriel," "Gaspereau," "Hiawatha," and "Grand-Pré."

The examples were endless, and at the end of the nineteenth century and beginning of the twentieth, *Evangeline* became a sought-after branding among anglophone populations located near the old French Bay. In 1893, the steamboat *Evangeline* crossed the Minas Basin, while the Ganong company across the bay in anglophone New Brunswick, printed the heroine's face on their chocolates. For the celebration of the four-hundredth anniversary of the foundation of French Acadie (1604–1904), the company produced a one hundred-kilogram chocolate sculpture of Évangéline. In 1896, novelist Carrie Jenkins Harris published a novel, *A Modern Evangeline*, which attested to the popularity of Longfellow's heroine among English-speaking Nova Scotians at the end of the nineteenth century. Harris humorously summarized the frenzy by describing the little town of Wolfville a few kilometres away from the old village of Grand-Pré where Harris was born.

*There is the cutest little steamer up in Wolfville! I think she is called the 'Evangeline.' By the way, 'most everything is named Evangeline around here. The place might well be called the 'Land of Evangeline.'*

*There is Evangeline Hall, Evangeline Beach, Evangeline Hotel, and hundreds of other Evangelines too numerous to mention.*

*A Modern Evangeline,* original text by Harris (1896, p. 8)

All of this was taking place in the absence and indifference of Acadians. They did take part in the commemoration and were in tune with the monumental spirit of the turn of the twentieth century. Since the middle of the previous century, massive Catholic churches could be seen across the landscape of poor villages, which contrasted greatly with the rustic nature of Protestant churches. Following the death of Father Lefebvre, founder of Saint-Joseph college, a building—Monument Lefebvre (1897)—was erected in his name, then a statue sculpted by Philippe Hébert, an artist who played an important role in the construction of the statue of Évangéline in Grand-Pré, as we will see later on. With its monuments, Memramcook—the place where the first national convention had been orchestrated—with its college and its peculiar status as the one of the only original settlements that had not been destroyed in the wake of the 1755 deportation, was becoming the symbolic capital of the new Acadie. In 1912, on the eve of his death, the valiant Father Richard was build- ing, in his colonial parish of Rogersville, a monument to *Notre-Dame de L'Assomption* (Our Lady of the Assumption).

Acadian leaders, being too busy marking the territory of the new Acadie, did not demonstrate much interest in the commemoration of the places of old French Acadie until the 1920s. Along with the poem, Grand-Pré and the event of the Deportation had evidently taken a central role in the Acadian collective imaginary. But the Acadie from before 1755, to borrow the lyrics from André-Thaddée Bourque's song, corresponded more to a "dream of youth" (rêve du jeune âge), a golden time that, like in the beginning of Longfellow's poem, did not refer to a specific physical space. Pastor Brown had noticed this as soon as the end of the eighteenth century, Thomas Haliburton had repeated it in the middle of the nine- teenth century, and Lionel Groulx—this time taking offence—repeated it at the beginning of the twentieth century: Acadians did not have specific demands regarding their old territory.

This apparent ambivalence could have stemmed from a healthy form of realism…maybe. These lands and settlements, as we have seen, after having been destroyed and distributed to Planters—Anglo Protestant settlers from New England—had been redesigned and most villages and landscapes had been renamed. "Naught but tradition remains of the beautiful village of Grand-Pré" had written Longfellow, "another race, with other customs and language" had settled there permanently. This country was now Anglo Protestant. The new Acadie, Rameau had noted, had migrated north, and that was where it should expand. Grand-Pré and the landscape of old Acadie were therefore not the place where the new Acadie would spontaneously impose its monumental presence. What is more, Acadian leaders were very careful not to escalate their exchanges with the anglophone majority. They used with moderation, at least when they spoke to the "others," the explosive charge that was the Acadian memory.

We can now understand why Acadian leaders may have seemed indifferent when initially invited to transform Grand-Pré into a high place of national memory. According to Placide Gaudet, in 1894 Acadian leaders received a proposal from John Frederic Herbin to participate in the erection of a monument on the old territory of Grand-Pré in honour of Longfellow's contribution. The statue would be one of an all-republican Évangéline holding above her head a shield with an effigy of Longfellow and wrapped in an American flag. It would be the grateful homage of Acadians to Longfellow and the United States of America. The Acadian leaders showed little interest, and the project was abandoned. Herbin later expressed his disappointment to Placide Gaudet.

John Frederic Herbin did not give up. He was an influential public figure in the small town of Wolfville that bordered the old Acadian Grand-Pré—he was the mayor of the town for two years. He claimed to be of Acadian origin—his mother was Acadian and his father was a French Protestant—though he did not speak the language—French—nor did he practise the religion—Catholic. He had a personal dedication to his ancestors. An occasional poet, Herbin praised the beauty of the land of Grand-Pré as Longfellow had done before him. In 1907, he convinced a few notables from Wolfville to purchase in trust and to transform into a memorial site the lands where the old St. Charles church had once been. This was the church in which Lieutenant-Colonel Winslow had imprisoned the inhabitants and which had become famous thanks to the descriptions of Longfellow.

Even though the province of Nova Scotia recognized the area as a historical site the following year in 1908, Herbin did not succeed in rousing sufficient interest nor leveraging the funds required to develop the land. He built a cross made of stones from an old French cemetery—Herbin's cross remains to this day on the site—and that was all. By 1916, a little tired, he sold the property to the railway company, Dominion Atlantic Railway (DAR), which served the route near Grand-Pré and which, through Halifax, connected to the rest of Canada, and through Yarmouth, connected to the New England ferries. Despite this setback, Herbin remained faithful to his mother's ancestors. In the transaction with the railway company, he insisted on adding a note in the contract that ensured the company would give a parcel of the land to Acadians so that they could build a monument, a church, and so on, to pay tribute to their ancestors.

The company supported this addendum. It had itself recently been sold to one of the two major Canadian players, the Canadian Pacific Railway, and CP wanted to develop along its lines a series of historical tourist attractions. Grand-Pré would be one of them. The company reached out to the Acadian leaders to give them a small lot of land located in front of the planned train station and hotel, and parallel to the old road where the Acadians had marched in procession toward the ships, they would build a small church. The church would be financed by and remain the property of the *Société nationale de l'Assomption* the organization created during the great conventions and representing Acadians. In so doing, the railway company found a way to finance a part of its historical park. With the new church acting as a landmark, the site would attract French Canadian nationalists to the land of Évangéline, adding to the Anglo-American tourists who already visited the area.

The Acadian leaders were aware of the mercantile nature of the project and that the memory which was projected unto the site was not entirely theirs. This was especially the case since the company had decided to put an imposing statue of Évangéline on the same lot, in front of the projected church. The statue was commissioned to a French Canadian artist, Henri Hébert, and inspired from a terracotta created by his father Louis-Philippe Hébert. Henri Hébert was well known among Quebec sculptors; he had recently created a statue of Madeleine de Verchères on the banks of the St. Lawrence River in Verchères, and a more modest one of Father Lefebvre in Memramcook.

The Héberts were a family of Quebecers of Acadian descent. A family rumour even claimed that one of their ancestors, Étienne Hébert, had found his fiancée in Quebec many years after his return from exile in Baltimore. His travels were said to the source of the inspiration for Longfellow's poem. Napoléon Bourassa, the author of *Jacques et Marie* (1866), a novel that was central to the French Canadian reception of *Évangéline*, was said to have shaped the Hébert family artistically. Hébert's statue of Évangéline was imbued with the French Canadian narrative: a woman standing proudly, arched, with her head turned back, looking at her lost country. Placide Gaudet later said in 1920 that the "attitude" of the statue meant to represent "Évangéline crying as she leaves the country that she will never see again and casting a painful glance behind her." She was inspired from the phrase "pleurant le pays perdu" ("crying over the lost country").

But this phrase did not exist in the poem. The formulation was less prosaic. In the work by Longfellow, the Acadian women who brought food to their loved ones imprisoned in the church struggled on, "Pausing and looking back to gaze once more on their dwellings." In the translation by Pamphile Lemay, the "dwellings" became a village: "Et puis, de temps en temps, elles s'arrêtaient toutes—Pour regarder encore une dernière fois— Le clocher de l'église et leurs modestes toits—Et leurs paisibles champs et leur joli village."[36] For the Hébert and Gaudet alike, this last time looking back meant contemplating a "lost country."

---

36. Translator's note: In English, this passage from Lemay's *Évangéline* (1870) would read as follows: "And, every now and then, they [the women] all stopped / To look again one last time at / The church steeple and their modest roofs / And their peaceful fields and their lovely village."

It was not the statue that bothered the Acadians. After all, the image that it projected was not that different from their own memory, other than the fact that in their narrative, Évangéline did finally see the lost country in the end. It was the attitude of the company and the ambiguity of building a memorial site on Anglo Protestant soil. In 1920, the inauguration of the statue took place without a single representative from the Acadian society. The ceremony was organized by the railway company, in English only, before a panel of journalists from the Commonwealth who were visiting from Canada. In full Canadian "nation-building" mode, the railway took the opportunity to praise the merits of the coexistence of nationalities and the integration of Canada in the British Empire.

*L'Évangéline*—not the character imagined by Longfellow, nor the statue, but the Acadian newspaper that had borrowed the heroine's name since 1887—was offended. "An imperialized Évangéline" ("*Une Évangéline impérialisée*") ran the editorial headline. One of its readers, Father F. Léger, fuelled the debate a few days later by writing that he "wondered whether the president of the C. P. R. or another would show up sometime to plant, in front of the statue of Évangéline, a bronze of the famous Lawrence or of the unjust Winslow."[37]

The Acadian leaders did not make much of the event. The fact was that the railway company had an agreement with the Acadian committee in charge of the Grand-Pré lot with whom it was negotiating the land owner-ship transfer. It had been determined that the inauguration of the statue and the official donation of the land would take place in 1920 at Grand-Pré on the occasion of the eighth Acadian Convention. But the Acadian elite cancelled the convention, giving as an official reason that their president, Pascal Poirier, was too ill to attend. In their negotiations with the railway company, the Acadians had insisted that the monument they would erect would be a real church, not a museum, and that they could hold conven-tions and gatherings on the land. They wanted the Grand-Pré site to be a memorial in honour of their French Catholic ancestors. They were thus

---

37. In Léger's words: "[se] demandant si le président du C. P. R. ou autre ne viendra pas quelqu'un de ces jours, planter, en face de la statue d'Évangéline, un bronze du fameux Lawrence ou de l'inique Winslow."

uncomfortable with the railway company's goal to make it a tourist park solely in memory of the poem and the great American poet.

The Acadian leaders might also have been afraid of negative reactions from the Anglo Protestant communities of Horton and Wolfville regarding a festive return of Acadians to Grand-Pré. They adopted an attitude that began to be noticed at the time, and that they would be criticized for in contemporary times: that of an excessive complacency toward the negative reactions of the anglophones. Marking these events, the newspaper *L'Évangéline* critiqued the servile attitude, which could be described as "colonized" nowadays, of some Acadian leaders who always needed to recall, through references to the Deportation, its loyalty to the Dominion of Canada and the British Empire.

In any case, the Acadian Convention took place the following year, with the notable absence of Pascal Poirier, but in less hostile territory, in an Acadian cluster about one hundred kilometres south from there, in Pointe-de-l'Église (Church Point), in the Baie Sainte-Marie area. The convention kicked off a vast national campaign for subscriptions that would finance the construction of a church in Grand-Pré on the land that had been transferred by the railway company and on which they "compulsorily" needed to spend ten thousand dollars. They had also obtained permanent rights to use the entire area of the memorial park for patriotic ceremonies. Senator Poirier of the faraway federal capital, in Ottawa, wrote to the delegates with this explanation: "What of the form, be it train station or sumptuous hotel, that will take the monument they will build next to ours? Each people knows what suits them best. Our own monument will be a commemorative chapel, where we shall piously communion with the souls of the exiled who were our ancestors."[38]

The 1921 convention included a solemn one-day round trip to Grand-Pré, to confirm that Acadians were taking possession of the land. The following year, they returned with more assurance—in a sort of procession of more than two thousand pilgrims—to assist to the blessing of

---

38. In Poirier's words: "Qu'importe la forme, gare de chemin de fer, ou hôtel somptueux, que prenne le monument qui sera érigé à côté du nôtre? Chaque peuple sait ce qui lui convient. Notre monument à nous sera une chapelle commémorative, où nous viendrons pieusement communier avec les âmes des proscrits qui furent nos aïeuls."

the cornerstone of the church led by Acadian Bishop Édouard Alfred Le Blanc—assumed grandson of notary LeBlanc, the one who had presided over Évangéline and Gabriel's engagement ceremony. "The son of the outcast, the Moses of the Acadian people, has come to bless the cornerstone of the second temple of Grand-Pré, erected over the foundation of the ruined temple,"[39] affirmed Father Thomas Albert in the sermon he prepared for the event.

In reality, the church of Grand-Pré would never be consecrated by the Catholic Church. It remained a commemorative monument in recognition of the Deportation of Acadians. But the children of Évangéline—they were an aging generation by then; Grand-Pré would be one of their final contributions—perceived this transmission of memory as a victory. Placide Gaudet, who had been asked to write a book titled *Le Grand Dérangement*, with profits invested into the construction of the church, spoke of this convention where Acadians returned to Grand-Pré with Évangéline as the convention of the "great arrangement" (*"grand arrangement,"* which rhymed with *"Dérangement"*).

For the children of Évangéline, the gesture represented a hijacking of Évangéline the American to benefit Évangéline the Acadian. The church of Grand-Pré would soon host the symbols of the nation that Rameau had recommended they build. In 1923, they placed a statue of the patron saint, Notre-Dame de l'Assomption, and later a cross on the beach described in the poem as the place of embarkment, then came charts recalling the Deportation and plaques in the church where would forever be engraved, as on the tablets of stone, the names of the deported families.

\* \* \*

Nowadays if you visit Grand-Pré, the memorial park is dedicated to the Acadian society that developed there before 1755. The references to Évangéline and Longfellow—who is entitled to a modest bust at the entrance of the park that was given by the government of Nova Scotia in

---

39.  In Father Albert's words: "Le fils du proscrit, le Moïse du peuple acadien, vient bénir la pierre angulaire du second temple de Grand-Pré, élevé sur les assises du temple ruiné."

1955—are demonstrably timid. But the statue of Évangéline still reigns majestically in front of the memorial church, and it is for her that visitors come to the site. The statue of Notre-Dame de l'Assomption has not eclipsed that of Évangéline. As for the surrounding landscape, it is still anglophone, far from the new Acadie that spread out farther north to those areas where the upheavals of the wars of the 1750s had pushed its inhabitants.

# References

BOURGEOIS, Philéas-Frédéric. "Évangéline." Conference presentation in celebration of the centennial of the birth date of Longfellow in Moncton, Shédiac, Typographie du *Moniteur acadien*, 27 February 1907, 22 p.

BRUCHESI, Jean. *Rameau de Saint-Père et les Français d'Amérique*. Montreal, Les Éditions des dix, 1950.

CLARK, Patrick D. "Rameau de Saint-Père, Moïse de l'Acadie?" *Journal of Canadian Studies/ Revue d'études canadiennes*, n° 28, summer 1993, p. 69-95.

DOUCET, Camille-Antonio. *Une étoile s'est levée en Acadie: Marcel-François Richard*. Rogersville, Les éditions du Renouveau, 1973.

FARAGHER, John Mack. *A Great and Noble Scheme*. New York, W.W. Norton & Company, 2005.

GAUDET, Placide. "Généalogie des familles acadiennes." Rapport des archives canadiennes, vol. 2, 1905, Ottawa, C. H. Parmelee, 1909.

GAUDET, Placide. *Le Grand Dérangement: Sur qui retombe la responsabilité de l'Expulsion des Acadiens*. Ottawa, Ottawa Printing, 1922.

GRIFFITHS, Naomi, E. S. "Longfellow's Évangéline. The Birth and Acceptance of a Legend." *Acadiensis*, vol. 11, no 2, spring 1982, p. 28-41.

GRIFFITHS, Naomi, E. S. *The Acadians: Creation of a People*. Toronto, McGraw-Hill Ryerson Limited, 1973.

HARRIS, Carrie Jenkins. *A Modern Évangéline*. Windsor, J.J. Anslow Printer, 1896.

LEBLANC, Barbara. *Postcards from Acadie*. Kentville, Gaspereau Press, 2003.

LEBLANC, Ronnie-Gilles. "Du dérangement des guerres au grand Dérangement: la longue évolution du concept." *Du Grand dérangement à la Déportation, Nouvelles perspectives historiques*, R.-G. Leblanc (ed.), Chaire d'études acadiennes, Moncton, p.11-20.

MAILHOT, Raymond. *Prise de conscience collective acadienne au Nouveau-Brunswick (1860-1891) et comportement de la majorité anglophone*. Doctoral dissertation in history, Université de Montréal, 1973.

MAILLET, Marguerite. *Histoire de la littérature acadienne*. Moncton, Les Éditions d'Acadie, 1983.

MARTIN, Ernest. *L'Évangéline de Longfellow et la suite merveilleuse d'un poème*. Paris, Hachette, 1936.

PLESSIS, Mgr Joseph-Octave. "Le journal des visites pastorales en Acadie de Mgr Joseph-Octave Plessis, 1811-1812-1815." *Cahiers de la Société historique acadienne*, vol. 11, n° 1-2-3 (mars-septembre 1980), p. 11-311.

POIRIER, Pascal. "Des Acadiens déportés à Boston en 1755. Un épisode du Grand Dérangement." *Mémoires de la Société royale du Canada*, 1908, section 1, p. 125-180.

POIRIER, Pascal. *Le père Lefebvre et l'Acadie*. Montreal, C. O. Beauchemin & fils, 1898.

POIRIER, Pascal. *Les Acadiens à Philadelphie, suivi de Accordailles de Gabriel et d'Évangéline*. Les Éditions d'Acadie [1875], 1998.

POIRIER, Pascal. *Origine des Acadiens*. Montreal, E. Sénécal, 1874.

RAMEAU de Saint-Père, François-Edme. *La France aux colonies: Études sur le développement de la race française hors de l'Europe. Les Français en Amérique. Acadiens et Canadiens,* Paris, A. Jouby, libraire-éditeur, 1859, 2 vol.

RAMEAU de Saint-Père, François-Edme. *Une colonie féodale en Amérique: L'Acadie 1604-1881.* Paris, Librairie Plon, Montreal, Granger frères, 1889, 2 vol.

RICHARD, Édouard. "Préface," in Pamphile Lemay, *Évangéline et Autres Poèmes de Longfellow.* Montreal, J.-Alfred Guay, 1912, p. 7-15.

RICHARD, Édouard. *Acadie. Reconstitution d'un chapitre perdu de l'histoire d'Amérique.* Quebec, Published and corrected by Henri d'Arles, Typ. J.-A. K.-Laflamme, 1921.

ROBIDOUX, Ferdinand J. (editor), *Conventions nationales des Acadiens. Recueil des travaux et délibérations des six premières conventions,* vol. 1, Shédiac, Imprimerie du *Moniteur acadien,* 1907.

ROSS, Rita. *Évangéline: an Acadian Heroine in Elite, Popular and Folk Culture.* Doctoral dissertation in anthropology, Berkeley, University of California, 1993.

RUDIN, Ronald. *Remembering and Forgetting in Acadie.* Toronto, University of Toronto Press, 2009.

THÉRIAULT, Léon. "L'Acadie de 1763 à 1900, synthèse historique." *L'Acadie des Maritimes. Études thématiques des débuts à nos jours.* Moncton, Chaire d'études acadiennes, Université de Moncton, 1993, p. 1-43.

THÉRIAULT, Léon. "L'acadianisation de l'Église catholique en Acadie, 1763-1953." Jean Daigle (ed.), *Les Acadiens des Maritimes: études thématiques.* Moncton, Université de Moncton (CEA), 1980, p. 293-369.

TRÉPANIER, Pierre. "Rameau de Saint-Père et Proudhon." *Les Cahiers des dix,* no. 45, 1990, p. 169-191.

TRÉPANIER, Pierre et Lise. "Rameau de Saint-Père et le métier d'historien." *RHAF,* vol. 33, Dec. 1979, p. 331-35.

VIAU, Robert. *Les visages d'Évangéline. Du poème au mythe.* Longueuil, MNH, 1998.

VIAU, Robert. *Grand-Pré. Lieu de mémoire, Lieu d'appartenance.* Longueuil, MNH, 2005.

# ÉVANGÉLINE THE SECOND

*Évangéline the first, they deported her to the sout'. An' she stayed there.*
*Well then as for us, I came back through the woods, on foot, for ten*
*years. And us I rebuilt.*

—Antonine Maillet, *Évangéline Deusse*

## Anti-*Evangeline* Anger

In the fall of 1969, the Quebec cultural magazine *Liberté* gave way to the
new Acadian ideologues and artists. Its pages featured a text by a filmmaker
and poet—the pioneer of Acadian documentary film—Léonard Forest,
who had just travelled to the islands of the ancient Acadian people, from
Belle-Île-en-Mer on the coast of Brittany in France to St. Martinville in
Acadian Louisiana, including, of course, Acadia of the Maritimes. He was
preparing a film, an inventory of the situation after two hundred years of
settlement, of these "new Acadies": *Les Acadiens de la Dispersion* (ONF,
1968). His text is entitled *Évangeline qui es-tu?*

Forest starts on these sentences: "Évangéline wears a miniskirt badly.
Her glance is turned toward the past. She weeps at length for a lost homeland. Standing stoically in Grand-Pré, Nova Scotia, and sitting inconsolably
in St. Martinville, Louisiana, Évangéline broods over happiness that ended
in a nightmare."[40] And concludes with this wish: "Perhaps we should now
let Évangéline, who has travelled a lot, sleep."

40. "Évangéline porte mal la mini-jupe. Son regard est tourné vers le passé. Elle pleure longue-
ment une patrie perdue. Debout et stoïque à Grand-Pré (Nouvelle-Écosse), assise et in-
consolable à Saint-Martinville (Louisiane), Évangéline rumine un bonheur qui s'est terminé
en cauchemar." Forest, *Les Acadiens de la Dispersion*

175

Forest puts on white gloves to attack *Evangeline*. He recalls, by borrowing Ernest Martin's work title, *Les suites merveilleuses d'un poème* (1936), how *Evangeline* provided a structure for Acadians to recognize themselves in a "poetic and mythical" place. The next generation will not show such decency to *Evangeline*—Forest was born in 1928, he is not of the contesting generation of the 1960s. "The violence," he insists, "with which a part of the current youth denies his sweet Évangéline betrays the significance she had in the prehistory of the contemporary Acadia."

Indeed, the youth of the 1960s is iconoclastic. The anti-*Evangeline* anger was to come from all sides. The references to the foreign, American origin of its author multiplied. Évangéline projects a victimizing vision of Acadia, making it an object of folklore. As a Romantic character, she has nothing to do with the harsh reality experienced by Acadians and particularly Acadian women. Incipient feminism would add to this, seeing her as the servile image of the procreative mother that the clergy wanted to instill in Acadian women, the famous *revanche des berceaux* ("revenge of the cradles"), and yet Évangéline never had children. What's more, she would have become a laughable commercial object, as the Acadian singer from Prince Edward Island, Angèle Arsenault, proclaimed in a popular song of the 1970s:

**Évangéline Acadian Queen**
Lyrics: Angèle Arsenault

*I'm going to tell you about someone you know*
*Yes, but make no mistake, she's not from the States*
*Even though a particular fellow named Longfellow*
*Popularized her two hundred years ago*
*Her name was Évangéline, she was really, really nice*
*She loved Gabriel on earth as in heaven*
*They lived in Acadia, they were made of money*
*But one day, the English were not satisfied*
*So they deported them, Gabriel disappeared*
*Disheartened, Évangéline looked for him as long as she could*

*She looked for him in Acadia, in Quebec, in Ontario*
*An' in the United States, in Florida, in Idaho*
*Arrived in Louisiana with her cousin Diane*

*Said now I won't misspend my time*
*She was seventy-five years old*

*Hired at the hospital, she was taking care of the sick*
*Then she saw her Gabriel leaving for heaven*
*Jumped at his neck*
*Told him thank you very much*
*Now that you're buried I can go back*
*I'm going to invest in the companies of the future*
*So that the name of Évangéline will be hella known*

*Évangéline Fried Clams*
*Évangéline Salon Bar*
*Évangéline Sexy Ladies wear*
*Évangéline Comfortable Running Shoes*
*Évangéline Automobile Springs*
*Évangéline Regional High School*
*Évangéline Savings Mortgage and Loans*

*Évangéline the only French newspaper in New Brunswick*
*Évangéline Acadian Queen*

The myth calling is a reminder of the inability of the previous century "elites" to propose a bold program, one that stuck with the living Acadia. Évangéline is a passive figure—she would have accepted the Deportation in a very Christian resignation—which was used to legitimize the Acadian "elites'" age-old fear of confrontation and their willingness to compromise, understood here as "compromission," with the anglophones. The use of the term "elite" to refer to the Renaissance artisans underlines the distance that the youth want to establish with them: "They are not our fathers," "we refuse the legacy."

Besides, the attack against *Evangeline* is only the tip of the iceberg. Because, as Forest says in his farewell to *Evangeline*, this anti-*Evangeline* violence is ultimately an attack against the Acadian reference. "Ultimately, it is not Évangéline that Acadia contests, but itself." In 1966, the Acadian youth gathered in a large assembly, le Ralliement de la jeunesse acadienne (the Acadian Youth Rally), which was intended to be the youthful counterpart of the great national conventions, proposed to put away in the sheds of history—the expression used is "in Acadia's folklore"—all the panoply of national symbols developed in the previous century during the *Evangeline* moment: national patroness, national holiday, national anthem, flag. On the Memramcook hill where the *Ralliement* took place, the mythical place of the century rebirth that had just ended, the young Acadians made a symbolic descent of the flag.

The youths' reproach to these symbols is that they no longer represent them—nor have they ever represented them, vectors of development and identity—that they do not reflect the pluralistic character of modern society, and that they unduly associate religion and nationalism. The word "Acadia" itself is questioned. They prefer the name "Francophone from Nouveau-Brunswick." The Acadian reference, they claim, is a reference that closes itself off from the "other"; this other being indiscriminately, according to the speakers, the Maritime francophones whose ancestors were not Acadians, or the Maritime anglophones and, in particular, the French Canadians. Moreover, in the province of Quebec, the latter is preparing to reject the "French-Canadian" reference and adopt the "Quebecois" one. It is time for openness, for anti-*Evangeline* anger, for anger against oneself.

## The Reference Tilts

Two books give a good account of this disillusionment, violence, and anger toward the old reference elaborated in the previous century. They come from two different places, which are like the two sources of the violent storm that hit Acadian nationalism at the time and that made *Evangeline* waver on its foundation. The first is Jean-Paul Hautecœur's *L'Acadie du discours* (1975), the second, *L'Acadie perdue* (1978) by Michel Roy. Both books explain how the anti-*Evangeline* anger was rooted in a much deeper wave, a rejection of the reference, the anger against oneself.

Jean-Paul Hautecœur's *L'Acadie du discours* (1975) is a scholarly study, originally a doctoral dissertation, on four bodies of writing covering the period from 1955 to 1971. These include the work of the Société historique acadienne, founded in Moncton in 1960; the Société nationale des Acadiens (SNA) which, from 1957 onward, replaced the old Société nationale l'Assomption, an organization that had emerged from the previous end-of-the-century conventions and was perceived as the guardian of the Acadian reference; the *Ralliement de la jeunesse acadienne* of 1966, of which we have just said a few words; and, finally, "neo-nationalism" which would have begun with the student protests at the University of Moncton, particularly the strike of 1968. In short, Hautecœur's study is an analysis of the discourses of Acadian society at a pivotal moment in its development, the turn of the 1960s.

Jean-Paul Hautecœur is of French origin but was a professor of sociology at the newly created University of Moncton in the late 1960s. The University of Moncton was born (1963) from an amalgamation of the three Catholic colleges (universities) that Acadian New Brunswick equipped itself with over the years, Collège Saint-Joseph (Memramcook, 1864), Collège Sacré-Coeur (Caraquet, Bathurst, 1899), and Collège Saint-Louis (Edmundston, 1946). The new institution is public—the amalgamation was created under the aegis of the provincial government—and is located in Moncton, in an urban setting, some thirty kilometres from the site of Father Lefebvre's former college in Memramcook. It embodies Acadian modernity. Students vaguely inspired by the student revolts of the 1960s— May '68 uprisings on American campuses—were quick to experiment.

Student unrest broke out, targeting the university administration, which was considered backward and complacent with political power; North American imperialism, which had relegated the Acadians to a state of underdevelopment worthy of third-world countries; the English-speaking leaders of the city of Moncton, who were resistant to the presence of this French-speaking youth in their midst; and, finally, the Acadian elite and its backward-looking reference system, which, according to the students, was responsible for maintaining all of its alienation. During this period of unrest (1968–69), a march to demand French-language services from the City of Moncton turned into a confrontation with the mayor, and a student strike against the underfunding of the French university was followed by an occupation of the university's premises that required police intervention. These events will be the subject of a film, *Acadie, l'Acadie?!?* (1971), directed by Quebec filmmakers Michel Brault and Pierre Perrault, which gave them an even more symbolic impact.

Such agitation was not usual in Acadia, a society whose leaders had erected "prudence" and "adherence" as virtues historically responsible for its survival. Évangéline embodied precisely this figure of submission that was all the more acceptable to the anglophone authorities because she—Évangéline—was also part of their cultural imagination. The university administration thought it was helpful at the time to attribute such behaviour to foreign influences, particularly those present in the sociology department, where three French cooperative professors were teaching, notably Jean-Paul Hautecœur. The department was closed because of its teachers' incompetence, sending the agitators, including Hautecœur, but also Camille Richard, the young Acadian recruit and inspiration for the 1966 Ralliement de la jeunesse, on to other matters.

Hautecœur and his colleagues had undoubtedly been involved in the rising anger of students at the fledgling university. They had been, in a way, the ideologues, although the multiplicity of protest registers made it impossible to attribute this anger to a single source. To hold them responsible for such agitation was to give a lot of weight to the influence of a few professors and very little to the structural upheavals that Acadia was then undergoing. Hautecœur left for Quebec City to complete his doctoral thesis under the Quebec sociologist Fernand Dumont, a great specialist in the Quebec reference. He will try to understand—with great empathy for the students' words, much less for those of the notables—the protagonists' discourse of which he had been both a stakeholder and a victim.

It was dispelling a myth that Acadian youth had revolted, Hautecœur finally concluded in *L'Acadie du discours*. Of course, all societies are built around a particular mythical account of their origin. But Acadia would have remained at the stage of the myth, of the word, without succeeding in clinging to some tangible realities. "Acadia had only the creative force of the words of its rhetoricians and priests to impose its existence on the world. It tried to preserve churches and classical colleges to perpetuate her word. Against the aggression of the fact, its only weapon was its value."[41] A myth

41. "L'Acadie elle n'eut que la force créatrice de la parole de ses rhéteurs et de ses prêtres pour imposer au monde son existence. Elle s'efforçait de conserver églises et collèges classiques pour perpétuer sa parole. Contre l'agression du fait, sa seule arme était la valeur."

that has prevented Acadia from becoming a society. Hautecœur has little regard for the institutions built in New Brunswick in the previous century, in the wake of the reference invention. These institutions would have been no more than a pretext for the perpetuation of power by word that was continually forced to re-edit the myth in the absence of social foundations.

This is what happened, Hautecœur believes, when, starting in 1955, Acadian nationalist elites wanted to modernize the reference by proposing to (re)found the old national society (Société Nationale l'Assomption). They were unable to present a realistic program, adapted to modern society, and were forced to re-edit the myth. The same thing happened to the ideological historians studied in the *Cahiers* of the Société historique acadienne (Acadian Historical Society): they had to dive back into the Deportation myth as "Longfellow had helped to define it." Because "Acadia is not a society," it is only a myth.

Paradoxically, the militant Acadian youth found itself in a similar dilemma. Its anger against the old reference did not find Acadian places to anchor itself. It had to conclude that its own society did not exist. In the same magazine issue where Forest made his farewell to Évangéline (*Liberté*, No. 65, 1969), Raymond Leblanc mourned the loss of his country: "People of my country without identity and without life," while at about the same time, in *L'Acayen* (1972), Ronald Desprès sang about a country he had to leave: "You are my Acadia—And without pain this time—country of departure."[42] Hautecœur concludes by asking whether Acadia is not indeed "condemned to be only in value, a hopelessly ideological fact, a 'country of departure.'"[43]

Brault and Perrault's film, *Acadie, l'Acadie?!?*, which relates the agitation of the University of Moncton's students—Perrault will sign Hautecœur's book preface—ends with the departure of the top Acadian student leaders toward Quebec, bitter, disappointed of the failure of their claims: there, it seems, the reference was able to be reforged. Irene Doiron, the one we see in the film responding in stammering English to Mayor Jones's questioning

---

42. "Tu es mon Acadie—et sans douleur cette fois—pays de partance."
43. In Hautecœur's words: "condamnée à n'être que dans la valeur, fait désespérément idéologique, 'pays de partance.'"

during the confrontation at Moncton City Hall, "Everybody understands English here?"—colonized behaviour she confessed afterwards—finally said: "Acadia is a detail."

Michel Roy's book, *L'Acadie perdue* (1978), is of a different nature. It is an essay by a local, "pure brand" or "tightly knit" Acadian, to use the Quebec expression. He is from Pointe-Verte, a small town in northern New Brunswick along Chaleur Bay, within sight of the Quebec Gaspé Peninsula, and in the mid-twentieth century home to the largest battalion of Acadians in the Maritime provinces. This is a scholarly book as well. Roy is a historian by training, educated at the University of Montreal's school of Quebec neo-nationalists. He returned to his village to teach history at Bathurst College (University of the Sacred Heart) in the mid-1960s, at the same time as he became a lobster fisherman.

Roy's essay is the most potent and disheartening essay on Acadia written by an Acadian. The book oscillates between memories of his life in Acadia—the carefree nature of his childhood in the 1940s in this small Acadian fishing village, the economic poverty of the area, which he describes with great empathy, the dark years of his time as a student at the College of the Sacred Heart under the alienating rule of the clergy—and original historical considerations on Acadia that the preparation of a doctoral thesis drives. This thesis was never finished, but it will lead him to write a second book: *L'Acadie des origines à nos jours* (1981).

Roy's anger is fundamentally anti-religious. He is still seething about the dumbing down of his people by the small religious elite that imposed itself as the guardian of the faith and language in the second half of the nineteenth century. The elite had it all wrong. At the beginning, religion only maintained the Acadians in a paralyzing and degrading religiosity that hindered the person development. "I have heard hundreds of sermons where, from Évangéline to Mary, the priest swam around like a fish in water, to finally conclude with the traditional depreciation of all mothers."[44] The nationalism then, based on the illusion that Acadia is reborn,

---

44. "J'ai entendu pour ma part des centaines de sermons où, d'Évangéline à Marie, le curé se promenait comme un poisson dans l'eau, pour finalement conclure par la traditionnelle dépréciation de toutes les mères."

that Acadia will always be reborn, that the Deportation was only a moment in the divine providence's plan. "A century after the dispersion ... a clergyman ... who told us that the dispersion was a grace ... gave us Évangéline so that we could dream even more."[45] Religion (under the protection of the Assumption) and nationalism (under Évangéline's protection) got along like thieves to hide the terrible reality from the Acadians. "We are now witnessing a sort of back and forth from one virgin to another, a place of sublimation and a source of appeasement for men who have been cut off from their nature [...] Longfellow's poem and this vague religious nationalism of the end of the last century were feeding a power whose weft was slowly being woven in the heart of our regions and our souls."[46]

His anger is also directed against the colonization project, the cornerstone of the national project proposed by Rameau de Saint-Père as early as 1860, implemented by the clergy in the footsteps of the "little nation delegate," Monsignor Marcel-François Richard. Failure on all levels. He only succeeded in attracting a few thousand Acadians to the back of the coast, on sandy lands, where they were condemned to a life of misery. As a result, the Acadians did not move into the city, leaving it to English society; they did not confront the powerful Jersey companies that exploited the Acadian fishermen on the coast. Hence the chronic underdevelopment of Acadian's regions.

The period when Roy was teaching at Bathurst College in the late 1960s was particularly marked by widespread protests against regional underdevelopment and against attempts by governments to close down certain inland villages. Léonard Forest, the author of *Évangéline, qui es-tu?*, produced two films chronicling the stakes of these struggles: *La noce est pas finie* and *Un soleil pas comme ailleurs*. The northeastern region of New Brunswick was indeed where "Acadian colonization" had been most

---

45. "Un siècle après la dispersion…un clergé…qui nous a dit que la dispersion était une grâce… qui nous a donné Évangéline pour que nous rêvions encore plus…

46. "On assiste désormais à une sorte de va-et- vient d'une vierge à l'autre, lieu de sublimation et source d'apaisement tout à la fois pour des hommes retranchés de leur nature [...] Le poème de Longfellow et ce vague nationalisme religieux de la fin du siècle dernier nourrissaient à merveille un pouvoir dont la trame doucement se nouait au cœur de nos régions et dans nos âmes."

successful. During the previous century, the territory had mainly become French-speaking, to the point of turning into the most dynamic region of French life in Acadia. But this had come at the price of collective impoverishment. Because of their unprofitability, the very villages that were to be closed were those that had been the pride of the previous decades colonizing priests. This reinforced Roy's conviction that Acadian nationalism had colluded with Anglo-American imperialism: "In 1847, Évangéline appeared in the Acadian sky and since then, [we have] known our past only by the false images conveyed to serve the conqueror's domination."[47]

Imperialism was not, however, responsible for Acadians' alienation and poverty. Their Quebec neighbours, it was thought, were taking control of their own destiny. It was the refusal of the nationalist elites to face it. All this depended, according to Roy, on a misperception at the very heart of the Acadian reference's existence. It's that Acadia had never existed. It was, at the time of the French Empire, a province of Canada that could testify to certain specificities, but certainly not enough to make it the beginning of a nation. This was not a war against Acadia but against New France. Acadia was lost in 1710 and given to England in 1713. The dispersion put an end to its existence. It was a foolish fantasy, he thinks, on the part of the Renaissance Fathers, to try to rebuild it. We pretended to ignore that what remained of the Acadian settlement had moved north. We stayed attached to the French Bay, making Memramcook and later Moncton the centre of New Acadia. These places were frontier places and New Acadia, which was never assumed, had moved closer to Quebec, Chaleur Bay at its centre, in chiasm with Quebec. "The Acadian renaissance is like Acadia itself: it is a construction of the mind."

Roy is angry but sorry. A tie-up with Quebec (French Canada) would have solidified the consciousness of a French nationality, which the dream of consolidating a new Acadia in the mirage of the old Acadia sung by Longfellow did not. He laments that he could not find the political will among his contemporaries to create an Acadian political space or annex the northern territories of New Brunswick to Quebec. "If there

---

47. "En 1847, Évangéline parut dans le ciel acadien, [nous connaissons] depuis là notre passé par les images fausses véhiculées pour servir la domination du conquérant."

had never been an Acadia, except for the resonance of this extraordinary word to cradle the sorrow of a great tear and to console us for not being in the right province, soon perhaps in the right country." Here, at the birth of the Parti Acadien that will follow this path. But Roy doesn't believe it. His anger and desolation are too deep. The northern college where he taught has closed its doors in the face of the young University of Moncton's rising strength, adding to the territory's desolation where Acadian life persists.

His book ends on the scene of the last fishing. He will leave the lost Acadia for Quebec, will devote himself to more bourgeois activities, as if there was nothing left to think about.

## The Évangéline of Memory and the Évangéline of Society

The reference's rejection was short-lived, an interlude between what the lyricists of Acadia will call, afterwards, the traditional Acadia and the modern Acadia. Jean-Paul Hautecœur had already perceived the phenomenon. After the anger came neo-nationalism (its fourth corpus). As we have just seen, Roy will participate in the emergence of an Acadian political movement in the north, as he had wished, but too late...too unassertive for him. However, the reference will resume with surprising strength, bringing back with it Évangéline's petticoat, challenging at the same time the assertion of a discontinuity between traditional Acadia and modern Acadia.

To put this second Acadian renaissance in context, let us return to our guide Évangéline, where we left her in the previous chapter, on her pedestal at Grand-Pré and, hiding behind her while glancing at it, the statue of Our Lady of the Assumption, patroness of the Acadians. This reunion of the Acadia of memory's symbols, of blood, of the Deportation, in short, of Longfellow's Acadia, with the religious symbols of the Acadia of the Renaissance, that of the new territory to be occupied, of the society to be built dreamed by Rameau, had seemed to close a chapter of the Acadian reference. Had the myth become a reality?

Not quite. Grand-Pré will never become the memorial of Acadia as some nationalists had hoped at the time of the temple's inauguration in the early 1920s. "We will come," said Senator Poirier, "piously communing with the souls of the outcasts."[48] The union of myth and reality was never fully embraced by Acadian Renaissance artisans, no matter what the angry youth of the 1960s would say. It was too far removed from the living Acadia that was unfolding farther north, too tied to a memorial Acadia that was foreign to them. We will return, as we will see, for solemn moments, the commemoration in 1930 of the Deportation 175th anniversary and the bicentennial "celebrations" of 1955.

Certainly, Évangéline had her hour of glory. Now enthroned in the centre of a tourist park, she slowly descended from the figure of Acadia's founder, in which the Quebec sculptor Hébert had cast her, to become a popular figure, a figure of Acadian folklore. It was around the 1930s that the commercial craze, already noted among the English-speaking populations of the "Land of Évangéline/pays d'Évangéline," spread to the Acadian population. People got used to naming businesses after her. At the same time, this general recognition will diminish the name's popularity among the descendants of the Planters who had settled in the area since 1760. In response, the residents of Horton asked that a monument be erected in honour of Colonel Noble, who had died in 1747 while attempting to save Grand-Pré—already under English rule but still inhabited by Acadians—from a French attack. The federal county in which Grand-Pré was located was also refused the name Évangéline. The dispute over historical responsibility was still ongoing.

In 1930, an Acadian delegation from Louisiana, led by Dudley J. LeBlanc—who likes to recall that he was the grandson of the notary LeBlanc, immortalized by Longfellow in Philadelphia, looking for his children and grandchildren—visited Grand-Pré as part of the activities to commemorate the Deportation's 175th anniversary. The event had little fanfare, the Acadian elites did not want to create friction with the surrounding English-speaking population, and the Acadians were not yet accustomed to practising "ethnic pride"; this would happen later, as we were about to see, during the two-hundredth anniversary "celebrations" in particular. LeBlanc, who would be a legendary figure in the political

---

48. "Nous viendrons pieusement communier avec les âmes des proscrits."

and identity life of South Louisiana until the 1960s (see Part III), was accompanied by twenty-five "Évangéline Girls."

The Louisiana Évangéline steals the show of the commemoration. The newspaper *L'Évangéline* and even the historian Antoine Bernard referred to this event as "the return of Évangéline." The Évangéline Girls are young girls representing Louisiana's "Acadian" villages. They had long blue cotton dresses with a black bodice placed over a white blouse and wore white Perette-styled headdresses. The whole thing looks strangely like the representations of Évangéline in the American tradition of the late nineteenth century: Évangéline a shepherdess, a milkmaid, in the Germanic forest. The Acadians of the Maritimes became accustomed to having a couple, Gabriel and Évangéline, symbolically preside over patriotic events, dressed in Teutonic fashion, in cotton from the southern United States—a fabric that was unknown at the time in French Acadia.

*Down the long street she passed, with her chaplet of beads and her missal,*
*Wearing her Norman cap, and her kirtle of blue, and the earrings*

*Evangeline*, original verse by Henry Wadsworth Longfellow

Grand-Pré became the meeting place of the great Acadia, one that was not yet called diasporic Acadia. The trip of the Louisiana Acadians and of Dudley LeBlanc, who had already visited Grand-Pré in 1928, is there to confirm it. Sharing the same place of memory, Acadia of the south and Acadia of the north met again, for the first time after nearly two hundred years, in the shade of the great willows under which Évangéline would have strolled. Several Acadian descendants were among the American tourists, not the children of the 1755 exiles, who had never found refuge there, but immigrants from Acadia, more recently arrived in New England.

The Quebec nationalist newspaper *Le Devoir* organized two significant trips to Grand-Pré in 1924 and 1927. These were nationalist excursions that included preparatory conferences, pamphlets, and patriotic speeches. Acadians from Quebec participated, but mostly the history-loving Quebec nationalist elite. Henri Bourassa, the founder of *Le Devoir*, the son of Napoléon Bourassa, author of *Jacques et Marie*, and above all, the great political tribune of the two nations, was there. He will take advantage of this forum to encourage Acadians to refuse assimilation and join the great adventure of French Canada. Lionel Groulx, the master nationalist historian, was also there. He will note, with regret, that "the crime of the Deportation" has never been atoned for and that the Acadians have little eagerness to claim their rights on the soil of Grand-Pré.

Grand-Pré created the illusion and distanced these foreign eyes from what was happening in Acadia-society. These people thought they were coming to Acadia, but they were coming to Grand-Pré. The Acadia of the soil and the Acadia of memory were not wholly reunited. While the Acadia-memory of the dispersion was being played out at Grand-Pré, the Acadia-society continued to consolidate its societal hold on the land.

The first generation of nationalist elites, the children of Évangéline, had died out around the 1920s—they were born around 1847, it should be remembered—having laid the institutional foundations of an Acadian church. Acadia institutionalization was nevertheless taking place farther north, in New Brunswick. It was there that the Acadianization of religious structures took place, notably with the appointment of an Acadian bishop in Chatham in 1920 (moved to French territory in 1938), the establishment of an archdiocese in Moncton in 1936, whose cathedral would be called a "monument to the Acadian Renaissance," and the establishment of a third diocese in Edmundston in 1945. It was through the Church that northern Acadia began its resurrection. Robichaud, the Archbishop of Moncton in the mid-1950s, would rightly say that the creation of the Archdiocese of Moncton and the Vatican's recognition of Our Lady of the Assumption as patroness saint of the Acadians were the first acknowledgements since 1755 that the Acadian people were a distinct entity.

This was realized in the north, but not only, as Michel Roy postulated, because after 1755, the Acadians had been displaced in that direction, on the shores of the Gulf of St. Lawrence and Chaleur Bay. Until the middle of the nineteenth century, the proportion of Acadians from the three Maritime provinces living outside New Brunswick was still significant—about 40 percent in 1871—but it declined steadily thereafter, to 15 percent today. The Great Upheaval began this shift, but it was the building of so-cietal institutions from the late nineteenth century onward, as proposed by Rameau, that made the difference. On this success, the angry youth and its interpreters will be blinded by their all-modern conviction to end tradition once and for all.

The consolidation of institutions under the clergy's aegis—parishes, convents, colleges, hospitals, newspapers, national institutions—never-theless had the effect of establishing a duality within the social structures in which the Acadians lived. Only what was under the symbolic or real direction of the Acadian reference and its institutions was considered Acadian; everything considered external, belonging to the other society, did not fit into such boundaries.

As was the case with politics and economics, Acadians participate in these spheres of activity, but not as Acadian subjects. After unsuccessful attempts to enter provincial politics in the middle of the previous century, nationalists abandoned politics, so to speak, in the hands of patronage and petty politics. There were no great nationalist politicians or perceived nationalists in the first part of the twentieth century.

The same thing happened in economics; Acadians were mostly small-scale, overexploited, "fishermen-farmers-lumberjacks" in any order you like. No one was putting together an Acadian representation of this eco-nomic production, except the exaltation of farming as a career in all co-herence with the colonial ideology. Under the dominance of merchants from the Jersey Islands and Halifax, even fishing took time to acquire the noble identity value it has today. A song like *Partons la mer est belle* ("Let's leave, the sea is beautiful"), falsely associated with a traditional Acadian song, arrived from France in the early twentieth century. A small Acadian merchant class existed but was little associated with the national cause, this elitist activity being reserved for the clergy and a few lay profession-als—lawyers, doctors, journalists.

The nationalist leaders had thus developed a kind of happy reserve giving them autonomy in their affairs, leaving the elites of English society surrounding them to manage the rest. There were, however, some attempts to move the boundaries of such a "compromise." In education, for example, from the 1930s onward, Acadian elites attempted to enlarge the narrow public space that had been granted to them following the school crisis of the 1870s, by creating the Association acadienne d'éducation (AAE), which was responsible for negotiating this relationship with the state on behalf of the Acadians. Acadia created its own economic space through mutual insurance associations, fishermen's cooperatives and credit unions. All of this was done within a logic that was more about expanding the institutionalization organized by the clergy than about breaking down its boundaries. These institutions were the natural extension of the parish organizations, the cornerstone of the entire Acadian societal edifice.

## Évangéline Gets Out of Her Reserve

It was this dual structure that, as the mid-century arrived, seemed outdated to the very leaders of the Acadian communities. They felt they had to modernize the old reference, to adapt it to a world that had changed a lot since the previous century. Paradoxically, this desire for change will appear around the organization of the Deportation's bicentenary "celebrations" (1955), which aimed primarily at commemorating the memory of the Deportation of 1755.

Since the 1930s, the Société nationale l'Assomption (SNA), which was the great guardian association of the reference, had fallen into a dormant state. The conventions of 1930 and 1937, in the absence of the founding fathers, had not had the panache of those at the beginning of the century. It had been almost twenty years since the Acadian people had met in conventions. Therefore, it was proposed to organize a grand reunion as part of the bicentennial "celebrations." These celebrations would have a double mission: to renew the national memory while reorganizing the "Acadian" organizational structure on a more modern basis. They would be reflecting the desire for preservation and renewal. The use of the term "celebration" (*fête* in French) for such an event underlines the tortured nature of the project. This is because Acadian leaders were both optimistic and pessimistic. Optimistic because the project of the last century had taken hold in New Brunswick, where Acadians had solid institutions and by the middle of the twentieth century made up nearly 40 percent of the provincial population. For the first time since the Great Upheaval, they could even hope that they would soon be the majority in a political space. Pessimistic because they felt they gained nothing. Acadia was fading at its borders. In Nova Scotia and Prince Edward Island, the numbers dwindled either through assimilation or immigration. These populations had not followed the same path as those in New Brunswick. Overall, the old reference seemed to lack appeal to new generations while being essential to the imagined community that was Acadia.

The 1955 celebrations were the swan song of this old Acadia, its moment of glory. Significant events in Grand-Pré to commemorate the Deportation and in Moncton–Memramcook to celebrate the subsequent "blossoming" of Acadia—the triumphant Acadia—were organized. It was a sort of attempt to (re)weld the Acadia of memory to the Acadia of society. Every Acadian parish was asked to participate. Parades, "historical pageants" re-enacting the Acadians' return, the streets decorated with the Acadian flag—the star-spangled tricolour—and that of the Vatican, arches covering the streets, and this, even in the still Anglo-Protestant city of Moncton. A festive committee in each community was mandated to promote the costume of Évangéline and Gabriel in the apparent "Teutonic Forest" fashion. They were placed on floats. Invitations were sent to the Acadians of the dispersion, those of Quebec, New England, Louisiana, and France.

This was an important event; it was the first time that the Acadians organized popular demonstrations around the Deportation. In 1855, Bishop Walsh of Halifax had asked that a mass be celebrated in commemoration of the event, at a time when the English Catholic Church leaders in the Maritimes still saw the Acadians as resources to be conquered. In 1904, the English-speaking world celebrated the three-hundredth anniversary of the now-English town founding—Annapolis Royal, formerly Port-Royal, Saint Andrew near the historic site of Saint Croix Island where Champlain and his party had spent the first winter—which had replaced the old French settlements. But the Acadians were not invited, except for a belated invitation to Pascal Poirier and Pierre-Amand Landry to encourage Acadians to contribute to a plaque fundraising in honour of Champlain's passage through Saint John, New Brunswick. In 1905, the 150th anniversary, which coincided with the 200th anniversary of the founding of Acadia (Port-Royal), had gone unnoticed. In Caraquet, where the sixth Acadian National Convention was held, attention was focused on appointing an Acadian bishop, but there were only vague references to 1755. In 1930—the 175th anniversary of the Deportation—a meeting was held at Grand-Pré, but still, as Ronald Rudin recalled in *Remembering and Forgetting in Acadie* (2009), in hushed tones, in "silence" and fear of offending the memory of the dominant.

In 1955, something will remain of the habit of Acadian nationalists to mourn among themselves, or in silence, the tragedy of a people and to exalt the happy historical coexistence in public. A letter was written to the Queen of England inviting her to the ceremonies in the old tradition of colonial submission, reminding her that it was under the structures of the British Empire that the Acadians had been able to flourish. We will ask to modify the "offensive" passages of the "*Pageant de l'Acadie*" presented in Moncton and written by a Quebecer, not always sensitive to peaceful coexistence. But the essential remains: Acadia went out into the street for the first time, proclaiming its existence.

The reference, formerly essentially of the second culture, not to say elitist, was democratized, popularized…while becoming trivial. Going out into the street also meant going out of Grand-Pré. Unbeknownst to the organizers, the parish celebrations had a magnitude that overshadowed the more solemn ones in Grand-Pré, place of memory—and Moncton–Memramcook—place of the renaissance. Five thousand people gathered at Grand-Pré; twenty thousand at the "celebrations" in Caraquet, a large village in northern New Brunswick. As has been noted, this corresponded to the tension between the Acadia of memory and the Acadia of society. If the Acadians did not travel to Grand-Pré to commemorate, Évangéline, still in her German dress, travelled to the Acadian villages.

In a sense, 1955 inaugurated the "modern" Acadia, the one whose identity would get out of its reserve and occupy the public square. It happened through tradition. To illustrate this, let us recall that Bishop Robichaud of Moncton, after the religious ceremonies that marked the opening of the bicentennial celebrations, called upon "his" people to make "*tintamarre*" ("din"). It was a reference to a vague Acadian tradition according to which, at the time of happy events, one went outside to alert the neighbourhood with a din. It was René Lévesque, future founder of the Parti Québécois, and at the time a journalist with Radio-Canada, who reported live on this first din of the modern era. In various forms, the cacophony will never stop.

## The Political Shift

Beyond the desire to rekindle the nationalist flame, another objective animated the bicentennial "celebrations" organizers. They wanted to adapt the organizational structure of Acadian life by reviving its master association, the Société nationale l'Assomption (SNA)—the "Nationale" as it was called at the time. This was done in 1957 when the "Nationale" was given a new name, the *Société nationale des Acadiens* ("National Society of Acadians") while keeping its acronym SNA. At the same time, the new SNA proposed to be Acadia's place of "governance" to use a modern term. Its unique structure will be similar to a form of corporatism. It was to transform the reference guardian's institution into an organization, master of the society's stewardship. The SNA was to bring together and oversee the associations of Acadian civil society. There was a plan to make it a quasi-Acadian government capable of negotiating with the real government. It was a matter of formalizing the duality between the two societies while providing itself with a more operational, more modern tool.

In June 1960, a major political event disrupted the political modernization of the Acadian reference and institutions: the election of the first Acadian premier in New Brunswick, Louis J. Robichaud. There had been Peter John Vienot (Pierre-Jean Vigneau by name), at the beginning of the twentieth century, who had been interim premier, but his brief presence had somewhat consolidated the divorce between the nation's business world of Acadian society—"Politics" with a capital "P"—and the participation business with the other society, partisan politics—"politics" with a small "p." Vienot had been able to integrate minor Acadian notables into the patronage network of the Liberal Party, but he had not integrated Acadia into provincial politics.

The election of Louis J. Robichaud was a different story. Not that he was initially a fervent nationalist. If he came from Acadian society, he was a classic politician at the time of his election, a product of the Liberal Party establishment. But the political situation in New Brunswick has changed dramatically. In 1861, Acadians represented 17 percent of the provincial population; by the end of the 1950s, they accounted for over 36 percent. The Acadians voted overwhelmingly for the young Liberal candidate and found themselves with a government in which their own people formed a virtual majority.

Acadians were given a royal road to provincial politics for the first time. Nationalist leaders jumped at the chance, especially since they looked for a way out of tradition. They saw in the Robichaud government's program of social reform—*Chances égales pour tous* ("equal opportunity")—the means to modernize the old institutions of Acadian society and open up to English-speaking society. Robichaud had been elected on the promise of standardizing public services across the province and creating a set of other services worthy of a welfare state.

This involved a transfer of the institutions that had developed over the past a hundred years—convents, colleges, hospitals, social services—through the clergy to the provincial state. It involved the centralization of government structures at the government level—the abolition of county political-administrative bodies—which reduced the narrow spaces where Acadian civil society had traditionally managed to exercise some power. We have said elsewhere that this process can be compared to a real expropriation of Acadian civil society.

This expropriation was accepted, desired, and even organized in large part by the Acadian leadership of the day. These reforms were necessary for Acadians and their institutions to catch up with the backwardness that the old formula would have caused in education, social services, hospitals, etc. They were also intended to better integrate the economically underdeveloped Acadian regions into the province's development. In a way, the reserve autonomy was traded for equality. This was accepted more quickly because we had the impression that we were now present within the political apparatus. It was also made more accessible by the promise that both the provincial and federal governments would be bilingual from now on.

This promise was made in the wake of the Bilingualism and Biculturalism Commission (1963–68), which established bilingualism as an official doctrine of the Canadian state in response to political unrest in Quebec. Under pressure from Acadian circles, New Brunswick followed suit. Some would say it would lead the way, its bilingualism act being a year ahead of the federal one, but this is not true. The great debates on bilingualism in New Brunswick follow those launched by the Quebec-Canada quarrel of the 1960s. The Robichaud government was not in a hurry to get started; it had to wait until its second mandate.

By happily associating themselves with the political project of the province of New Brunswick, the Acadian leaders accentuated the rift they had begun to create with their own tradition. In 1960, at the opening of the SNA's annual meeting, its president Louis Lebel could say of the Deportation: "On these painful events let's keep silent, otherwise let's decide to forget it." This was the case with Father Clément Cormier, who was invited to give an overview of Acadia. He was a central figure in those pivotal years. In the early 1940s, he founded the School of Social Sciences at Saint-Joseph University, organized training for the new Acadian elite, was involved in the creation of the Acadian Historical Association, and presided over the founding of the University of Moncton, of which he was the first rector, and became a member of the Royal Commission on Bilingualism and Biculturalism, all the while being an eminence grise with both civil society and government leaders. He encouraged his compatriots to move away from the "isolationist thesis"—with respect to both French Canada and English-speaking society—that he felt the Renaissance generation had been forced to adopt. His wish was widely heard. For example, in 1970, the daily newspaper *L'Évangéline*, the official newspaper of Acadian institutions, changed its name to *Progrès—L'Évangéline*, as if in the face of progress, Évangéline had to fade away.

Integration into provincial political life also rendered obsolete, in a sense, the project of renewing the Acadian government. Acadians did not need an intermediary; they were part of the New Brunswick government and society by right. Or so they thought. This is why, without a reference point and much use in the new political situation, the new SNA never really took off.

The anti-*Evangeline* anger of the 1960s youth is therefore not so surprising. They were ultimately much closer to their fathers than they thought. They radicalized their premises, but their judgments about tradition were the same. The idols of the past had to be destroyed in order to enter modern society. Excited by the impatience of the 1960s, more hurried, more radical than their elders, they did not grasp that the tradition they were fighting against was already no longer that of their fathers.

However, this anger was short-lived, at least in its anti-*Evangeline*, anti-memory dimension. Much like in the nineteenth century, when Acadians wanted to enter provincial politics without a label, they were quickly reminded that they were different. If young people wanted to reject the reference a century later, it was as Acadians that they were answered, notably at Moncton City Hall during their demonstration for linguistic equality. "If you are not Acadians, you are nothing," the Quebec essayist Jacques Ferron reminded them some time later. Premier Louis Robichaud had not put forward Acadia, nor its origins, in his 1960 campaign; it would be as an "Acadian" favouring the development of French-speaking regions that he would be criticized and finally defeated. At the same time, it was also because they were Acadians that the popular movements in northern and eastern New Brunswick fighting against poverty and rural depopulation believed they were not being heard. A banal labelling process: the other returns you to your identity, you can only defend yourself by claiming that identity.

In the film *Acadie, l'Acadie?!?*, there is a scene where the young protesters feel the need to return to the village to see if they can find there the meaning of their protest. It is a powerful image of the emergence of neo-nationalism. After having bitterly criticized the very existence of the reference, at the turn of the 1970s, the nationalist protest resumed with renewed vigour, especially among the youth who had just rejected it. As we have just seen, the other's reference to their rejected identity (labelling) is not the only reason. The rapid social changes of the post-war period and the growth of a welfare state everywhere in the West have profoundly disrupted identity references. We will then witness a sixty-eight-year-old Romanticism that aims at answering the expressivity deficit of modern society. The hippie movement is an example of this. In regions where capitalist homogenization had been slow to take hold—we are thinking of Quebec, Brittany, and Catalonia in France, Flanders in Belgium, and, of course, Acadia and Louisiana—and where there was, within reach, so to speak, a tradition that was still alive, the counter-cultural movement took the path of revalorizing it. The young protesters returned to the village.

In Acadia, this search for expressiveness was strongly fuelled by the strength of Quebec nationalism in the 1960s. This was not new. Despite the separation of the 1880s, the two nationalisms had been working symbiotically for a century. Most Acadian intellectuals were educated in Quebec, and they were convinced to link politics and identity by reading their poets and essayists.

Neo-nationalism presented itself as another possible path, just as political, leading to political integration into New Brunswick society. To the unqualified equality that the Acadian elite was henceforth proposing, the militant youth opposed the equality of historical communities. In 1972, the Parti Acadian was founded in the north, in Bathurst, which at the outset was intended to be the voice of economically disadvantaged and Acadian communities, voiceless communities according to its promoters. The party's nationalist tendency became more pronounced and, in the late 1970s, it called for the creation of an Acadian province for the northern and eastern parts of New Brunswick. The "separatist" demand was never a popular one, and the Parti Acadian had insignificant scores in the elections in which it ran candidates. It will, however, inject into the reference two notions that will politicize its meaning: the question of territory and that of autonomy.

The territory question is as old as the reference itself. One remembers that Rameau de Saint-Père already made it the *sine qua non* condition for the rebirth of an Acadia. This conception opposed the reality born of the Great Upheaval: Acadians dispersed on two continents, a fragmented universe even in the Maritimes. The impossibility of the territory was why, according to Roy, Acadia was forever lost or doomed, according to Hautecœur, to remember the myth. Contrary to the latter's judgment, it will be said that the renaissance partially remade a society, particularly in New Brunswick. However, it did so by referring to memory without territory, that of a dispersed people. The statue of Évangéline on its pedestal in Grand-Pré and that of Our Lady of the Assumption, behind it, in its church, symbolized this tension that constituted the first century of the Acadian reference.

Neo-nationalism thought to put an end to this tension. The Acadia they seek will be a territorialized Acadia, an Acadia-society. The magazine *L'Acayen*, which was the spokesperson for Acadian neo-nationalism during the 1970s, very close to the Parti Acadien, clearly stated this principle in June 1972:

> We at L'Acayen *do not believe in an extra-spatial or extra-temporal Acadia. For us, Acadia is not the bayous of Louisiana, the rocks of Belle-Île-en-Mer, nor even the coasts of Prince Edward Island or Nova Scotia (where most of those of French origin can no longer speak French). Nor is Acadia, that of the Great Upheaval, an interpretation that divided New Brunswick francophones into two classes: the so-called "pure-bred" Acadians, that is, the descendants of the deportees, and the others, such as those from Madawaska.*

Acadia is the territorial space where the Acadian culture spreads in a hegemonic way, that is to say, the north and the east of New Brunswick. Similar statements can be found in the Parti Acadien's program or in a book that marks a political shift in the reference, *La question du pouvoir en Acadie* (1982) by Léon Thériault.

During the same years, the Société nationale des Acadiens (SNA) was multiplied into different provincial societies confirming a territorial shift: Fédérations des Acadiens de la Nouvelle—Écosse (FANE), Société des Acadiens du Nouveau-Brunswick (SANB)—Prince Edward Island already having its association since 1919, the Société Saint-Thomas d'Aquin. As nothing was definitely abandoned in Acadia, the old SNA will remain the organization responsible for the cross-border dimension of the Acadian nation. Nevertheless, the Acadians are now advancing in scattered territorial battalions, and only the Acadia of New Brunswick, according to the neo-nationalists—there was no neo-nationalism in the other Maritime provinces—would have the territorial concentration necessary to take over the project.

Despite the mixed electoral success of the Parti Acadien, neo-nationalism would permeate a much larger segment of the population. It was more significant than its electoral echo. Throughout the 1970s, when the Robichaud government was a thing of the past, Acadian circles succeeded in having the notion of duality recognized as legitimate in political discourse. This notion, which ran counter to the unqualified equality of the Robichaud era, was based on the idea that there were two societies in New Brunswick and that these two societies should be built on different projects. It is also based on the idea that autonomy is an essential historical intention of the Acadian community. If an Acadian province or an attachment to Quebec is a chimerical project, the reorganization of New Brunswick based on community equality and autonomy is not.

The Acadians achieved some political success by taking this path. They were granted educational duality, a dual structure allowing each community—English-speaking and French-speaking—to be autonomous in the design and management of education. Bill 88, which was enshrined in the Canadian Constitution in 1993, recognized the equality of the province's two linguistic communities and their right to their own cultural institutions. More recently (2010), health institutions were reorganized around two autonomous boards, each serving one of the linguistic groups.

## A Territorialized Reference

This politicization of Acadian identity, which was not without practical effects, was based on the reappropriation of the reference. A reappropriation that nevertheless proposed a different narrative of Acadian history. A narrative better articulated to the notions of territory and autonomy. There was less emphasis on the Deportation and more on the historical continuity between the bucolic Acadia of New France and that of the re-establishment of the Acadians after the Great Upheaval. Jean-Paul Hautecœur can say: "The idyllic village of Évangéline country recounted by Longfellow and by Anselme Chiasson is not without a deep relationship to the collective farm imagined by the first ideologues of the Parti Acadien."[49]

Léon Thériault's book *La question du pouvoir en Acadie* is representative of this neo-nationalist thinking. Thériault was a history professor at the University of Moncton whose courses on the history of Acadia in the mid-1970s were highly regarded. He would become a representative of the so-called nationalist wing of the Parti Acadien. As a historian, he was particularly interested in the nationalist struggles of the last century to Acadianize the Catholic clergy. In *La question du pouvoir en Acadie*, Thériault reminds us that the Acadians made collective political choices before 1755, such as neutrality. That they already possessed, since 1713, (delegated) mechanisms of collective representation that distinguished them from the English power and project in the Maritimes. This awareness survived the Deportation. After 1755, "They got it into their heads," he says, "to find a new Acadia." For him, the scattered debris discovered by Rameau de Saint-Père was the result of an "Acadian" desire to regroup.

Such an interpretation also had the effect of relativizing the clerical-national elite role of the previous century. The role it played was not as central as traditional history would have it, and as we would have it here, that of literally founding Acadia. Rather, its action was part of the long term, a step in the long march from the French era toward the political institutionalization of Acadia. Thériault blamed Michel Roy for attributing the Acadians' alienation and socio-economic backwardness to this group action.

It was no longer the Deportation but the establishment of an Acadian society for nearly four hundred years on the territory that signalled the existence of a people and its attachment to a territory. This thesis of continuity in the collective consciousness between French Acadia and

---

49.  "Le village idyllique du pays d'Évangéline raconté par Longfellow et par Anselme Chiasson n'est pas sans profonde relation avec la ferme collective imaginée par les premiers idéologues du Parti acadien."

contemporary Acadia will be best supported by the British-Canadian historian Naomi Griffiths—one thinks in particular of *Acadia: the Creation of a People* (1973). Although far removed from Acadian identity concerns, her work will have great resonance with neo-nationalists.

In 1979, the Acadians celebrated the 375th anniversary of their settlement in America with great fanfare. The slogan was "We came to stay." There was no official celebration the following year, which was the 225th anniversary of the Deportation. The theme of aboiteaux became omnipresent, in poetry, in song, as well as in history. The aboiteaux were the dykes the inhabitants built to drain the marshes on which they practiced agriculture and grazed their herds before 1755. "Water clearers," one might say. The aboiteaux became the symbol of the autonomist tradition. This, we insisted, is proof of the Acadian culture union with the territory. In the early 1970s, a historical village was built in Caraquet, focusing on the return of the Acadians and their resettlement in continuity with the aboiteaux's country. Évangéline and Gabriel were stripped of their German shepherdess costumes, and we created for them a new suit in linen, the country's fabric, a country they inhabited since 1604.

The Acadians were portrayed from then on as proud peasants, people of the frontier, resisters who had led struggles against the oppressor. Longfellow was criticized for depicting the deportees as poor, destitute, submissive peasants marching and singing hymns to the ships that would deport them. His description of Father Félicien exhorting the Acadians to Christian resignation in the face of Basil the blacksmith's attempt to stir up revolt inside the church at Grand-Pré was considered more accurate.

This seemed to them to be more in keeping with the resignation that the clergy had preached for a century, and that would have prevented the Acadians from showing their rebellious character.

They looked for "real" heroes to replace the imaginary and passive figure of Évangéline. The renaissance fathers, including Monsignor Richard, were excluded because if the anger against Évangéline was waning, the anger against the clergy was not. Joseph Broussard, known as Beausoleil (Beausoleil-Broussard—a group of famous singers in the 1970s—was named after him) was put forward. He was born in Port-Royal in 1702 and moved as a young man with his brothers to the northern part of French Bay—an area that remained under French control after 1710—at the top of the Petitcodiac River near present-day Moncton. In 1747, Broussard assisted the French and Indigenous peoples in their attacks on the English garrison at Grand-Pré. In 1755, he led groups of Acadians in a guerrilla war against the English, both on land and at sea. He joined the French battalion led by Boishébert and became a negotiator between Colonel Monckton and the Indigenous peoples at the time of the French defeat at Fort Beauséjour.

His character will be recognized in "Jacques" of the novel *Jacques et Marie* by Napoléon Bourassa and consequently in *Les Acadiens à Philadelphie* by Pascal Poirier. Thus, Beausoleil Broussard can hardly be the hero of territorial Acadia. Taken prisoner in 1762, he stayed in the Halifax prison, where he negotiated his departure from Acadia, along with six hundred other Acadians, for Saint Domingue. He was finally found with his group in 1764 in Louisiana. He is better known as the founder of the Cajun country than of the new Acadia.

Louis Mailloux was another candidate. He died under the bullets of the "Canadian" militia corps that came to ensure order during the Caraquet riots of 1875. The village inhabitants were protesting against King's Law, which prohibited Catholic (and French) education in the schools. Mailloux is hardly more genuine than Évangéline. He was a nineteen-year-old boy who happened to be in the Albert house when the militia wanted to arrest those allegedly responsible for the attempted violence against the Protestant and anglophone notables. His death is not accompanied by any political move. His heroism came from the pen of Calixte Duguay, who dedicated a song and a musical play to him in the mid-1970s.

## From Reference to Pride

The excitement of the 1970s did not last. Gains had been made. Acadia had built institutions adapted to the new reality. Acadians had learned to play politics. But this was far from the young neo-nationalists' dream of the previous decade, that of an Acadian province, or even an Acadian country. In 1979, the Acadians—or more accurately, the nationalists—met in a national convention, the *Convention d'orientation nationale acadienne* ("Acadian National Policy Convention" or CONA), as they had done since the last century, to make public their nationalist mood. They still expressed a preference for a political option of autonomy, but their hearts were no longer in it. The enactment of Bill 88 (1981), recognizing the equality of New Brunswick's two linguistic communities—which was the government's response to neo-nationalist demands—and its subsequent incorporation into the Canadian constitution will be described by one of the leaders of Acadia in the 1980s as the confiscation of Acadian political discourse by provincial and federalist politicians (*Le discours confisqué*, Michel Doucet, 1994).

The political claim will diminish, or at least take a new, more legal form, that of right claims. The Canadian political situation changed in the early 1980s. The failure of the first referendum on Quebec sovereignty necessarily cooled, by ricochet, in Acadia, the impulse to create a "country." The creation of the Canadian Charter of Rights and Freedoms immediately followed, giving a more individualistic meaning to the Canadian language claim. It was one of the explicit goals of then Prime Minister Pierre Elliott Trudeau to replace the nationality feud inherent in Canadian political culture with a culture of legal equality.

The Canadian Charter of Rights and Freedoms created a new legal reality, the "rightful claimants" to Canadian minority language status. The struggle to expand the Acadian political space would largely be defined through the law from that moment on. Acadian lawyers from the University of Moncton's new law school took over the political leadership of the priests of the beginning of the century and the politicians of the 1960s and 1970s. Such a "judicialization" of the political space will necessarily have the effect of pushing the Acadian reference toward denationalization. It was no longer Acadia, the bearer of national history, that demanded recognition, but the Acadian individual, the bearer of a right. Sociologists and literary scholars will start using the Canadian-style language of minority and pluralistic identities, while historians will no longer talk of Acadia.

The Acadianity's expressiveness was not meant to disappear. On the contrary, one could even say that it will increase, will take on a new life. As early as 1955, as we recalled, at the time of the bicentennial "celebrations," Évangéline had come down from her pedestal to become a popular figure. After the short-lived anger of the 1960s, the democratization of Acadian identity will resume in earnest. Acadian identity would no longer be closely associated with the reference elite guardians. Poets, novelists, songwriters, popular festivals, cultural tourism, helped by the technical tools of the modern world, will participate in the development of a "pride" in their identity.

In the 1970s, a coalition of regional protests, nationalistic claims, and political affirmation was formed around identity pride. This coalition broke up. The regional and political dimensions of the protests have largely vanished or been mutated, as we have seen, into legal language. Pride, however, survives the coalition's erosion. But it was no longer connected to anything collective. It now became more of an individualized expressiveness. It would be a matter of a relationship that the individual has directly with "their" roots, "their" genealogy. Hence the idea, in a complete reversal of the Acadia of the 1970s, that Acadia would be plural, according to the artistic assembly that each Acadian makes of their relationship to their roots. Acadia would no longer be a reference, a place that institutes a plurality of humans in society, but a raw, folkloric expression of human plurality.

Thought of in this way, Acadia no longer has any boundaries—neither institutional, like the renaissance Acadia, nor political, like the desired Acadia of the 1960s and 1970s—other than the one set by the individual imagination of the person who call themselves Acadian. "Acadia is where Acadians exist." Here, the reference individualization and the logic of the law come together; it is not Acadia that is recognized, but Acadians, no matter where they are located in the territory. We thus witness a curious reversal as Acadia becomes timeless, a pure object of memory, equally present in Saint John, New Brunswick; Edmonton, Alberta; Montreal, Quebec; Grand-Pré, or Caraquet. Precisely what the imaginary of Évangéline the Elder was blamed for, that is to say, for being situated in the myth. That said, the reference individualization does not erase the search for an anchor. It is superimposed on it. In Acadian culture, a pathos of the lost country and a society to be remade, "the wound of Évangéline's country," said Philéas Bourgeois in the nineteenth century, persists. This is why Évangéline is attacked but does not die.

The more Acadia considers itself a country without borders, a society without politics, the more it submits to the imaginary realm. It is a culture that in recent years has tried to cover this wound. We understand "culture" here in the sense of cultural expression, of cultural production—arts, literature, cinema, etc.—and not in the sense of anthropogenic culture, identity-based culture. In recent years, artists have occupied the reflective foreground in New Brunswick's Acadia, they have recovered a part of what the legal word has left aside, the field of the symbolic. In 2004, for example, Acadian nationalist circles organized a major national convention for the thirteenth time. What had been, at the turn of the twentieth century, large-scale events showing the other its existence have today become manifestations of its existential anguish. From now on, we meet when the nation is out of order. This had already been the case in 1979 at the time of the previous convention (CONA, 1979), and it will be the case for the 2004 convention. The desire for a political form for Acadia in New Brunswick was again expressed. But there were no more ball carriers than in 1979, except for the cultural community, which took up the ball by announcing in ceremonial Estates General of Culture—Caraquet, 2007—that the Acadian project was above all a cultural project and that they were its custodians.

Cultural production, by the game it plays between reality and fiction, by the blurred use of the *I* and the *We*, can create an illusion—let us think that it has filled the chasm between the real country and the mythical country, between identity and reference, between Acadia-society and Acadia-memory. Moreover, it is most probably there in this never-ending quest between the real country and the imagined country that the truth about Acadia lies. Insofar, of course, as the word can become flesh, that is to say, embodied in a policy, which is not the case today.

These ambiguities, which are those of contemporary Acadia, and even our societies, can be found in the two portraits we are about to present of the two most emblematic cultural figures of contemporary Acadia, Antonine Maillet and Herménégilde Chiasson. As we will see, it is difficult to get rid of the wound of Évangéline's country.

# Evangelist: "I Know You Are, But What Am I?"

It is safe to say that Antonine Maillet is the honorary president of contemporary Acadia. Chancellor of the University of Moncton from 1989 to 2000, she has been called upon over the past forty years to give the "inaugural lesson" at almost every major symbolic event in Acadia. When New Brunswick's Acadia hosts, its "first lady" is constantly called upon to inaugurate the party. This was the case at the First World Acadian Congress in Moncton in 1994 and at the meeting of political leaders from the Francophone world (Sommet de la Francophonie-Moncton, 1999). At the time of her "inaugural lessons," she tirelessly repeated her optimistic account of Acadian history. French people by language, even before it was the language of France, Acadians have kept from this deep relationship to the old guttural French a joy of living, authenticity, a stubbornness that has allowed them to go through the trials of history joyfully and to leave an indelible mark in the great book of words. If real Acadia can die, the Acadia of words will never perish.

Antonine Maillet owes this notoriety to a gigantic fictional and theatrical body of work that has been in the making for over fifty years now. Of particular relevance to our topic are three major works: *La Sagouine* (1971), *Évangéline Deusse* (1975), and *Pélagie-la-Charrette* (1979). Maillet is not the first Acadian novelist, but her work is, by all accounts, the first Acadian work. The previous novels, written by Acadians, were isolated experiments. As the literary like to say, she ushers in the Acadian literary institution. This means that we must immediately reject the proposition, raised notably by Herménégilde Chiasson in *Oublier Évangéline*, that the "folkloric" image Maillet would project of Acadia and the Acadians would be one essentially imposed from the outside, from Quebec and its institutions. Apparently, one can self-folklorize.

Yes, Antonine Maillet is an Acadian writer, the greatest of Acadian writers. Born in 1929 in Bouctouche, in eastern New Brunswick, she was educated in Acadian schools, colleges, and universities before studying French literature in Quebec and returning, for a time, to live on Acadian territory. She draws much of her inspiration from the Acadian imagination, both historical and popular. A tourist site has been dedicated to her characters in Bouctouche, her native village. *La Sagouine's* famous monologue on the census, where she asks why Acadia is not on the "censusors" list of possible answers—yet I am neither "American" nor "French Canadian" nor "Quebecois"—is a true anthology piece on which both humanities scholars and Acadian literary scholars rely today.

It is not so much the popular reception of her work, which, in my opinion, remains relatively modest in Acadia, as the institutional reception that has made Maillet one of the chroniclers of the contemporary Acadian narrative. It is not Quebecers who invite Antonine Maillet to be chancellor of the University of Moncton or hostess of special occasions, but the natives themselves who see her as a worthy representative. The reception of her work in Acadian institutional circles is integral to her legitimacy as an artist.

Certainly, Maillet's work is recognized far beyond Acadia, which does not take away her place in it, on the contrary. She has been awarded more than thirty honorary doctorates. Quebec, France, and Canada have buried her under a mountain of prizes, awards, ribbons, and crosses of all kinds. She is notably the winner of the Goncourt Prize (1979), the most prestigious literary prize in the French-speaking world. She was the first writer outside of France to receive this award, and no other Acadian or Quebecer has received it since. This popularity led to her being mummified during her lifetime. She publishes in Quebec and lives in Montreal on a street that bears her name.

With her credibility and Acadianity established, let's look at her relationship to the poem *Evangeline* and her contribution to the Acadian narrative. By most literary critics, she is considered to be the anti-*Evangeline* par excellence. Her entire work is an attempt to debunk Longfellow's heroine, to do away with the false image of Acadia projected by a writer whose imagination is utterly foreign to Acadia. She would have wanted, will one go so far as to say, to kill Évangéline to bring out the truth about Acadia. La Sagouine, Évangéline Deusse ("Évangéline the Second"), Pélagie, central characters of her imagination, would all be candidates to replace Évangéline the first. They are inverted figures of Évangéline.

While Évangéline was the ideal image of the Victorian woman, pious, faithful, and passive—we forget that she had nevertheless crossed America in search of her lover—Maillet's female characters are irreverent, critical, and beautiful. La Sagouine is an impoverished woman who sees the world from below and casts a caustic eye on today's society. Évangéline Deusse also is of modest means, fiery and combative, a figure of the modern deportee, she tries to transplant her identity in Montreal, where life circumstances contributed to her failing. As for Pélagie, she would be the inversion par excellence of Évangéline. With her cart and her oxen, this woman brings back to Acadia, along the American coasts from Georgia, the exiled Acadian people. Évangéline Deusse will announce Pélagie by saying:

> "Évangéline the first, they deported her to the sou'.
> An' she stayed there.
> Well then as for us, I came back through the woods, on foot, for ten years.
> And us I rebuilt."

Whereas Longfellow's poem would have served as a victimizing, revanchist, and plaintive reading of Acadia, Maillet's work presents funny, hopeful characters fighting for the country to be built.

The idea that inverting the myth would give birth to a true history of Acadia is one that Maillet herself has suggested to literary critics. "I wanted," she said, commenting on the publication of *Pélagie-la-Charrette*, "to present a new Évangéline, my own vision of Évangéline." To another journalist, she will say: "If Longfellow had set up one of these women in front of the troops, I don't say he would have saved Acadia from exile, but he would have given the Great Upheaval a certain tone of truth that would have made it more real to us and, who knows, less tragic." In a little book that was intended to be a touristic-intellectual travel guide to New Brunswick's Acadia, she states: "Instead of Évangéline Bellefontaine, sitting by the well, you will see a woman going to put out the church fire with her bucket; and instead of Gabriel, the angelic one, you will see Captain Belliveau overpowering the English crew, taking the helm and setting sail for Quebec. Throughout her work, Maillet spread snarky comments against Longfellow's Évangéline. Thus in the little story *La tireuse de cartes,* the narrator will say, sarcastically: "Then a virgin-heroine stood up amid her people, and led them into the land of exile chanting the song of longing and loyalty... The beautiful tale!"

Her words flow with authority. Maillet, after all, is an expert on folk traditions in Acadia. She is the author of a doctoral thesis (*Rabelais et les traditions populaires en Acadie,* 1971) in which she sought, in the Acadian language and popular traditions, the correspondences with the fantastic world described by François de Rabelais—one thinks of Pantagruel (1532) and especially of his son Gargantua. It is because Acadia's initial settlement culture, which dates from the first part of the seventeenth century, would be impregnated with the quasi-medieval universe described by Rabelais. The characters in Maillet's novels, which she says she draws from the Acadian folk tradition, are Rabelaisian, that is to say, joyful and irreverent. One understands then this disobliging remark about Évangéline in one famous tale: "if you think we produce virgins-to-make-statues in the land of sea cows and aboiteaux!"

The popular tradition of which Maillet claims to be a part of would have been ignored, covered up, voluntarily repressed by the elites of the renaissance, supported in this by the reference to Évangéline. In the introduction to her book *Rabelais et les traditions populaires en Acadie,* she says: "But let us be clear, the goal of the elite who propose a new ideology made up of a mixture of Assumption, starry tricolour, loyalty to language, religion, and the land of the forefathers, which we would call 'evangelism,' if we dared, has nothing to do with Acadia's true popular traditions."

"I know you are, but what am I?" So it was said when I was a child, and someone tried to insult us.

"Fat pigs!"

"I know you are, but what am I?"

"Evangelist!"

"I know you are, but what am I?"

Like Monsieur Jourdain, Antonine Maillet would be "evangelizing" without knowing it, or rather, in her case, while denying it. One must agree that inverting the plot of a story does not make it disappear; one remains in the same textuality, the reference is intact. Maillet does not end Évangéline's story, she simply reverses the terms.

Those who see the end of "evangelism" in Maillet's work are mistaken. They act as if only emptiness filled the time between the writing of Longfellow's poem (first part of the nineteenth century) and Pelagie's story (second part of the twentieth century). They contrast the Deportation narrative—Longfellow—to that of the return—Maillet—the submission narrative—*Evangeline*—to that of joyful resistance—*Pélagie*. They are quite right. *Pélagie* is indeed the inversion of the American story of Évangéline or Father Casgrain's *Pèlerinage au pays d'Évangéline*—the Quebec tale—which was interested in mapping the dispersion. With Maillet, Évangéline (Pélagie) has returned to (re)build her country. However, this inversion is not Maillet's, but rather that of the work done by Acadian intellectuals on Évangéline. *Pélagie-la-Charrette* is only the reworked Acadian version of Évangéline, which has been running for more than a century in Acadia.

Under the sign of the return, Rameau de Saint-Père already announced in 1860 that Acadia had survived the tragedy of 1755. The first work of fiction written by an Acadian in the nineteenth century—Pascal Poirier's *Les Acadiens à Philadelphie* (1875)—features an Acadian privateer (Jacques) who comes to Philadelphia to find his deported fiancée (Marie). Poirier had borrowed this idea from the novel *Jacques et Marie,* where Jacques, already the figure of Beausoleil Broussard, was a resistance fighter allied with the French. Unlike Bourassa, who ends his love affair in Quebec—and of course, Longfellow, who ends his in Philadelphia—the lovers' return, in Poirier's little play, is to Acadia. From Pascal Poirier, *Les Acadiens à Philadelphie* (1875), to Claude LeBouthillier, *Le feu du mauvais temps* (1989)—through Jean-Baptiste Jéco's *Le drame du peuple acadien en neuf tableaux* (1932), Antoine J. Léger's *Elle et lui, tragique idylle du peuple acadien* (1940), or J. Alphonse Deveau's *Le chef des Acadiens* (1956)—all the pastiches of Évangéline written in Acadie during the last century will speak of return and resistance.

"Evangelism" thus this love encountered in Philadelphia, in 1776, the year the independence of the American colonies was promulgated, between "Pélagie" born in Grand-Pré, in English Acadia, who takes her people up north in a cart, and "Beausoleil Broussard," the Acadian privateer of the Petitcodiac River who, by sea, chases the English and regroups the Acadians dispersed in the new Acadies of the south and the north. Pélagie, like Moïse, will die at the gate of her country without being able to see Beausoleil Broussard again, in contrast to the poem where Évangéline survives Gabriel who dies in her arms.

"Evangelism" is also the national narrative plot found in the novel *Pélagie-la Charrette*. Pélagie is aware, as with the Hebrews, of bringing a people back to the ancestors' promised land. The odyssey that Longfellow had traced to inaugurate the American journey exceptionalism is reversed but remains intact. The waters part to let the promised people pass. These people, whom Pelagie brings back to the north, are already imbued with the democratic virtues of equality and pluralism. A people sympathetic to the War of Independence that breaks out during the long march backwards (1770–80) of the Acadians across America, Pelagie's son marries an Iroquois woman along the way, an enslaved Black person is freed in Charleston, South Carolina, who will be added to the marching nation.

Pelagie will not reach the promised land. On the heights of the mountains from which one can see the Memramcook Valley, near the old French fort Beauséjour, she will pass away. Having learned that Grand-Pré had now become an English country, she told the Acadians to go farther north and hide for a century: "don't wake the sleeping bear." She will not go to Grand-Pré but will say, like Pascal Poirier in 1930: "You will return on pilgrimage to bloom the graves of your forefathers."[50]

There is no doubt that this story is "evangelism," an Acadian adaptation/inversion of Longfellow's story. In her scholarly work on popular traditions—*Rabelais et les traditions populaires en Acadie*—Maillet rightly recalled that there were no popular traditions in Acadia relating the Deportation and the return of the inhabitants. All this, she said, is the renaissance elites' ideology.

In reappropriating the story, she also re-edits its pitfalls. Maillet is a wordsmith. The language spoken by the Acadians in her books is an old

---

50.  "Vous y reviendrez en pèlerinage pour y fleurir les tombes de vos aïeux."

French language that she has purged of anglicisms, in other words, of the corrosive effect of real life in a minority setting on language. All this leads her to propose an Acadia of memory that distances itself from the Acadia-society. "Grand-Pré no longer exists; no one remembers it—But it lives in history, it lives in romance."[51]

Acadia, she had already said in her Rabelais, may have said its last word, but "at least we can take solace in knowing that...this last word was well said." More recently, she had Jeanne Valois (*Les confessions de Jeanne Valois*, 1992), this pioneer woman of education in Acadia, say: "One day we will have forgotten even the name of Acadia. It will be a pity. It was so harmonious. But the generations that will succeed us on American soil, even if they forget the colour of the tribe that we were, will receive by osmosis the culture that now soaked the ground that their feet will tread." "They sleep under the walls of a Catholic temple!—Their names are ignored; the simple and rustic cross—Which told the passerby the place of their rest / Can no longer be found!"[52]

The "Evangelism" distances the story from reality and pushes Acadia into the memory. It was to get away from such a danger that the anti-*Evangeline* anger arose.

* * *

Herménégilde Chiasson is the other great figure of contemporary cultural Acadia. His notoriety is more circumscribed to the Acadian cultural space than Maillet's. Still, it is more prevalent there, although he too benefits from an institutional recognition that goes far beyond the Acadian universe. Prestigious prizes, honorary doctorates, and all kinds of recognition have been awarded to him by Acadian, Canadian, Quebecois, and French

---

51. "Grand-Pré n'existe plus; nul n'en a souvenance—mais il vit dans l'histoire, il vit dans la romance," *Évangéline*, translation by Lemay.

52. "Un jour on aura oublié jusqu'au nom d'Acadie. Ce sera dommage il était harmonieux. Mais les générations qui nous succéderont en sol d'Amérique, même si elles oublient la couleur de la tribu que nous fûmes, recevront par osmose la culture dont nous aurons imbibé le sol que fouleront leurs pieds. » [...] « Ils dorment sous les murs d'un temple catholique!—Leurs noms sont ignorés; la croix simple et rustique—Qui disait au passant le lieu de leur repos / Ne se retrouve plus!" *Évangéline*, translation by Lemay.

institutions, and those of the Francophonie. He is a versatile artist like few others, with a considerable body of work in painting, visual arts—cinema, photography—as well as in poetry, theatre, and essay. He served as New Brunswick's lieutenant governor from 2003 to 2009.

Chiasson, who studied at the fledgling University of Moncton in the mid-1960s and Mount Allison in New Brunswick, and was educated in Paris and Boston, is said to have deliberately chosen Acadia. At least, this choice has become one of his intellectual postures. A large part of his reflections deals with the issues of the artist's recognition in a minority environment, in an exiguous culture. He has been a tireless champion for the institutionalization of the arts, seeing the establishment of publishing houses, theatres, film institutions, etc., the essential tools for producing a "modern" Acadian culture. He has since constantly criticized the detour, or more bluntly the departure, of Acadian artists to Quebec, seeing it as a kind of alienation and an impediment to Acadian cultural empowerment. However, as an artist producing in French in Canada, a large part of his consecration comes from Quebec.

Born in 1946 in the small village of Saint-Simon in northern New Brunswick, a homogeneous French-speaking region near Quebec, he is critical of the natural inclination of Acadians, particularly in the north, to see themselves as an extension of Quebec culture. "Quebec has always been a disruptive element in the Acadian consciousness." Chiasson will be an Acadian of the frontier, the one farther south—Moncton—continually interfacing with anglophone and American culture. He will be the champion for a time of miscegenation, the hybridity, the diversity, the Americanness that this proximity of the other produces, without being naive, knowing well that there is another alienating slope for Acadia. This is why, in the last stage, one can perceive a move away from such an approach, which leads him to the retrieval of something approaching an Acadian tradition.

Let us not anticipate. Chiasson has been called the father of Acadian modernity. It is difficult to understand what he or his interpreters mean by this. It is undoubtedly not technical modernity; the renaissance fathers arrived by train, the tool par excellence of modernity, at the Memramcook

Convention (1881), which was to self-found Acadia. Nor is it a question of societal reflexivity, the awareness of making its history, which sociologists associate with modernity. Here again, all the work on the Évangéline narrative that we reconsider in this book is modern: Acadians receive, interpret, and modify their founding narrative. Traditional societies don't. Perhaps it is the changes that occurred at the turn of the 1960s, which we like to think of as Acadia's entry into modernity, to indicate the distance between "us," the "moderns," and "them" our fathers, the "ancients." Chiasson could not be the father of such a movement, as he was not a central figure in the angry Acadian youth of the 1960s.

Nevertheless, there is a dimension to Chiasson's approach that seems to us radically modern. From his earliest writings, such as *Mourir à Scoudouc* (1974), he is obsessed with the excessive weight of the past. The Acadia of memory is an oppressive, alienating society. He proclaims to have shared for a while the idea of getting rid of the Acadian reference, of the word itself, until the moment—in the film sequel *Acadie, l'Acadie?!?*—where Jacques Ferron will call out to the angry Acadian youth by telling them: "If you are not Acadians, you are nothing." Chiasson will reclaim the word, if not the identity, without, however, ceasing to lament the excessive weight of the past that it carries. He will never be a true neo-nationalist, preferring to emphasize, at first, wandering and hybridity as central characteristics of Acadian culture rather than a revisited memory.

Radically modern, because it was a question of thinking of Acadia without filiation, without memory, even without its national reference, in its pure immediacy. The artistic modernity of the West's history wanted to be iconoclastic and break the idols of the past. "We are the heirs of no tradition." Long after the 1960s, Chiasson still claims to be part of this modernist "tradition." This led him to want to think of Acadia as a simple place, in America, where culture lives, a place that is self-produced by the very dynamics of its institutions. Thus opposing the Acadia-society (network) to the Acadia of memory.

Chiasson was not alone during these years to make this link with the land and, beyond, the continent. Think of Gérald Leblanc and his *Éloge du chiac* (1995), this hybrid language spoken by Acadians in southern

New Brunswick. This modernism animates Moncton's cultural school, notably around the Aberdeen Cultural Centre—whose English name has been retained to demonstrate that culture is not a place of memory but of openness to the world. We will say that these artists are modern because they strive to create works whose themes do not make explicit references to an Acadian tradition. Chiasson would be the father of Acadian modernity because he would be the first great Acadian artist who expresses Acadia without referring to tradition.

A culture without memory, purely immanent. Something possible. Can such a culture be the place of an identity reference that allows a national minority to build a society? Chiasson and Moncton modernism will soon come up against this problem. I use the expression "national minority" to recall the inexistence of political boundaries and the weakness of the few public institutions associated with the minority space. Without political borders, what will limit identity, if not memory? This question is significant because Moncton modernism affirmation, of which Chiasson is the herald, coincides with the fading of the neo-nationalist political claim.

Will such a perspective not dilute the expression of identity and language in a mixture that would make the old autonomist dream of society impossible? For Acadia without memory is hardly a society. It has no territory of its own. Its societal space always refers to a skein with the other society...the Quebec society...the American continent...the anglophone society of New Brunswick. Is society not called upon to make itself invisible by opening itself up to these places? This question, not to say this contradiction, will be raised by Chiasson's consent to take the position of lieutenant-governor of New Brunswick (2003–09). This position, however symbolic, is the ultimate symbol of the harmonious coexistence of New Brunswick's two linguistic communities. Beyond the political, linguistic and cultural differences, it is meant to show the cohesion of the New Brunswick community. Acadians before Chiasson had occupied this position, such as Hédard Robichaud (1971–81), Gilbert Finn (1987–94). They were not reference virtuosos, and they were typical old elite Acadians, proponents of good-accordance, an ideology that Acadian autonomists rightly contest.

Such a judgment on Chiasson is a bit unfair. Chiasson is not a sociologist whose job is to produce coherence from the plurality of the world. He is an artist who expresses the questionings, the wanderings, the contradictions of his society. This is why, at the same time that he is called the father of Acadian modernity—the one who expresses Acadian society without recourse to memory—he is the most "evangelistic" of Acadian artists. His work is littered with references to Évangéline and memory. And, surprisingly, in contrast to what his "modern" posture and writing— *Oublier Évangéline*, for example—suggest, his references to Évangéline and tradition are marked by a great empathy.

His vocation as a visual artist would be born, he says in an autobiographical text (*Brunante*, 2000), from a pact made with his mother. She would finance him a complete set of paint tubes in exchange for a reproduction, "a copy of Évangéline's portrait, looking off into the distance where the Acadians were being shipped away from their land." In his first collection of poetry (*Mourir à Scoudouc*, 1979), amid the anti-*Evangeline* period, he recalls, with nostalgia, the days in the village when his brother painted Évangéline and especially "Eugénie Melanson," that lost youthful love: "You were the most beautiful though—When you disguised yourself as Évangéline so you could recreate with Gabriels-of-parades the memorable dates of an unglamorous past, swallowed up in the dreams and poems of yesteryear that you had never read (Eugénie Melanson)."[53] In 1982, he produced a theatrograph, *Évangéline: Mythe ou réalité*, at the Escaouette Theatre in Moncton.

In 1997, at the invitation of the University of Moncton's Acadian Museum, on the occasion of the 150th anniversary of the publication of Longfellow's poem, he accepted to inaugurate an artistic adventure, *À l'ombre d'Évangéline*. Thirty artists will eventually be invited to produce a work based on one of the three elements of Évangéline's name: "Eve," "Angel," and "Line." Of the serie first works already produced (about ten), Chiasson's painting *EVE* (1997) is the most directly related to Longfellow's

---

53. "Tu étais la plus belle pourtant—quand tu te déguisais en Évangéline pour pouvoir recréer avec des Gabriels de parade les dates mémorables d'un passé sans gloire, englouti dans les rêves et les poèmes d'antan que tu n'avais jamais lus Eugénie Melanson."

work. An angel walks over translated verses of the poem and, in the background, over texts by contemporary Acadian artists.

Yet another painting, *Évangéline Beach: an American tragedy* (2002), depicts a scene from the poem—the one source of the pact with his mother, the genesis of his artistic career—where the Acadians on the beach are waiting to be loaded onto the boats. This is not an exhaustive list. Évangéline appears everywhere in his work, as in this play, *La Grande Séance* (2004), in which the author parodies the historical "pageants" of the bicentennial "ceremonies" in 1955 by parading Évangéline and Gabriel on floats.

In fact, Chiasson acts as if he is aware of the cul-de-sac of the dead end, with regard to Acadia, in which his artistic modernity leads him. As Forest said, and as already mentioned: "In the end, it is not Évangéline that Acadia is contesting, but itself." To think of Acadia as pure immanence, a simple factuality of cultural networks, is to immediately note its fragility, its incompleteness. "The name I bear constitutes an identity crisis in itself." To historian Ronald Rudin, who was preparing a research paper on the 2004–05 commemorations in Acadia, he would say: "We must forget the Deportation," while agreeing, with some chagrin, that the Deportation remains for Acadians the "founding myth, the year one of Acadian history."

In *Les années noires*, a film Chiasson produced in 1994, he attempted to tell the story of the Great Upheaval's years by distancing himself from the mono-referential obsession, born of Longfellow's poem, for Grand-Pré and 1755. Like the people of his generation, like Antonine Maillet, it is the Acadia of resistance, that of Beausoleil Broussard, that he wants to put forward. In *Oublier Évangéline*, he recalls that this simplification of history to a single "us" event has made us forget that there was never a "surrender," that "we fought to the end," and that "Beausoleil Broussard went all the way to Louisiana to continue a fight that he did not want to interrupt."

The one who embodies the artistic modernity in Acadia expresses a lot of memory, even if he would like Acadia to leave it. He does it with a certain embarrassment, refusing to be part of a filiation, claiming that it is the "others" who are incapable of getting out of the too-heavy weight of the past. These "others," one wonders if they are not a creation of the artist, allowing him to seize again symbolically the past under cover of criticizing it. For, with the exception of artistic circles, there are no longer any other spokespersons of a second culture—historical, sociological, political—who speak of memory in Acadia, which is reserved for a primary reality, the identity pride.

\* \* \*

Herménégilde Chiasson and Antonine Maillet do not recognize that they are the children's heirs of Évangéline, that they carry the plague of Évangéline's land that Philéas Bourgeois stated at the 1881 convention. They are ungrateful moderns. They are—in the manner of the hip-hop group Jacobus and Maleco's song titled "La nouvelle génération remplace la Déportation" ("The New Generation Replaces the Deportation")—those who reiterate within the new generation the memory of the Deportation under the guise of replacing it. "We know you are, but what are we?" This is to say that Acadia is hurting for its memory. Chiasson is somewhat aware of this, which is why we will find him when we talk about postmodern Évangéline.

# References

BÉLIVEAU, Joël. *Tradition, libéralisme et communautarisme durant les «Trente glorieuses» : les étudiants de Moncton et l'entrée dans la modernité avancée des francophones du Nouveau-Brunswick, 1957-1969.* Doctoral thesis, Université de Montréal, 2008.

CHIASSON, Herménégilde. "Traversées." *Tangence,* n° 58, 1998, p. 77–92.

CHIASSON, Herménégilde. "Oublier Évangéline." *Aspects de la nouvelle francophonie canadienne,* S. Langlois and J. Létourneau, (dir.), Québec, Presses de l'Université Laval, 2004, p. 147–63.

CHIASSON, Herménégilde. *Brunante.* Montreal, XYZ, 2000.

CHIASSON, Herménégilde. *Mourir à Scoudouc.* Moncton, Les Éditions d'Acadie, 1979.

DOUCET, Michel. *Le pouvoir confisqué.* Moncton, Les Éditions d'Acadie, 1994.

FOREST, Léonard. "Évangéline. Qui es-tu?" *Liberté,* vol. 11, n° 5, August-September-October 1969, p. 135–43.

HAUTECŒUR, Jean-Paul. *L'Acadie du discours.* Québec, Presses de l'Université Laval, 1975.

LANDRY, Michelle. *La question du politique en Acadie: Les transformations de l'organisation sociopolitique des Acadiens du Nouveau-Brunswick.* Doctoral thesis in sociology, Université Laval, 2011.

MAGORD, André. *The Quest for Autonomy in Acadia.* Bruxelles, P.I.E. Peter Lang, et al. Études canadiennes/Canadian Studies, 2008.

MAILLET, Antonine. *Pélagie-la-Charrette.* Montréal, Leméac, 1979.

MASSICOTE, Julien. *L'Acadie du progrès et du désenchantement: 1960-1994.* Doctoral thesis, Université Laval, 2011.

ROY, Michel. *L'Acadie perdue.* Montréal, Québec Amérique, 1978.

RUDIN, Ronald. *Remembering and Forgetting in Acadie: A Historian's Journey through Public Memory.* Toronto, University of Toronto Press, 2009.

THÉRIAULT, Joseph Yvon. *Faire société: Société civile et espace francophone.* Sudbury, Prise de Paroles, 2007.

THÉRIAULT, Joseph Yvon. *L'identité à l'épreuve de la modernité.* Moncton, Les Éditions d'Acadie, 1995.

THÉRIAULT, Léon. "L'acadianisation de l'église catholique en Acadie, 1763-1953" in Jean Daigle (dir.) *Les Acadies des Maritimes.* Moncton, Centres d'études acadiennes, 1980, pp. 293–370.

THÉRIAULT, Léon. *La question du pouvoir en Acadie.* Moncton, Les Éditions d'Acadie, 1982.

VIAU, Robert. *Antonine Maillet 50 ans d'écriture.* Ottawa, Les éditions David, 2008.

VIAU, Robert. *Grand-Pré, Lieu de mémoire, Lieu d'appartenance.* Longueuil, MNH Publications, 2005.

VIAU, Robert. *Les visages d'Évangéline: Du poème au mythe.* Longueuil, MNH Publications, 1998.

WARREN, Jean-Philippe and Julien Massicotte. "La fermeture du département de sociologie de l'Université de Moncton: histoire d'une crise politico-épistémologique." *The Canadian Historical Review,* vol. 87, n° 3, 2006, pp. 463–96.

# PART III

## ÉVANGÉLINE THE CAJUN

♦ *indicates a publication.*

## XV CENTURY

**1492**
Europeans discover America through Christopher Columbus.

## XVI CENTURY

**1524**
Giovanni da Verrazzano explores the east coast of the Atlantic in the name of the king of France. He names the present Virginia and Maryland coasts "Arcadia."

## XVII CENTURY

**1603–13**
Samuel de Champlain names Maine and Nova Scotia "Arcadia" then "Acadia."

**1604**
Acadia is founded with the installation of a first settlement on Sainte-Croix Island.

**1605**
Port-Royal (capital of Acadia) is founded.

**1613**
Port-Royal is destroyed and the British take control of Acadia.

**1606**
Samuel de Champlain establishes the Order of Good Cheer.

♦ *Le Théâtre de Neptune en Nouvelle-France* [first play in Classical French], Marc Lescarbot.

**1621**
The king of England claims Acadia and names it Nova Scotia.

**1628**
Sir William Alexander Jr. establishes a settlement of seventy men in Port-Royal, renamed Fort Charles.

**1629**
Treaty of Suza: Nova Scotia is given back to France. Acadia and Port-Royal keep their names.

**1632**
Isaac de Razilly arrives with three hundred French settlers.

**1654**
England declares that Acadia is "illegally taken by the French." Major Sedgwick attacks and conquers Acadia.

**1667**
Treaty of Breda: England gives Acadia (Nova Scotia) back to France.

**1680**
Pierre Thérriot, with a few other Acadians, leave Port-Royal for Grand-Pré.

**1690**
Admiral Phips takes control of Port-Royal.

1692

Robert Cavelier de la Salle names the valley of the Mississippi "Louisiana."

**1697**
Treaty of Ryswick between France and England: Acadia becomes French once again.

**1699**
Louisiana is founded, and two hundred French colonies are formed.

## XVIII CENTURY

**1710**
Port-Royal surrenders.

**1713**
Treaty of Utrecht: Acadia is definitely surrendered to England and is renamed Nova Scotia.

**1718**
New Orleans is founded.

**1719**
The beginning of the importation of enslaved Black people to French Louisiana.

**1755**
The English seize Fort Beauséjour and force Acadians to swear fealty to the English Crown.

The Deportation of the Nova Scotian Acadians.

**1763**
Treaty of Paris: France gives Canada to England and Louisiana (Mississippi) to Spain.

**1764**
Around twenty exiled Acadians in New York establish themselves in Louisiana.

**1765**
Three hundred Acadians from Nova Scotia, under the direction of Beausoleil-Broussard, settle along Bayou Teche.

**1766-70**
Seven hundred exiled Acadians from Maryland and Pennsylvania settle in Louisiana.

**1785**
One thousand six hundred Acadians who had been deported to France are transported to Louisiana.

**1791-1809**
More than ten thousand refugees from the Caribbean, most notably Santo Domingo—including Creoles, enslaved Black people, and free Black people—arrive in Louisiana.

**1794**
♦ *Histoire philosophique et politique des découvertes et établissements des Européens aux deux Indes*, l'abbé Raynal.

## XIX CENTURY

**1800**
Napoleonic France acquires Louisiana.

**1803**
The United States purchase Louisiana from France, leading to American immigration to Louisiana.

**1812**
Louisiana becomes an American state.

**1843-46**
Alexander Mouton (an Acadian) is governor of Louisiana.

**1861**
Louisiana withdraws from the American Union.

**1861-65**
American Civil War.

**1865**
Slavery is abolished.

**1807**
♦ *Voyage to Louisiana: 1803–1805*, C. C. Robin.

**1829**
♦ *An Historical and Statistical Account of Nova Scotia*, Thomas Chandler Haliburton.

**1844**
♦ *Life in the New World*, Charles Sealsfield.

**1847**
♦ *Evangeline: A Tale of Acadie*, Henry Wadsworth Longfellow.

**1866**
♦ "Acadians of Louisiana," *Harper's Weekly*, A. R. Waud.

**1880**
♦ *The Grandissimes: A Story of Creole Life*, George W. Cable.

**1888**
♦ *Bonaventure: A Prose Pastoral of Acadian Louisiana*, George W. Cable.

**1894**
♦ *Bayou Folk*, Kate Chopin.

**1897**
♦ *A Night in Acadie*, Kate Chopin.

**1896**

Plessy v. Fergusson in Louisiana.

The US Supreme Court legalizes racial segregation.

**XX CENTURY**

**1901**

Discovery of an oil field in Jennings, Louisiana, in Cajun country.

**1904**

Birth of the expression "Jim Crow Laws," which refers to a set of anti-Black discriminatory laws (1876–1964).

---

**1901**

♦ *The Breaux Manuscripts* [anonymous manuscripts about the Louisiana Acadians, attributed to Judge J. Breaux].

**1906**

♦ *The Acadians: The Historical Basis for the Longfellow Poem of Evangeline*, George P. Bible.

**1907**

♦ *Acadian Reminiscences: The True Story of Evangeline*, Felix Voorhies.

---

**1909**

W. E. B. DuBois founds the National Association for the Advancement of Colored People (NAACP).

**1916**

Schooling becomes obligatory in Louisiana.

**1917**

The United States enters the war against Germany (First World War).

**1921**

A new constitution is adopted in Louisiana that forbids French in public schools.

**1941–45**

Cajun participation in the Second World War.

**1960**

John F. Kennedy, the first Catholic president, is elected in the United States.

---

**1919**

Theatrical release of *Evangeline*, produced by the Fox Film Corporation, directed by Raoul Walsh and starring Miriam Cooper.

**1922**

Suspension of the publication of the last French-language newspaper in New Orleans, *L'Abeille*.

**1929**

Theatrical release of *Evangeline*, directed by Edwin Carewe and starring Dolores del Río.

**1931**

Unveiling of the statue of Évangéline in St. Martinville, Louisiana.

**1932**

♦ *The True Story of the Acadians*, Dudley LeBlanc.

**1934**

Opening of Evangeline State Park in St. Martinville, Louisiana.

**1955**

Bicentennial commemoration of the Deportation of the Acadians.

**1964**
Dewey Balfa and his band perform at the Newport Folk Festival.

**1966**
◊ *The Acadian Miracle*, Dudley LeBlanc.

**1974**
Creation of the Center of Acadian and Creole Folklore at the University of Louisiana at Lafayette.

**1977**
Recognition of Acadians as an ethnic group protected by the Civil Rights Act.

**1996**
Unveiling of the Acadian Monument in St. Martinville, Louisiana.

**2005**
Hurricane Katrina.

**1974**
CODOFIL presents the first Tribute to Cajun Music concert in Lafayette.

**1976**
◊ *Don't Drop the Potato (Lâche pas la patate)* [the first book written in Cajun French], Revon Reed.

**1980**
◊ *Screaming on the Bayou: the Birth of Acadian Poetry in Louisiana (Cris sur le bayou: naissance d'une poésie acadienne en Louisiane)*, Jean Arceneaux.

**1994**
First Acadian World Congress in southeastern New Brunswick.

**1995**
Zachary Richard creates Action Cadienne (literally: Cajun Action) to preserve, promote, and defend French language and culture in Louisiana.

**1999**
Second Acadian World Congress in Louisiana.

## XXI CENTURY

**2004**
Third Acadian World Congress in Nova Scotia.

**2005**
◊ *Acadian Redemption: From Beausoleil Broussard to the Queen's Royal Proclamation*, Warren Perrin.

**2008**
Creation of the zydeco music style, a popular style in southern Louisiana that combines French tunes with elements of Caribbean music and the blues.

**2009**
Fourth Acadian World Congress on the Acadian Peninsula.

**2014**
Fifth Acadian World Congress in Quebec, Maine, and New Brunswick.

# ÉVANGÉLINE OF TROY

*On the banks of the Teche are the towns of St. Maur and St. Martin.*
*There, the long-wandering bride shall be given again to her bridegroom;*
*There the long-absent pastor regains his flock and his sheepfold.*
*Glorious is the land, with its prairies and fruit-tree forests; Under the*
*feet, a garden of flowers, and the bluest of sky Bending above, and*
*resting its dome on the walls of the forest. They who dwell there have*
*named it the Eden of Louisiana.*

—Henry Wadsworth Longfellow, *Evangeline*

## The True Story of Évangéline

In 1907, E. P. Rivas publishing house in New Orleans published a small book of about one hundred pages called *Acadian Reminiscences: The True Story of Evangeline.* The author is a judge, Felix Voorhies, a native of St. Martinville on the banks of Bayou Teche in southwest Louisiana. The shore of Bayou Teche—the towns of St. Maur and St. Martin—is precisely where, in Longfellow's poem, Évangéline finds an Acadian community and Gabriel's father—Basil the blacksmith—now a wealthy cattle owner.

Felix Voorhies was of Dutch descent on his father's side and Acadian on his mother's, a Mouton of the great Mouton family, one of whose ancestors, Alexander (1802–85), was the first Democratic governor (1843–46) of Louisiana, a senator in the US Senate (1837–42), and president of the convention that declared the state's secession in 1861. It was during his meeting with this former governor that Father Henri-Raymond Casgrain, making his pilgrimage to the "pays d'Évangéline" ("the Land of Évangéline") at the turn of the 1880s, though he saw in his son, returning from a visit to the family property, the figure of the proud Basil the blacksmith as described by Longfellow. *The True Story of Evangeline* is a story that Voorhies says he got from Governor Mouton's own mother, his maternal grandmother. He never claimed to be a historian but, as he later put it, an "authentic" recorder of the stories his grandmother told her grandchildren so that they would be remembered.

The grandmother, who is said to have lived for a hundred years, was apparently born in the parish of Saint Gabriel, in French Acadia, before the expulsion of its inhabitants. She had taken under her care a poor orphan, Emmeline Labiche, who was nicknamed "Évangéline" ("God's Little Angel"). Emmeline was engaged to a Pierre Arceneaux, and the couple was separated when the English scattered the inhabitants on the American coast. Just before that, however, the grandmother's proud and courageous family had attempted to flee from Saint Gabriel, prior to being recaptured and deported to the New England colonies. Emmeline and her family ended up in Maryland, where they were kindly welcomed for a few years by a Catholic family. Having heard that their people were well established and prosperous in lush Louisiana, they decided to travel there, crossing the Appalachian Mountains to reach and then move down the Mississippi, almost to its mouth. On the way, in Tennessee, notary LeBlanc, who was their leader and guide, died, unable to reach the promised land. Arriving after many challenges on the banks of the Bayou Teche, at the Attakapas post, Emmeline found Pierre Arceneaux, her fiancé. He had taken a wife and country there. For years, Emmeline mourned the betrayal of her lover under an oak tree at the back of the Saint Martin de Tours church in St. Martinville, Louisiana. She had fallen into a melancholy madness that would cause her death.

Voorhies had already published fragments of this story in the local newspapers of St. Martinville and New Iberia, two small towns with a Creole cultural background, located on Bayou Teche in the heart of Cajun territory, around 1890. *The True Story of Evangeline* soon became part of local folklore, especially since Philadelphia historian George P. Bible had already "accredited" it, under a certain prestige, in a 1903 book, *The Acadians. The Historical Basis for Longfellow's Poem of Evangeline*, published before Voorhies's book. Bible confirmed this story from the account of

Alexander Mouton's grandson, Charles Homer Mouton. The latter said that Alexander Mouton himself, the ex-governor, would have told this story to Longfellow, who apparently counted among his friends. Later, the great American poet's story recount was attributed instead to Judge Edward Simon, also from St. Martinville, and who was a student at Harvard when Longfellow was teaching there. Regardless of the source, Longfellow would have romanticized a "true" story, that of Emmeline, known as Évangéline. In 1955, historian Harry Lewis Griffin of the Southwestern Louisiana Institute (now the University of Louisiana at Lafayette) claimed to have found traces of Évangéline's fiancé Pierre Arceneaux. That same year, a monument was erected in Evangeline State Park in St. Martinville to honour Voorhies and his contribution to the Acadian community in southwest Louisiana.

Like Longfellow's poem, Judge Voorhies's *The True Story of Evangeline* is based on a romantic conception of Acadian history. The Acadians came from a peaceful and happy pastoral society, one they would have carried to Louisiana. In contrast to the poem's narrative, in which Évangéline makes only a furtive passage (two nights) to Louisiana, the real Évangéline (Emmeline) wishes to settle in the Eden of Louisiana, land of promise. She and her family are welcomed there, although Grandmother Mouton has reservations about the Americans' "materialism" that could corrupt her grandchildren. The story told is ultimately a happy one. The Acadians have a new homeland except, of course, for Emmeline, who "lived in the past, and her soul was absorbed in the mournful regret of that past."[1] To the "Acadians," he wants to instill a sense of pride and ends the little tale with these words: "Your Acadian fathers were martyrs in a noble cause, and you should always be proud to be the sons of martyrs and men of principle."[2] Grandma Mouton's grandchildren would then respond in unison: "We are proud now of being called Acadians."

Voorhies nonetheless does not want to only instill pride in the French-speaking population of southwest Louisiana by praising the merits of a

---

1. "vivait dans le passé et son âme était absorbée dans le triste regret de ce passé." (Online version courtesy of Project Gutenberg.)
2. *Ibid.*

people with a glorious past and gentle ways. The publication of his story has another educational purpose. The story, after all, is written in English, even though the author was known to write small plays in French. He wanted above all else to introduce a gentle and welcoming image of the French-speaking people of Louisiana to the American public. They are descendants of Acadians who found refuge in America. Their expulsion from historic Acadia was due to their desire not to betray their French homeland; they are valiant patriots. They have a glorious history and do not live in the past. Like Pierre Arceneaux, they have taken roots in their new country and accept their integration into the surrounding society (America).

## "White Trash"

Voorhies's little text is better understood in the literary imaginary in which it is inscribed. Or one could say—to use the language of literary essayists—in its "intertextuality." As we have already recalled, *Evangeline* had an immediate and immense success from the moment it was published as a poem of the American frontier. From then on, Louisiana and the Acadians will be part of its literary landscape. As early as 1852, five years after Longfellow's work was published, the novelist Harriet Beecher Stowe would initiate this cycle in *Uncle Tom's Cabin*, a novel that would become an icon of American literature. Éva (short for Évangéline—little angel) will welcome and protect Uncle Tom in his French Canadian planter family of New Orleans.

As Beecher Stowe's novel announces, America is on the eve of civil war, and Louisiana is one of the states that will soon rebel against the Yankees of the North. That is to say, the image of a pastoral Louisiana, the "Eden of Louisiana," as described by Longfellow, did not fall on fertile ground. The literary establishment, led mainly by New England anti-slavery advocates, saw the South as an un-American space because of its undemocratic—slave-owning—and Franco-Catholic character. It was not until the post-bellum and reconstruction periods that America again took an interest in the South, sometimes as a means of reconciliation with the battered part of the country, sometimes as a reminder of the radical eccentricity, the un-American character, of the region and its people. Journalists from the northern city's major newspapers, like the novelists of the *Local Colour Story*, revisited Louisiana and discovered the Acadians of the poem.

It was not the Acadians of the poem that they discovered or, at least, described. Instead of the idyllic portrait that Longfellow had painted, they portrayed a primitive and ignorant population living in miserable conditions. Thus, as early as 1866, in the aftermath of the Civil War, the journalist of New York's *Harper's Weekly*, A. R. Waud, following a visit to southwestern Louisiana, published a series of articles in which he identified as Acadians the French descendants living there: "Acadians of Louisiana" (October 20, 1866). "These primitive people are the descendants of French Canadians [...] and by intermarriage have succeeded in carving out for themselves a shallow place in the social scale. [...] An effortless life is their apparent goal in life. [...] Their language is a mixture of French and English, which can be quite confusing to the uninitiated."[3] This population would be a good example, he says, of "white trash"; those white people in the southern American states who live in social conditions comparable to Black people, if not worse. Moreover, the "Negroes," when they want to express their disdain for one of their own, call him "Acadian [N-word]." Waud accompanies this description of the moral decay of these "Acadian [N-word]" with a photo of the day, depicting the wash along Bayou Lafourche. These women "who have never seen a washboard" are presented without any modesty, the oldest one smokes a corn cob pipe, the young girls have their skirts raised beyond their knees, and the presence of strangers does not seem to bother them.

Longfellow had used William Darby's *The Geographical Description of the State of Louisiana*, published in 1816, and Charles Sealsfield's *Life in the New World* (1844) to describe Evangeline's passage through southern Louisiana. The former had said that this region was "the most magnificent country in the universe," the latter that it was the "paradise of Louisiana," and, to use Longfellow's words, "the Eden of Louisiana." The poet's inspiration came from Sealsfield, the Austrian monk who described the

---

3. "Ces gens primitifs sont les descendants des Français du Canada [...] et par intermariage ont réussi à se tailler une place très basse dans l'échelle sociale. [...] Une vie sans effort est leur but apparent dans la vie. [...] Leur langue est un mélange de français et d'anglais assez troublant pour les non initiés."

democratic virtues of the American "frontier" and visited the region in the early 1820s. Longfellow, however, retained from Sealsfield only the spectacular description of nature, the giant cypress trees and Spanish moss that drape the bayous-like banners, the birdsong, and the romantic-sounding names of the villages.

Longfellow had retained nothing—or wanted to retain nothing—from Sealsfield's terrible description of the Acadians he had met on the Louisiana–Texas border, then under Mexican rule. According to him, they were awful fighters, more enraged than the Indigenous peoples, more ferocious than the Texans (Spanish), more clever than the Americans. These "savages," "barbarians," "inveterate drinkers" were possessed, he would have one of the Americans in the essay say, by an "eternal" madness of always wanting to dance, which is why he—this American—did not want to settle near them. This image of Acadians as crazy dancers, loudly partying rather than working, would stick with them. According to Frederick L. Olmsted, a New York landscape and urban planner sent to Louisiana in the early 1850s to denounce slavery, a prominent planter even bought the land of Acadians near his property to keep them away from his plantation for fear that their laziness would affect the morale of his slaves.

## Creoles, Cajuns, and "Negroes"

Longfellow also failed to recognize the distance Sealsfield describes between Acadians—the small white inhabitants—and Creole people—the large landowners of French and Spanish origin. He said the two groups hated each other like monarchists and republicans in France, like two humanities that disdained each other. Longfellow will knowingly confuse them. The Acadian Festival that marks the reunion is likened to a Creole ball: "It was the neighbouring Creole people and small Acadian planters, Who had been summoned all to the house of Basil the Herdsman." (*Evangeline*, original verses by Longfellow). Basil himself is described as a wealthy landowner, more Creole than Cajun, acculturated to the country as evidenced by his "broad, brown" appearance and his "Spanish sombrero."

No wonder then that Harriet Beecher Stowe in *Uncle Tom's Cabin* had her Louisiana Évangéline born into a prominent Creole family in New Orleans.

In the *Local Colour Story* of the 1880s, this distinction between Creole people and Acadians will appear with more force. It will be at the heart, as Maria Hebert-Leiter has just recalled in *From Acadian to American: The Literary Americanization of Cajuns*, a series of works bringing the Louisiana Acadian universe into the world.

Kate Chopin's short stories, initially published in magazines and newspapers and collected in two books, *Bayou Folk* (1894) and *Night in Acadie* (1897), are probably the most explicit on constructing social representations and distinctions in late nineteenth-century south Louisiana. These essays mainly describe the world of a vanishing Creole society, although it is not insignificant that she chose titles for these two collections of short stories that recall Acadia and the land of the bayous. Chopin was born in St. Louis, Missouri, to a mother of French descent and an Irish father (O'Flaherty). Married to a Creole (Chopin) from Louisiana, she lived at the turn of the 1880s in New Orleans and, following financial problems on her husband's family plantation, in Cloutierville in the northern Cajun country. Évangéline country was an entry card for the American public, not the Creole one.

The Acadians are described by Chopin with a certain empathy, but they nevertheless remain a little stupid, lazy, clumsy. They are small people who, unlike the Creole people, have no Black servants. They are situated somewhere in the social scale between the Black people, former slaves, and the Black people descended from the "Free People of Color." Chopin's willing confusion of identities and social classes makes her short stories so delightful. In *A Gentleman of Bayou Teche*, she portrays an Acadian, Évariste, who an American photographer asks to pose as he leaves the bayou. The small inhabitant wants to dress appropriately, but his Black neighbour reminds him that the American wants a poor white man's face. He wants, she says, to be able to write in his journal: "Dis heah is one dem low-down 'Cajuns O' Bayeh Têche." Black people and Acadians are socially close. Even the "Negress" is called Aunt Dicey by the Acadian's daughter and speaks condescendingly to the Acadians from her "cabin," more comfortable than that of Évariste's family. Therefore, small white people who nevertheless remain white people can transgress the social ladder, which is denied to Black people. Évariste, who has saved the photographer's son from drowning, is finally invited to lunch at the wealthy white American planter's table in whose house the northern traveller is staying, much to the displeasure of the Black servant. In "Cadian Ball," Cajun people and Creole people finally marry.

In addition to this complex relationship between Creole people and Acadians, Chopin introduces another nuance to the naming of the group in question. She uses the term "Acadian"—Chopin writes in English—to refer, in a general sense, to the modest French-speaking inhabitants; she prefers the expression "Cajun" to refer to them in a pejorative way, in the sense of "white trash," usually through the mouths of her Black characters, like Aunt Dicey in *A Gentleman of Bayou Têche*. And finally, they would call themselves "Cadians." It could only be a nuance of style to account for the phonetic deformation of the Acadian word, in the Afro-American dialect, "Cajun," and, in Acadian French, "Cadien." But we will see that she is referring to something more profound.

If Kate Chopin describes with accuracy the identity porosity between Acadian, Creole, and Black people, at the time when Voorhies writes *The True Story of Evangeline*, George Washington Cable (1844–1925), in *Bonaventure*, will propose a programmatic that we will find thereafter in the Acadian recovery of *Evangeline*. Cable was born in New Orleans to an Anglo-American family. He is one of the most brilliant American writers to emerge from the South in the postbellum period. He participated in the Civil War on the Confederate side but later became a champion of American democratic ideals, to the point of becoming a harsh critic of the South and its un-American culture. His book *Grandissimes* (1880) critically describes the undemocratic and aristocratic nature of New Orleans Creole people—Remember child, you belong to a race that has never bowed to man or God—making him an ostracized character in Louisiana literary circles. He believes the South is impossible, as it is undermined from within by an undemocratic culture.

*Bonaventure: A Prose Pastoral of Acadian Louisiana* (1888) is of a completely different nature than *Grandissimes*. The story is not set in the Creole milieu of New Orleans but among the small French-speaking inhabitants of southwestern Louisiana, "the land of the Acadians," he said. Cable stayed there around the 1880s to write a description of Louisiana, a work done for the Tenth US Census. He found there, as the subtitle of his work indicates—*A Pastoral Prose of Acadian Louisiana*—the pastoral charm of Louisiana as described by Chateaubriand and Longfellow, a charm that he had not found among the Creoles of New Orleans.

Cable describes the Acadians with empathy, thus not condemning them to be "white trash." He is careful to call them "Acadian," and, in the novel, they themselves would self-define as such. The diminutive "Cajun" will appear rarely and exclusively in the mouths of Black people, like this one who wonders why these friendly, but somewhat slow, people do not like being called that. The expression "Cadian," also rarely used, is the way Creole people name Acadians.

They are still poor, ignorant, and prone to celebration in Cable's work. But, unlike the Creole people, Acadians are healthy. "Look at their history, all poetry and pathos! Look at their character, brave, peaceable, loyal, industrious, home-loving." They are worthy of rescue. True American frontiersmen who will benefit from the regenerative effects of such an ordeal. These are, he will make say to one of *Bonaventure*'s characters, "the only whites who settled on this continent without ever oppressing anyone." Their story is tragic and beautiful. They were under the colonial yoke in French Acadia…exiled and alienated in the American colonies…poor, sick and rejected in Santo Domingo and…under the rule of the great Creole for a century. The French and Americans gained freedom a century ago, the enslaved Black people are now free, it is the turn of the Acadians to be free. If only they could learn English—"the world's greatest language," which they apparently do less well than Black Creole people—they could become proud Americans. Didn't three of them become governors of Louisiana precisely because of their education in English?

The entire history of *Bonaventure* is centred around education and learning the continent's language. "Make haste to know English; in America, we should be Americans" is repeated like a slogan throughout the novel. Bonaventure, a young Creole orphan raised by an Acadian family, will make it his mission to teach English to his people. He is an Acadianized Creole, which for Cable makes him a suitable candidate for salvation, for Americanization. He will fight against the reluctance of the Acadian community toward education. He personifies the future, openness to American society—the "good fortune"—while his rival in love, Tanase Beausoleil, who embodies the Acadian tradition, dies early in the novel—Beausoleil is the name of the Acadian privateer who, we think, settled in St. Martinville. We will come back to this. As in the story of Grandma Mouton, the old Acadia must die for the new one to be born.

This link between the novel's ideology and the word that the Acadian narrative will seize is not fortuitous. During his stay on the shores of Bayou Teche, Cable frequented what would later be called the "Genteel Acadians," those educated, English-speaking Acadians comfortable in American society. In his travel journal, he reports that a Mrs. Voorhies told him how her family, exiled in Maryland, had moved through mountains and forests to settle in St. Martinville—the story of Émmeline/Évangéline, the young orphan, had not yet been told. The novel is launched by the patriarchal figure of the Acadian ex-governor of Louisiana (Mouton), who will take young Bonaventure under his guardianship, direct him to a good Acadian family and see to his education. The preoccupations of the "Genteel Acadians" in the face of their own people's ignorance were reflected in *Bonaventure*. Bonaventure, the Creole orphan, becomes a good American by passing through Acadian purgatory, a kind of frontier test. The reverse, the Acadian becoming a Creole, would be a regression, as Marguerite, the Acadian, is reminded in a Creole family in New Orleans. "Creolity" is for George Washington Cable associated with an aristocratic world separate from America's democratic virtues.

It is, however, a plea such as this one—that the Acadians make themselves Creole people—that Sidonie de la Houssaye will propose in one of the last books published in French in Louisiana for a long time, *Pouponne et Balthazar* (1888). Paradoxically, Cable, a friend of Madame de la Houssaye, suggested that she writes small local histories about the Acadian environment. They both share the conviction that education will bring the Acadians out of ignorance. But the similarity ends there. Sidonie de la Houssaye came from an old Creole family long established in Cajun country and received a bilingual education in French and English. After the death of her husband during the Civil War, her family experienced financial problems that led her to devote herself to teaching in southwest Louisiana, in Franklin and St. Martinville. She published short stories in the French newspapers of New Orleans—including *Pouponne et Balthazar* in parts—which will succeed in the Creole community. She will not show Cable's empathy for the Acadians, whom she condescendingly calls "Cajuns," but rather the prejudices of her caste. A predisposition that also applies to the Black population in the short essays she will devote at the end of her life to interracial circles—*Les Quarteronnes de La Nouvelle-Orléans* (1895).

*Pouponne et Balthazar* is a pastiche of *Evangeline*. One could say a pastiche in the style of *Jacques et Marie*, the novel by Napoléon Bourassa published twenty years earlier in Canada. Both stories are set in a place called "Petite-Cadie" and immediately after the events that expelled the inhabitants. De la Houssaye uses the first sentence of Bourassa's novel in its entirety to describe the Acadians' place of exile: "It is said that the exiled Trojans gave beloved names to the unknown places where they had come to seek a new homeland." Petite-Cadie, whether along the Richelieu River (Bourassa) or on the banks of the Mississippi (de la Houssaye), is on the margins of the surrounding French society, as if the Acadians resettled in new lands practiced integration with difficulty. In both books, the romantic framework is the same. Alone, the heroines are deported to the American coast; their respective lovers, patriots and activists, joined the French regiment of Boishébert before the English abduction and participated in the battle of Quebec; they will find their respective fiancées at the end of the hostilities, fiancées who lived with the missing lover's father, bruised and aged by the Deportation; the two older men will die in the arms of their son, unlike Gabriel's father, the Basil of Longfellow's poem, which the Deportation had revived. As for the lovers, they got married, lived happily and had many children in their new part of the world...French Canada for one and Creole Louisiana for the other.

However, in Sidonie de la Houssaye's novel, integration comes at the price of denying one's origin. Pouponne befriends Madame Bossier, a Creole woman, the author's presumed great-grandmother, who teaches her to write and to live according to Creole ways. This education is presented as a change in humanity; Petite-Cadie is perceived as a sordid place and the Cajun culture is described with obvious contempt. Cajuns are coarse peasants, drinkers, and fighters who speak a rough and vulgar language. The "Cajun wedding" is an occasion for debauchery where … even the women get drunk. Fortunately, Balthazar Landry, Pouponne's fiancé (Thériot), also learned to write during his stay in the Quebec prison following the French troops' defeat. After the marriage, the couple, now educated and civilized, will integrate into Creole society. Balthazar became a judge and supported the American rebels during the American Revolution. As for Pouponne, she will educate the little Cajuns while having inherited the Creole contempt for her own. The "Cajun wedding," she will go so far as to say, speaking of her marriage, is a real "cannibal wedding."

As with Cable, the Acadians are capable of salvation through education. This salvation in de la Houssaye's book does not announce any direct passage to the American society, except by a detour through the Creole society. Nor does it involve the rehabilitation of tradition; Cajun rusticity does not yield the democratic virtues described in *Bonaventure*. The Cajuns must deny what they are and what they were to reach the white civilization. Through the words of Sidonie de la Houssaye, the Creoles who, as Cable would say—*Creoles in Louisiana*, 1895—had agreed to the naming of all sorts of local Creole objects—from peas to Creole chickens and ponies—but who had denied this privilege to the "Acadians," were proposing that, at the very moment when their privileged status was collapsing in the Civil War aftermath, the Cajuns should come to join them through education.

Voorhies's short text, *Acadian Reminiscences: The True Story of Evangeline*, will be a direct repudiation of Madame de la Houssaye's appeal. The Cadians will not become Creoles. They will become true Americans while learning to be proud of their origins. This is how we must understand the Acadian appropriation of the poem. It will be so successful that the white Creole identity will fade away and merge into this new identity.

Before describing this process, let us return to the "true" story of the Lower Louisiana Acadians.

## Let's Stay in Louisiana

In February 1765, 193 Acadians arrived in New Orleans on the ship *Santo Domingo*, under the command of Captain Joseph Broussard, known as Beausoleil. They were followed in the months afterwards by a hundred more—for a total of about three hundred—all from the same group, all Acadians who had been held in Halifax Prison. When the war ended in 1763, the Nova Scotia authorities did not know what to do with them. They were forbidden to stay in this colony as colonial authorities were reluctant to send them to Canada—too close to their former Acadia—where the new English governor was willing to take them in for fear that they would try to return to claim their former lands; the American colonies faced with the same problem refused to let them be dumped back on their territory; and returning to France was costly and raised diplomatic questions. After all, they were British "subjects."

At their request, they were allowed to join the French colony of Saint Domingue—"a climate deadly to men born in the northern countries," Governor Wilmot had said while blessing their departure. Six hundred of them will leave, at their own expense, that is to say, by preparing a boat with the money they had just received for having repaired the dikes protecting their former French Bay lands from the tides so that the new colonists who arrived from New England could settle there. Broussard-Beausoleil, negotiated the departure after they were refused entry to Canada or to the islands of Saint-Pierre and Miquelon, the small archipelago in the Gulf of St. Lawrence that remained French. Broussard-Beausoleil would have planned to take his group to Canada or the Illinois country by going up the Mississippi. This is why, as soon as he arrived in Santo Domingo, he changed ships and headed for New Orleans.

Louisiana was no longer French. By a "family pact" between the French and Spanish royal dynasties (Fontainebleau, 1762), the territory was transferred to the Spanish Crown. At the time of the Treaty of Paris

(1763), the Louisiana territory east of the Mississippi (minus the city of New Orleans) would be ceded to England, while the western part would remain with Spain, which would, however, cede Florida, thus making the entire eastern part of the Mississippi an English territory...soon-to-be American. In 1765, when Broussard-Beausoleil, arrived in New Orleans, it was still a French governor, Jacques Charles Aubry, who was administering Spanish Louisiana while waiting for Madrid to appoint a governor. The latter received the Acadians with open arms. He needed new populations, especially farmers, to feed New Orleans, whose eastern hinterland— Mobile, Fort Toulouse—was now English territory.

Aubry offered Broussard-Beausoleil's band to settle farther west of New Orleans, on the other side of the Atchafalaya Basin, where the plain was beginning to emerge with difficulty from the innumerable quiet waterways known as "bayous," at the post known as the Attakapas, along Bayou Teche, in what would later be named St. Martin parish. They were given food, an allowance, and equipment. They will be associated with the Frenchman Antoine Bernard Dauterive, who has just been allocated large tracts of land in the region and proposes to supply New Orleans with livestock. The Acadians will be his herdsmen. And thus, Broussard-Beausoleil's band became the first cowboys west of the Mississippi.

Father Jean-François, who accompanied the Acadians from New Orleans to their new location, will name the place "Nouvelle-Acadie." Joseph Broussard-Beausoleil, born in Port-Royal in 1702, will be appointed captain of the militia and commander of the Attakapas's Acadians. He who, with his family, had left English Acadia well before the events of 1755 to settle on the French side, he who had led, with his people and the Mi'kmaq, a ceaseless guerrilla war against the English, he who had been at the battle of Grand-Pré (1747) and Fort Beauséjour (1755) finally found, at the end of his days, a land where he was welcome. Sadly, he would not be able to enjoy it, dying a few months later.

Broussard-Beausoleil's band was not the first group of Acadians to settle in Louisiana after 1755. The previous year, nearly twenty exiles had left New York to embark on boats bound for Mobile (now in Alabama) and from there joined the French populations of Louisiana, which had become

Spanish. They had settled on the right bank of the Mississippi, east of the Atchafalaya Basin and a little higher than New Orleans, almost opposite to Baton Rouge, which was at the time only a place-name in the Anglo-American territory and would therefore never be a French city, let alone an Acadian city. The little band was living next to a small German colony lured to the New World. These places became known as the "German Coast" and the "Acadian Coast," names that will soon disappear in favour of Parishes of Saint James and Ascension. This group was quickly joined, between 1766 and 1770, by nearly seven hundred people who had been deported to Maryland and Pennsylvania and who, having been informed of the warm welcome given to Broussard-Beausoleil's band, reached Chesapeake Bay and sailed to Louisiana. It was the new Spanish governor Ulloa who received them, happily, but demanded that they settle along the Mississippi with the small New York group and even farther up toward Fort Saint Gabriel and San Luis de Natchez (what would become the "second Acadian Coast"). Ulloa thus wanted to protect his eastern frontier, now English, by populating it.

The bulk of the battalion that would settle in Louisiana was still to come. More than twenty years after the first Acadians settled in the Spanish colony and thirty years after the edict that announced their expulsion and the confiscation of their property in Nova Scotia, in 1785, nearly sixteen hundred new immigrants landed. They were a new generation, many of whom had never known the land of their birth. They were Acadians who France had repatriated after the loss of Île Royale or brought back from England after a few years in prison there. They had been vegetating in the maritime regions of western France for more than twenty years, especially near the seaport of Nantes. Without land, accustomed, by more than one hundred years of life in Acadia, to the freedom of the small farmer, their reintegration had not been done. One had thought of re-establishing them in a colony in Saint-Domingue—and Bougainville will transport some of them to the Falkland Islands. But all these efforts had failed. Just like this attempt—"the Acadian line," 1773—by the Marquis Pérusse de Cars to make them French peasants, on his land, in Archigny, in the Vienne region.

Two entrepreneurs, the Frenchman Henri Peyroux de la Coudrenière and the Acadian Olivier Terrio (Thériault), organized this trip. They imposed themselves as immigration agents to the Spanish Crown, which was still trying to populate the land it had just acquired from France. Spain would pay them for each Acadian they convinced to join their Louisiana "cousins." The story goes that Olivier Terrio was punished for paying off his brothers in this way. He was cheated by his partner de la Coudrenière. So the ancestor Terrio did not make a penny in the business…but settled in the Eden of Louisiana.

The authorities insisted that the latter group also settled on the west coast of the Mississippi to protect the border from the now-American enemy. But many of them wanted to join a group of Acadians who had already left the great river Acadian shores to settle farther south, still east of the Atchafalaya and almost at the Gulf of Mexico, along Bayou Lafourche. These lands were thought to be less flooded than the Mississippi shore and more suitable for smallholdings, a mode of occupation that seemed to suit their way of life better.

Except for about twenty Acadians who arrived a few years later from the French archipelago of Saint-Pierre and Miquelon, this is the end of the Acadian settlement of Louisiana. Approximately three thousand Acadians would have settled there between 1765 and 1785, all of them by boat and none emerging from America's bowels by crossing the Appalachians and descending the great river, like Évangéline or Emmeline Labiche.

At that time, the number of Acadians who remained in the former French Acadian territory was no more than four thousand.

## What Happened to These Acadians?

Some Acadians had found a new ecological niche. Indeed, the waves of the settlement had drawn a quadrilateral around the Atchafalaya Basin, which would become the centre of Acadian settlements in Louisiana. The "Acadian Coast" to the east, above; the "Bayou Lafourche" below; the "Opelousas" plains west of the basin, to the north; and the "Attakapas" to the south. A circumscribed place, relatively restricted, whose centre—the basin of the Atchafalaya—is too marshy and almost uninhabitable, making communication difficult and isolating the communities that live there. A niche, in apparent contrast with the scattering of their brothers of the north who found themselves scattered on thousands of kilometres in the lands and islands of the *foggy Atlantic* and who would end up grouped under at least five different political administrations.

This territory is the gateway to Lower Louisiana, where the Mississippi, before flowing into the Gulf, bifurcates eastward because its own alluvial deposits block it; where the Atchafalaya, for more than 220 kilometres, remains as a road that seems to indicate the direction the river was supposed to follow; where the river flows sinuously over waterlogged lands and divides into the multiple small arms of the old Mississippi, forming many bayous where Longfellow would, a century later, make his heroine travel. He knew the outline well. "It was a band of exiles: a raft, as it were, from the shipwrecked Nation…" He takes them down the big river to Bayou Plaquemine, where the group will turn its gaze west to reach the towns of St. Maur and St. Martin through the beautiful Opelousas.

*Men and women and children, who, guided by hope or by hearsay,*
*Sought for their kith and their kin among the few-acred farmers*
*On the Acadian coast and the prairies of fair Opelousas.*

*[…]*

*They were approaching the region where reigns perpetual summer,*
*Where through the Golden Coast, and groves of oranges and citrons,*
*Sweeps with majestic curve the river away to the eastward.*
*They, too, swerved from their course; and, entering the Bayou of*
*Plaquenime, Soon were lost in a maze of sluggish and devious waters.*

*[…]*

*Over their heads the towering and tenebrous boughs of the cypress*
*Met in a dusky arch, and trailing mosses in mid air*
*Waved like banners that hang on the walls of ancient cathedrals.*

*Evangeline*, original verses by Longfellow

When the Acadians arrived, the bayou country was not the Eden described by the Romantics and Longfellow. The land of Spanish moss, lush vegetation, cypress trees, semi-tropical climate, and stagnant waters. It is a jungle full of insects, a hostile environment conducive to infectious diseases, with wet soils difficult to cultivate. Not much better than the climate of Santo Domingo, where Governor Wilmot had authorized Broussard-Beausoleil to go, finding it helpful to emphasize that it was "deadly" to the men of the north. This territory, sparsely inhabited by the Indigenous populations, had been largely shunned by European settlers until now. It is not for nothing that the Louisiana authorities welcomed these landless beggars with open arms.

Unexpectedly, the Acadians quickly acclimatized to the land. In 1803, when Louisiana was sold to the United States, the small colony had melted into the territory. It had changed its agricultural habits, had adopted a new cuisine—gumbo was already there—and had regained and surpassed its standard of living of the old French Acadia. The Frenchman C. C. Robin, who made a trip to the region at that time— *Voyages à l'intérieur de la Louisiane...* (1807)—will say that the Acadians have adopted a certain nonchalance proper to the southern climate, that they like dancing more than any other group in the region, that they already have dances in the manner of the Creole people and that one walks more than fifteen leagues to get there and ... that even the grandfathers and grandmothers attend. A new society was born with little resemblance to the old Acadia or the one being recreated there. The cultural mix with the African population is evident but also, unlike the rest of the tribe who stayed in the north, a return to the roots of French culture.

What seems to have persisted from this mutation is the production model of the small frontier inhabitants.

The small frontier inhabitant lives in relative autarky on their small family property. To achieve this, they practice pluriactivity: subsistence agriculture, which can include some products for sale, supplemented by hunting, fishing, and gathering to meet the family's needs. Like the old European peasant family, they do not have a special attachment to the family land; it is the environment they cherish. Hence their propensity—which the abundance of land in New World countries allows them to do—to move as soon as there are too many inhabitants in the hamlet—almost every generation—to a new settlement area, not very far from the old one, but where the new land allows them to reproduce, with their children, the pluriactivity.

For over a century, this mode of production, of the modest frontier dweller, had presided in French Acadia over the successive displacement of Acadian families on thousands of kilometres from Port-Royal to the Minas Basin, to Beaubassin, to the Petitcodiac. Pluriactivity made it difficult, if not impossible, for the group to reintegrate into the French peasantry, which was too rigid, too locked into its hierarchical framework. We saw the same thing happening all around the Atchafalaya. Along the Teche, the group of Broussard-Beausoleil, who had been transported to participate in the great cattle production, quickly abandoned the proximity of the large property to settle on small plots along the bayous, between La Manque and Fausse. At the end of the eighteenth century, the Acadians left the Acadian coasts en masse. The Creoles and the Americans will quickly covet the land for the large sugar and cotton plantations. They went south to Bayou Lafourche and west to the Opelousas plains, where land was plentiful and where pluriactivity—small-scale farming, hunting, and fishing—was more accessible. There was talk of a "second deportation," as if they had been driven out by Creole people and American planters who wanted to take over their lands. Instead, they sold them, unfit for large-scale exploitation, attracted by what Carl A. Brasseaux, the best historian of Louisiana's Acadia, would call an "agrarian frontier society."

Between 1765 and 1785, the typical Acadian family moves at least once as soon as they settle down. As a result, the original settlement quadrangle around the Atchafalaya Basin extended westward across the prairies to the Texas border. It was there, around the 1820s, that Sealsfield, Longfellow's guide, had found them. They were now true frontier beats who would have then moved farther south, forming a triangle that covered all of Lower Louisiana, with Bayou Teche as its centre, near St. Martinville and Vermilionville (now Lafayette).

The small Cajun settler not only had the economic qualities of the frontier, but they also had the spirit of it: the independence of the new society. On the Acadian coasts, the houses had hardly been built, and in

1768, the Acadians took part in the uprising against the installation of Ulloa, the new Spanish governor. This almost stopped any possibility of new establishments on the part of the Spanish authorities. Otherwise, they never showed any particular interest in the institution, which was confirmed by the fact that their settlements were scattered outside of real urban, religious, or village structures. They will also live relatively in the margin of the political institution. It was family, just as in the old country and as Rameau de Saint-Père had stated in 1860—the Bourque meadow, the Béliveau Cove—that was their only real institution. The frontier society was not a society of order; quarrels between neighbours ended more than elsewhere in duels, the "house ball," which was also called "*fais dodo*" ("go to sleep"), late at night, turned into a pitched battle. The transgressions of the order are frequent and not only at Mardi Gras. As the mid-century approached and inter-racial tension developed in the region—the "know-nothing" movement—Acadians participated in these vigilante committees. However, the latter, in addition to controlling enslaved Black people, attacked the poorest and the Catholics, which the Cajuns were. They were also the most numerous to flee the Confederate states' conscription at the time of the Civil War, "a war that was not theirs," as Cable will say.

The Acadians did not arrive alone in these lands of Lower Louisiana. They will become part of a region that will prove to be the most complex of North American regional societies in terms of identity. As we have seen, they settled in Louisiana at the time when France, which had colonized the territory for nearly sixty years (1699), had just ceded the territory to Spain. France had left nearly ten thousand settlers if one does not count the Indigenous populations, which were few south of the Mississippi, but very numerous—more than five hundred thousand individuals—farther up in the former French Empire. Since slavery had been introduced in the region as early as 1719, half of the ten thousand settlers were enslaved Black people. The rest of the population was made up of large French landowners and Canadians who were often the first inhabitants. The French had already established, as we have seen, a small German colony along the river.

The arrival of the Acadians had a significant impact on the white population: it almost doubled the number. The Atchafalaya area and the western prairies where they settled were not colonized. They were the first sedentary inhabitants, along with a few French and Canadians who moved from the territories farther east—Fort Toulouse—ceded to the English, to the west, especially in the Opelousas prairie. They were quickly followed in the 1770s by former settlers—here again French and sometimes Canadians—who imposed themselves as an aristocracy among them. The Spanish administration tried to introduce a Spanish population but it succeeded only in establishing a small colony along the Teche River in Nueva Iberia, which was first assimilated by the French Creoles.

## Acadia Blends Into Cajun Country

The population complexity increased during the Spanish period (1762–1801), during the short period of Louisiana's return to France (1801–03), and during the early years of integration into the American Union (1803 and after). Paradoxically, at first, it became more French. As we have just seen, the arrival of the Acadians took place at the very beginning of the Spanish government. Between 1792 and 1809, eleven thousand refugees from Santo Domingo settled in Louisiana, most of them having passed through Cuba. One third of them were French Creoles fleeing the slave insurrection in the Caribbean Island; another third was their Black slaves who were transported to re-establish their privileges in this new colony; the last third were free people of colour. This last category was an original feature of French colonialism, which allowed for the emancipation of former slaves under certain conditions (*Code Noir* of 1724). Although this population did not exist in the slave model of English-speaking America, it already existed in small numbers in Louisiana. Some enslaved people born out of white masters' wedlock, or others who had participated in the Natchez War (1729–31), had acquired their freedom. Their number was multiplied by the arrival of more than three thousand freed Black people.

These refugees from Santo Domingo settled mainly in New Orleans. They gave the city its flavour during the first part of the nineteenth century, a flavour that combines aristocracy and freedom. Aristocracy by the dominance of white French Creoles; and freedom by the breeze that smelled of new times, by the presence of a free Black population, often educated, fed with French culture. This population would spread to the whole of Louisiana, where the Creoles—accompanied by enslaved people and free people of colour who often worked as artisans—established plantations, thus pushing back the Acadians. They had settled there from the Mississippi's "Acadian shores" deeper into the bayous. The Creoles, Cajuns, and free people of colour spoke French; the enslaved Black people spoke Creole, a Franco-African dialect that was not yet considered a language.

During these years, the French presence was further expanded by a continuous flow of Frenchmen fleeing the Revolution of 1789 or by military families who had received land from Napoleon during the French interregnum (1801–03). These new arrivals were more significant symbolically than demographically. Symbolically—their number did not exceed a thousand—because rumour had it that they were nobles, which enhanced the Creoles' prestige. In St. Martinville, where many of them settled, it was said for a long time that, throughout the first part of the nineteenth century, it was a Petit-Paris ("Small Paris"), where people spoke, listened to the opera, and danced—the Creole ball—as in the French court. This was more a way to identify with the white Creole aristocracy and distinguish oneself from the Cajun peasants than historical truth. St. Martinville, let us not forget, was in the heart of Cajun country and would be the place where the "true Évangéline" would appear.

The Napoleonic wars did not only bring reinforcements to the Creole aristocracy. Louisiana was retroceded to France in 1800 through Napoleon's takeover of Spain in the artifice. It will be short-lived; after some hesitation as to whether the dream of the French Empire of America would not be repeated, Napoleon decided to sell Louisiana to the United States for eighty million francs, to finance his wars—fifteen million dollars today, a considerable sum for the time, representing one and a half times the American GDP. This was done in 1804. The ceded territory was vast: the whole western part of the Mississippi basin up to the Illinois country in the north—about fifteen American states would be drawn there. This change would open the great adventure of the American western border.

All in all, Acadians were still the plaything of economic transactions. For a large part, they had just been bought by Spain from France—the sixteen hundred French Acadians of 1785—and were integrated by a commercial act into the anglophone and Protestant United States.

In 1812, the Lower Mississippi River became the eighteenth state of the United States, under the official name of Louisiana. The Americans were quick to establish a population in their own image. As early as 1810, they brought 3,100 settlers (English-speaking), who were added to the American people already present east of the Mississippi—Baton Rouge and its surroundings were reintegrated into the new state. Planters from the southern United States will gradually settle there with their Black and Protestant slaves. The Americans settled mainly in the northern part of the new state. Still, New Orleans quickly Americanized itself, and American populations were inserted into the French-speaking islands of Lower Louisiana. From this latter group, the merchant and later industrial elite of southwest Louisiana will be formed. Louisiana will quickly lose its French majority. Only a Creole elite persisted until the Civil War in New Orleans and the French-speaking world of the small frontier farmer. The Cajun population was not in the majority in the bayous and the southwest prairies, although they did form a relative prevalence among the white population and gave the region its local colour.

In Cajun country, which would become Acadiana, the ancient Acadians thus quickly cohabited with a mosaic of groups that intersected and dissociated at the same time. On the one hand, there was the division between the white and Black populations, the most significant one, the one whose border seems impassable were not for the mixed-race children resulting from white masters sexually assaulting enslaved Black women, and also because of the presence of the free people of colour, who sometimes owned enslaved people and whose socio-economic status is higher than that of the small inhabitant of the border. There was, on the other hand, the division between the white Creoles, essentially of French and assimilated Spanish origin, the large landowners and their professional associates, and the small peasants of the frontier, who may also own some slaves, rejected by the white Creoles but whose frontier with them will never be watertight. There were also the divisions based on language and religion, the new masters, the "Americans" as they are called, with whom they will mix little. The Creoles were Catholic and French-speaking, like the Cajuns, the free people of colour, and the enslaved Black people from French colonialism; the Americans were English-speaking and Protestant, as were their Black slaves from the United States. Finally, there were islands of German, Irish, and Scottish settlers, who, depending on their economic status, will assimilate to the Americans or small French-speaking peasants, but rarely to the Creoles, who will reserve their caste for French or Spanish descendants in Louisiana. One can understand how the region became the place of an inextricable identity complexity.

What became of the Acadians in this mix? Until the Civil War (1864), their integration into the surrounding society, a society becoming more and more American, continued. In 1804–05, Governor Clairborne, in charge of organizing the new American administration, appointed Joseph Landry as commander of the Lafourche District and five other Acadians of origin as justices of the peace. In 1805, three Acadians were elected to the territorial legislature; only one, however, was elected in 1812, the first in the new state. At that time, northern Acadians were still prohibited from holding public office and sitting in the legislature. At the time Longfellow wrote his poem, a native Acadian, Alexandre Mouton, was governor of Louisiana (1843–46). As has already been mentioned, he had been a senator from Louisiana in the US Senate and chairman of the Commission that would decommission Louisiana from the American Union. A few years after Mouton, Paul Octave Hébert will also become governor (1853–56). Henry Schuyler Thibodeaux had already been governor for a time in 1824. Thibodeaux was an orphan of Acadian origin from the northern United States who settled on Bayou Lafourche. Not a true example of Acadian integration, but still proof that an Acadian surname was not a stigma at the time. Others became members of Parliament, judges, or army officers like General Alfred Mouton, son of the other, who fought on the Confederate side during the Civil War. By 1810, it is reported, most "Acadian" families owned slaves, and by the 1830s and 1840s, a group of prosperous merchants and farmers were emerging in the Acadian patronymic. Marriages between

Acadians and Protestant Americans were infrequent, with those between Acadians and Creoles being somewhat more numerous—especially between Acadian men and Creole women, more inclined to jump the class barrier as they were sorry for their men's attraction to Black women.

It is true that an elite integrated into Louisiana's "aristocracy," one that had emerged from the small deportee community of the previous century. But it did not mean that the Acadians had melted into Creole or even American society. It does, however, remind us that we should not completely overlap the Acadian origin and the small frontier farmer world; that we should not, in the middle of the nineteenth century, completely overlap the "Acadian" and the "Cajuns." Before the Civil War, before the popularization in American literature of *Evangeline*'s poem, the descendants of Acadian immigrants in Louisiana did not form an identity or ethnic group. Here too, as in the north, in the territory of old Acadia, there is no living memory of the events that led this group to settle in Louisiana. There is no trace of folklore either. Songs, for example, were built on the French ballad tradition and the rhythm of African origin, never in continuity with the Acadian memory.

In the early days, the place of their settlement was called Côte acadienne ("Acadian Coast") or Nouvelle-Acadie ("New Acadia"). These names quickly disappeared under the new administrative realities of the Spanish and American governments: Ascension Parish, St. James Parish, St. Martin Parish. The first historians of Louisiana certainly mentioned the arrival of the Acadians on the territory but never described—until recent years—the persistence of an Acadian community afterwards. Rare were the travellers who would refer to the existence of such a group, especially at the end of the eighteenth century. As time went on, the word "Acadian" would appear less and less. This population was sometimes called Creole (small), sometimes French, rarely Acadian. Darby and Sealsfield, who speak of "Acadians" and whom Longfellow consulted, are exceptions in this regard.

## When Being a Cajun Meant Belonging to a Class

What is this group that emerged after the Civil War that is called "Cadjin" ("Cadien") in French and "Cajun" in English? It is a social class, or a social state, more than a memory group—for the small peasant of the frontier. The name had no historical resonance at the time, except that it remained attached to the most significant historical component at the origin of the group. Joseph A. Breaux, who is credited with writing the *Breaux Manuscripts* at the end of the nineteenth century, a sort of historical and lexical inventory of the French-speaking people of Lower Louisiana, makes clear the meaning that was given to the term at the time:

*Cajun (pron, "Cadjen"), country boy. Air Cajun. Cajun habit; à la cadienne, in the manner of the Cajuns. This name is sometimes given in irony, but most often in contempt. It does not seem at all the abbreviation of Acadian; for it is applied indiscriminately to any Creole, whatever their origin, who smells of the country and looks like a peasant. He is a Cajun.*

Joseph A. Breaux, who participated at the end of the century in transforming the Cajun "class" into an Acadian "identity," did not define himself as a "*Cadien*" ("Cajun"). He was a justice of the Louisiana Supreme Court and came from a family of planters, but he was a Creole of Acadian origin. In the same way that Alexandre Mouton, his son Alfred, or his nephew by marriage, Judge Voorhies, were never Cajuns. For the Moutons probably... Creole people, but this is not certain. If many Acadians in the antebellum period assimilated into the Creole world, many were simply Americans. Far from New Orleans, where the Creoles were still accustomed to educating their children partly in French, the "Genteel Acadians" had been educated in English in American colleges. Until the Civil War, the elite from the Acadian milieu was more Americanized than the Creole elite, part of whose prestige still emanated from its old European culture.

Conversely, the small frontier farmer, whether of French, Canadian, Spanish, Irish, German, Acadian, or even American origin, was a "Cajun" as long as they spoke French and were Catholic. But it is not sure that they identify themselves as such, if not, as Justice Breaux says, "by irony," as in the expression "He's a Cajun like us," to qualify someone who would exalt his social success too much, thus denying his low birth. And here again, there is no certainty. In *Bonaventure*, we remembered how Cable made a Black character say to another Black character that he could not understand why these otherwise lovely people refused to be called "Cajun." In 1893, a reporter for *Harper's New Monthly Magazine*, Julian Ralph, "Along the Bayou Teche," made the same point in a report:

> *Nearly all the white folks who trudged along the highway were Acadians, all but hallowed by the magic of Longfellow, and it was strange indeed to hear that we must not call them "Cajuns" to their face lest they be offended that the term is taken as one of, and that the negro farm hands taken care of on the white men's places look down upon these people who have to take care of themselves, as the darkies elsewhere look down upon "poor whites."*

—*Acadians at Home,* Julian Ralph

The word "Cajun," pronounced "cadjin" in popular French and "cadjun" in English, certainly existed before it appeared in postbellum writing. After all, it was not novelists or journalists who coined the term, although Madame de la Houssaye's Petite-Cadie seems to be a borrowing from the French-Canadian novel *Jacques et Marie*. "Cadie," "Cadien," "Cayen," "Cadgiens" are diminutives that seem to have existed already in the days of French Acadia. It is reported that the expression was used by a certain Jean-Baptiste Cyr around 1785, when American loyalists fleeing the Revolution were pushing the Acadians on the Saint John River, farther north toward Madawaska: "My God, is it true that you no longer make land for Cayens."[4] In his *Glossaire acadien*, Pascal Poirier states that the inhabitants of French Acadia identified themselves as "*Acadgiens.*" The Louisianan Désirée Martin, in an autobiographical work in 1877, speaks historically of the "Franco-Cadian colony" and the "Franco-Cadians of 1754." However, the way the word has been preserved in Louisiana is more pejorative labelling of a group with low socio-economic status than a self-identification. It is not without significance that it was in a Creole woman's writing, the author of *Pouponne et Balthazar*, that it first appeared in written form in the late nineteenth century. At least it was against the use

---

4.   "Mon Dieu serait-il vrai que vous ne faites plus de terre pour les Cayens."

of this word and against what it represented that Felix Voorhies and Joseph A. Breaux wanted to give the Cajuns an Acadian affiliation, an expression ennobled by the American popularity of Évangéline's poem. Évangéline's romance served as a riposte to the contempt with which the French-speaking population of Louisiana was regarded in the postbellum period.

## Acadia Postbellum

Louisiana was then a defeated country. The economy was devastated. The old social structure where the great Creoles were enthroned had collapsed. The Creoles themselves were ruined, replaced by American merchant capitalists. As a class, white Creoleism was discredited, becoming little more than the romanticized object of a glorious past. Most of them will assimilate, trying to fit in with the new American elite. Having never thought of the people in democratic terms—i.e. as a "we" enlivened by common citizenship and culture—but rather as distinct humanities, Creoles versus Cajuns, they will not have the reflex to rely on the substantial dimension of their francophone culture to break their fall. They had asked for little or no special protection for their culture when they entered the American Union (1812), and they did not protest when the new Constitution (1864), shortly after the Civil War, abolished the few remaining provisions recognizing French. The French of New Orleans and the predominantly Creole areas of Louisiana perished with the class that had carried it: the white Creole.

Things were different in southwest Louisiana. Certainly, the economic devastation was just as great, if not greater, due to the great plantation collapse. The economic recovery was slower to occur, and it would not be achieved until the oil industry boom of the early decades of the twentieth century.

The postbellum economic disaster acted as a real steamroller, levelling down socio-economic differences. In the white population, we saw a real Cajunization—downward mobility—of the people. Ruined Creoles join the way of life of those they despised—the small white Cajun peasants— or become culturally close to them by becoming judges, civil servants, and teachers in Cajun country (like Madame de la Houssaye). The group of small planters, among whom were many descendants of Acadians, collapsed and joined the socio-economic status of the Cajuns. As for the Black population, the same thing happened to the free people of colour: their socio-economic situation deteriorated, bringing them closer to the former slaves who had been freed but whose well-being had improved little. Carl Brasseaux will say that the region inherited a third-world social stratification…a small ruling elite…and a largely poor population mass.

The socioeconomic race to the bottom did not have the effect of culturally homogenizing these populations. The legal distinctions disappeared thanks to the abolition of slavery, the ways of life became more and more similar due to the levelling of standards of living—Blacks people and petits blancs ("small whites") now broadly shared the same way of life, the same food, and the same music—but the identity distinctions became more pronounced. Southwest Louisiana became the stage of a strange ballet of identity, the "ballet of small differences." The free people of colour claimed the title of Creoles to differentiate themselves from the former slaves who had become free like them. Cajuns claimed the title of Acadians to distinguish themselves from the discredited Creoles and the Black populations with whom they are assimilated. Former Creoles affirmed their difference with the small whites (Cajuns), others assimilated with the Americans, and others joined the new Acadian identity. The Americans were taking over prestigious economic and intellectual niches and setting themselves apart with their specific religion and language. This phenomenon was happening all over the United States, but particularly in the South, against the backdrop of the new racial segregation policy—which would become known as Jim Crow Laws—enacted to sanction the new post-slavery distinctions.

Let's take a closer look at the Cajuns' situation. If the Civil War had resolved the white Creoles' dissolution as a group, the Cajun's issue had not. Their economic and ecological marginality in the bayous of Lower Louisiana had helped preserve their cultural and linguistic differences; the fact that they were illiterate, largely without schools, had preserved them from learning English. Their "society" had even grown through the influx of fallen Creoles who had come to join them. As the end of the century approached, the question of integration into American society became more pressing. In 1890, the railroad finally connected the main towns of southwestern Louisiana to the main American cities. The rural exodus that would typically follow was blocked by two seemingly contradictory things: illiteracy and the discovery in 1901, in Jennings west of Lafayette, of an oil deposit. Indeed, as illiteracy slowed down their exit to the continent, the oil economy allowed them to remain in a territory they had occupied for more than a century. The oil would even help them expand their group to the Cajun community, toward Texas (Spindletop Field).

The regional Cajun niche was destined to survive. The question remained of its integration into America. This would be done primarily through the spread of education.

As we have seen, the literary imagination that presided over the birth of the group's identity—Cable, de la Houssaye—encouraged it to educate itself. This was made mandatory by Louisiana's 1916 enactment of compulsory schooling; in English, the Louisiana Constitution of 1921 will see to it. The Cajuns would later say they were humiliated and forbidden to speak French in school. But this was done without much resistance. If "American" teachers participated in the anglicization of the little Cajuns, "Genteel Acadians," and former white Creoles—like Bonaventure in the novel of the same name—will also participate. After 1920, Acadian families gave English names to their children and once they knew English, stopped speaking French at home. The transition was rapid and brutal.

It seems paradoxical at first glance that the appropriation of Évangéline in the Cajun imagination occurred when the Cajuns were assimilating linguistically and economically into American society. An apparent paradox. *Evangeline* will serve as a Trojan horse for Cajun's Americanization. It was draped in the glorious banners of this great American poem that they announced their arrival as an ethnic group in American society. As Cable had suggested, the Cajuns were ripe for redemption, they were not "white trash," they were not former regime Creoles, they were a frontier people, they were frontier Americans. Elites from Cajun country would use *Evangeline* to be nobly accepted in a space that had become Americanized.

*Evangeline* stands up to the Cajun fact, as the pastoral and bucolic past of Acadia will replace the "trashy" image of the "white trash." As we will see, from the beginning of the century to the 1970s, the Acadian notables will know the term "Cajun" as an ethnic insult. Indeed, the depiction of the Cajuns as poor, ignorant, and violent will persist. In the 1926 play *The Cajun* by Louisiana American Ada Jack Carver, Cajuns are still associated with the illiterate and poor French of South Louisiana. Such stigmatization is usually done by outsiders, as in the Cajun humour that emerges simultaneously, initially exogenous humour deriding the group. In contrast, narrators mainly indigenous to the Acadian identity will from this point on portray the group as gentle people, in the romantic image of *Evangeline*. As in the poem, the image of the border as a romantic place of origin will be substituted for the rough and wild one. This is how Voorhies in *The True Story of Evangeline* described the people of this community as humble and straightforward. Alcée Fortier, although of Creole origin, invited in 1894 to a Cajun house ball, praised the pastoral charm of the Acadians, "whom education will easily elevate to the ranks of illustrious characters of Louisiana," he said. When, at the beginning of the twentieth century, Gustave A. Breaux, a former army officer, undertook the translation of *Evangeline* (which was not published in his lifetime), he dedicated his work to his race "simplicity."

The same is true of the presumed author of the *Breaux Manuscripts*, Justice Joseph A. Breaux, who is also involved in developing a memorial park for Évangéline's character near St. Martinville at the turn of the century. The *Breaux Manuscripts* are from the late twentieth century and would have been completed in 1901. They contain a glossary and a description of certain Acadian traditions. "Cadien" is by no means a synonym for "Acadian," the glossary states. There are two French traditions in Louisiana, that of the Creoles and that of the Acadians; it is the latter that Breaux wants to describe with sympathy. If there was a certain "rusticity" in the Acadian past, things, he believes, have changed since the Civil War. Customs had to be adapted to the new reality, including the language. He reminded the historian Bible in 1903 that few Acadians still spoke French. This is undoubtedly a gross exaggeration; at the turn of the 20th century, Cajun country still spoke French. But like Voorhies, Breaux aimed more at rehabilitating the "memory" of the French of Lower Louisiana (Acadians) than at exalting the "persistence" of a linguistic difference.

Felix Voorhies and Joseph A. Breaux are judges, Gustave A. Breaux is a lawyer and an officer. They are the first lyricists of the Louisiana story of *Evangeline*. They were "Genteel Acadians," educated, English-speaking Acadians, closer to Americans than Creoles. During the reconstruction period, they were the ones who saw the value of promoting the Acadian identity to negotiate their return to prestigious positions. It was not until the beginning of the twentieth century that an Acadian elite reintegrated the Louisiana power structures, following the disaster of the Civil War and the anathema that had fallen on all that was French. In a democratic society, the elite could not be legitimate without defining a common belonging with the people. By constructing a new identity, it redefined what remained of the Louisiana Francophonie under, from now on, the Acadian reference hegemony.

The Acadian identity would quickly become hegemonic. By the end of the twentieth century, southwestern Louisiana began to be proudly referred to as "pays d'Évangéline" ("the Land of Évangéline"). Along the Bayou Teche, in St. Martinville, an oak tree is designated as "the Évangéline tree," the one under which Emmeline Labiche would have taken refuge to mourn the loss of her lover. It will become one of the most photographed trees in America.

*Ah! how often thy feet have trod this path to the prairie!*
*Ah! how often thine eyes have looked on the woodlands around me!*
*Ah! how often beneath this oak, returning from labour,*
*Thou hast lain down to rest, and to dream of me in thy slumbers!*
*When shall these eyes behold, these arms be folded about thee?"*

—*Evangeline,* original verses by Longfellow

Couples of Évangéline and Gabriel, in northern forest peasant costume, now grace the floats of Mardi Gras parades. At the turn of the century, subdivisions of St. Landry Parish adopted the names *Evangeline Parish* and *Acadia Parish*. These were probably the first official reappearances of the word Acadian since the group had settled on the "Acadian Coast" 150 years earlier. It is also a sign that the Creole descendants—for the former St. Landry Parish is an old Creole area—now identify themselves as Acadians rather than Creoles.

\* \* \*

Despite its modest claims, Felix Voorhies's book *The True Story of Evangeline* had enormous repercussions. It heralded the transformation of the "Cajun fact" a class reality into an Acadian identity. The new identity allowed former Cajuns to enter America disguised as Acadians like a Trojan horse. Three conclusions can be drawn from this mutation:

1. By adapting the story of Évangéline to that of the Cajuns, the new narrative allowed their "Americanization" by inscribing their group history in the grand national narrative as Longfellow had already formulated it. It allowed for the dissociation of the Acadians' history from that of the Creoles, disgraced by their participation in the history of American slavery. The Acadians were, Cable said, the only white people who immigrated to America without ever having dominated any other people. Acadian lyricists would insist, until recently, that the Acadians never owned slaves.

2. In doing so, the Acadian narrative of Évangéline "whitewashed" the Acadians, dissociating them from the stereotype of "white trash, Acadian [N-words]." Today, whitewashing reintroduces domination—segregation—between white and Black populations. This is true, even if whitening the Cajuns did not legitimize dominance over the Black people; the Acadians remained a community of "small whites."

3. Finally, all of this contributed to "ennobling" the Acadians, giving them a democratic past as frontiersmen fit for the American dream. Their gentle ways and happy lives made them worthy representatives of the American dream romantic version. The romance of Évangéline made them an identity group, an ethnic group, proud of their roots.

Voorhies's account ended with this cry from Grandma Mouton's grandchildren, in the language they had just learned: "We are proud now of being called Acadians."

# References

BIBLE, George P. *The Acadians. The Historical Basis for the Longfellow Poem of Evangeline*. Gretna, Pelican Publishing Company, (1906) 1998.

BRASSEAUX, Carl A. *In Search of Evangeline, Birth and Evolution of the Evangeline Myth*. Thibodeau, Blue Heron Press, 1988.

BRASSEAUX, Carl A. *Louisiana's Historic Cajun Country*. Baton Rouge, Louisiana State University Press, 2011.

BRASSEAUX, Carl A. *The Founding of New Acadia: The Beginnings of Acadian Life in Louisiana, 1765-1803*. Baton Rouge, Louisiana State University Press, 1987.

BRASSEAUX, Carl A. *Acadian to Cajun. Transformation of a People, 1803-1877*. Jackson, University Press of Mississippi, 1992.

BRASSEAUX, Carl A. French, Cajun, Creole, Houma: *A Primer on Francophone Louisiana*. Baton Rouge, Louisiana State University Press, 2005.

BRUNDAGE, W. Fitzhugh. "Le réveil de la Louisiane: Memory and Acadian Identity, 1920–1960", in W. Fitzhugh Brundage (dir.) *Where these Memories Grow: History, Memory and Southern Identity*. Chapel Hill, N.C. Press, 2000, UNC Press, p. 271-298.

CABLE, George W. *Bonaventure. A Prose Pastoral of Acadian Louisiana*. New York, Charles Scribner's Sons, 1888.

CHOPIN, Kate. *Bayou Folk* [1894] and *A Night in Acadie* [1897], Penguin Books.

CONRAD, Glenn R. (dir.) *The Cajuns: Essays on their History and Culture*. Lafayette, University of Southern Louisiana, 1978.

DE LA HOUSSAYE, Sidonie. *Pouponne et Balthazar: Nouvelle Acadienne*. New Orleans, Librairie de l'Opinion, 1888.

DITCHY, Jay K. *Les Acadiens louisianais et leur parler* [*Les Manuscrits Breaux* 1901], Montréal, Comeau & Nadeau, publishers, 1997.

DOMINGUEZ, Victoria R. "Social Classification in Creole Louisiana." *American Ethnologist*, vol. 4, n° 4, p. 589-602, 1997.

HEBERT-LEITER, Maria. *Becoming Cajun, Becoming American: The Acadian in American Literature from Longfellow to James Lee Burke*. LSU Press, 2009.

HENRY, M. Jacques et Carl L. Bankston, *Louisiana Cajuns in the New Economy of Ethnicity*. Westport, Praeger, 2002.

LAUVRIÈRE, Émile. *Histoire de la Louisiane française, 1673-1939*, Paris, Librairie Orientale et Américaine, 1940.

PARKER, Alice. "Evangeline's Darker Daughters: Crossing Racial Boundaries in Postwar Louisiana," in D. H. Brown et Barbara C. Ewell (dir.), *Louisiana Women Writers*, Baton Rouge, Louisiana State University Press, p. 75-98, 1992.

RALPH, Julian. "Acadians at Home," *Harper's Magazine*, reprinted in *The Indianapolis Journal*, p. 2, November 3, 1893

VOORHIES, Felix. *Acadian Reminiscences: The True Story of Evangeline*, New Orleans, Éditions E. P. Rivas, 1907.

# FROM "CADJIN" TO "CAJUN" BY WAY OF ÉVANGÉLINE

*Let the good times roll.*
*"Those people really know how to have a good time!"*
*An idyllic, carefree race,*
*Crawfish, potatoes, and raccoon ass,*
*As if we were still in the forest primeval.*
*Strolling with Mademoiselle Bellefontaine*
*In Acadie, Home of the Happy*

—Jean Arceneaux, "La nouvelle valse du samedi au soir," *Cris sur le bayou*

## The Ethnic Entrepreneur

In August 1930, Dudley J. LeBlanc (1894–1971) of Abbeville, a small town in southwestern Louisiana, led a delegation to the 175th anniversary commemoration of the Deportation at Saint Charles Church in Grand-Pré, Nova Scotia, Canada. He was accompanied by some forty Acadians from Louisiana, including twenty-five young girls dressed in "Évangéline costume," each representing a village in Lower Louisiana. These "Évangéline Girls" dressed as Normand peasants overshadowed the Grand-Pré commemoration ceremony and amazed the northern Acadians, who were thus confronted for the first time with the existence, far to the south, of a living Acadian community. Dudley J. LeBlanc himself created a slight commotion among the northern notables when, in the presence of English-speaking dignitaries, he severely condemned British imperialism for its responsibility in the Deportation. This form of democratic rudeness was not yet practiced, at least in public, by his northern brothers.

On the way, the delegation stopped in Washington, DC, where it was received by President Herbert Hoover and photographed in the White House gardens. The delegation stopped again in Cambridge, Massachusetts, where they met Anne Allegra Longfellow Thorp, the daughter of Henry Wadsworth Longfellow, author of the famous poem. This was the first of three delegations that Dudley J. LeBlanc would lead to where Évangéline (Emmeline Labiche in the Louisiana version) was born, in Grand-Pré, Nova Scotia. Each time, in an apparent effort at publicity, the delegation stopped at the White House and was photographed in the gardens: in 1930 with President Herbert Hoover, in 1936 with President Franklin D. Roosevelt, and in 1963 with President John F. Kennedy.

Dudley J. LeBlanc is an ethnic entrepreneur as only multi-ethnic America can produce; he will play the identity card to promote his business and will manufacture and sell identity as if it were a commercial good like any other. In 1930, he was a candidate for governor of Louisiana. He displayed, defended, promoted, and sometimes invented an Acadian identity, all the while relying on it to create an electoral base from which he thought he could conquer the whole of Louisiana. In the 1920s and 1930s, America was still marked by the fusional ideology of the melting pot. LeBlanc was one of the first American politicians to understand that social integration, as a policy, would henceforth take the form of ethnic diversity promotion. He failed to become governor of Louisiana, but he had a long political career, serving four non-consecutive terms as a Louisiana state senator between 1940 and 1971, not to mention a term as a Louisiana congressman in the mid-1920s. He was the "Acadian" politician par excellence in the second quarter of the twentieth century, without ceasing to be an entrepreneur.

As early as the mid-1920s, LeBlanc was involved in the appropriation of Évangéline's figure for touristic-commercial purposes. It was he who, in 1926, proposed to the State Congress the granting of ten thousand dollars to support the creation of a park near St. Martinville to commemorate the heroine: Évangéline Park. He used the park's support committee to build his political base of support, just as in the late 1940s and early 1950s he would use the Cajun network and its voter base to launch one of the

ÉVANGÉLINE

most original economic ventures in postwar America: Hadacol. Hadacol was supposed to be a multi-variety vitamin that had the distinction of containing 12 percent alcohol, so much so that the drink would be on the menu of some bars. LeBlanc used various marketing tools, some of which would become standard practice, and relied on his support in the Cajun country. Large radio campaigns were proclaiming the product's rarity—he himself hosted a radio show—and people could only acquire the product in exchange for tokens bearing LeBlanc's effigy. However, the thing that helped him gain considerable recognition everywhere in America was the "Hadacol Caravan." This caravan travelled through the cities of the southern United States, offering shows with a Cajun sound, the "Hadacol Boogie," but it was not limited to it. Big Hollywood celebrities—Bob Hope, Chico Marx, Hank William—participated. Jazz and blues were in the spotlight because LeBlanc wanted to offer his product to the Black population. In the early 1950s, LeBlanc sold his company for eight million dollars. It would soon become apparent that both the product's benefits and sales figures were largely fabricated.

Dudley J. LeBlanc would write two books on the Acadians of Louisiana, *The True Story of the Acadians* (1937) and *The Acadian Miracle* (1966), the second being a revised and expanded version of the first. *The True Story of the Acadians* was the first "history" book explicitly written about the Acadians of Louisiana. LeBlanc drew heavily on the historiographical debate that raged in the early century in French Canada about the responsibility of the British in the Deportation, adding to the warm welcome his group would have received from the Americans. His hymn to America will continue with an account of the role that the Acadians played in the American Revolution. At the time of independence, they would have participated massively with the Spaniards in the war against the English—Louisiana being at the time under Spanish domination. The decision of the Marquis de Lafayette to come and support American Independence would even have been primarily motivated by his desire to punish the English for the atrocities they had inflicted on the Acadians at the time of the Deportation—the story would have been told to Lafayette by Silas Deane, delegate of the Thirteen Colonies to the French government.

Finally, LeBlanc insists on the Acadian loyalty to the Americans during the War of 1812 or at the time of their participation in the First World War.

LeBlanc is trying to make sure Acadians' history is remembered, not that of the Cajuns, whose names he rarely mentions. He begins his story by recalling how, despite the immense popularity of *Evangeline*, neither "our mothers nor our teachers" took the trouble to familiarize them with these peoples' "history and tradition." He took up Voorhies's story to explain their settlement in Louisiana. He tells the story of the notary LeBlanc—the poem's real character—of whom he claims to be a great-grandson. Louisiana was, for the expelled, a "land of opportunity"; the successive waves of emigration will be the consequence of the "flourishing conditions" that await the first settlers. He describes the Acadian dimension in the tradition of Longfellow's Romantic scheme, as pastoral and gentle people. The Acadian language is not a dialect, he insists, we speak French, not Cajun. To the surprise of his opponents, he uses this language in his electoral campaigns to show that he is from the "country" and he introduced French on the radio, hosting a political commentary program. However, LeBlanc is not there to fight for the survival of the French language or the French society. He wants to showcase his origins, nothing more. In 1930, he told a visiting French Canadian that, unlike in Canada, "We [Louisiana Acadians] have never had to fight for the survival of the French language."

Dudley J. LeBlanc was not the first to instrumentalize Évangéline for commercial or political purposes. While Évangéline had arrived in northern Acadia in the wake of a national reference development (a second culture that would take some time to become popular), she will penetrate southern Acadia directly as a popular icon, a first culture. Why? Because the type of grouping that was being put in place in Louisiana's Acadia was very different from the one that had developed a few years earlier in the former territory of French Acadia. Here, Acadia was a heritage, the memory of a group that wanted to instill pride to participate with dignity in the American dream: this is what sociologists call an "ethnic group." There, farther north, in mimicry with French Canada, the group proposed to constitute itself as an autonomous society, to do a work of civilization by turning its back, so to speak, on America; this is what sociologists call "a nationalistic grouping" or "a national minority." However, the two characters, Évangéline the Acadian and Évangéline the Cajun, will have different fates.

## Evangeline Country

We saw in the previous chapter that upon entering Cajun country, Évangéline appears in the form of a tale (*The True Story of Evangeline*, Voorhies) unique to the initial culture; the history will come later as a confirmation of this tale. By the end of the century, the region was proudly called "le pays d'Évangéline" ("the Land of Évangéline"), and the Évangéline Oak in St. Martinville was used for tourism purposes. A campaign was launched not much later to erect a statue of the heroine in a future park, a project in which Joseph A. Breaux and Dudley J. LeBlanc took part. At the turn of the 1920s, these activities intensified. Susan Evangeline Walker Anding of St. Martinville created a committee to promote the park, again for tourism and identity purposes. She was the first to have the idea of dressing up girls as Évangéline the Norman to promote her project and attract political support. She exhibited her "Évangéline" at the Philadelphia Sesquicentennial Exposition in 1926, commemorating the 150th anniversary of the American Revolution. The event was a success, and a department store on Fifth Avenue in New York displayed Évangéline's costumes. She took her lobby, seventeen Evangeline Girls, to the Demo Convention in Houston two years later.

While the Evangeline Girls' offensive failed to convince the US government to make the land near St. Martinville a national park, the Louisiana government did agree to make it Louisiana's first state park: the Longfellow-Evangeline State Park (1934). The presence in the park of a house said to be the home of Louis Arceneaux—the Gabriel of *The True Story of Evangeline* (Voorhies)—is reasonably representative of the identity issues at work in Louisiana re-approval of the poem. The rich house belonged to Charles de Closel Olivier. Olivier was Creole and had his residence built in the early nineteenth century, too late to have been inhabited by the Louis Arceneaux of "the true story." Unless one considers them as pure idiots, one can say that the notables of St. Martinville were undoubtedly aware of these facts. All the more so since St. Martinville had been the great Creole city of Cajun country in the very recent past. But it must be seen that this did not bother them, for their plan was to ennoble the Cajuns. In so doing, the new Acadian identity has in fact appropriated the Creole past of the region, for, in their decline, a part of the Creoles had indeed "cajunized" themselves.

During the 1980s the Louisiana State Parks Administration, in the name of historical truth, forced Évangéline Park's officials to rename the Louis Arceneaux House the Olivier House. A Cajun cabin was built a little ways away, better reflecting the state of poverty of a large part of the Acadians of the time.

At the forefront of this promotion of *Evangeline* were, at the turn of the 1930s, the local economic elites. St. Martinville had had its glory in the days of the Grand Creoles. The oil economy and the continental railroad running farther north made Lafayette the regional economic centre. Competing with New Iberia, another Creole city in economic decline, the St. Martinville Chamber of Commerce saw the promotion of *Evangeline* as a way to revitalize the regional economy of deep south Louisiana. The road system development announced the rise of automobile tourism.

The identity issue was no less present. By promoting the "pays d'Evangeline," an ennobled image of the Cajuns was also presented to America. Tour guides began to present the region's inhabitants as the descendants of the famous Longfellow lovers. The terms Cadiens and Cajuns (except to remind us that they distort the name "Acadian") do not appear in these advertisements. Hence, the inhabitants are Acadians with a gentle and peaceful way of life, primarily confused with the Creoles, whose name is usually kept silent. And it works. As early as 1928, the great French writer Paul Claudel, French ambassador to the United States, visited St. Martinville and the Évangéline tree. His daughter was given a copy of Longfellow's poem, and he was given an autographed copy of Voorhies's *True Story of Evangeline*. The *New York Times* reported on Claudel's visit using terms in stark contrast to the "white trash" that Waud had used in *Harper's Weekly* some sixty years earlier. According to the *New York*

*Times*: "In the Bayou Teche country of Louisiana he [Claudel] found them: gentle, merry but determined farmer folk, the kinsfolk of Évangéline and Gabriel Lajeunesse."

The figure of Évangéline will reach its zenith of popularity with the production (1929–30) of the second great American silent film based on Longfellow's poem: *Evangeline* (1931), by Hollywood Edwin Carewe Production. William Fox had directed the first in 1929. Carewe's film would be the last major "American" film production of the poem, as the 1920s will become the time of Longfellow's fading from the niche of great national poets (see Part I). Carewe's *Evangeline* is a pivotal film; from then on, the heroine will be a minor character associated with American history, an "ethnic" figure, that of the "Acadians." Carewe was convinced by André A. Ollivier, secretary of the St. Martinville Chamber of Commerce and the excellent local authority, from the 1930s onward, of "the true story of Évangéline," to shoot the film in Louisiana. He insisted that such a film could not be made anywhere but in the "pays d'Évangéline." The choice of a well-known actress of Mexican origin, Dolores del Río, to play the role of Évangéline also contributes to this ethnicization. Up to this point, Évangéline had always been portrayed as a European, a mainstream Anglo-European American; now, she is portrayed as a slightly swarthy woman. If the Cajuns were using Évangéline to penetrate America, it was done in conjunction with the redefinition of a multi-ethnic America.

During the filming, Dolores del Río was made aware of "the true history of Évangéline" and the existence, according to André A. Ollivier, of Emmeline Labiche's tomb near the church of St. Martin of Tours. After that, she agreed to finance the installation of a statue. This statue will be similar to the first famous portrait of Évangéline painted in 1854 by the Scottish artist Thomas Faed: Évangéline looking for her family in a cemetery. "Written their history stands on tablets of stone in the church-yards" (*Evangeline*, original verses by Longfellow). Dolores del Río herself will serve as a model for the famous character. The statue, ready in 1930, was inaugurated only in 1931, awaiting a delegation from Canada (from Acadia and French Canada) of about one hundred notables on a tourist pilgrimage who were returning Dudley J. LeBlanc's visit, the year before, to the other Évangéline from Grand-Pré, whose statue had been inaugurated about ten years earlier. The two Évangélines were somewhat competitive. In 1930, at the time of LeBlanc's trip to Canada, the Lafayette and St. Martinville newspapers—*Lafayette Tribune*; *Weekly Magazine*—will state that the Canadian Acadians want the body of Emmeline Labiche, the real Évangéline, back in Grand-Pré where she was born and...where her true homeland is.

The Canadians' visit takes place in an Évangéline carnival. In each town and village where the delegation stopped, they were greeted by young girls dressed as Nordic peasant women who, as in ancient Greece, were wrapped in flowers that they handed out, forming alleys to lead the guests to the reunion agape. At the lavish ceremony for the unveiling of Évangéline's statue in St. Martinville, it is once again through the figure of Évangéline that the Acadian's pastoral simplicity is sung. Lafayette Bishop Jeanmard will describe to the guests the people they are called to discover: "They are hospitable and generous. They have retained the simplicity of the dove and the gentleness of the lamb; they are hospitable and generous, sometimes in spite of their poverty, forgiving their enemies and not wishing them ill."[1] Longfellow described their character well in these apt lines: "Men whose lives glided on like rivers that water the woodlands."

The Canadian delegation's trip was the second rediscovery by French Canada that Acadians had survived the Deportation. The first had been that of the Acadians, in the middle of the nineteenth century in the Maritimes, following the publication of Rameau de Saint-Père's book: *La France aux colonies* (1859). In Canada, it was believed that the French in Louisiana had died out with the Creoles' assimilation. As early as 1831, the Canadian journalist Étienne Parent will say, speaking of the difficult survival of French in America: "*Le sort de la Louisiane nous fait trembler*" ("The fate of Louisiana makes us tremble"). The more the century

---

1.  "Ils sont hospitaliers et généreux. Ils ont conservé la simplicité de la colombe et la douceur de l'agneau; ils sont hospitaliers et généreux, parfois malgré leur pauvreté; pardonnant à leurs ennemis et ne leur voulant pas de mal."

progressed, the more Louisiana would serve in French Canada as a repellent to any annex attempt with the American Republic. Therefore, it was with amazement that the patriotic delegation organized by the newspapers *Le Devoir* (Montreal) and *L'Évangéline* (Moncton) noted the presence of over five hundred thousand Acadians. Bishop J. H. Prudhomme, reporting on this trip to Louisiana in the newspaper *Le Devoir*, titled his article "Les morts qui vivent" ("The Dead Who Live").

For the Cajuns, the *Evangeline* pilgrimage was an opportunity to establish ties with their "brothers" from the north, confirm their Acadian origins, and ascertain that the language they spoke was indeed French. As early as 1905, Joseph A. Breaux—the alleged author of the *Breaux Manuscripts*—attended the Acadian Convention in Saint-Basile, New Brunswick. In 1928, Dudley J. LeBlanc, accompanied by a small delegation, went to the New England Acadians in Waltham, Massachusetts, where he began to spread the fabulous story of "the true Évangéline." Contacts were established. Some priests and religious communities from the north settled in Louisiana to try to spread the Catholic and French spirit there, especially after establishing the Lafayette diocese in 1903, which made the Cajun country almost an autonomous religious entity. Dudley J. LeBlanc himself will point out that his love and knowledge of Acadia came, for the most part, from his meeting with a priest from northern Acadia, a certain Father Chiasson.

The patriotic-religious feeling of the northern Franco-Catholics did not take root in the south, nor did the tradition of large patriotic gatherings—the national conventions—which had come to give rhythm to the nationalism life up there. The Cajun identity will be less tragic, less institutionalized, more popular, more festive…a happy encounter with America. It is rather they—the Cajuns—who will come to infuse the tragic identity of their northern cousins with a sense of pride, dressing up as Évangéline and Gabriel for every happy event, and placing them on floats in the many parades and festivals that marked life in the Eden of Louisiana.

## Cajun Renewal

In the fall of 1964, Dewey Balfa—a Cajun fiddler and singer—returned from the reception he and his band (Gladius Thibodeaux, Vinesse Lejeune) had received at the great American folk music festival in Rhode Island: the Newport Folk Festival. Anxious "to bring home the echo of the standing ovation" they received there, he will be, for the next quarter-century, one of the most active artists involved in the revival of this music. He will also be its greatest ambassador in the rest of the United States, in France, Quebec, and Acadia. His many awards and recognitions— National Heritage Award (1982); Grammy Award nomination for his album *Souvenir* (1986); professor of Cajun music at the University of Louisiana at Lafayette (1988)—testify to the recognition acquired over the years by the Cajun sound.

Cajun music had fallen into a kind of disgrace, swept away by the Americanization and Anglicization that had been blown through the Cajun country like a hurricane since the 1920s. It was also too much associated with the "white trash" image that the promoters of Évangéline wanted to attack in their attempt to Acadianize the Cajuns. The latter were the heirs of a rich musical tradition. Since the beginning of the nineteenth century, all observers have noted the Cajun's propensity, some would say almost diabolical, to dance to the rhythm of a particular sound. To tell the story of this music would be to pick up the thread of the many encounters that have shaped the country. French ballads; African, Irish, and Scottish sound; blues of the southern rural Black Americans; Celtic music; guitar and accordion borrowed from Europeans of passage; and American folk and western, are elements that, through borrowings, hybridization, and reformulations, have produced this particular music. Cajun ballads never speak of the country's identity. They are instead love stories that nevertheless broadly define its identity.

The 1930s, with the first recordings of Cajun music—"Allons à Lafayette," recorded by Joe Falcon and Cléoma Breaux in 1928; and "Jolie Blonde" by Amédé, Ophé, and Cléopha Breaux—will establish a certain classicism, if one can use this expression for a musical tradition that was essentially vernacular until then. The entry of Cajun music into the electronic age almost destroyed it right before American music reached the Cajun country. After that, Cajuns began to sing in English and adapt their music to the American sound. In the dance halls, which after the 1930s replaced the inhabitants' "fais dodo"[2]—the term used for the Cajun dance—country music and swamp pop (a Cajun adaptation of rock and roll) replaced the old Cajun sound. In 1955 the indefatigable Dudley J. LeBlanc and Roy Thériot, mayor of Abbeville, under the high patronage of Évangéline, organized throughout Lower Louisiana, "pageants," parades, and popular festivals to commemorate the bicentennial of the Acadian "migrations." During this time, the American radio station kept playing Bill Haley & His Comets's *See You Later Alligator* on its swamp pop, lyrics, dance, and music by Cajun Bob Charles Guidry. Cajun music seemed to be relegated to a few old stoops and dance halls in small towns on the plains, far removed from New Orleans and even from Lafayette, as in Mamou, for example, the neighbouring town where Dewey Balfa comes from. The festival audience gave Balfa a standing ovation, justifying his emotion: the Cajun sound could still please!

It was the beginning of the 1960s. What had been emerging since the Anglo-American fusion identity crisis of the 1920s, which had already signed Longfellow's fall as the narrator of the American narrative, was confirmed. The civil rights movement was in full swing. After his election, John F. Kennedy immediately visited Ireland and recalled that he was an Irish-American. America had changed; it was no longer the recent era when President Roosevelt could say that there was no such thing as a hyphenated American and that the American melting pot could only have one language: English. The Black struggle for emancipation and the valorization of ethnicity were not of the same nature. American multiculturalism carries with it a certain distancing from the civil rights movement through the valorization of small white cultures of European origin—as was the case with "Cadianity." But the two movements converged in the America of the

---

2.   Translator's note: It was believed for a time that "fais dodo" referred to "fait de dieux" (act of God) but it was a bad translation of the well-known French expression "fais dodo," meaning "go to sleep."

1960s to a certain glorification of the difference: "Black is beautiful." Alex Haley worked in the 1970s on his great novel *Roots*—published in 1976—on the history of Black people and American slavery, the popularity of which confirmed the infatuation of the new America with its plural roots.

If America had changed and was ready to hear the Cajun sound, the Cajuns themselves had to be willing to say: "I'm proud to be Cajun." But there was reluctance. At the time when Balfa and his band were invited to perform at the Newport Folk Festival (October 1964), the Opelousas *Daily World* editorial writer wondered: "What is this noise called 'Cajun music' that wants to represent the Cajuns at the festival?" It is not, he thinks, "the discovery of something great that was hidden all these years from the rest of the country." Instead, it was something shameful that had to be put out of one's mind. It took ten years for Balfa's wish to publicly revive Cajun music in Louisiana to come true with the 1974 Tribute to Cajun Music Festival in Lafayette. It was the first time that Acadian culture and Cajun music were publicly associated in the most official way possible, under the patronage of the new organization dedicated to the defence of the French language, CODOFIL (Council for the Development of French in Louisiana). Still, it was necessary to convince the new organization's leader, mainly its president Jimmy Domengeaux, that such an association was not incompatible with their desire to preserve the French in Louisiana.

The creation of CODOFIL as a state organization dedicated to preserving French in Louisiana (1968) was both the accomplishment of the Évangéline generation's efforts to restore Acadia to the Cajuns and an admission of failure. Even though it was a state agency, CODOFIL was the first francophone institution in Louisiana since the fall of the great Creoles and their institutions. As for the Cajuns, as has already been pointed out, their only institution had been the family one and its network. Around the 1960s, encouraged by the wave of identity pluralism sweeping America, we could feel the need to perpetuate the heritage. In 1965, Thomas J. Arceneaux, Dean of the Faculty of Agriculture at Southwestern Louisiana Institute (now the University of Louisiana at Lafayette), inspired by the Canadian Acadians' experience, proposed a distinctive flag for the Acadians of Louisiana. The flag was officially recognized in 1974 by the

Louisiana government as the flag of Acadiana; the twenty-two parishes in southwest Louisiana had formally been recognized in 1971 by the same government as a distinct cultural and tourist region. The great Tribute to the Cajun Music gathering (1974), which we have just mentioned, will continue to this day in the Acadian Festival—another manifestation of Cajun's recognition outside the soothing figure of Évangéline.

However, this official recognition by the state felt like an admission of failure for a generation that had believed they could preserve their heritage on the strict level of their pride. "We never had to fight for our language," Dudley J. LeBlanc proudly reminded visiting Canadians in the early 1930s, just as French was being banned from Louisiana's schools. But it had to be agreed, and LeBlanc was one of the promoters of CODOFIL, that French was fading away. Jimmy Domengeaux, the organization's first president, never ceased to remind us throughout his term of office that they did not want to re-Frenchize Louisiana, much less politicize the language issue in the way that Quebecers and northerner Acadians were doing. Yet he was strongly inspired as the first director of CODOFIL by a British-Canadian professor of public administration, Robert Spencer Rodgers, who, in light of the Canadian linguistic conflict, believed that the preservation of French in North America required a concerted political effort. Inspired by the domino theory—we are in the Vietnam War era—Louisiana was the outpost that had to be defended, or all of French America would be lost.

Jimmy Domengeaux (1907–88) was from an old family of German descent that had long been "Cajunized"—his mother was a Mouton— although he did not particularly identify with Acadian pride until he was appointed founding president of CODOFIL. He was a successful Lafayette lawyer who had served in the US Congress during the 1940s. He was soon associated with those "Genteel Acadians" who had wanted, since the turn of the century, to shed the "trashy" image associated with Cajuns and who, to do so, had promoted the figure of Évangéline and Acadian docility. For him, the preservation of French in Louisiana still required a particular mutation of Cajun culture and a struggle against the stereotypes that were still attached to it. His initial reluctance to associate the Cajun sound with the revalorization of French in Louisiana can be explained in this way, as can the other battles waged by CODOFIL—against ethnic humour, against the use of the terms like "coonass" and "Cajun" against Cadjin patois, and for the teaching of standardized French. These battles were poorly received by a new generation of young Cajuns who saw in them the rejection of a grassroots culture.

In the wake of this, Domengeaux led a critique in the south Louisiana newspapers in 1974 against Cajun humour, which he considered to be mainly foreign to the Acadian tradition, humour that would ridicule the Acadians. He particularly attacked Justin Wilson, a famous comedian of the time, who had never lived in Cajun country but portrayed Cajuns, especially on a PBS cooking show, by parodying their accent when speaking English, as "dumb." But Wilson was not the only one of these Louisiana humourists. Ethnic humour "against" "Cajuns" is a constant in their history. Sealsfield, the Austrian adventurer who inspired Longfellow's Eden of Louisiana, wrote about how in the 1820s, the "Americans" ridiculed the behaviour of the Acadians. In the novels of Chopin, La Houssaye, or Cable, the condescending discourse on the Acadians by Creoles, Americans, and even Black people is often associated with scathing humour. From the 1920s on, however, this humour was broadcast and accessible to Cajuns, who now knew English and listened to the radio. Walter Coquille, also of non-Cajun origin, hosted a radio program of political satire from New Orleans. He popularized the character of Télesphore Boudreaux, "Mayor of Bayou Pom Pom," who spoke English poorly and poorly understood the tricks of modern American life. The "Boudreaux and Thibodeaux" repertoires of jokes will become, until today, classics of Louisiana laughter. In addition to seeing in them external humour pejorative toward Cajun culture, Domengeaux was shocked to see that Acadians, practicing self-mockery from then on, claimed to be part of it.

The same is true for the word "coonass," an extremely pejorative term whose origin remains a matter of controversy. Domengeaux associated this term with the French expression "connasse," which refers to the sex of a woman and, by extension, in a derogatory way, to a dirty and infected sex worker, or, more broadly, to any dirty and stupid person. French officers, who worked with Cajuns as translators during the Second World War, apparently called them "coonass" to ridicule the dialect of French the Cajuns spoke. American soldiers picked up the term, carrying it to Louisiana. But the word seems to have a much older usage. Some trace it back to the Spanish era when "cunaso" meant a "person living simply." The term is also associated with a distortion of the English word "raccoon," which would refer to an insult to the Acadians—literally raccoon's ass—referring to the Cajun delicacy, or referring to Cajuns' stooped posture (that of the women particularly) as hunter-gatherers in the bayous. Finally, folklorist Barry Ancelet recalls that *Coontown* was a Black neighbourhood in Lafayette in the 1920s, so "coonass" would refer to the "Acadian [N-words]" who lived there.

In any case, the term has a history of denigrating Cajun culture. In 1977, Calvin J. Roach, a Cajun, sued his employer, Dresser Industrial Valve and Instrument Division, for attributing, in his presence, a robbery to "cheap crooked coonass…unreliable…and …no good." Domengeaux and Thomas Arceneaux, a long-time advocate of Acadian identity, supported the case. The judge ruled that the Acadians are an immigrant community protected under US law and the Civil Rights Act of 1964—a group protected from discrimination based on national origin. Following this ruling, Acadian elites attempted to have their group recognized as a minority under the preferential policy. However, they were unsuccessful in the face of opposition, particularly from some Black members of Parliament, who questioned how the group had been discriminated against. In 1981, the Louisiana legislature recognized the "offensive," "vulgar," and "obscene" nature of the name "coonass" and condemned its commercial use. On the eve of his death in 1983, Domengeaux still wanted to bring a class-action suit on behalf of all Acadians against Golf Oil, which had distributed a promotional mug illustrating a cartoon character, Crawgator, from the marshes, who supposedly gave birth to the Cajuns.

Here again, Domengeaux was not only angry at the pejorative use of the term but also at the tendency of Cajuns to call themselves "coonass." In 1943, the word "Cajun-Coonass" was proudly inscribed on the cockpit of an American plane piloted by Cajun Albert Burleigh. This makes Domengeaux's explanation that the word originated from the participation of Acadians in the French war, dubious. But until the ethnic pride of the

1960s, few Acadians would positively use the term. This will not be the case afterwards. Domengeaux even criticized the governor of Louisiana at the time, Edwin Washington Edwards, a Cajun, for defining himself as a "coonass."

The election of Edwards—the first Cajun governor since Paul O. Hébert (1853–56), on the eve of the Civil War in the middle of the previous century—also demonstrated that the name "Cajun" was no longer a stigma. Edwards had campaigned for office in the early 1970s under the banner of "Cajun power," which would have been an insult a few years earlier. Dudley J. LeBlanc had certainly used Acadian ethnic identity in the 1930s to promote his candidacy for the same position. It was a political failure, but more importantly, LeBlanc was putting forward his "Acadian" roots and the image of *Evangeline*…not the ignoble word "Cajun." Domengeaux still thought the term was stigmatizing, worse than the term "redneck" used to denigrate Anglo-Protestant white boys.

Domengeaux's success in denouncing the use of the word "coonass" will not extend to the revalorization of the term "Cajun." The election of Edwards and his "Cajun power" was confirmation of this. Cajuns had reappropriated the term, a sign of Americanization and Anglicization. By speaking American, the Acadians started recognizing themselves in the word that had long served to ostracize them. It was also part of the young Cajun activists' desire to root Acadian identity in lived culture, as had been the recognition of Cajun music as a valued element of Acadian heritage. In 1974, while denouncing the use of the word "coonass" to refer to Acadians, Cajun circles would agree that the English translation "Cajun" for Acadian was correct.

## "Don't Give Up the Word"

It was on the issue of language that Domengeaux's activism was most felt and most controversial. In 1968, the year COFODIL was created, a body of legislation was adopted allowing the return of French language teaching in primary and secondary schools; it required universities and colleges to train qualified teachers in French; recognized French as an official language for legal notice publications; and authorized the establishment of a French-language radio and television station (which was never implemented). As of the 1970 census, CODOFIL estimated the population of French origin in Louisiana to be over 1.4 million of which 750,000 still spoke French. This population, especially those still speaking French, largely inhabited Acadiana—an expression born a few years earlier from a typographical error of the word "Acadian"—those twenty-two parishes in Cajun country officially recognized in 1970 as a region of Louisiana for cultural and tourist purposes.

Estimating Louisiana's French population, let alone the Cajun population is challenging. American censuses lack the subtlety of Canadian censuses in measuring linguistic affiliation. The questions change from one census to another, and all languages except English are generally considered second languages. The figure of 750,000 in 1970 is misleading because it was derived from how people answered the following question: "What language did you speak as a child?" While it reflects a certain knowledge of French among people born after 1900, it was not a reflection of the actual importance of the French language in 1970. It is estimated that at the beginning of the twentieth century, 80 percent of the population of French or Acadian origin spoke French regularly in the Cajun country. Compulsory education in English (1916) would change those numbers, and assimilation would proceed at a rapid pace, following the disappearance of the generations who spoke French in their daily lives with the family. The 1970 figure probably reflects the highest number of French speakers Louisiana has ever had. Those still using French at that time were most likely around 400,000 to 500,000, and were exclusively in Acadiana; the presence of French in the rest of Louisiana, such as New Orleans, has become negligible. In 1980, the number of French speakers decreased to 240,000; today, it is estimated at less than 200,000, an ageing population representing less than 15 percent of the population of Acadiana and less than 5 percent of the total population of Louisiana.

These numbers do not reflect the Cajun population. Many residents of Acadiana consider themselves Cajuns and do not speak, or no longer speak, French. Since the late eighteenth century, the influence of the

Cajun dimension largely exceeded the Acadians' direct descendants and even today of French speakers'. In 1990, more than 400,000 Louisianans declared themselves Cajuns. The 2000 census, which dropped the name for self-identification on ethnic origin, found only 44,000—the others were of French Canadian or French origin. The best connoisseurs of the Cajun world estimate the population to be closer to 400,000 and 700,000 (a third of the population of Acadiana), including 50,000 Texans living on the Louisiana border in cities such as Port Arthur, Beaumont, and Orange.

The transmission of French no longer takes place. The founders of CODOFIL had already made this observation and it is one of the reasons behind the Cajun militancy that had long been thought to be dispensable. Jimmy Domengeaux believed that what remained of the French language in Louisiana was a "Cajun patois," a second-level French that had no literature or grammar and had never been formalized. Was "patois" taught in the French schools and "joual" in the Quebec schools? Therefore, the French language revival was based on the learning of standard French, bilingualism that would give the Cajuns an "international" prestige we saw in Europe at the time of the Second World War when Cajuns were praised for their work as translators. For another reason, the transition to standard French was also necessary. No Louisianans had been educated in the French language since the turn of the century and, therefore, there was no Cajun expertise to teach it. CODOFIL called upon the French, Quebec, Belgian, and northern Acadian cooperation to launch its program for the French renewal in Louisiana.

The reintegration of French in the schools was more difficult than expected. The Cajun population showed little enthusiasm. Many parishes, including some of Cajun, refused to participate in the re-Francization programs. The working classes still associated French with the "white trash" stigma and English with social success, as they had long been taught. Anglicization continued. Young Cajuns immediately attributed this failure to Domengeaux's snobbery and to the contempt of Évangéline's generation—the "Genteel Acadians" of whom Domengeaux would be a worthy successor—for popular culture. If Cajuns showed little enthusiasm for the re-Francization programs, it was because the language they were being taught—"French"—was not theirs—"Cajun"—and that the foreign teachers were ignorant, even contemptuous, of true Cajun culture.

The protesting Cajun youth was in itself a curious paradox. They were the children of the first generation to abandon French as a common language. Their knowledge of French often came from their grandparents or, for the more educated, from study and exchange trips organized by CODOFIL to France, Quebec, and northern Acadia. The best example is Zachary Richard, who popularized Cajun culture more than any other in the French-speaking world outside Louisiana from the 1970s on. A trip to France made him (re)discover that the Cajun language and sound, almost forgotten by him, were treasures. He is the prototype of a generation of young Cajuns at the centre of the cultural revival, which, while being closely associated with the action of CODOFIL, were its first critics. The ethnologist Barry Ancelet and the historian Carl Brasseaux studied in France; the Cajun French teaching activists Richard Guidry and Amanda Lafleur stayed long in French-speaking countries; and Zachary Richard launched his career as a Cajun singer from Montreal. The "exile experience," to use Ancelet's expression, was a kind of catharsis. They came back convinced that they had to fight for their language, just like the Quebecers and Acadians of the North.

At the same time, they were equally convinced that this language should be inscribed, if not written, in Cajun country. This is the criticism that they will address to Évangéline's generation: to save the heritage, they have distanced themselves from popular culture, from Cajun's culture. Évangéline was an exported myth, not Cajun, a kind of outer cloak used by the "Genteel Acadians" to dress the Cajuns. A "fakelore," described by the historian Brasseaux as false tradition. In 1988, in a small book entitled *In Search of Evangeline Birth and Evolution of the Evangeline Myth*, Brasseaux tried to systematically deconstruct the poem's historical foundations and, even more, the Acadian version of Judge Voorhies. No, Emmeline Labiche never existed, the character who might have corresponded to her was never an Évangéline, the tree under which she presumably died is continually moving due to the sinking effect of the bayou—we would be on the third tree since its discovery at the end of the nineteenth century. Barry Ancelet agrees, *Evangeline* does not emanate from Acadian popular culture. She is an American whose narrative has distracted Cajun consciousness from the real issues, the real heroines, the real language: "They are not virgins who give birth. If all Acadian women had been like Évangéline, we wouldn't be here anymore." In "The New Saturday Night Waltz," under the pseudonym Jean Arceneaux, he ridicules this idyllic view of Louisiana Acadians.

**La nouvelle valse du samedi au soir (The New Saturday Night Waltz)**
Lyrics: Jean Arceneaux

*Let the good times roll.*
*"Those people really know how to have a good time!"*
*An idyllic, carefree race,*
*Crawfish, potatoes, and raccoon ass,*
*As if we were still in the forest primeval.*
*Strolling with Mademoiselle Bellefontaine*
*In Acadie, Home of the happy*

*Laissez le bon temps rouler.*
*«Those people really know how to have a good time!»*
*Une race idyllique sans souci,*
*Des écrivisses, des patates et des culs de chaoui,*
*Comme si on était toujours in the forest primeval*
*Après se promener avec Mlle Bellefontaine*
*En Acadie, home of the happy*

Same thing in this rewriting of "Gabriel's Waltz" by Alex Broussard in the mid-1960s:

**Gabriel's Waltz**
Lyrics: Alex Broussard

*Gabriel was my godfather,*
*Évangéline was my godmother.*
*Gabriel, he was not pretty,*
*Évangéline, she was no better.*
*Gabriel had a beautiful hat,*
*It was a pity, he had no cap.*

*Évangéline had beautiful shoes,*
*It was a pity, they were tennis shoes.*

*Gabriel, c'était mon parrain,*
*Évangéline, c'était ma marraine.*
*Gabriel, il était pas beau,*
*Évangéline, elle valait pas mieux.*
*Gabriel avait un beau chapeau,*
*C'était dommage, il avait pas de calotte.*
*Évangéline avait des beaux souliers,*
*C'était dommage, c'était des tennis shoes.*

They will assert themselves as Cadjins and then Cadiens, that is to say, a sort of in-between Cajun, which they will never wholly reinstitute, and Acadian, too much linked to the "fakelore" of *Evangeline*—although the term Acadian persists as in the Acadian Festival hosted by Ancelet since the late 1970s. They will try to prove wrong Domengeaux's belief that Cajun culture could only produce pop music. The language could be written. Thus, in 1980, Ancelet, still under the pseudonym of Jean Arceneaux, collected an anthology of Acadian writing, *Cris sur le bayou: naissance d'une poésie acadienne en Louisiane.* The work was published in Quebec and was born of the absence of Louisiana writers during the programming of a large gathering of American francophones in Quebec City. The book would have convinced Domengeaux that the Cajun language was indeed a variety of French and not a patois. An earlier work by Revon Reed, *Lâche pas la patate* (1976), still published in Quebec, appears to be the first book written in Cajun French and even the first Louisiana book in French since the end of the nineteenth century. Revon Reed—who didn't mind calling himself a Cajun—hosted a radio music program in Cajun beginning in the early 1960s from the small town of Mamou (*Fred's Lounge*) in the Cajun country northwestern plain. This program did much to keep Cajun culture alive during the years of disgrace, both in music, humour, and language. And the Saturday morning show from *Fred's Lounge* still exists.[3]

---

3.   Translator's note: As of 2022.

As with the young northern Acadians of the time who were evangelical without saying so (see Part II), the anti-*Evangeline* criticism is excessive. The quarrel over language and the denigration of the Cajun language is an old dispute that goes back to the opposition between Cajuns and Creoles in the nineteenth century. The promoters of *Evangeline* wanted to dignify the Cajuns, but they did not denigrate their language. The author of the *Breaux Manuscripts* (circa 1901), Judge Joseph A. Breaux, already speaks of two varieties of French in Louisiana. According to Breaux, if Cajun French was riddled with old French expressions and sometimes corrupted by English, it was still French, something he denied to the "negro language" that we now refer to as Creole. Again, Dudley J. LeBlanc, in his 1937 short history of the Acadians in Louisiana, *The True Story of the Acadians*, makes it clear that Acadian speech was not a dialect.

The work of the French revival young leaders (Richard Guidry, Amanda Lafleur, Barry Ancelet) in the early 1980s to (re)valorize Cajun French as a local variety of French is largely in continuity with *Evangeline* promoters' idea that Acadians were of French descent but of different origin from Creoles. They had and still have to contend with the non-formalization of Cajun French and the lack of local resources to teach it—just like Domengeaux at the time. Barry Ancelet recently reminded us that it is delusional to think Cajun culture can do without the language. "It is not enough to drink beer, eat fries, cook gumbo, and say Poo-yaie. With such commitment, our culture will soon be reduced to a few pages in a tourist brochure. "*Lâche pas la parole*" ("Don't Give Up the Word") is a recent slogan of CODOFIL, in continuity with its founder's inspiration.

## The Return of the Cajuns

Further from *Evangeline*'s story is the view, among a new Cajun youth, that identity could do without language. Shane P. Bernard, in *The Cajuns: Americanization of a People* (2003), defends such a proposal. Most Cajuns, he says, now see themselves as an English-speaking ethnic group, albeit with a French linguistic heritage. After abandoning their traditional values, they have abandoned their language for the "American dream." Bernard, who calls himself a "Cajun," a term he prefers to "Acadian" or "Cadian," and he recalls that the little French he knows is a standard French far removed from the Cajun dialect. The use of the word "dialect" throughout the book to refer to Cajun French is a way of dissociating Cajuns' identity from their language. The image of *Evangeline* would have been a way for the elites of the first part of the twentieth century to please white America while turning their backs on Cajun popular culture.

Deborah Royer Richardson, in a doctoral dissertation on Cajun humour in which she attempts to rehabilitate Cajun-deprecating humour as authentic group humour—the group would have reclaimed it, a kind of spoils of war, in other words—says the same thing: "I am no longer concerned about my place in my culture. I'm a fence-jumper: no French, exogamous marriage, and I am not Catholic anymore." She goes so far as to say that the attempt by CODOFIL and Domengeaux to ennoble Cajuns by rejecting ethnic humour and valuing French, in the wake of a fabricated historical interpretation—*Evangeline*—was the second "great and noble scheme" to obliterate Cajun culture. The return of the word would be a cultural recovery with its authentic culture.

In her book *Becoming Cajun, Becoming American: The Acadian in American Literature From Longfellow to James Lee Burke* (2009), Maria Hebert-Leiter demonstrates, without qualms, how the Louisiana Acadians became Americans, adopting English and freeing themselves from Évangéline's narrative. Their Americanization would not be a loss, for, in the process, they developed an astonishing new liveliness of identity: they became Cajuns.

Indeed, the Cajun identity is a real success despite its apparent failure to promote the language. The Cajun sound has acquired since the 1970s a pan-American reputation—in 1994, the guitarist D. L. Menard was awarded the National Heritage Fellowship by the National Endowment for the Arts from Hilary Clinton—and even worldwide (Cajun clubs are springing up all over the world). In particular, great American stars—Mary Chapin Carpenter—distinguish themselves with their Cajun songs. Between 2008 and 2011, there was a Grammy Award specifically designated for southwest

Louisiana music: the Zydeco/Cajun Grammy. Following Dewey Balfa, who in the late 1980s wondered if Cajun music was too commercial and if its success would destroy it, some today wonder who will define its sound and language if its judges are now in California? The question was directly posed for the first Zydeco/Cajun Grammy in 2008 after the nomination of Lisa Haley, a Californian. Had "Cajun music" lost its connection to any regional or Cajun identity?

We see the same phenomenon occurring in gastronomy: "Cajun is hot." In the 1970s, large restaurants like Mulate's and Prejeans, lined the region and entwined Cajun cuisine and music. Initially oriented toward tourism, these restaurants nevertheless popularize among Cajuns a regional cuisine under the label "Cajun." Paul Prudhomme, originally from Opelousas, opened K. Paul's in 1979, a restaurant in New Orleans that became famous for its Cajun cuisine. In the 1990s, he participated in a national PBS show that significantly contributed to popularizing Cajun cuisine throughout the United States. Today, Cajun restaurants can be found in every American city and even in Australia. New Orleans, long a graveyard for Cajun culture, now proudly calls itself home for Cajun and Creole cuisine. The Louisiana authorities even had to intervene in 1988 to prohibit the appellation to non-Louisiana products. The time is long gone when one could say, "you're Cajun…if your mother can do a roux."[4]

The return of the once-hated word is well demonstrated by Barry Ancelet's compilation of identity referents used in commerce in Lafayette since the early twentieth century—from telephone books (*"From Evangeline Hot Sauce to Cajun Ice: Signs of Ethnicity in South Louisiana"*). *"Evangeline,"* which first appeared in 1906, was the preferred term until the early 1960s. The word "Acadian" replaced it from 1955, the year of the Deportation bicentennial commemoration, and it was predominant until the 1970s. Then the word "Acadiana" imposed itself and will become the most used reference today. But the term "Cajun," which appeared for the first time in 1965, will also impose itself; in the 1990s, it became the second ethnic sign, declassifying *"Evangeline"* and "Acadian" in apparent regression.

4.   Translator's note: A Cajun roux is made with flour and oil (not butter, as would be the French version). It is used as thickener in many dishes, including étouffée, jambalaya, and gumbo.

Already in the 1970s, while Governor Edwards was proclaiming "the Cajun Power," *The Louisiana Tour Guide* described Lafayette, in French, as the city of the "Cajun spirit." The word "coonass," although appropriated by some Cajuns on plaques or T-shirts—"I'm a coonass"—remains banned from commercial signage.

Observers of the Cajun scene conclude from this transformation that the identity referent is the regionalization of identity. In this way, the "Cajun" becomes less and less a memorial or linguistic reference and more and more a regional belonging—Acadiana—and cultural—the "Cajun spirit." Already, in Edwards's "Cajun power," the reference was to a regional political base rather than a memorial one. The romantic dimension of Acadian bayou country described by Longfellow—a more middle-class expressiveness—has metamorphosed into something more popular, a regional ecological niche where the Cajun is the one who has a special relationship with the wilderness of southwest Louisiana—the bayous, the plain, the fishing, the hunting. Through gastronomy, music, and dance, the Cajun spirit is best defined.

The Cajun culture would have been maintained as a popular, largely working-class culture—blue-collar bayou, to use the title of the book by Jacques Henry and Carl L. Bankston. As we have seen, the oil industry transformed the small Cajun inhabitant into a worker, making it unnecessary to emigrate to distant cities. Through professional proximity, the old Cajuns still form a relatively homogeneous group, a socioeconomic class whose members still marry each other, like an ethnic group—a high rate of endogamous marriages—and this, in spite of the language border dissolving. In this light, the *Evangeline* narrative and Cajun Acadianization would have been attempts to transform the former class of petits habitants ("smallholders," or Cadjins) into an ethnic group (Acadians). These attempts that would have been partially unsuccessful, as the withdrawal of Évangéline's narrative would coincide with the return of the Cajuns as a cultural identity defined more in relation to a regional socioeconomic than to an ethnic memory. This is why the group's culture has, as in the days of the smallholder dimension, a tendency to aggregate, on a regional basis, individuals of similar socioeconomic status across ethnic lines—even people of American origin now call themselves Cajuns. *Evangeline* appears as a parenthesis between the world of the small nineteenth-century inhabitant (the Cadjin) and the socioeconomic dimension of the late twentieth-century blue-collar worker (the Cajun). The path through *Evangeline* and Acadia will nevertheless have ennobled this Cajun. They can take back the old name they had been ashamed of because it is no longer a stigma.

The regionalization of Cajun identity has its science. Scholarly studies of Acadian culture are relatively recent. The history books by Dudley J. LeBlanc (1937, 1962) were more narrative than historical. Except for a few forays into confirming the true history of *Evangeline* around the 1950s, systematic study of the Cajun world began with the French/Cajun revival of the 1970s. The Center for Acadian and Creole Folklore, founded in 1974 and later renamed the Center for Louisiana Studies at the University of Louisiana at Lafayette, spearheaded this work.

These studies will never be in continuity with the Acadian narrative. Instead, they attempted to draw out the underlying truth. This was consistent with Cajun culture's distance—in keeping with American empirical liberalism—from any form of primary culture institutionalization. At the outset, the *Evangeline* story was not presented as a reference or founding myth, as it was among the northern Acadians, but rather, in both Voorhies and Leblanc, as a "true story." The distance from the northern narrative will be further accentuated by the fact that such works will not pretend to be a reading immanent to Cajun's dimension—made from a perspective indigenous to Cajun culture. After all, the Cajuns themselves did not claim to belong to a Cajun society with its historicity. This work will be done from an outside perspective, that of ethnic America, of Louisiana regional history, but especially of the frontier theme.

To illustrate this point, the work of Carl Brasseaux, who was in recent years director of the Center for Louisiana Studies, is typical of the evolution of Acadian studies in Louisiana. Born in Opelousas in 1951 of Cajun's origin, Brasseaux belongs to the Cajun awakening generation of young people. He even published a series of Acadian stories in Cajun French in 1988, *Trois saisons*, under the pseudonym Antoine Bourque—it is a tendency among Cajun academics to dissociate their scholarly work from their participation in the identity narrative; Ancelet published his poems and stories under the pseudonym, Jean Arceneaux. Brasseaux's initial interest, in a doctoral dissertation completed in France, was in Acadians' settlement in Louisiana as a consequence of the expulsion of neutral French from Acadia in the middle of the eighteenth century (published in 1987, under the title *The Founding of New Acadia. The Beginning of Acadian Life in Louisiana*, 1763–1803). Already, his work tends to re-establish the facts. The Acadians did not arrive in Louisiana, as Longfellow describes and as popular culture remembered it, from the centre of the United States down the great river. Most of them—Broussard-Beausoleil's group, the Acadians from France—did not transit through the United States.

Later, Brasseaux will be interested in defining the Acadian settlement in Louisiana through the notion of the frontier. Dear to American historiography, the "frontier" has long been used to demonstrate the construction of the democratic man in America. It is not a boundary marker but an experience of continuous peoplehood in the New World, one that transforms the old European man into a new man, a democratic one. Longfellow's poem is a frontier poem, but a poem of a romantic frontier that tends to insist on communal continuity (see Part I). Brasseaux's frontier is more liberal, more in keeping with the dominant version that makes the frontier a site of social unbinding at the root of American individualism. The first chapter of *Founding of New Acadia*, about the French period, was already called "Children of the Frontier." The Acadians brought the frontier spirit to Louisiana. They were the first Europeans to develop a distinctly North American identity. They would carry it all the more as the rebellious Acadians—Broussard-Beausoleil—were the first to move to Louisiana. Historically, the Cajun country would be the prototype of a frontier experience. Glenn Conrad, the founding director of the Center for Acadian and Creole Folklore, said of the Cajun frontier that it was a "total democracy."

As we have seen, Brasseaux would continue his scholarly work by restoring the "truth" of the *Evangeline* story—*In search of Evangeline*—through a systematic deconstruction of the story as a mere myth. He writes that such a narrative leads to a distorted view of the people. As a historian, he participated—without total success—in bringing the story interpretation of *Evangeline* and Acadia proposed at the Évangéline Historical Park and the Acadian Memorial in St. Martinville closer to the historical reality. His great interest in "true history," to the detriment of representation or memory, led him to reduce the history of *Evangeline* in Louisiana to a simple commercial enterprise linked to the local tourist industry.

His subsequent work will be less focused on the history of the Acadians and more on the overall dynamics of southwest Louisiana society. In a final work, he focuses on Acadiana (*Acadiana: Louisiana's Historic Cajun Country*, 2011) as a region, demonstrating its multiple influences: French, Acadian, African, Creole, American, Indigenous, etc. In an earlier book, he presented Louisiana's Francophonie (French, Cajun, Creole, Houma) as a reality born of diversity. In short, his approach, which could be found among other researchers and which we consider typical of recent identity transformations in Cajun country, can be summarized as follows: a shift from the Acadians (memory group) to the Cajuns (regional group).

The return of the Cajuns is further confirmed by the reevaluation of the role of violence. Brasseaux contrasts the idyllic pastoral frontier, the Jacksonian egalitarianism of Évangéline country, with the real frontier of southwest Louisiana. Without endorsing the "white trash" reading—the frontier harshness is above all a fertile ground for democratic independence—he is not afraid to recall the violence concealed in the world of the small frontier farmer—between "small whites," but also toward the Black population. If there are still people today who complain about the "trashy" image projected on the Cajuns, especially in the movies, the fact remains that people are becoming more tolerant. Shane Bernard does not hesitate to consider as Cajun the police series by James Lee Burke and his inspector Dale Robicheaux, whose action takes place mainly in Cajun country and largely revives the group's image as a violent one. The same is true of Deborah Royer Richardson's rehabilitation of self-deprecating humour.

If the regionalization of identity must be freed from language, which some people contest, the region "Cajunization" also poses a particular problem for the Black population. Black people will challenge the regional appropriation of identity that the Cajun discourse tends to achieve. This tension will be revealed, in particular, when the adjective Cajun is applied to sports teams and venues. "There are no Blacks who should consider themselves 'Cajuns,'" said a student leader when the University of Louisiana at Lafayette named its soccer stadium the "Cajun Field." We saw the same reaction with the naming of the stadium, the "Cajundome," and its soccer team the "Ragin' Cajun." The Cajun identity is not inclusive; it cannot claim to encompass all the identities of Southwest Louisiana. The name "Ragin' Cajun" is, to some Black people, particularly offensive because "Ragin" backwards is "Nigar"—although the idea of a "Ragin' Cajun" is a reappropriation of an ethnic slur.

These comments must be read in the context of a Creole affirmation movement that started in the 1980s to promote the identity of Black Catholics of French cultural origin. In its opposition to Cajun identity, this statement is a sign that tension persists on the racial border. In the previous chapter, we saw how *Evangeline*'s narrative and Acadian identity participated in the construction of a symbolic boundary between the "Blacks" and the "less than Blacks," the "Cajuns." *Evangeline* whitened the Cajuns by giving them a definitively white ancestry and a pastoral romance, while their peaceful and gentle morals excluded them from any connection with slavery. Black people and Acadians had little contact during the twentieth century despite their cultural proximity in food, music, and language. At the turn of the 1960s, during the civil rights movement and the Cajun revival, Black Catholics and "Negro-speaking" defined themselves as African American. This accelerated their assimilation, faster than that of the Cajuns, into the Anglo-American world—no more than thirty thousand people would still speak Creole. It was not until the 1980s that they began to self-identify as a particular cultural group. They then took the name that the "free people of colour" had already taken from the grandissimes French and Spanish Creoles after the Civil War in the nineteenth century, both to designate themselves as a group (the Creoles) and to designate their language (Creole).

The deconstruction of *Evangeline*'s romance and the regionalization of identity again blurs the line between the two groups. The statement presents both a stiffening of this border and its weakening. The Creoles will challenge the Cajuns' claim to define the region's cultural identity, a claim that is realized at the expense of their recognition (one would even speak of genocide). In St. Martinville, a former Creole (white) town now predominantly Creole (Black), Évangéline's myth centrality is being challenged in the town promotion. Could it be, two Creole city councillors wondered, that Black citizens were hanged from Évangéline's oak tree? On the other hand, Cajuns who visit the Acadian Monument complain that the history of diversity they are taught in school is often reduced to the history of Black Americans.

The assertion of a Creole identity by Black Americans is also a sign of recognition of their cultural proximity to Cajuns, a weakening of the border. It is true that in contrast to Black people—Madame de la Houssaye's Quarteronnes, unlike their cousin Évangéline, could never claim to be fully American—the Cajuns were able to transgress ethnic boundaries more easily. The fact remains, however, that they (the Cajuns) would remain a group on the bangs of America, with no direct socioeconomic dominance over the Blacks. Acadian affirmation was one of integration into White America before the birth of a racial distinction movement. The Creole affirmation acknowledges this somehow and demands inclusion as it is a protest against the usurpation of regional identity by the Cajuns. Bands are increasingly mixing Cajun and Creole, Cajun sound and zydeco sound, as evidenced by the creation of the Best Zydeco/Cajun Album category at the Grammy Awards. Creole musician Dopsie named his band the Cajun Twisters. Creole Clifton Chénier, associated with popularizing the zydeco style, was nicknamed "The Black Cajun." Restaurants advertise Creole and Cajun cuisine as if Creoles now knew how to make a roux. CODOFIL, which in the early years had not thought to include Creoles in its concerns, is doing so more and more. The Cajuns said Melvin Ceasar, president of a Creole organization, "didn't come with all this food and music and all these varieties of folklore. We contributed. Life is a big mix in this part of the world."

Whether that "big mix" has enough consistency to meet the expressive needs of the groups involved remains to be seen: Cajuns versus Créoles. Évangéline may not have said her last word.

# References

ANCELET, Barry. "Elements of Folklore, History, and Literature in Longfellow's Evangeline." *Revue de Louisiane/Louisiane Review*, no 2, 1982, p. 188–126.

ANCELET, Barry. *Cajun Music: Its Origins and Development*. Lafayette, The Center for Louisiana Studies, 1989.

ANCELET, Barry. "From Evangeline Hot Sauce to Cajun Ice: Signs of Ethnicity in South Louisiana." *Louisiana Folklore Miscellany*. 1996, p. 29–42.

ANGERS, Trent. Dudley LeBlanc, *A Biography, Lafayette*. Acadian House Publishing, 1993.

ARCENEAUX, Jean. *Cris sur le bayou: naissance d'une poésie acadienne en Louisiane*. Montréal, Éditions Intermède, 1980.

BERNARD, Shane K. *The Cajuns. Americanization of a People*. Jackson, University Press of Mississippi, 2003.

BRASSEAUX, Carl A. *The Founding of New Acadia*. Baton Rouge, Louisiana State University Press, 1987.

BRASSEAUX, Carl A. *Acadian to Cajun: Transformation of a People*. Jackson, University Press of Mississippi, 1992.

BRASSEAUX, Carl A. *In Search of Evangeline: Birth and Evolution of the Evangeline Myth*. Thibodeaux, Blue Heron Press, 1988.

BRASSEAUX, Carl A. *French, Cajun, Creole, Houma: A Primer on Francophone Louisiana*. Baton Rouge, Louisiana State University Press, 2005.

BRASSEAUX, Carl A. *Acadiana: Louisiana's Historic Cajun Country*. Baton Rouge, Louisiana State University Press, 2011.

CONRAD, Glen (dir.). *The Cajuns: Essays on their History and Culture*. Lafayette, The Center for Louisiana Studies, 1978.

DORMON, James H. *The People Called Cajuns: An Introduction to an Ethnohistory*. Lafayette, Center for Louisiana Studies, 1983.

HEBERT-LEITER, Maria. *Becoming Cajun, Becoming American. The Acadian in American Literature from Longfellow to James Burke Lee*. Baton Rouge, Louisiana State University Press, 2009.

HENRY, Jacques M. et Carl L. Bankston. *Blue-Collar Bayou: Louisiana Cajuns in the New Economy of Ethnicity*. Westport, Praeger, 2002.

HÉROUX, Omer. *En Louisiane*. Montreal, Le Devoir, 1931.

LEBLANC, Dudley J. *The True Story of the Acadians*. Lafayette, Tribune Publishing Company, 1937.

# AFTERWORD
# POSTMODERN ÉVANGÉLINE

*Gabriel was not forgotten.*
*Within her heart was his image [...]*
*He had become to her heart*
*as one who is dead, and not absent.*

—Henry Wadsworth Longfellow, *Evangeline*

## Cosmopolitan Longfellow

*Evangeline* is still out there. She lost her grandeur of the 1900s when the poem was arguably the best known in Anglo-American schools worldwide. She no longer sits atop Acadian nationalism either, as she did in the 1950s when the Deportation bicentennial was commemorated. She no longer brings, as in the 1920s, Hollywood producers to St. Martinville, Louisiana, introducing America and the world to Cajun country. Already, in the first decades of the twentieth century, literary modernity had confined Longfellow to the rank of a minor poet. *Evangeline*, the Catholic romance of Anglo-Protestant fusion America, no longer fit into the multicultural America that had emerged. *Evangeline* would remain a popular icon through the 1960s, until, as Longfellow predicted in the poem's final passage, our founding couple of America would be largely forgotten: "Under the humble walls of the little Catholic churchyard, / in the heart of the city, they lie, unknown and unnoticed." (*Evangeline*, original verses by Longfellow.)

Driven out of the American imagination, Évangéline will take up residence in her land up north, in the former French Acadia, and down

293

south, in Louisiana, in the land of the Cajuns, where she will take a central place in their respective stories. For a while, it is through "her" that these countries will tell their stories. But, there too, the irreverent young people of the 1960s will chase her away: not "political enough," the Acadians of the north will say, not "authentic enough," those of the south will reply. They wanted to forget her, they ridiculed her, in song, in literature, in poetry, in painting, but they never succeeded in getting rid of her completely, so much the genesis of their existence story as a group was due to her.

*Evangeline* is still out there…and so is her author. Longfellow was said to have been forgotten, ostracized from the American literary field. Newton Arvin's early 1960s biography, *Longfellow: His Life and Work*, had been one of the few works devoted to the poet since some publications at the turn of the century. And even then, Arvin was reluctant to reinstate the ancient bard in the pantheon of national poets and refused to consider *Evangeline* a great epic poem, reducing it instead to a "minor poetic form." Such was not the judgment of Dana Gioia, chairman of the National Endowment for the Arts from 2003 to 2009, who, in the name of poetry that still knows how to tell stories, made a passionate plea for the rehabilitation of the poet as a great American lyricist (in *The Columbia History of American Poetry*, "Longfellow in the Aftermath of Modernism," 1993). Already in 1984, John Seelye, specifically regarding the poem *Evangeline*, had rung the bell in "Attic Shape: Dusting Off Evangeline," asserting that *Evangeline* still deserved to be included in the great book of national poems. With *The Long Life of Evangeline* (2010), Ron McFarland completed a book on the history of Évangéline's image in Anglo-American books and popular culture, still relevant in his view. Maria Hebert-Leiter, in *Becoming Cajun, Becoming American: The Acadian in American Literature From Longfellow to James Lee Burke* (2009), provided a broad portrait of the presence of Louisiana Acadians in American literature since and because of Longfellow's publication of *Evangeline*.

However, it took two critical intellectual biographies—the first ones in forty years—that aim to rediscover or reread the forgotten poet with empathy, to confirm a certain rehabilitation: *A Rediscovered Life*, by Charles C. Calhoun (2004) and the brilliant work of Christoph Irmscher (2006),

*Longfellow Redux*. It is a "new" Longfellow that these two authors make us (re)discover—no longer, like Gioia or Seelye, the Longfellow poet of the national narrative, "the one who would have named America" (to use the Bowdoin College exhibition title for the bicentennial of the poet's birth). It would rather be the singer of diversity and lover of Europe and foreign languages Longfellow, the one who practiced democratic sentimentalism that made him commune with all humanity. This is the Longfellow who, after reading Goethe one evening, felt the need to walk toward the ocean because its waves touched both Europe and America and who, on his return, in the omnibus, felt as if bewitched by the sweet sound of the foreign languages still spoken by recent immigrants to Boston. He is the Longfellow of the Protestant romance of American Catholicism or the friend of Emerson, proponents of pantheism, that sort of civic religion of humanity. In short, a Longfellow more cosmopolitan than nationalist.

Charles Calhoun reminds us that Longfellow, this professor of modern languages at Bowdoin College and later at Harvard, more or less invented the discipline of comparative literature in the United States. As a sign of this new recognition—a pluralist and cosmopolitan Longfellow—the Department of English and American Languages at Harvard University named one of its centres the Longfellow Institute in 1994. This centre is dedicated to works written in the United States in languages other than English and their influence on the evolution of the English language in the context of multiculturalism. Longfellow would be the most "ambitious multiculturalist" of nineteenth-century American writers. Christoph Irmscher goes further, erasing any nationalistic approach in Longfellow's work. For Irmscher, Longfellow is resolutely a poet who prefers diversity to unity, or the multiplicity of the worlds and its regions to the nation. Longfellow would thus be a precursor of postmodernity. He would refuse poetry committed to one language and one "place," in this case to the English language and the American nation. His writing would challenge the very idea of a narrative written by an author. Instead, he believed in the "great cosmopolitan literature"—Goethe's *Weltliteratur*—where writing becomes the act of borrowing and adding one's experience into the great book of humanity. The propensity to "plagiarize," which Edgar Allan

Poe condemned in Longfellow, is elevated by Irmscher to a postmodern virtue. Longfellow would practice or even radicalize "intertextuality" before the letter.

Should we see a contradiction between the proposals of one Dana Gioia or one John Seelye to reintegrate Longfellow into the grand American narrative—or even the proposal of this book to read *Evangeline* as a great American poem—and that of one Charles Calhoun or one Christopher Irmscher to read Longfellow as the builder of a "cosmopolitan enterprise"? Between, thus, Gioia's or Seelye's Longfellow and a Longfellow who sees the world as his horizon and reject the nation, who exalts diversity and denies rootedness, who offers no narrative but the great enigmatic book of humanity's march? Not if we recall American "exceptionalism" (see Part I). That is, the propensity of the American narrative to see in America's singular history—its Protestant and English past—the realization of the modern promise of democracy and cosmopolitan identity. The meaning of America is immense, Longfellow once remarked; it refers to a "celestial mechanism." Like a new Jerusalem, the universal story had a land of choice: the United States of America.

This American story, however, has a history. At the time Longfellow wrote *Evangeline*—the first half of the nineteenth century—America was constructing a narrative in which the diversity of its population was merging into an Anglo-Protestant republic that was supremely capable of accommodating that diversity. *Evangeline* was a founder of America, but…no one remembered; there were no "names" written on the graves of her descendants. She and Gabriel lay "under the humble walls of the little Catholic cemetery" in Philadelphia, while thousands of hearts, thousands of minds, thousands of arms, thousands of feet continued to make America. *Evangeline* and what it represented, the old society, were to die a gentle death to make way for democratic America and its civic religion—an expanded Protestantism.

Judeo-European America would replace Anglo-Protestant America. The narrative of its founding moved from the *Mayflower* to Ellis Island. In this passage, the American narrative will come to define itself less by its fusional capacity than by the recognition of its diversity—another way of thinking about modern individuality, either by equality (fusional) or by authenticity (diversity). The America of ethnic recognition began to assert itself at the start of the twentieth century and found its consecration during the 1960s in the civil rights movement; a movement that forced the integration of Black people into the ethnic mosaic and forced multicultur-alism; a movement that broadened the list of founders to include groups other than Judeo-Europeans. Some will call the foundations of this new narrative the "ethno-racial pentagon" because of the five races listed in the US Census: European-Americans, African-Americans, Asian-Americans, Hispanic-Americans (Latinos), Indigenous Peoples (Native Americans). In this multi-ethnic America, identities will no longer be merged but called upon to coexist, the melting pot replaced by the "salad bowl," a process by which, after mixing, the constituent parts remain visible.

Longfellow's eclipse of the grand national narrative effectively cor-responds to this period. He presented these communities as the image of Gabriel, "dead" but not "forgotten," or as the "ghost" pursued by the Shawnee on the frontier of the American west. These stories of other-worldly, foundational, but unhistorical communities will not survive the multicultural narrative: the Jews and *The Jewish Cemetery*, the Indigenous people and *Hiawatha*, the Acadians and *Evangeline*. The latter needed com-munities that were still alive. Unless, of course, you truncate the meaning, which is what will be done for *Evangeline* to revive her, no longer as an American heroine but as the heroine of a lost nationality: Évangéline the Acadian, or resolutely ethnic, Évangéline the Cajun.

Multicultural America would be outdated today. Ethnic identities, compartmentalized, neatly nested, exclusive, integrated in a multicul-tural republic, would be over. We would now share several identities: those of our fathers, of our mothers, sometimes of our grandfathers or grandmothers—"plural identities." These identities would cross borders—"diasporic identities," "ethno-scape." They would no longer be linked to a real community existence, the old ethnic or even national community, but to that of an imagined community—"symbolic identity." They would be less the effect of history burdens than a "choice," a memory reconstituted, cobbled together by individuals—"individual identities."

These new forms of identity, this "post-ethnicity," would also require a redefinition of the American republic and its narrative: a republic that would be called "cosmopolitan" because it would bring together individuals—no longer communities—whose memory would henceforth be drawn in a vagrant way from the storehouse of plural humanity. "Gabriel was not forgotten. Within her heart was his image [...] He had become to her heart as one who is dead, and not absent. (*Evangeline*, original verses by Longfellow.)

The romantic proposal to merge the individual with a universal community is now admissible again, and America would be the prototype. It is to such a portrait that the "new" Longfellow presented by Irmscher is associated: a cosmopolitan Longfellow for an America that one would like to be just as cosmopolitan.

## The Return of Évangéline the American

The idea for this book occurred to me in the mid-1990s. I was participating in a work session with university colleagues in preparation for a book, an inventory of minority francophones in Canada. It was summer. We had chosen to meet at the small Université Sainte Anne, located in Church Point, in the Baie Sainte-Marie region of Nova Scotia. We chose this location because we wanted to experience the atmosphere of a minority francophone community (the region has about ten thousand inhabitants) and because the mild maritime climate is unmatched at this time of year. The scenery is beautiful, although it does not rival that of the village of Grand-Pré, located two hundred kilometres farther up on the Bay of Fundy.

Baie Sainte-Marie, as its Acadian inhabitants call it, or the Municipality of Clare as the colonial power called it at the time of the Great Upheaval, is now known to the readers of this book. It is the place where Thomas Chandler Haliburton, in his 1829 history of Nova Scotia, says he knew descendants of Acadians who lived in pastoral simplicity, as Abbé Raynal had described French Acadia. This was the only remaining French settlement on the coast of the Bay of Fundy, formerly the *Baie Française* and the heart of historic Acadia. Some refugees and exiles returning from

Boston had been allowed to settle on these lands, less rich and therefore less adapted to agriculture, less protected from the foggy Atlantic than those of the Port-Royal valley or Minas Basin. Longfellow certainly drew on this population to write the poem's last lines, as Haliburton was the primary source for his knowledge of the Acadian reality:

> *Still stands the forest primeval; but under the shade of its branches*
> *Dwells another race, with other customs and language.*
> *Only along the shore of the mournful and misty Atlantic*
> *Linger a few Acadian peasants, whose fathers from exile*
> *Wandered back to their native land to die in its bosom.*

—*Evangeline*, original verses by Longfellow

Since the end of the nineteenth century, St. Marys Bay, a continuous stretch of fifty kilometres between the towns of Yarmouth—where there is a ferry to New England—and Digby, Nova Scotia, has been a must for American tourists visiting "the Land of Évangéline." Grand-Pré was owned by a railroad company before becoming a historic park and national monument. The automobile era has not denied this vocation: the municipality is crossed by the "Route panoramique Évangéline/Evangeline Trail." At the time of our visit, in an explicit attempt to exploit this tourist potential, a local artistic producer, Normand Godin, was presenting a translation of "Evangeline" performed by local people and, more authentically, in the local French variety. Our little group of scholars was invited to attend this performance.

Indeed, I knew or thought I already knew, *Evangeline*. My family genealogy, going back to the mid-seventeenth century, is essentially Acadian. The Thériault family is less well known than that of the notary LeBlanc, immortalized by Longfellow. But it was a Thériault ancestor—Pierre Thérriot—who co-founded the settlement of Grand-Pré in 1682, and it was a Thériault—Olivier Terrio—who organized the 1785 emigration of Acadians from France to Louisiana. Pouponne, the Évangéline of Madame de la Houssaye's novel (*Pouponne et Balthazar*), was also a Thériot. I spent my youth in Caraquet, on the coast of Chaleur Bay in northern New

Brunswick, a community that has emerged over the past sixty years as the cultural capital of Acadia. I was immersed in "évangelism." I am old enough to remember the appearance of the first Évangéline (and Gabriel), in Norman (or northern forest) costumes woven from southern US cotton thread, around the Deportation bicentennial celebrations (1955). The couple was subsequently present at all the city's festivals and ceremonies, welcoming passing travellers and inaugurating major events on their float—their costume was later modified to make it more in keeping with historical "truth," but their presence survived the anti-*Evangeline* wave of the 1980s. *Évangéline*, by André-Thaddée Bourque, "Je l'avais cru ce rêve de jeune âge" ("I had believed it this dream of a young age") will serve as a national anthem for all these years. I learned to read on a daily newspaper called *L'Évangéline*, which died out in 1982 after nearly a century of life. I even married a pretty Acadian woman who lived in a village called Évangéline. Évangéline was a serious, patriotic affair, it did not (yet) refer to a commercial or tourist display.

I belong to the generation that wanted and thought it had gotten rid of *Evangeline*. A mythical conception of Acadia that deterritorialized the Acadian fact, referring the identity experience to genealogy rather than to living together. I thought I knew Évangéline, and…had forgotten her. I was struck by the spectacle I heard that August evening on the shores of St. Marys Bay. Basil the blacksmith is extolling the virtues of his new country—the United States—finding his new home more comfortable than his old one, railing against the rocky lands and winter of old Acadia, refusing to return to that monarchical country still ruled by a king who burns and steals the barns and farms of the inhabitants. I heard again the notary LeBlanc, who had remained in Philadelphia, remind Évangéline of how the egalitarian (democratic) qualities of her new country and its inhabitants—the Quakers of Pennsylvania—reminded him of Acadia before the fall.

It was not the Évangéline I thought I had forgotten. It was not the Évangéline of my childhood, nor was it the more literary Évangéline I had learned through my association with Acadian poetry, literature, and theatre—my Évangéline was *Pélagie-la-Charrette*, the one who had returned to "make a country" in the north. As many Acadians of my generation probably did, I realized then that I had never read the work in its original version, that of Longfellow, which I did promptly. Indeed, what I was hearing at St. Marys Bay was closer to Longfellow's version than what I had learned from my long association with Évangéline, the Acadian. There was an "American Évangéline" different from the "Acadian Évangéline." There would also be a "Cajun Évangéline," which I would learn to discover. And I would remember what an old aunt, on her return from Grand-Pré, had announced to us, all proud, mainly that she had been told that the real Gabriel was an Arceneau(x), like my maternal grandmother, and that they—Gabriel and Évangéline—had lived there, in Louisiana.

I was not surprised that *Evangeline* was still being played. Rather, my surprise was that what came out of the translation was the American version of the story, not the patriotic Évangéline, the country builder. What was happening in Acadia that made this audible today? Will Acadia refuse to be a country from now on? Would it perceive itself, like Gabriel for Évangéline, as "something dead but not forgotten"? There will be voices thereafter that will confirm to me—particularly at the margins of northern Acadia—that this was the case. Normand Godin, commenting on his translation of *Evangeline*, said he wanted to present "the universal story of lost paradise: that of being driven from the Garden of Eden. It is the search for the Holy Grail."

"There is no Acadia, there are only Acadians," corrected the poet Georgette LeBlanc, a native of Saint Marys Bay who acted in Godin's play when she was a student at the Université Sainte-Anne. She later completed a doctorate in the form of a performance at the University of Louisiana at Lafayette, *Alma: An Acadian Performance* (2007), which virulently rejects the institutional Acadia of her childhood—that of Évangéline the Acadian—for a popular, authentic, complex, trilingual vision of Acadia.

Clive Doucet, in *Notes From Exile*, written in the wake of the 1994 World Congress, still speaks of an Acadia of exile, of a "cosmopolitan" attempt to attach his identity to the memory of the visits he made in his youth to his grandfather in Cheticamp, Cape Breton. At the turn of the 1980s, Acadian poets from Moncton had already tried to define the

Acadian through wandering—*Les cents lignes de notre américanité* ("The Hundred Lines of our Americanness")—or through linguistic hybridization—*Éloge du chiac* ("In Praise of Chiac"). The "linguistic schizophrenia" will be celebrated by others as a break with the homogeneous Acadia of the past and an opening to otherness, to plurality. Jean Morency's program of study on the interculturality of Acadian literature seeks to break away from a national and territorial vision of the Acadian literary field: Acadia is from nowhere.

The plural Acadia, the hybrid Acadia, the diasporic Acadia, the Acadia of Americanness—whether one refers to it by taking up *Evangeline* or by wanting to deconstruct the myth—was for me a curious return to *Evangeline* the original: Longfellow's cosmopolitan *Evangeline* for whom Acadia was "an image not forgotten" before being a society. Like American literary scholars (Calhoun, Irmscher) who reread a pre-national Longfellow to understand their postmodernity—were the northern Acadians drawing a line under the history of their nation-building by returning, even unwittingly, to the cosmopolitan Évangéline of the poem? I doubt that the cosmopolitan adventure will have the same effect in a small, fragile culture—Acadia—as it has in the culture of the greatest world power, America. In any case, it seemed to me that *Evangeline* was still revealing the deployment of an identity. I had wanted to make her story.

## AND (and) And

Herménégilde Chiasson, who in the 1980s flirted with the Acadia of hybridity, wandering, Americanism, and "linguistic schizophrenia"—Acadia without a place or language—thus defined the journey of Acadian identity in *Oublier Évangéline*. There was the "tradition" in which Acadia took pleasure in reproducing its past in such a way as to ensure its survival under the high patronage of *Evangeline* and the painful memory of the Deportation. There was "modernity" where, starting from external forms, one liked to destroy the idols and everything that seemed to be related to tradition. This had the effect not of abolishing tradition but sending it back, by depoliticizing it, to popular folklore. There would be, finally, "postmodernity" where it would be necessary to relearn to conjugate *And* the tradition, *And* modernity, *And* the culture's substantive contents, *And* the abstract forms, *And* the local rooting, *And* the belonging to the world, *And* the storyteller's presence, *And* that of the historian's censors. Postmodernism had wings and roots, it was from here and there, from the past and the present…at the same time. Chiasson himself would be an eloquent example of this approach. "Local poet" *And* "poet of modernity" and of "openness" to the world, he wants to "forget Évangéline," *And* yet he sprinkles his work with references to her. He asserted himself as a great critic of tradition *And* as the guardian of what is the most dusty about tradition (he was the lieutenant-governor of New Brunswick).

I entirely agree with this portrait, even if I integrated into the reading more continuity and less rupture: tradition is less immobile than it is said to be, modernity more dependent on tradition than it is believed to be, in short, postmodernity less original than its sycophants claim. Finally, the amalgam between the Évangéline moment and the Acadian nationalist project is overdone. The clergy had its reluctance in the face of Évangéline's idolatry, her patron saint was Our Lady of the Assumption, and her project was the institutionalization of the Acadians by the Church, not the fusion of identity. But Chiasson is right, *AND* (and) *And* is indeed a feature of the hypermodern representation in which we live—postmodern, as he likes to call it. Postmodernity is not only the deconstruction of grand narratives of tradition and modernity, it is their reuse under minor, random forms. Évangéline reappears in contemporary works, in Chiasson's paintings or literary works in northern Acadia, in George Rodrigue's magnificent paintings or sculptures, or novels written in English—like those of Tim Gautreaux—among the Cajuns. The story of the Acadians inaugurated by the poem *Évangéline* is not dead, it reappeared surprisingly in the 2000s, as we are about to see.

Before doing so, however, I would like to point out an unforeseen logic. In the *AND* (and) *And*, what is unheralded is the lower case "*and*," the link that unites the two "*And*," the mediation between tradition "*and*" modernity, between the local "*and*" the global, between the past "*and*" the future, between the critic of tradition "*and*" the guardian of tradition.

This "and" is the mediation that allows the conjugation of sometimes contradictory elements to take shape. This "and" is the narrative that gives meaning to a reality that without it would present itself as a multiform reality, unreadable, outside the narrative. Tradition and modernity merge, except that the modern narrative must undergo the test of historical science, the trial of modernity. This "and" is also the political, cultural, state, religious, and civil institution—as long as one does not make it an elusive reality—the territory in its socio-economic configuration—the ecological niche. The "and" is also a historical weight, a set of elements which, by and through the narrative, transform a multitude of individual paths into a community...into a society.

Thus, before being a realistic description of the social reality, postmodernity is a question to the men and women of our time: do we still want to have narratives, do we still want to "make society"? Or, on the contrary, do we want our individual and collective destinies to be governed from now on by a tiny "and" that we no longer pretend to control? Unthought of, that is to say, without a narrative, without institutionalization, this tiny "and" condemns us to be directed by forces that do not come from us: a dead past that we resurrect without reflexivity, the forces of a nebula that we call globalization or the world cosmopolitanization.

## Superimposing Narratives

I am writing these words at a time (July 2012) when UNESCO has just listed Grand-Pré landscape as a World Heritage Site. Two criteria were put forward to justify the nomination. Grand-Pré is an "exceptional landscape," sculpted from the end of the seventeenth century by the Acadians and maintained by the Planters, the settlers from New England who succeeded the Acadians on this land. This landscape results from an ingenious vernacular technique of collective draining of the marshes called the *polder*. The Grand-Pré landscape is also a major "symbolic place of memory" for the Acadian diaspora—"the most evocative of its collective memory and awareness"—a diaspora whose Deportation, beginning in 1755, is known as the Great Upheaval.

Grand-Pré is no longer officially a park dedicated exclusively to Évangéline, at least for its promoters. Already in the 1920s, Acadian notables were adamant that the site not be, according to the railroad companies' tourism aims, only a hymn to Longfellow and Évangéline Land. "Everyone knows what is appropriate for them. Our monument to ourselves will be a commemorative chapel, where we will come to commune piously with the souls of the outcasts who were our forefathers," Pascal Poirier recalled. The Acadians built a chapel behind the statue of Évangéline, in which they inserted a statue of Our Lady of the Assumption, inscribed bronze plaques with the names of the families deported, and erected the Deportation Cross to mark the place where their ancestors would have boarded the ships. In the 1950s, the Government of Canada took ownership of the site with a promise to keep the Acadian memory alive. This was done, although some Acadians complained that the "British" version of the Deportation and the Planters' occupation of the area were overemphasized in the interpretation and artifacts of the Commemorative Church. In 1960, for example, a monument was erected near the Deportation Cross at Horton Landing to commemorate the New England settlers who came after 1760 to occupy the former Acadian lands. After the 1980s, a committee of Acadians became partners (with the state) in managing the site. The site then refocused on the Acadian memory, not so much of the Deportation as establishing an Acadian community in Grand-Pré from 1682 to 1755, which ingeniously adapted to the surrounding nature.

It is for the adaptation to this "exceptional landscape," partly sculpted by man, and not for the recognition of the story that took place there, that UNESCO has recognized the candidacy of Grand-Pré. The landscape is said to encompass the cultural characteristics of the Mi'kmaq, Acadian, and Planter populations that have shaped the area's history. In defining Grand-Pré as a "place of memory" and not as a "historic site," one avoids deciding on the singular or particular character of the events that took place there. Regardless of one's judgment on the Deportation or the importance of Grand-Pré—did the poem magnify its historical significance? The Acadians have made it a place of memory of the period of the Great Upheaval. It is not the Deportation that is recognized as such, but its memory. Finally, there is a furtive reminder that this place of memory owes its birth in the mid-nineteenth century to a work of fiction, *Evangeline*, by the American poet Henry Wadsworth Longfellow.

The multiplication of narratives around the Grand-Pré landscape is presented as a victory of diversity over homogeneity, unifying narrative over the divisive one. The local Anglo-Protestant population, which has historically been kept away from the site construction since its appropriation by the Acadians, is now recognized as the guardian of this exceptional site, which was once inhabited by the Mi'kmaq, carved by the Acadians, and maintained by the Planters.

A site that is everyone's memory can also be nobody's memory. Except for the Deportation's great romantic moments—the 175th, 200th, and 250th—Grand-Pré has always had difficulty establishing itself as the centre of Acadian memory, too far away from the settlement of the new Acadia located farther north. This is why the Acadian village of Caraquet, which commemorates the (re)settlement (return) of the Acadians after the Great Upheaval, is much more visited by Acadians. The Mi'kmaq and Planters will not make Grand-Pré a place of remembrance; it is too associated with Acadian memory.

There is still Évangéline; she is still present, with her statue still in the middle of the garden in front of the church, her well; next to it is the bust of Longfellow, hidden in the shade of the tall willows, which reminds us that he is the first author of this story. I have the impression that the visitors present during my visit were there above all for Évangéline ... the cosmopolitan. Because, for everyone to celebrate Grand-Pré, the village must be "dead but not forgotten," no longer the place of an ever-living memory ready to rebound, but the place of a dead memory belonging to humanity. "Naught but tradition remains of the beautiful village of Grand-Pré." (*Evangeline*, original verses by Longfellow).

I had the same feeling in December 2008 when I visited the Acadian Memorial in St. Martinville in the heart of Cajun country. This museum was inaugurated in 1996 in the old municipal buildings behind the St. Martin de Tours Church. Here, too, the aim was explicitly to depart from the "fakelore" of Évangéline and present an account according to the most up-to-date scientific knowledge. The best specialists in Cajun history, such as Carl Brasseaux, participated in elaborating the scenario. The memorial is a tribute to the three thousand Acadians who were expelled by the British from their ancestral land and who found refuge in Louisiana. The tone is more realistic, more serious than the "true" accounts of Judge Voorhies or Dudley J. LeBlanc. The arrival of the Acadians in Louisiana was, on the whole, a happy adventure. Here is the tragic story of dispersion, the description of a diaspora. All the more so since the Acadian Memorial and its accompanying museum share their space with the African American Museum. A common focus points to either the history of the Acadian diaspora or the African American diaspora, nothing else can help understand their shared history.

As with the African American diaspora, the "global" character of the Acadian dispersion is emphasized. Geographical maps reproduce with large arrows the Acadian migrations from 1755 to 1785—a crossroads between Acadia, New England, France, Louisiana, Santo Domingo, and the Falkland Islands. These maps provoked the curiosity of frontier historian John Mack Faragher and led to the publication of this great work on the Deportation: *A Great and Noble Scheme* (2005). A mural created by Robert Dafford of Lafayette depicts the arrival of Broussard-Beausoleil's group of Acadians at St. Martinville. An exact copy of this mural can be found on the rue des Acadiens in Nantes, France, where the largest contingent of Acadians left for Louisiana. For more realism, the refugees' faces are actual portraits of Acadian descendants. A wall—like the Vietnam Veterans Memorial in Washington, DC—displays the names of the three thousand Acadians who arrived in Louisiana; it is also the counterpart to the plaques in the Grand-Pré Church on which the names of the families expelled from French Acadia are displayed. On the shore of Bayou Teche, just behind the building, the Deportation Cross has been installed, a replica of the cross erected in 1924 at Horton Landing, the Grand-Pré beach where Longfellow described the outcasts' boat. Finally, an eternal flame reminds us of the link between the Acadian tragedy and that of the great wars in human history.

The Cajuns are the descendants of victimized people, like Blacks Americans. Their bucolic integration into the Eden of Louisiana is not far off. The memorial adjoins the garden that houses the Évangéline Oak, and near it is a plaque honouring Judge Edward Simon, a St. Martinville resident who studied at Harvard in the 1840s and is said to have told Longfellow the "true story of Évangéline." Across the street, near the Church of Saint Martin de Tours, where Emmeline Labiche is supposed to have been buried, is a statue of Évangéline in the image of the Mexican actress Dolores del Río, who played the role of Évangéline in the 1929 film. On the tables, in the Memorial Museum, a small text recalls the local version, "the true story of Évangéline" of Voorhies. For many people, this story still seems more "real" than the boring version of the historians. As the ethnologist Barry Ancelet said, reporting the words of Madame Guirard, interpreter of *Evangeline*'s story, who was accused of having embellished the tale: "Les Acadiens ont bien le droit d'ajouter une fin heureuse à leur légende" ("The Acadians have every right to add a happy ending to their legend").

## Universalizing the Narrative

"Forgetting Evangeline." August 2009. In front of the church in Caraquet, in northern Acadia, stands a large stage. More than thirty thousand people—some say thirty thousand Acadians—gathered to watch the Fourth World Acadian Congress closing ceremony. Among the invited artists, two great Acadian performers for whom the song "Évangéline" by Michel Conte was one of the big hits. In Quebec, Annie Blanchard has just received a Félix for the song of the year, "Évangéline" (2006); and Marie-Jo Thério, in an admirable performance, has made the song known in France. We expect a duet or a quartet of women singing the great heroine. Even the folklorist Édith Butler and the popular singer Natasha St-Pier are also present. After all, "Évangéline" is the most famous song associated with Acadia, and the show is broadcast on the National Television Channel.

But no, "Évangéline" will not be sung. The show organizers want to give a modern image of Acadia, an Acadia open to the world, turned toward the future, a cosmopolitan Acadia. They want to forget *Evangeline*. If they will allow the Cajun Zachary Richard to perform his engaged anthem

"Réveille," it is as long as the anti-English words—"C'est les goddams qui viennent / Vole la récolte" ("It's the goddamns that come / Steal the harvest")—are modified by evocations of great world genocidal disasters and ethnic cleansing: Sarajevo, Kosovo, South Africa, Rwanda, etc. Acadia must become universal, its history should no longer be read in its historical singularity. Although the singers performing that night are all from the real Acadia of the south or the north, none of them are natives of the great diasporic-cosmopolitan Acadia that we would like to represent: France, Quebec, New England, or Santo Domingo.

**Évangéline**
Lyrics: Michel Conte

*The stars were in the sky*
*You were in Gabriel's arms*
*It was a beautiful day, it was Sunday*
*The church bells were about to ring*
*And you were going to be married*
*In your first white dress*
*Autumn was well underway*
*The flocks had all returned home*
*And all the teal ducks had flown*
*And in the evening, to the tune of the fiddle*
*The girls and especially the boys*
*Would have told you that you were beautiful*
*Évangéline, Évangéline*

*But the English arrived*
*In the church they locked up*
*All the men of your village*
*And the women had to wait*
*With the children who cried*
*All night on the shore*
*In the morning they boarded Gabriel on a big sailboat*
*Without a farewell, without a smile*
*And all alone on the dock*
*You tried to pray*
*But you had nothing more to say*
*Évangéline, Évangéline*

*And so, for more than twenty years*
*You've searched for your lover*
*All over America*
*In plains and valleys*
*Every wind whispered his name*
*Like the sweetest music*
*Even though your heart was dead*
*Your love grew stronger*
*In memory and absence*
*It was your every thought*
*And every day it bloomed*
*In the great garden of silence*
*Évangéline, Évangéline*

*You lived with a single desire*
*To relieve and to heal*
*Those who suffered more than you*
*You learned that at the end of sorrows*
*A way can always be found*
*That leads to the one who loves you*
*And so, one Sunday morning*
*You heard in the distance*
*The chimes of your village*
*And suddenly you understood*
*That your trials were over*
*And so was your long journey*
*Évangéline, Évangéline*

*In front of you was lying*
*A stranger on a sickbed*
*An old man dying of weakness*
*In the morning light*
*His face suddenly seemed*
*To take on the features of his youth*
*Gabriel died in your arms*
*On his lips, you bestow*
*A kiss as long as your life*
*One must have been greatly loved*
*To have been able to find*
*The strength to say "thank you"*

*Évangéline, Évangéline*

*Still today, there are*
*People who live in your homeland*
*And who recall your name*
*For the ocean speaks of you*
*The southern winds carry your voice*
*From the forest to the plain*
*Your name is more than Acadia*
*More than the hope of a homeland*
*Your name goes beyond borders*
*Your name is the name of all those*
*Who, although they are unhappy*
*Believe in love and hope*
*Évangéline, Évangéline*
*Évangéline, Évangéline*

However, the show organizers are wrong. The song "Évangéline," written in 1971 by Michel Conte, is a cry toward the universal. One only has to remember these final stanzas: "Your name is more than Acadia / More than the hope of a homeland / Your name goes beyond borders / Your name is the name of all those / Who, although they are unhappy / Believe in love and hope." Conte, a Frenchman living in Quebec at the time, wrote this song outside the Acadian story of Évangéline. It is not the return to the country that interests him but the universal cry of human distress. His interpretation is close to a romantic, cosmopolitan reading, à la Longfellow. In Quebec and Acadia, Conte's song, written in 1971, did not reach great popularity until the 1990s. It then again picked up at the beginning of the 2000s, years of a nationalist chill following the failure of the 1995 Quebec referendum.

This is not the only paradox. The World Congress, for which this show was intended as the closing event, is in itself a curious mixture of "dead but not forgotten" Acadia and "living Acadia," of local Acadia and globalized Acadia. The idea is said to have originated in the mind of a recent Acadian exile—André Boudreau—in faraway Alberta during a speech by the well-known Acadian activist Jean-Marie Nadeau. The idea was to organize a grand celebration, a "great reunion" of the dispersed sons and daughters of 1755 worldwide. A first World Congress was held in Moncton, in New Brunswick's Acadia, in 1994. The event was to be repeated every five years. A second occurred in Acadiana in 1999, marking the tercentenary of French Louisiana's founding. A third took place in Acadia, Nova Scotia, in 2004, in conjunction with the four hundredth anniversary of the founding of French Acadia. The Fourth Congress, as we have just seen, took place on the Acadian Peninsula of New Brunswick in 2009, and the fifth is planned for 2014 in the Acadia of Madawaska and Témiscouata, a territory bordering the United States, Quebec, and New Brunswick.[1] The theme will be, of course: *The Acadia of the World*. Each of the previous gatherings was a tremendous popular success, attracting tens of thousands of participants and creating a great identity pride revival in the regions where it was held.

**Réveille ("Wake Up")**
Lyrics: Zachary Richard

*Wake up, wake up,*
*The goddams are coming,[2]*
*To steal the harvest.*

*Wake up, wake up,*
*Acadian men,*
*To save the village.*

*My great-great-grandfather*
*Came from Brittany,*
*The blood of my family*
*Has wet Acadia.*
*And now, the damned are coming,*

---

1.  Translator's note: The Fifth Congress was held in 2014 in northwestern New Brunswick, but also in Maine and Quebec. The Sixth Congress was held in 2019 in southeastern New Brunswick and Prince Edward Island, with the objective of promoting a contemporary, cooperative, urban, and rural Acadia. The Seventh Congress is scheduled for 2024 in southwestern Nova Scotia as of 2022.

2.  Translator's note: The term "goddamns" was used by the French for the English soldiers during the Hundred Years War of 1337–1453. Indeed, English soldiers were notorious for their frequent use of profanity and in particular "God damn."

*To hunt us like beasts,*
*To destroy families,*
*To throw us all to the wind.*

*Wake up, wake up,*
*The goddams are coming,*
*To steal the harvest.*

*Wake up, wake up,*
*Acadian men,*
*To save the village.*

*I heard about*
*Going up with Beausoleil.*
*To take arms*
*Beat the damned.*
*I heard about*
*Going to Louisiana*
*To find some good peace*
*Down there in Louisiana.*

*Wake up, wake up,*
*The goddams are coming,*
*To steal the harvest.*

*Wake up, wake up,*
*Acadian men,*
*To save the village.*

*I saw my poor father.*
*He was taken prisoner.*
*While my mother, my dear mother*
*Was bawling.*
*I saw my beautiful house*
*Set on fire,*
*And I remained an orphan,*
*Orphan of Acadia.*

*Wake up, wake up,*
*The goddams are coming,*
*To steal the harvest.*

*Wake up, wake up,*

*Acadian men,*
*To save the village.*

*Wake up, wake up,*
*The goddams are coming,*
*To steal the children.*

The borrowing of the event name, Congrès mondial acadien (World Acadian Congress), from the Congrès juif mondial (World Jewish Congress), defined the Acadians for the first time, in contemporary times, as a diaspora. The Acadian world would include between three and six million Acadians depending on its driving forces. One would have to go back to the first invocations of the Deportation, notably the 1855 letter of Bishop Walsh to the Acadians, directly inspired by the poem "Exil sans fin et sans exemple dans l'histoire" ("Exile without end and example in history") to define the Acadians as a diaspora. Traditional Acadia never had this ambition. Its great gatherings and its national conventions were limited to bringing together the Acadian "people" dispersed over the northeastern territory of America—where the Cajuns were not—where, according to the wish of Rameau de Saint-Père, Acadia could hope to "(re)make society." In the World Acadian Congress, there was no intention to bring the exiles back to Zion, nor even, according to the old tradition of the national conventions, to discuss the state of the nation's institutionalization. At one point, there was a certain political intention. The First World Congress in Moncton in 1994 included a vital conference component aimed to reflect on Acadia in the near future (Acadia in 2004). But successive congresses have eliminated this component, making it an essentially cultural and touristic-identitarian event dedicated to gathering and promoting the pride of the diaspora Acadians.

The reunion of the diasporic "families" made the World Congress successful. At each congress, special celebrations are organized around family names—the LeBlancs, Landrys, Thériaults, Thibaudeaus, Arceneauxs, Richards, etc. These family gatherings are not limited to the old family names of French Acadia. It is estimated that there are about 60 stem families of French Acadia (pre-1755), and nearly 120 family reunions are expected at the 2014 convention. This means that Acadia has assimilated new families over the last 250 years. Nevertheless, the phenomenon is genealogical and participates in identity individualization. One clings onto Acadia through one's family roots, not through living together.

If we can thus exalt the Acadian plurality—the members of these families do not all speak French and they live in different regions and countries—this is done at the expense of the societal identification of the two Acadians. In such a process, the Cajun country becomes Acadian again, putting its French origins in tension with the regionalization of Cajun identity. In doing so, the Cajuns accentuate their distinctness from the Black Creoles, who do not have Acadian origins even though they largely share the same Cajun culture. In 1995, the president of CODOFIL told a predominantly African-American audience that Acadians were the only group forced to immigrate to the United States. The same is true in northern Acadia: the World Congress seems to go against the trend going on since the 1960s, i.e. that of territorializing (regionalizing) national identity. At that time, there was a consensus that any francophone living in the Maritime provinces was Acadian, whether their ancestors came from French Acadia or settled there through successive waves of immigrants that assimilated into the Acadian culture while shaping it.

"Territorial" Acadia would not be universal enough, too homogenizing, enclosing the Acadian within a border, referring them to a particular culture. Couldn't we be *AND* (and) *And*? *And* Acadian of the diaspora *And* Acadian of a place? This is what the World Congress does, but the place of mediation between the two—the lower case "and"—is no longer a malleable component, sociologists would say "reflexive," like the region, the nation, or the territory as a cultural space. No, the place of mediation is now a fixed form of grouping: the family genealogy. This is why there is nothing more "Évangéline" than the World Congress, a universal sentimentality carried by an individualized memory, a memory that does not refer to or pretend to refer to the historicity of a particular human group. Someone dead and not forgotten. If we strip Acadian narratives of their anchorage in a singular history, then the wandering Acadians of the poem can resume their place without obstacles. One then substitutes the Acadian (national) wandering for the American one—such is the proposal asserted in this "new" proposal to define the Acadian journey in the Americanness imaginary. Already Michel Roy said in *L'Acadie perdue*: "Acadia is everywhere. It walks through the world with the dreams of its wanderers, the memory of a thing lost at the edges of memory."[3] And yet, "Évangéline" will not be sung that night on the stage in front of the Caraquet church. One is led to believe that the closing show organizers were even more modern than postmodern.

## Victimizing the Story

In December 2003, the Canadian federal government Cabinet endorsed a royal proclamation recognizing the wrongs done to the Acadians during the deportations of the mid-eighteenth century. The idea of demanding an apology from the British Crown has been in the air since the early 1990s, a proposal mainly carried by Warren Perrin, a Cajun lawyer living in Erath in the southern plain of Cajun country. In 1993, Perrin became the third president of CODOFIL, the organization charged by the Louisiana government with promoting French in Louisiana.

Stéphane Bergeron, a Quebec MP and member of the sovereign-ist Bloc Québécois, decided to demand an apology from the Canadian Parliament following his participation in the Second World Congress in Louisiana. The motion caused confusion both among Acadian members of parliament, who saw such a move as a trap by a "sovereignist" member to annoy Canada, and among leaders of Acadian nationalist associations, who had never before thought it worthwhile to inscribe their actions under the umbrella of an "apology" for a historical crime. Without "apologizing," Cabinet, as a trustee of the British Crown, acknowledged the "wrongs" done to the Acadians and proclaimed August 28—the date on which Governor Lawrence of Nova Scotia signed the banishment of the French Catholics from his province in 1755—a Canadian day of commemoration

---

3.   "L'Acadie est partout. Elle se promène par le monde avec les rêves de ses errants, souvenir d'une chose perdue aux confins de la mémoire."

of the Great Upheaval. The Deportation, first recounted in the poem *Évangéline* in 1847, was thus introduced into the pantheon of great moments in Canadian historical memory.

The Canadian commemoration of the Great Upheaval and the apology from the British Crown are part of the new constitutive position that the Deportation occupies in northern and southern Acadia's memory. It goes without saying that the Deportation has always been central to the Acadian narrative, but its revelation in the poem *Evangeline* set in motion the memorial narrative and identity effects that this book narrates. However, except Évangéline the American, whose tragic fate referred to something universal—the exceptional fate of America, a microcosm of cosmopolitanism—*Evangeline*'s Acadian and Cajun narratives told the story of a historical singularity. The Acadians retained the memory of the Deportation to vivify their singularity in the face of French Canadian and English-Canadian narratives that ignored them; the Cajuns wanted to dissociate themselves from the white Creoles and Black populations to present themselves as true Americans with a distinct memory. Their respective narratives were understood only in tension with the national narrative(s) they were negotiating.

The singularity was further accentuated by the fact that the "Deportation" could not be understood without the "Recovery." In Acadia, the first reactions to the poem were to run to New England—to Boston, to Philadelphia—to attest that the Acadians had not taken up residence in those foreign lands but had indeed returned. The "return" will always have been more central to the Acadian imagination than the "Deportation"; it was the explanation for the "people" existence. From the 1970s onward, the Acadian narrative even wanted to get rid of the Deportation to attest to the practical and continuous presence of a francophone (Acadian) community in the Maritimes since 1604.

In the Eden of Louisiana, the idea of a joyful Acadian recovery has always overshadowed that of the Deportation. In *The True Story of Evangeline*, the Acadians are welcomed in Maryland and Évangéline (Emmeline Labiche), who still dreams of the loves of her lost country, finds an Acadian community that has integrated so well that Gabriel

(Louis Arceneaux) has already taken a wife there. In his *Pèlerinage au pays d'Évangéline* ("Pilgrimage to the Land of Evangeline"), Father Casgrain said in the 1880s that in Louisiana, "the Acadians speak without bitterness of the Great Upheaval." This was still true. Until recently, the Deportation, if not in the form of the joyful reunion in the Eden of Louisiana, was not part of the story.[4]

Things have changed in this regard. The identity (re)shaped by the World Congress no longer insists on recovery. Acadia is everywhere and nowhere at the same time, or, more accurately put, there is no longer an Acadia but only Acadians. In this new imaginary, the diaspora wants to replace the return. The image of the Jewish diaspora—not that of the return to Israel, which is today stigmatized—has become the archetype of postmodernity. However, such an opening toward the universal (re)popularizes the Deportation or victim identity question. In a world where all identities are equal and reduced to individual tinkering, the only way to gain recognition for small cultures with neither a robust political system nor a powerful cultural industry is to argue that they have suffered a universal wrong. The cosmopolitan identity no longer recognizes singular ethnic or national paths, it only recognizes universal victims. Hence, there is a proliferation of requests for forgiveness, apologies from former victimizers, and races for victim recognition in post-national societies. Small cultures use this stratagem to affirm their participation in the universal wandering and equally demand universal recognition. This is also how the logic of the law, which is universal in principle, works: it only recognizes the equality of individuals unless that individual has suffered a collective wrong that has prevented them from achieving that equality.

Sometimes, the demands for victim recognition are linked to national community reconfiguration or reparation of wrong policies. The South African experience, which has served as a model for these practices, was a matter of "making society" following years of apartheid. The Acadian "apology" had nothing to do with a demand for collective reconstruction or redress of grievances—which would have repoliticized the issue—it was instead a demand for symbolic recognition, referring primarily to personal

---

4.  "les Acadiens parlent sans amertume du grand dérangement"

identity. Warren Perrin was very conscious of this fact, insisting that his request was not political, that it was intended to give him the power to pass onto his child a memory of which he would be proud. If the Canadian government finally agreed to incorporate the Great Upheaval into the pantheon of Canadian commemorations, it was more to consolidate Canadian unity than to encourage any particular remembrance efforts to be made in Acadia. Senior Canadian government officials who participated in the formulation of the Royal Proclamation understood the individualized and decommunized nature of the "apology" thus demanded and partially granted. They—including the Minister of Canadian Heritage, Sheila Copps, and the Governor-General of Canada, Michaëlle Jean—immediately asserted that they had Acadian ancestors and that this recognition was also for them.

The *Société nationale de l'Acadie* (name taken in 1992 by the *Société nationale des Acadiens*, still retaining its acronym SNA) traces its genesis in the nationalism formulation of northern Acadians at the end of the nineteenth century. Since the 1970s, the SNA has aimed to represent the territorial Acadias of the Atlantic provinces of Canada, but recently, the organization started opening up to worldwide representation. The SNA is responsible for the World Acadian Congress, and Acadians from Louisiana, Quebec, France, and New England are now invited to join. In 2005, it launched a major international project to commemorate the Great Upheaval. This project aimed to erect monuments to commemorate the Great Upheaval in northern Acadia, southern Acadia, England, France, and the United States—in places where Acadians were expelled and where they were exiled. These monuments include a replica of the Deportation Cross erected in the 1920s at Horton Landing, where the prisoners of the Grand-Pré church boarded the boats. A copy of this cross is already present on the banks of Bayou Teche, behind the Acadian Memorial in St. Martinville. Beyond Acadia, the Deportation is an event of international significance that transcends Canadian borders.

In a book published in 2005, *A Great and Noble Scheme*, the American historian John Mack Faragher will confirm the universal and victimized nature of the Acadian odyssey. This book is one of the few historical books written about the Great Upheaval. Strangely, Acadians, like Cajuns, have done little research on the events leading up to their expulsion as if, to paraphrase the 1960s Acadian ethnographer and folklorist Anselme Chiasson, the Acadian story was too good to be distorted by history. The children of Évangéline, in the south as well as in the north, appropriated the Deportation narrative by counting the "returns" (re-establishments), much more than the "departures." Faragher's book, which describes the phenomenon from an American perspective, a northeastern "frontier" war, had an immediate identity resonance for the latter. Faragher was one of the few speakers at the 2009 World Congress. At the University of Moncton, the Centre d'études acadiennes ("Acadian Study Centre") quickly commissioned a translation. Faragher confirms that the Acadians are indeed a victimized population, from a point of view that is no longer endogenous to Acadia and is taking place outside of the Acadian narrative. They would have been, he suggests, the victims of the first "ethnic cleansing," that is, the first attempt by a modern state to systematically remove a population from its territory because of ethno-religious incompatibility.

The victim narrative can be all the more radical as it is unmoored from any socio-political anchor, as it no longer speaks in the name of a particular community, as it does not have to deal with the other groups that occupy the same space as it. Warren Perrin recently published a book, *Acadian Redemption: From Beausoleil Broussard to the Queen's Royal Proclamation* (2004), which tells the story of the Cajuns back to Broussard-Beausoleil, the "rebel" who in 1764 led the first significant group of Acadians on Louisiana soil. Beausoleil is the ideal candidate to replace Évangéline as the great hero of the Acadian story—he was the lover of Pélagie-la-Charrette (Évangéline the Acadian) in Antonine Maillet's great novel of the same name. He was neglected precisely because of his "rebellious" character, which did not fit in with the pastoral image that Acadia in the north and the south had given itself. Moreover, in the north, it must be remembered that Beausoleil left Acadia…and never came back. This is why today Perrin, a legal activist—he intends to reactivate the legal proceedings against the use of the word "coonass"—can without embarrassment present Beausoleil-Broussard as both the founder of Acadiana and its direct ancestor by maternal descent. The book's cover features a Che Guevara–like revolutionary waving a northern Acadian flag.

The idea of a victimized but rebellious Acadia seems to be gaining ground as the real Acadia fades away. As we saw in the case of the Acadian Memorial, the description of a pastoral Acadia—the land of Évangéline— has been replaced by the story of a forced diaspora. The Cajun discourse became more radical in the wake of the World Congresses. Freed from the constraints of living in a society, speech can wander. Upon his return from the 1994 Congress, Zachary Richard founded *Action cadienne*, dedicated to renewing the fight for the French. He revived "Réveille," a militant song he wrote during the effervescence of Quebec and Acadian nationalism in the 1970s—which included a reference to Beausoleil the rebel—but which had not had much of an impact until now. "Réveille" became one of the fetish songs of the World Congress and the diaspora Acadia. Beausoleil reappears in "Réveille," in Perrin's book, and in the film *Acadie liberté*, a historical film in the glory of rebellious Acadia presented as an introduction to Acadiana in Jean Lafitte's cultural centres in Cajun country. The Deportation, absent from popular song, makes its entrance, for example in "Acadie à la Louisiane" by Bruce Daigrepont (1989) and "La valse de l'héritage" by Ivy Dugas (1987).

Acadian poet Serge Patrice Thibodeau has just translated, into French, The Diary of Colonel John Winslow (2011)[5]. From this diary, which Thomas Haliburton consulted to write his history of Nova Scotia in 1829, Longfellow drew the description of the Deportation scenes to Grand-Pré. Thibodeau is a poet of wandering Acadia. He wants to return to the Deportation sources to reach a universal truth about it, a truth that would be rid of the nationalistic jeremiads produced over a century by the children of Évangéline. A human rights activist, he wants to return to the Deportation's original meaning, a history that is not Acadian but a "crime" against humanity "for which those responsible must be named." This was precisely what Longfellow wanted to do with his poem *Evangeline*, a great idyll to the glory of the "celestial mechanics" that he saw unfolding in young America: the fusion of humanity into one nation.

---

5.    In its new French version, the book is titled *Le Journal de John Winslow à Grand-Pré*.

\* \* \*

No one knows what will happen to Évangéline's story. Will the men and women of the future still use it to "make society" or, on the contrary, to free themselves from the constraints of identity? Will they succeed in forgetting Évangéline? Then, as Longfellow imagined, could the poem's loving couple quietly disappear from our imagination, their story over for good?

\* \* \*

In this book, I wanted to pass on the American tales presented to us in the *Evangeline* poem. The following generations will decide if they deserve to be continued.

# References

BELKHODJA, Chedly. *D'Ici et d'Ailleurs. Regards croisés sur l'immigration.* Moncton, Perce-Neige, 2011.

BOUDREAU, Raoul et Jean Morency. « Le postmoderne acadien », *Tangence.* no. 58, October 1998.

CALHOUN, Charles C. *Lonfellow. A Rediscovered Life.* Boston, Beacon Press, 2004.

CHIASSON, Herménégilde. « Traversées », *Tangence.* no. 58, 1998, p. 77–92.

CHIASSON, Herménégilde. « Oublier Évangéline », in S. Langlois and J. Létourneau (ed.), *Aspects de la nouvelle francophonie canadienne.* Québec, Presses de l'Université Laval, 2004, pp. 147–63.

DAVIS, Marc. "The Acadian Memorial as Civic Laboratory: Whiteness, History, and Governmentality in a Louisiana Commemorative Site Museum." *Museum Anthropological Review,* vol. 4, no. 1, 2010 (online).

DOUCET, Clive. *Notes from Exile: On Being Acadian.* Toronto, McClelland, 1999.

FARAGHER, John Mack. *A Great and Noble Scheme.* New York, W.W. Norton & Company, 2005.

GIOIA, Dana. "Longfellow in the Aftermath of Modernism" in Jay Parini (ed.), *The Columbia History of American Poetry.* New York, Columbia Press, 1993, p. 64-96.

HEBERT-LEITER, Maria. *Becoming Cajun, Becoming American: The Acadian in American Literature from Longfellow to James Lee Burke.* Baton Rouge, Louisiana State University Press, 2009.

IRMSCHER, Christopher. *Longfellow Redux.* Chicago, University of Illinois Press, 2006.

LEBLANC, Georgette. *Alma: An Acadian Performance.* Doctoral dissertation, University of Louisiana at Lafayette, 2007.

MORENCY, Jean. « Les visages multiples de l'américanité en Acadie », in Madeleine Frédéric et Serge Jaumain (ed.), *Regards croisés sur l'histoire et la littérature acadiennes.* Bruxelles, Peter Lang, 2006, p. 55-66.

PERRIN, Warren A. *Acadian Redemption: From Beausoleil Broussard to the Queen's Royal Proclamation.* Erath, Acadian Heritage and Cultural Foundation, 2004.

RUDIN, Ronald. *Remembering and Forgetting in Acadie: A Historian's Journey through Public Memory.* Toronto, University of Toronto Press, 2009.

THIBODEAU, Serge Patrice. *Journal de John Winslow à Grand-Pré.* Moncton, Perce-Neige, 2011.

VIAU, Robert. *Grand-Pré: Lieu de mémoire, Lieu d'appartenance.* Longueuil, MNH Publications, 2005.

# ACKNOWLEDGEMENTS

A book is always the fruit of long companionship. This one, in particular, took time to grow, slowly, in my mind.

I started working seriously on this book at the University of Ottawa, at the Centre for Interdisciplinary Research on Citizenship and Minorities (CIRCEM) as the Chair of Research, Francophonie, and Identity. Ginette Peterson and Sophie Letouzé assisted me in the preparatory work for this essay. I continued this work at the Université du Québec à Montréal, as the holder of the Canada Research Chair in Globalization, Citizenship, and Democracy. Sophie Grenier was a great help to me in the many tasks related to the manuscript preparation.

During these years, I received support from the Social Sciences and Humanities Research Council of Canada and the Canada Research Chairs Secretariat. As a Trudeau Foundation laureate, I was able to make Évangéline's pilgrimage from the Maritimes to Acadia, Boston, New England, and finally Cajun country in Louisiana.

While in Louisiana, I was hosted by the Centre for Louisiana Studies, then directed by Carl Brasseaux, at the University of Louisiana at Lafayette. Brenda Mounier was the guide for my wife and me, and introduced us to a Cajun country that we did not suspect. We had the great privilege of spending Christmas Day 2007 with Richard Guitry, this living encyclopedia of Cajun identity and a great lover of Cajun French. He taught us how to make a "real" gumbo. That Christmas would be his last.

I often consulted my brother Daniel for his knowledge of both northern and southern Acadian culture. I had Annie Claude, my daughter, read a few chapters to test the argumentative coherence. Jacqueline, my wife, who had to accept my long association with Évangéline, was often a faithful listener as I read specific passages aloud. Patrick Clark, who has an exhaustive knowledge of the writing on Acadia, agreed to read the first version of this manuscript, pointing out to me the passages that surprised his historical eye. I did not always listen to him, but the manuscript was greatly improved thanks to his work.

Éditions Québec Amérique immediately believed in my project. Myriam Caron Belzile significantly improved the manuscript and transformed it into a beautiful book.

It goes without saying that I take full responsibility for any errors that may be found in this book.

This image by the Faed
Brothers—painted by
Tomas Faed in 1850 and
engraved by his brother
James in 1855—is one of
the first representations of
Évangéline. Longfellow
particularly liked this
Romantic depiction of her.

© ARCHIVES OF THE MUSÉE ACADIEN AT
L'UNIVERSITÉ DE MONCTON.

Henry Wadsworth
Longfellow (1807–82) on
the Isle of Wight, in 1868.
PUBLIC DOMAIN

*The memorial church of Grand-Pré was built in 1921 with funds from Acadian associations. The statue of Évangéline (1920) was designed by Quebec sculptor Philippe Hébert and built by his son Henry. The statue was sponsored by the railway company, which saw it as an opportunity to bolster tourism.*

© PARKS CANADA / CHRIS REARDON / 2003 / H.03.36.04.04.25

*This statue of Évangéline in St. Martinville, Louisiana, was inaugurated in 1931 and is located near the St. Martin de Tours Church— where the presumed tomb of the "real Evangeline" (Emmeline Labiche) rests. The statue was sponsored by actress Dolores del Río, who played the titular character in Edwin Carewe's 1929 movie. Del Río also served as model to build the statue.*

© CITY OF ST. MARTINVILLE, LOUISIANA.

*This image by A. R. Waud was on the cover of* Harper's Weekly *(1866) and illustrates the "white trash" perception of the Louisiana Cajuns following the American Civil War.* PUBLIC DOMAIN

*Dudley LeBlanc (1894–1971) was committed to popularizing Acadian culture among Louisiana Cajuns, and led three delegations of Cajuns to northern Acadia. Each time, he was accompanied by young Louisiana women, the "Evangeline Girls," each representing a town from Lower Louisiana.* © STATE LIBRARY OF LOUISIANA, HP00073.

*Project of a monument honouring Longfellow from the commemorative album of the 25-year anniversary of the Société Saint-Jean-Baptiste: "Standing on a podium depicting waves and the famous Nova Scotian aboiteaux, a young peasant symbolizing Acadie—Évangéline herself—holds up the medallion of Longfellow draped in American colours to honour posterity, and to inspire admiration for centuries to come."* © SOCIÉTÉ SAINT-JEAN-BAPTISTE.